WAIT TILL NEXT YEAR

WAIT
TILL NEXT
YEAR

THE STORY
OF A SEASON WHEN
WHAT SHOULD'VE HAPPENED
DIDN'T AND WHAT COULD'VE
GONE WRONG DID

WILLIAM GOLDMAN
AND
MIKE LUPICA

BANTAM BOOKS
TORONTO • NEW YORK • LONDON • SYDNEY • AUCKLAND

WAIT TILL NEXT YEAR
A Bantam Book / December 1988

*Grateful acknowledgment is made for permission to reprint
from* The New York Times, *Copyright © 1987
by* The New York Times Company. *Reprinted by permission.*

All rights reserved.
Copyright © 1988 by William Goldman and Mike Lupica.

Book design by Richard Oriolo

*No part of this book may be reproduced or transmitted
in any form or by any means, electronic or mechanical,
including photocopying, recording, or by any information
storage and retrieval system, without permission in
writing from the publisher.*
For information address: Bantam Books.

Library of Congress Cataloging-in-Publication Data

Goldman, William.
  Wait till next year.

  Includes index.
  1. Sports—United States. I. Lupica, Mike.
II. Title.
GV583.G65 1988   796'.0973   88-22181
ISBN 0-553-05319-1

Published simultaneously in the United States and Canada

───

*Bantam Books are published by Bantam Books, a division of Bantam Doubleday
Dell Publishing Group, Inc. Its trademark, consisting of the words "Bantam
Books" and the portrayal of a rooster, is Registered in U.S. Patent and
Trademark Office and in other countries. Marca Registrada. Bantam Books,
666 Fifth Avenue, New York, New York 10103.*

───

PRINTED IN THE UNITED STATES OF AMERICA

DH   0 9 8 7 6 5 4 3 2 1

When asked by Hugh McIlvanney on a Channel 4 programme whether he perhaps didn't understand the "poetry of baseball," Steinbrenner snapped: "Don't talk to me about poetry, I majored in English and there's nothing about Sheats and Kelly that I don't know."

From THE BOOK OF BASEBALL
by Derek Brandon and Jim Marooney

*Published in England for
British baseball fans*

For Minnie Barstad
who
in 1937
on North Linden Avenue
taught me how to hit a baseball

W.G.

For Taylor and Christopher,
who never make me wait till next year,
because we're all too busy celebrating
today, and Esther Newberg, whose gift
as an agent is only surpassed by
her gift of friendship

M.L.

ACKNOWLEDGMENTS

One last thanks to all the ones—players, front office types, PR men, clubhouse boys, agents, announcers, beat reporters—who were my eyes and ears when my own eyes and ears couldn't be there. Thanks for watching, listening, and remembering. Without The Network, this book would not have been possible. Sometimes, the clubhouse walls do talk.

M.L.

CONTENTS

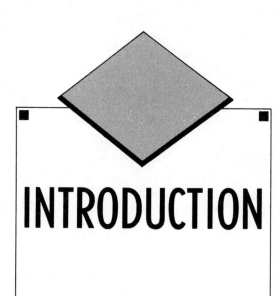

INTRODUCTION

Years are what they are.

(Everyone relax, philosophy class is now over.) Still, there's a certain truth involved. Wine growers know it. Sports fans, too.

We knew that this book had to be written about this 1987 year in New York sports (and by extension, sports in general) simply because for the first time in many too many years, we had two world champions prowling for repeats.

Would they? Neither of us—the fan or the reporter—are, by nature, as optimistic as we once were. So probably, we suspected, both would not turn out to be double champions.

But which would fail? The Mets were so clearly the best team in the majors. And they were so strong in most positions. And their pitching was not only remarkably deep, the arms were still young. (No starter yet thirty.) Plus this: They won it all without any of their stars having career years.

The Mets were a lock.

But try finding some negatives about the Giants. They won breezing. Destroying the enemy as the season went along. And they, too, were young in most positions. And yes, Joe Morris and Mark Bavaro had spectacular years, but they weren't over their heads; rather, they were extraordinary talents whose time, as they say, had very much come.

Sure, repeating is a bitch. (Only the Lakers have repeated this decade.) And repeating in New York, because of the media hype, poses particular problems—

—but—

—big but—

—the Giants were not the Chicago Bears. They were not loudmouth stars (McMahon) or freaks (William Perry). They did not have a defense with a catchy name. They did not do Superbowl Shuffles.

These were blue-collar workers with a blue-collar coach and during the preseason, amazing numbers of them clustered in the weight room at their Jersey training complex, quietly getting ready. The Giants might not win but they would not self-destruct.

And if they didn't self-destruct, they had to win. They were not just good, they were that much better than the other guys.

The Giants were a lock.

So '87 had these two. It also had the Yankees who might, if they caught a break, win it all. Winfield and Mattingly and Henderson were not only likely Hall of Famers, they were durable. Yes, the pitching was shoddy, but no one in the American League was long on pitching.

We had a shot, in baseball, for a Subway Series.

We had a shot, in football, for a *Semi-Tough* Super Bowl. Not that the Jets were that good. But the AFC had been blown out in many Super Bowl games this decade. The Jets, if they could survive their horrendous Decembers, were in it.

Four potential champions.

And for comic relief: Right in our own backyard, folks—who is funnier than the New York Knicks? (175 losses in the last three years.) But wait—the Nets were falling fast. Could they achieve their potential this year and surpass the Knicks in terms of bumbling? Possibly. All they needed was a few key injuries and they might never win a game on the road.

Obviously, you know the results as you read this. Maybe, it's been awhile in some cases, you've even forgotten the results. Matters not. This isn't a book about who won or lost and why. If it's about anything, it's this: reliving memories from maybe a different angle. What we wanted was for you to look up from the page and say, "I didn't know that." If you're a fan, that is. And if you're not, what we wanted, hoped for, was this kind of reaction: "Oh, no wonder they get that excited, maybe they're not so crazy after all."

Along with the six key teams, we had floods of ideas for ... well, *stuff.*

Like a day in the life of Andre the Giant.

And a day in the life of a bookie.

And a day in the life of a sports groupie. Coupled with one about an athlete's wife.

And maybe a day with Peter Ueberroth, and one with a pro basketball referee (what's hard?—who's easy?—) and Runyon's, where a lot of media people drink to forget, and Larry Bird and Kenny Anderson (maybe the best basketball prospect since Jabbar was Alcindor).

You like roundtable discussions? How about one on sports broadcasting with Madden, McCarver, and Marv Albert? And spotting talent with Al Davis and Red Auerbach.

Not to mention chapters on alcohol and race and money and tracing a trade from glimmer to contract signing and, of course, drugs, and again of course, the media—not why is it so good or why is it so bad but why is it so indifferent?

And the workings of Madison Square Garden and the U.S. Tennis Open and dog shows and cat shows and track and why New York does what it does to those that it does it to.

Interesting stuff? We thought so.

Alas, almost none of it got into the book.

Hard to say why. Probably because we were overtaken by events. And anyway, years are what they are. We tried to be mistresses to '87. And a lot of events happened in January and some things actually transpired in February. But for the True Believers, nothing of Consequence took place until late March.

When one of the great talents in the history of American sports picked up a bottle and absented himself to have a pee. . . .

WILLIAM GOLDMAN   MIKE LUPICA
New York City   *New Canaan*

BROKEN
PLAYS

THE REPORTER'S NOTEBOOK

"IT'S NOT TRUE, SWEAR TO GOD ..."

Dwight Gooden closed his eyes and began to cry.

It was the morning of April 1st, nine o'clock, Cashen's office, Huggins-Stengel Field, St. Petersburg, Florida. Until 1988, when ownership moved the entire spring training operation to Port St. Lucie, on Florida's East Coast, Huggins-Stengel was the spring training headquarters for the New York Mets once the schedule of exhibition games began. On April 1st, that schedule had nearly been completed. The regular season, the Mets' defense of their world championship, would begin in one week. Dwight Gooden, twenty-two years old and the most famous baseball pitcher alive, would start at Shea Stadium against the Pittsburgh Pirates.

But now as he slumped in the chair in front of the desk belonging to Cashen, the Mets executive vice-president and general manager, Gooden knew that had changed. Plenty had changed.

His life, mostly.

Cashen sat wordlessly on his side of the desk. Joe McIlvaine, the Mets vice-president in charge of baseball operations and the man who had drafted Gooden in 1982, sat in a folding chair to Gooden's right.

There was only one other presence in the tiny office.

A piece of paper in front of Cashen, sitting there on the desk, between him and Gooden, the kid pitcher from across the bridge in Tampa who symbolized the glorious rebirth of the Mets franchise.

A week before Opening Day, the baseball season suddenly began to move underneath the world champion New York Mets. The piece of paper was the lab report on the urine sample Dwight Gooden had given the Mets five days earlier.

The official name for urinalysis is the EMIT Screen Test. It screens a urine sample for barbiturates, amphetamines, opiates, cannabinoids (marijuana), cocaine, phencyclidine (various cough syrups). There was no name on the report, just a number. The sample had been sent to the hospital, it had been given a number, sent to the laboratory, tested, returned, the report delivered to the Mets.

This is how the EMIT Screen Test on Frank Cashen's desk read:

BARBITURATES: Negative.
AMPHETAMINES: Negative.
OPIATES: Negative.
CANNABINOIDS: Negative.
COCAINE: Positive.
PHENCYCLIDINE: Negative.

The lab report from the St. Petersburg hospital said that sometime during spring training, Dwight Gooden had used cocaine.

The Doc, Doctor K, the most electrifying presence on a pitching mound since Sandy Koufax in his prime, had tested positive. It was there, Cashen had just told him.

Right there on the paper.

Look at it.

Only Cashen did. McIlvaine, who had studied at St. Charles Seminary in Philadelphia and had once considered the priesthood instead of a career in baseball, looked at Gooden. Gooden picked his head up, imperceptibly swayed side to side in the chair, crying soundlessly. And in the reality of the moment at Huggins-Stengel, none of them—not Cashen or McIlvaine or Gooden—could immediately feel the baseball season give such a jolt that the Mets began to stumble up there at the top of the hill, where they had been since the previous October 27—Mets 8, Red Sox 5, Game 7 of the World Series. Cashen and McIlvaine said nothing, just waited for the best pitcher in baseball—58–19 before his twenty-second birthday, lifetime ERA of 2.28, 744 strikeouts already, $1.5 million in salary for the upcoming season, The Doc, Doctor Freaking *K*—to stop crying.

Much later in 1987, Joe McIlvaine would say, "April Fool's Day. The first symbol. In a series of bad symbols."

First nudge down off the top of the hill.

Like everybody was tripping on one lousy piece of paper or something.

Frank Cashen would later say, "It hit me later on the same day. The season was supposed to be beginning, and all of a sudden I felt like it was ending."

When Gooden finally began to speak, speak with the evidence right there in front of him—lousy piece of paper—the words tumbled out of him, running into each other, spilling onto Cashen's desk.

Make the paper disappear. That was it. Since he had come to the major leagues as a nineteen-year-old rookie who could strike out the world, Dwight Gooden could do anything.

He would make the paper (EMIT Screen? What was that? He was *The Doc*) disappear.

"Swear to God it's not true, swear to God, swear to *God!*" Dwight Gooden said, shaking his head from side to side.

Cashen is a former newspaper columnist, probably the only baseball executive in history to have had his work included in the book *Best Sports Stories*. He is the holder of a Bachelor of Laws degree from the University of Maryland. While at Baltimore's Loyola College, he wrote a campus musical comedy. He has worked at racetracks and breweries and in the office of the baseball commissioner. He and his wife Jean are the parents of seven children. He is a learned, literate man, uncommonly literate for a baseball executive, a lover of the language, a reader of books.

Cashen is the baseball genius of the 1980s for what he has done with the New York Mets, taking the team from its position as a baseball graveyard to the Tiffany's of the sport. His operation became the envy of everybody in baseball.

Doubleday and Company bought the team in 1980 and bankrolled Cashen's vision. But what has mattered most has been that vision. Cashen has made personnel mistakes, everybody does. For the most part, he has been right: building the farm system first, signing Darryl Strawberry, getting Keith Hernandez and then Gary Carter in trades, signing Gooden, and somehow, in his quiet way, assembling the sexiest team in sports. And the strongest organization. Cashen has built something that will last. The fruits of his vision will still be around in the year 2000. It is that simple. Shea Stadium will be gone and the Mets will probably be playing in high-tech digs somewhere else in Queens, perhaps under a dome, and they will talk about Cashen still, as if he were the Mets' Branch Rickey.

Words failed him in the face of the denial. He just stared at Gooden, finally sighed, then said, "Son. The report. It's there in black and white."

Like: The report card doesn't lie.

"You can read it if you want to. Do you want to read it?"

"No."

The report had been delivered to Cashen the previous afternoon, around five o'clock. He had called McIlvaine and Al Harazin, senior vice-president of the Mets and equal second-in-command to Cashen with McIlvaine. Harazin's primary responsibility is contracts. It was Harazin, with Cashen's approval, who had agreed to pay Gooden the $1.5 million for the 1987 season. The three of them had sat in Cashen's office looking at the lab report the way Cashen, McIlvaine, and Dwight Gooden would the next morning.

Cashen said, "Gentlemen, we have a tragedy on our hands."

McIlvaine said to Cashen, "What happens now?"

"We bring him in in the morning and confront him with the evidence, and then we're going to have to get him into some kind of drug rehabilitation." Cashen, upon receiving the results of the drug test, had placed a call to baseball Commissioner Peter Ueberroth's office in New York. Ueberroth, who had been vigorously attacking the cocaine epidemic in his sport since assuming the role of commissioner in 1984, was quite specific in his response to the fact that Gooden had been using cocaine:

Gooden would enter a rehabilitation program immediately.

Or he would be suspended from the sport for an indefinite length of time.

One or the other.

Cashen said to Harazin and McIlvaine, "We're going to need another Opening Day pitcher."

Now on the morning of April 1st, 1987, with the Mets scheduled to play an exhibition game against the Pirates in Bradenton, Gooden put his head down—he was almost shaved bald, said his momma thought his hair was too long last season—mumbled, "It's not true. Swear to God."

McIlvaine thought, Dwight, start owning up.

Gooden suddenly picked his head up, looked past the paper and directly at Frank Cashen.

"Do I gotta go to jail?" he said.

The previous December, Gooden had been involved in a much-publicized incident with the Tampa police. Gooden was driving his Mercedes. There were friends in another car. It was night. Gooden and his friends had been drinking. Both cars were pulled over. An altercation ensued. Gooden had one version, the police had another, eyewitnesses had another. (One said he heard a policeman growl, "Break his fucking arm.") The result was that Gooden was charged with resisting arrest, assaulting an officer of the law. Gooden was given a stiff probation.

It was the last troubling episode for Gooden in what had been an erratic 1986, both on and off the field. He had missed a spring training game after being involved in a mysterious car accident. There had been an incident with a rental car clerk at LaGuardia Airport in April, involving Gooden, his fiancée (at the time) Carlene Pearson, and Gooden's sister, Betty; a drink was thrown, the three of them ended up talking about it with the Port Authority police.

It did not end there. Gooden, after having a record of 24–4 in 1985, slipped to 17 wins. His strikeout total dipped from 268 to 200, and his earned run average rose from 1.53 to 2.84. It was still a season to be coveted by 99 percent of the pitchers in baseball.

There was just something different.

He was more Dwight Gooden than The Doc. Someday, when the knees and ankles go for good, Magic Johnson will turn back into Earvin Johnson, whether he wants to or not.

After a while, people did not go to Shea Stadium thinking this would be the night he would strike out twenty men. There was not the same commotion in The K Corner, the section of Shea high up and in left field, where two Mets fans named Dennis Scalzitti and Bob Belle had achieved local celebrity from the time Gooden was a rookie, hanging "K" cards over the railing (K being the shorthand in a baseball scorecard for strikeout) every time Gooden would strike out another man, turn another bat into dust.

The K was as old as baseball, but somehow it became the kid's monogram those first two years.

Only now, in the third year, he was great and no longer legendary and while no one came out and said it, Mets fans knew the difference. In sports, there are unspoken truths you feel before you verbalize.

Excuses were made instead. It is a rule someone passed in sports for that transition between legend and great.

No way he *could* repeat 1985. You kidding?

He's just having a natural letdown, son of a *bitch*, give the kid a break, he's twenty-one. You *know* how many pitchers would like to die for the season he's having right now.

What's the big deal, anyway? The Mets are twenty games in front of the field. *The Doc will be there in October.*

Except he wasn't, not exactly, not like everyone expected. Not like 1985. He lost the first game of the National League Championship Series to Houston's Mike Scott. He pitched bravely in Game 5, locked in a pitching duel with Houston's Nolan Ryan, and came away with no decision in a game the Mets eventually won 2–1 in 12 innings. Then he flopped in the World Series, gave the Mets no help at all. Two starts. Two losses. ERA of 8.00. Nine innings total in the two games.

Then he missed the Mets victory parade in Manhattan. Said he was in the process of breaking up with Miss Pearson, while everyone who heard about the story or read about the story just nodded knowingly, said, "Hangover."

Then there was a bizarre story of Miss Pearson getting picked up at LaGuardia for carrying a handgun through the security checkpoint.

Finally, he got pulled over and beat up by the Tampa police.

It was then that the rumors started up—again—that Dwight Gooden was using cocaine. There had been rumors during the season. Gooden and other Mets were supposed to be using cocaine.

Not a month went by during the season when one of the New York papers did not get a phone tip. Every New York sports editor turned narcotics agent, waiting to be the one who broke the story of Gooden, and others, or all, using cocaine. Reporters were dispatched to clubs the Mets frequented. Leads were checked out. Police informants were contacted.

The Number One rumor went something like this: Gooden and others had been seen snorting cocaine in a parked car, and had been spotted by police, but ignored.

Nothing checked out. The rumors never got near the newspapers.

But they were Out There. Any time an athlete slips now in sports, particularly a rich, young black athlete, they are fingered as dopers without any proof. It is part of the game. So throughout the summer of

1986, the glorious summer when the Mets went about the business of winning the National League East as if they were some baseball Secretariat, there was always someone on the phone to a New York sports department, and that somebody always had a friend or a cousin who had seen Gooden using cocaine.

When Gooden got himself arrested, the rumors went wild. The whispers. Sports editors heard them. Fans heard them. Gooden heard them. The Mets heard them. Gooden looked fat. You heard that.

Gooden was sweating an awful lot when he pitched.

Did he sweat like that when he was winning 24?

He's awful twitchy on the mound now, you know, between pitches.

The Doc look all that wound up last season?

"You get phone calls," Joe McIlvaine said. "You hear wild stories. It happens all the time. Sometimes you check. Sometimes you don't. Eventually, without hiring a battery of private detectives for all the stories about your players, you dismiss them. And hope to God they aren't true."

Over the winter, in the wake of the incident with the Tampa police, Dwight Gooden announced that he would voluntarily submit to drug testing if that's what it would take to stop the rumors circling above him like buzzards. You don't think I'm clean? I'll prove to you I'm clean. No problem.

Give me the bottle.

He showed up in St. Petersburg looking leaner than he had the previous season, with the new momma-said-so hair and, he said, a new attitude. "I don't know who that person was last season," he said one day in the Mets clubhouse. "But it sure wasn't me."

People believed because they wanted to believe. Like McIlvaine said: Hope to God. Hope it was just a bunch of shit in 1986. Run of bad luck. Except that the rumors would not go away

On March 11th, 1987, Joe McIlvaine attended a baseball game between the University of South Florida and Florida State. McIlvaine has the reputation of being a brilliant scout; his first job with the Mets had been as scouting director. During spring training, if there was a good college game in the St. Petersburg area, McIlvaine would go watch it. And there was this pitcher from South Florida McIlvaine wanted to take a look at.

The game was in Tampa. McIlvaine, as was his habit, sat in the scouts' section. He struck up a conversation with the stranger sitting next to him. The man asked McIlvaine who he worked for, McIlvaine said the Mets, the conversation finally got around to Gooden vs. the Tampa police. The story, like the rumors, would not go away. Gooden is a Tampa kid; he had played his high school ball at Hillsborough High, and still lived with his parents in the off-season. It was the kind of high-school-hero-goes-bad affair that a town gets into its teeth and worries to death, dog with a big, old bone.

The stranger defended the police to McIlvaine. There had been allegations, after the fact, that maybe things had gotten out of hand because the policemen were white and Gooden and his friends had been black; it was suggested that if it hadn't been a young black man in a Mercedes the car wouldn't have been pulled over in the first place. The stranger sitting with Joe McIlvaine at the USF–FSU game raised the argument, shot it down.

McIlvaine was tired of talking about Dwight Gooden and police officers. "Well," he said, "there's two sides to every story."

The man got up to leave at the end of the eighth inning. He said to McIlvaine, "I guess I should have told you at the start, but I'm a Tampa police officer."

McIlvaine said, "Oh, is that so?"

The Tampa police officer then said, "You take this for what it's worth, but the word on the street is that the kid is into cocaine a little bit."

McIlvaine remembers thinking, this is a little bit more than a crank call.

"I still didn't want to believe it," he said. "But I figured I better tell Frank."

Two weeks later, Cashen decided he would take Gooden up on his offer of voluntary testing. Clear the air, once and for all. "I thought, let's get it done before the season," Cashen said. "If anybody wants to confront us with the damn rumors, then our skirts are clean. We've tested the young man, and he's come up negative, seven ways to Sunday." Cashen went to Gooden and told him he wanted the test. Gooden said, Fine.

For months afterward, people speculated about why Gooden had agreed to take the test if he knew he had used the coke a couple of days before. Was it a cry for help? Did he want to get caught? Sports psychobabble. Gooden wasn't afraid of urinalysis. It turns out, he had used coke a few days before his rounds with the Tampa police, took a urinalysis then, beat it. Tested negative. Apparently thought he had some sort of lifetime exemption from ever testing positive. In his novel, *Baja Oklahoma,* writer Dan Jenkins listed the ten stages of drunkenness. No. 10 was "Bulletproof." When it came to peeing in a bottle, Dwight Gooden thought he was bulletproof.

In June, Gooden simply said, "I never thought I'd get caught." Illegal drugs are not called dope for nothing. Just because you have a 90-mile-per-hour fastball does not make you an entrant in the World's Smartest Man contest.

This time the EMIT Screen Test won.

It was now batting .500, one-for-two against Gooden.

Cashen said, "Son, who's close to you? Who can we call? We can't sit on this, we've got to move."

Gooden said nothing.

Cashen said, "Do you want me to call your parents?"

"No."

McIlvaine thought, the most famous player in the world maybe, and he's afraid to call his parents.

Cashen said, "Do you want me to call Jim Neader?" Neader was Gooden's St. Petersburg-based agent.

"Yes."

Cashen went outside to use a pay phone. The players were starting to appear in the clubhouse, sitting in front of lockers, reading morning papers, chatting near the coffee machine. Arrogant, supremely confident baseball team, winner of 116 baseball games the season before, getting ready to play out the Florida spring.

A couple of weeks before, at the Joan Payson Complex, on a similar spring training morning, Wally Backman had sipped coffee and smoked a Winston Light in front of his locker. Backman is a tough little man from Oregon, more a New Yorker in attitude than his teammates on a New York team, a baseball Dead-End Kid once he showed up in the clubhouse, a baseball citizen from some bygone, dirty-uniform era, incapable of ducking a reporter's question, of giving a dishonest answer. It had been suggested of Wally Backman more than once that if he ever tried to bullshit a writer on even the most innocent issue, he would get the bends.

On a team of brash talkers, Backman talked as much as anyone. It was not always politic conversation; Backman didn't care, he was a dirty uniform, used to leading with his face. The season before, he had been one of the Mets' offensive heroes, batting .320, backing up his mouth. He was a switch-hitting second baseman more effective batting left-handed against right-handed pitchers, a pest in the No. 2 hole behind his pal on the team, center fielder Lenny Dykstra.

Backman had been asked, "What will it take for you guys *not* to repeat?"

Backman dragged on the Winston Light and said, "Fifteen or twenty fucking car wrecks."

The other Mets were not so blunt, but felt as Backman did. So, in his quiet way, did Cashen. "I'm a pitching guy," he said. "The year before, I've got more pitching than anybody. I still figure I got more pitching than anybody."

But there was the lab report back in the office with McIlvaine and Gooden. Cashen called Neader, nodded to the players in the room, knowing what they did not know about the season, went out to the field to find manager Davey Johnson, carrying the news of the first fucking car wreck.

Cashen briskly gave Johnson the facts. Told about the test, the result, the need for Gooden to go away for treatment. By the end of the morning, Cashen would have called Hazelden, in Minnesota, and the Betty Ford Clinic, and the Smithers Center in Manhattan, trying to decide where his Opening Day pitcher would spend Opening Day.

Joe McIlvaine tried to get Gooden to talk about it. Looked at him and tried to feel like a father, wondered how he would handle it if this were his son. McIlvaine knew he was there with a twenty-two-year-old man, a man already owning baseball history and the biggest contract a pitcher his age had ever signed. But Gooden had never been treated that way, not by the Mets, by baseball. He was treated like a baseball Mozart. That's what one writer had called him. Boy genius. Magical child. He was the kind of talent a scout—and all baseball executives are scouts at heart—hopes to find once in a lifetime.

Gooden said, "I only tried it a couple of times at parties, swear to God."

"Did you use it during the season?"

Gooden said, "Never."

McIlvaine did not know what to believe. Positive on EMIT Screen could have meant anything from junkie to couple-a-times-at-a-party-swear-to-God. And as he sat there, not knowing what to say, waiting for Cashen to come back and Neader, the agent, to arrive, McIlvaine could not help thinking back to the night he signed Gooden to the Mets contract, back in 1982.

He had gone to the Gooden home. Dan Gooden, the father, was there, and Jim Neader, and Carlos Pascual, brother of the famous curve-ball pitcher Camilo Pascual; Pascual was the Mets scout in central and south Florida, and Central America. They sat in the Goodens' living room, and there was lot of conversation, and finally Dan Gooden wanted the deal.

McIlvaine said, "Eighty-five thousand."

The father said, "We'll take it." Neader started to say something, wanted to be an agent, negotiate it up another flight.

The father said, "We're done." He looked at Joe McIlvaine and said, "How about we go out and celebrate?"

McIlvaine said that sounded fine. He remembers, laughing, that all of a sudden relatives started walking through the door, like a fire drill in reverse, sisters and cousins, and he was introduced to them all quickly, and everyone got into cars and went to a nearby restaurant. McIlvaine remembers a party of twelve.

When everyone was seated, menus were being read, drink orders were being taken, McIlvaine looked around and noticed something was wrong with the picture.

"Where's Dwight?"

Dan Gooden said, "Oh, he went off with some friends."

Now, on April 1, 1987, McIlvaine sat there with Gooden, wondering if the kid had blown everything, and thought back to that restaurant.

"I couldn't get the irresponsibility of that out of my mind," he said. "At a time like that, you go back to the original."

Cashen came back. Neader arrived. Gooden asked for a couple of days before he would enter a rehabilitation clinic. Cashen said that was fine. Gooden and Neader left. Cashen was left alone in his office. He would address the Mets, explain to them what had happened, before they left for Bradenton. Now he sat. He had been named general manager of the Mets in February of 1980. In 1979, the team had won 63 games, lost 99, drew 788,905 fans to Shea Stadium, down nearly two million from the home attendance in 1970, the season after the Mets had won the World Series, been the Miracle Mets.

Cashen set out to build the team from the ground up, through the farm system, and the free-agent draft. Gooden became the symbol of the building, more than anyone else in the organization. The Mets finally got to 90 wins in the 1984 season. Gooden, who had been the Mets' No. 1 draft choice (fifth overall) in the 1982 draft, was nineteen years old. He won 17 games, had 276 strikeouts, averaged over 11 strikeouts per nine innings, had a one-hitter, became the first teenage rookie to ever lead a league in strikeouts. More than Davey Johnson, a rookie manager that season, more than Darryl Strawberry or veterans like Keith Hernandez and Gary Carter for whom Cashen would later trade, Gooden, the baseball Mozart, was the cornerstone. He was the ace for Cashen, the pitching guy. He was the draft reaping almost immediate benefits. He was the farm system. He was, by 1985, the brightest star in baseball, drawing huge crowds at home and on the road.

In 1986, the Mets won the 116, became champions of the world, drew 2,762,417 fans to Shea Stadium; it was an all-time baseball attendance record for New York City. Cashen, on the eve of the new season, felt the Mets would become the first "cold weather" (anyplace except Los Angeles) team to draw three million fans at home. And Cashen felt his team would be the first since the 1977–78 Yankees to repeat as world champions.

Now ... this ... shit. Up the kid's nose. All over the place.

Roger McDowell, the Mets' top relief pitcher the year before, would begin the season on the injured list, because of a hernia suffered during spring training. Dave Magadan, a Tampa prospect the Mets felt would someday be National League batting champion, would also begin the season on the injured list, because of minor surgery to remove an infected lymph node from under his arm. Cashen considered both incidents trifles. He felt Jesse Orosco, who had pitched so brilliantly during the playoffs and World Series, could carry the load until Mc-Dowell was ready to pitch, probably at the end of May. And Magadan had done nothing during the spring to earn the third base job away from incumbent Howard Johnson, anyway. And Cashen had traded for outfielder Kevin McReynolds, who would bat sixth behind Hernandez and Carter and Strawberry and, Cashen hoped, provide 30 home runs, as many as 100 RBI.

Gooden was different. In the parlance of professional sports in the 1980s, he was a franchise player. If there is such a thing as a quarterback in baseball, it is the ace of the starting pitching staff. Only he was a franchise player going away for a month—Hazelden, Betty Ford, Smithers, *someplace*—as soon as Cashen met with the team and met with the reporters and got on with one of the truly miserable, stinking days of his baseball life. April Fool's.

The rehab would take a month. When would Gooden be ready to pitch? Frank Cashen had no idea about that.

Or if Peter Ueberroth would suspend Gooden anyway, once the rehab was complete. Cashen had no guarantee from Ueberroth, one way or the other.

He slammed his fist on the desk in the empty office.

Cashen: "I had mixed emotions. I felt sorry for him. I was like Joe McIlvaine; I tried to imagine what my reaction would have been if he were one of my own children. I felt sorry for him, and his family. But more than anything else, I was angry. *Angry* about what he had done to himself and his family, and to our ball club. In that first day, and a lot of days that followed, there were a lot of people feeling sorry for Dwight, about this terrible mistake he had made, how terrible that was for him. I was not one of them. The more I thought about it, the more I was outraged at what this young man had done to his life, his career, the fans, the game of baseball, the New York Mets. *Outraged.* I have been around baseball a long time. I started with the Baltimore Orioles in 1966. I know how hard it is to win. You are given only so many chances. And only one team every year has a chance to repeat. And now I have to start the season shorthanded because Dwight Gooden used cocaine. Certainly, no one could have foreseen everything that would happen to us over the next six months. But I feel Dwight is the one who opened the door."

Cashen placed the EMIT Screen Test in the top drawer of his desk. Five months after Orosco had struck out Marty Barrett of the Red Sox to win the '86 World Series for the Mets, a week before the title defense would officially begin against the Pittsburgh Pirates at Shea Stadium, Cashen walked out of his office and delivered a terse keynote address to the baseball champions of the world.

"Dwight Gooden has tested positive for cocaine. . . ." the little man began.

One man's positive is often another man's negative.

LEVELS OF THE GAME

I don't even remember who told me. I think it was a phone call and probably the conversation went like this:

"They got Gooden."

"Cocaine?"

"Yeah."

"Fug."

"Yeah."

"Bye."

I do remember pacing after putting the phone into its cradle. I wasn't surprised—I don't think any fan really was surprised. We'd all known Gooden was... something. A drunk, a druggie, pick your poison. He'd been behaving so erratically for so long—the missed parades, the gun-toting girlfriends, the Hertz fights—that you had to assume it was a tad more than your standard problems with public maturation.

I also remember how I felt when I paced. I could say that I was a good neighbor and wished the kid well, hoped he'd come out of it, be able, eventually, to deal with reality. I could also say I was an obsessed fan and was furious that he'd screwed up the Mets' chances of repeating.

What I felt was this: deprived. Which can mean "divested of something enjoyed" or "stripped" or "bereaved."

Or all of the above.

Every athlete in the three major leagues possesses genuine quality. Even Buddy Biancalana with his lifetime average barely peeping over .200 would be a tiger on any playground in the Continental Forty-eight. But on a very much higher level there are a few, bless them, who are genuinely superb:

Andre Dawson
Steve Largent
Michael Cooper

Getting into a rarified atmosphere now. For above the superb there are a few, let us genuflect, who are great:

Pete Rose
Terry Bradshaw
Moses Malone

Hard to breathe now. But there is yet another level. Visited by so few. Nod in recognition please, for the unsurpassed:

Schmidt
Payton
Bird and Magic

The unsurpassed need but one name. I don't need to say "Jack" Nicklaus. If I have to say "Rod" Laver, I'm obviously not talking to a tennis fan.

So this is as high as it gets, then?

No.

But how can something surpass someone who is unsurpassed?

Can't.

So?

We are talking now about a different level altogether. Not higher. Not better, necessarily. Just different. It's as if the names thus far were hung on branches of a tree. And on the highest branch, that's where the unsurpassed belong.

But what if next to the tree is not another tree but something totally different, a pyramid? And, depending on your angle as you move, either higher or less high or the same height as the tree.

Legends live on the pyramid.

a. Who are they?
b. And why?
c. And why does it matter?

Nicklaus is not on the pyramid. You may call him the greatest golfer and you may be right. You're welcome to your opinion. You're wrong but you're welcome to it. But not Fat Jack. No mystery to the pharmacist's son. If the life of someone I loved was at stake, and that life depended on a single golf shot, I don't want the Golden Bear with his hands on the club. It's obvious who I do want.

And it's obvious to you, too. Think a minute. Someone you love. One single shot. If you follow golf, you're already nodding, thinking the name. There's only one possibility and it isn't Jones and it isn't Snead and, God knows, it isn't Palmer.

Hogan.

Has to be Hogan. When other golfers see Nicklaus they smile or nod. If they know him they say hello. When Hogan passes by they just stand there. And whisper, some of them, to each other: "It's Hogan."

Why does he cause that reaction? Two reasons, mainly. First, his record. Second, the car crash. It crippled him, that crash. That's what the early radio reports said. I remember sitting up in bed when I was a kid, listening to the sports news and hearing that: he might never walk again, he certainly would never play. I'd watched him. In those days, the biggest money tournament was outside Chicago, Tam O'Shanter. I spent one nine following Snead, the other Ben. (You could call him that. He wasn't a legend then.) They seemed, to my totally amateurish eye, equals. But all Snead did in the decades to come was win and win and win. Hogan damn near died.

And so he's on the pyramid. Wilt, too. And of course, the Babe. And Gehrig. But not because of his playing, great as that was. If Gehrig were alive today (and if he were, he'd be all of eight years older than President Reagan) and going to Old Timer's Days, there would be arguments about him—not who was the greatest first basemen but who was the greatest first baseman *of just the 1930s,* Gehrig or Greenberg or Foxx? And I'm not sure Gehrig would have won the argument. It was his death that brought him to the pyramid.

Here, alphabetically, are three running backs, all great. Which one's on the pyramid?

Brown
Sayers
Simpson

If you didn't say Sayers, you are wrong. At least in my pantheon. (All of this, understand, deals only with *my* pantheon. You may think Jimmy Connors belongs. I think he sucks. Probably the truth lies somewhere in between.)

Why Sayers? Not only because he was the most exciting runner of modern times. But because he was struck down. Unfairly. Pissed on by the gods.

I have seen a lot of pitchers in my life: Koufax and Spahn and Ford and Gibson and Marichal and Carlton and Seaver and a dozen more. But there are at least that many that I didn't get a chance, because of age, to watch. Which one do you think I most would want to see?

Grove
Johnson
Mathewson
Young

Answer? None of the above. The man I would have died for never made it to the majors. But you hear things, you hear things. I have seen much great acting but the two performances I most wish I had seen (I saw Brando in *Streetcar*) were Olivier's Oedipus and Laurette Taylor in *The Glass Menagerie*.

For pitchers, Steve Dalkowski is my man. Maybe, just maybe, the greatest fireballer in the history of the game. I've talked to people who saw him and that's what they say. No one even close. And he didn't look like a power pitcher, either; too chunky.

But he simply had no control. There are stories. (You hear things, you hear things.) My favorite is that he sometimes did have control. Could sometimes rip the corners, scorch high and rising. But only in practice when whoever his minor league manager was would place batters on *both* sides of the plate.

But if I am leading you to believe that mainly the maimed belong on the pyramid, let me correct myself now. Ali, of course, is babbling away on the pyramid as I write this. But not the Ali who was embarrassed by Spinks, humiliated by Holmes.

Legends, when they are healthy, and when it matters, truly matters, always come through. Legends are *there*. And I was there, in Comiskey Park when the man who, for any Chicagoan, is the greatest legend played his greatest game. To put it as briefly as possible: I saw Nagurski.

He was the Bambino of Football.

Grantland Rice went on record as saying that he obviously was the greatest football player who ever lived because eleven Bronko Nagurski's could beat eleven anyone elses. The point being, the man had a certain versatility.

Opening game of '27, his sophomore year at Minnesota, he started at end. But tackle was the weak spot so he shifted there. He had surprising speed for his size—six-two, 230—and also, for his size, shocking power. Red Grange used that word in describing what it was like to try and tackle the man. It was "strange; like getting an electric shock."

Why would you tackle a tackle? Because Nagurski played both positions, tackle and fullback, and was All-American at both positions *the same year*. But that was not the full extent of his versatility. Many feel he was surely the greatest blocking back. Hard to prove. Some evidence exists. And if you were a sports fan of my time in Chicago, these numbers meant something:

1,004–101

Beattie Feathers was a Bear rookie in '34, up from Tennessee. And those were his numbers that year—1,004 yards gained in 101 attempts. Almost all of it on one basic play. You know the famous University of Southern California basic play, made famous by O.J.? Student Body Left and Student Body Right? That's what the Bears had. Except Nagurski was the entire student body. He would go crashing off tackle or around end, Feathers riding him, then exploding on his own.

Nagurski will never be remembered as a great passer, but he threw the most important pass in pro football history. It came at the end of the championship game of '32.

The score as the game was ending was 0–0. The Bears were in deep but the entire Portsmouth team knew that Nagurski would carry the ball so they bunched in and stopped him twice. The third time was the charm.

He got the ball, bolted straight ahead toward the masses, then, almost daintily, at least for him, retreated a few steps and passed to Grange for the winning touchdown. (Not a bad battery, that.) It brought the Bears their first championship in eleven years.

Hysteria followed. Wild arguments all coming down to a single issue: Where was the Bronk when he released the ball? Because in those days, you had to be five yards *behind* the line of scrimmage to pass legally. The Bears won the argument that day, but the echoes built well into the off-season, at which point two men, Halas and George Preston Marshall of the Redskins, decided to hell with it, let's let them pass from *anywhere* behind the line of scrimmage. That decision changed pro football forever.

It also made things a lot easier for Nagurski. From then on, one of the Bears' best plays was sending him up to the line, letting him jump, loft the ball to Billy Hewitt (who sometime lateraled after the catch). When he retired, one Bears book gives Nagurski's passing totals as 38 completions in 80 attempts. (Considering that Payton is 11 for 34 and is the best at that play today, 38 for 80 will do.)

But all this, the blocking, the passing, the line play, the shuddering runs—I have to interrupt myself to tell about just one. In '33, in a run for the championship, the Bears had a 10–7 lead late in the game when the Bronk, playing defense, was caught holding, giving the enemy a first down. Long pass. Touchdown. The Bears are down now, 14–10. Kickoff to the Bronk. He bucks up to the Bear 45. Huddle. And he's crying. "It's all my fault," he says. "Just gimme the ball." Muddy field. Shovel pass right. He grabs it, chugs down the sideline. Hit. Hit. Everyone bounces off. Picking up speed now. The goal line closer. Roaring. Touchdown. Bears win.

Only he's going so fast and the field is so treacherous he can't stop. At the south end of Wrigley was a dugout. In those days it was kept open. The Bronk slams into the dugout before coming in contact with a brick wall. Later, groundskeepers swore there was a dent in the wall. Surely apocryphal. But what is known is from that day on, and for as long as the Bears played at Wrigley, the dugout was boarded up during football season. A leading sportswriter described the run: "Those who were unlucky got in his way. Those who were lucky got out of it. The only thing that could stop him was a brick wall."

Which finally brought him down.

Now to repeat—all this, the blocking, the passing, the line play, the shuddering runs, all that unparalleled versatility is only of value, meaningful value, if it helps the team. The year before Nagurski joined them, the Bears won four, lost eight. His first year with them, they lost four, won nine. His last year with them they lost one of eleven. The first year after he was gone, they lost five. They won 70 percent of their games during the Nagurski years.

I knew all this growing up. Pretty much of it, anyway. Mainly because my late Uncle Victor had gotten season tickets for the Bears somewhere in the (I think but maybe earlier) mid-twenties and was the first genuine sports nut I ever knew.

Pro football was like a heffalump when I was growing up, this weird thing that huffed along come Sunday. I remember in the playground, during the great Bear teams of the forties, arguing constantly their merits. What it came down to usually was this: Could the Bears, the 73–0 Bears, the four-time world champions between '40 and '46, *beat Notre Dame?* That was what I had to face. And the majority answer was this: They could not. Reason? Because the college teams *cared.* They played for love. And the pros were just a bunch of big fat guys who did it for money.

Hard times at Elm Place School.

I didn't really care. (I did, that's a lie, I knew how wonderful they were.) But I didn't care how great the derision because *I got to go.* As a consequence of my Uncle Victor's haranguing, my family got Bear season tickets from (I think) 1940 on. They were good seats. On the twenty. But not like my Uncle Victor's. His seats, having been present at the creation, were dead center. I can remember now sitting in his seat and following the fifty-yard line straight up to where it could cut me in half.

And we saw such players. Slingin' Sammy Baugh, most accurate of all passers. And Don Hutson, a legitimate legend at twenty-five.

And the Bears had Sid Luckman and wonderful runners—Gallarneau and Standlee—and whenever I raved on about them Uncle Victor would shake his head and say it: "You should have seen Nagurski."

God, I hated that taunt.

"You should have seen Nagurski."

Because I couldn't. He was gone. Retiring after the '37 season, becoming wrestling champion then of some pro world or other, finally leaving sports altogether, heading back to the Northland.

Every time I'd see a great run I'd ask, "Could he have done that, Nagurski?" Usually my uncle wouldn't even bother to dignify the question.

At nights after games I used to wonder: Was he real? Could they be true, the stories—not all the stories, no one really expected all the stories, but some of them, just some of them.

Please, just some of them.

In 1943, six years after retiring, first there were rumors, then the rumors were fact: War had sapped manpower. *Nagurski was returning!*

Ecstasy.

Then more facts: but not to run, never to run, only to help out at tackle.

Despair.

It was worse than not having him there at all. I watched him whenever he played. Big No. 3. At tackle. Big deal. I still don't know what a tackle's supposed to do. There's this snap and then everyone gets all squished together. I don't know what a center does, either. And guards I follow only when they pull.

Let him run, I thought. Just let me see him run.

But he didn't run. The season went on. The Bears were locked in it against the Packers. Season, as all seasons do, winds down. One game left. The Bears have to win it. Have to. If they do, they're in the championship game. If not, say hello to Green Bay.

But they will win it. It's a cinch. Because they're playing the worst team in the league, the winless Cardinals. Except in those days, these were still the Chicago Cardinals, the move to St. Louis still inconceivably in the future. And if you think of the Dodgers versus the Giants, that's what this was then. They always were playing for the blood-spilling rights to all Chicago.

The game was to be in their pen, Comiskey Park. We trooped in, my family, led by Uncle Victor. "Maybe Nagurski will play," he said on the drive in. "They might need Nagurski. Then you'll see something."

There was, as I remember, a certain distant logic to his pronouncements. Nagurski was listed all season as the fourth-string fullback on the talent charts. And then the game prior, the third-string guy got hurt. (This is all memory now.) So he was moved up. But it didn't really matter, once the game began.

November 28th, the South Side of Chicago, and the Cardinals were simply inspired. They owned the line of scrimmage. And their fans owned the air. First quarter, all Cardinals. Second quarter, still. Close, but they were better. And they knew it. And at halftime we talked about how we'd get it back together and kill them in the third.

But late in the third it was the Cardinals, 24–14. It was their day. The season was suddenly (we'd only lost once, up till then) dying on us.

Earlier, in the first half, the second-string fullback got hurt. And then, with the Bears trying to get something, anything going, they sent their fullback into the line.

Pileup.

Slow unpiling.

Everybody back on his feet.

Everybody except our first-string fullback.

And then (and I can see this as I write), far across the field, this lone
figure got off the bench, reached for his helmet. And slowly trotted
onto the grass.

Murmurs from the Cardinal fans. Murmurs that built. They checked
their programs. It was No. 3. And beside me, my Uncle Victor, who
was to die before his time, was out of all control, standing and screaming and pounding me on the back—"It's him—the Bronko—and
they're putting him in the backfield—now you'll see something—*now
you'll see something.*"

I don't know that I was ever so scared in my life. I was so frightened
that after all the dreams, all my ridiculous fantasies, it wasn't going to
be right.

And he looked, truth to tell, very slow as he came on the field.

And worst of all, I saw doubt in my uncle's eyes. " 'Course he's been
away six years," he said. "A lot can happen in six years."

Into the huddle now. Then out of it. Luckman, still for me the most
brilliant quarterback, moves behind center. Behind him now, waiting,
Nagurski. And in Comiskey Park, it was wild, because even though
they rooted for the wrong team they were fans and they knew what
everyone knew that Luckman was going to hand off to Nagurski for an
inside run.

The Cardinals knew it, too—you could see them inching closer
together. I sensed the disaster, I really did, and then I realized that
Luckman was too much the master to ever try the obvious, that what
he would do was either (a) fake to Nagurski and throw a touchdown
pass over the bunched Cardinal defense or (b) hand off to
Nagurski, who would do what he did that won the championship with
the pass to Grange: fake the run and do the passing himself.

Luckman counts cadence.

The Cards are waiting.

The snap.

Luckman turns.

Hands off to Nagurski.

Who runs. But slowly.

Too slowly.

The Cardinals are waiting.

It's not a fake. It's nothing at all but a plunge at the line. Only the
Cardinal line is there, surging forward, and as I stared I saw, after all
these years, I saw Nagurski being lifted up into the air by the enemy.
Frozen and helpless.

I just couldn't watch. I was so fucking mad. At Luckman for being suddenly now—*why now?*—stupid. At Nagurski for coming back. At the Bears for asking him.

All my years of waiting, all my hope, and I get an old slug who is going to leave us with a second down and 12 to go, maybe second and 13. I had no way of knowing then I was entering into the high point of my life.

I turned back to the field. Second and 6.

And 6?

"What happened?" I asked.

"I don't know," the guy next to me said. "He sort of fell forward."

I didn't get it but I decided not to turn away again.

Next play. Same play. Or sort of the same play, it was just the Bronk taking the ball from Luckman and ploughing ahead and the Cardinals zapped him again—

—only not before he'd made a first down.

And suddenly I remembered what the great Grange had said about trying to tackle Nagurski.

"Strange."

That was the word he used. It was "something strange."

And now something strange was starting to happen down on the field. Because it was clear that the Bears had no tricks today. They were going with the old man. And something strange was happening in the stands, too. The sounds were imploring, all home fans sound imploring a lot of the time. But it was different. I don't know about this, but what I like to think is that none of us would have rather been anywhere else in the world that November afternoon.

He just kept attacking the Cardinal line and the Bears moved down the field. There is an image I thought that day and it's this: If you've never seen an axe and you've never seen a tree and the one is swung at the other, you have no way of knowing what's going to happen. Maybe the tree will give. Or maybe the axe will bounce away.

He didn't bounce away. And the Cardinals were behaving differently too, slapping each other on the asses, trying to fire each other up.

They were ahead but they were already behind. This force was coming at them from God knows where and they couldn't get out of its way. Now the Bears are near the Cardinal ten. And the huddle. And the snap. And Luckman turns. And he takes the ball, Nagurski takes the ball and slices through to the eight and then a half a dozen men hit him and he falls forward and crawls, *crawls,* and more and more guys are dropping on him, diving at him. And finally, they stop him.

On the one.

They huddle in their end zone and they're shaking their fists and hitting each other but they know what's coming and they also know they are helpless, helpless to stop it.

We're all standing now, Bear fans and Cardinal fans and what I remember most is this: It was eerie. Everyone knew what was going to happen. We were all seers that Sunday.

The Bears break. The snap. Luckman turns. Hands off. The Bronk takes off. The Cardinals are the tree. He is the axe. They give it their best but the axe always wins.

Touchdown for the old guy.

That was the beginning of the beating. From being 10 down with the third quarter going, the Bears win by 11. Nagurski gains, in less than one quarter, 80 yards, maybe more. We're in the championship game, we win that too, he scores his final touchdown there, then back he goes to International Falls, this time forever.

Every time I see a runner I see him. Still. All the names we all know. All great.

He was just different. The Babe was different. Wilt was different. All of them sitting highest on the pyramid. Koufax sits there too.

Sanford Koufax, born Brooklyn, New York, December 30th, 1935, retired from baseball after the 1966 season, thirty years old. When he left, there were no more pitching legends. Not for nearly twenty years, when Dwight Eugene Gooden came along.

How did Koufax get there?

Very slowly.

What he had from the beginning was speed. He could, as they say in the trade, "bring it." Just precisely where he brought it, however, posed something of a problem. As a nineteen-year-old bonus baby rookie, he was used little, managed to strike out 30 and walk 28. The next year he got a little worse, striking out 30, walking 29. Two years later he had his first double-figure win, taking down 11 W's. He also had 11 L's, walked 105 in 159 innings, all with an earned run average of slightly under 4½ runs per game. After seven years in the majors, at the age of twenty-five, he was genuinely mediocre: 54 wins, 53 losses, an ERA of 3.97.

We in the East (I was a New Yorker by now) promptly forgot about him. He had been a Brooklyn Dodger his first three years and we had seen what there was to see: just another brainless power pitcher.

But Out There, where they don't know much, especially about sports, drums were beginning to beat. True, he did lead the league in K's in '61, but he still walked close to one hundred, his ERA was still high: 3.52. True, in '62, he did pitch a no-hitter and lead the league in ERA, but his record was a certainly modest 14 up, 7 down.

Then came '63.

Remember, there was no real National League baseball in New York during most of this time. The greedy Dodgers and cowardly Giants had long since gone, the funny Mets were something to be avoided. And so, when the idiots from La-La Land began talking about this *great* new creature in their midst, this *amazing* figure, well, we knew better: These were, after all, the folks who gave us *Cleopatra*.

Granted, he had put up some better-than-fair numbers in '63: 25–5, 306 K's in 311 innings, an ERA of 1.88. We New Yorkers remained unconvinced. This was merchandise we had seen. We knew how bad the Mets were. Let him do something against a *team*. Like, say, the '63 Yankees.

This edition wasn't the '61 monsters (109 wins, the M&Ms hit 54 and 61, respectively) but it was representative. Maybe a speck better. With the M&Ms mostly sidelined (167 games between them) they still eked out 104 W's, had four guys with more than twenty homers (as they were once, in olden times, referred to) and in Whitey Ford (24–7, 2.74), Ralph Terry (17–15, 3.22), and the not-yet-scandalous Jim Bouton (21–7, 2.53) they were well staffed.

It was truly a David and Goliath confrontation. Because the Dodgers were a mediocre ballclub. Yes, they had speed (Wills, Willie Davis) but only Frank Howard had hit more than twenty out and their other two pitchers, Drysdale and Podres, had won a grand total of four games more than they'd lost.

Besides, they were the *Dodgers*. Greedy, craven carpetbaggers; cowardly, swinish, grasping, dastardly milquetoasts; spineless, white-feathered, pussyfooting sneaks—you could only call them names like this if you fancied them. If you saw them for what they were—Benedict Arnolds all—you could only wish for one thing: blood. Their blood. Splattered all over the sunshine of Yankee Stadium.

And with that thought in mind, 69,000-plus went to the ballpark. I, along with some fellow haters, repaired to the trusty tube. Victory was taken for granted. Humiliation was probably a good side bet.

But curiosity was in the air, too: Had Sanford actually improved? Could he get it, with any consistency, over the plate? Was there any truth at all to the rumors or was it all Los Angeles horseshit, the production of which they excel?

(When it matters, truly matters, legends are *there*. Don't forget that. Never forget that.)

Ford humiliates them in the top of the first. Zero for them.

Then there he was on the mound. We studied. He looked like good old wild Sandy. Handsomer, if possible. But assuredly erratic. Under pressure.

Batter up and it's Kubek. Tony whiffs. Swinging.

Next: Bobby Richardson who doesn't strike out (22 K's in 630 times at bat). And this was one that did it. Swinging strike one. Foul strike two. And then the blazer. High. And the consummate contact hitter swipes at the ball. Flails at it. Whiffs. But a giant one. He looked—we had to admit it—funny. Bobby Richardson looked like a clown.

Someone in the room laughed.

Something a bit out of the ordinary was happening in the Bronx. Now Tommy Tresh. Called third strike.

So: He had struck out the side. On all of twelve pitches. Unnerving, sure. But we still had Whitey on the mound. The great cuffer. Ten World Series wins already in the bank. (The all-time you-could-look-it-up record.)

They belted the shit out of him for four runs. A *shot* and no one ever hit harder than Frank Howard did that day—we're speaking of a 460-foot *line drive* off the center field wall. I don't think it ever got much higher than when it left his bat. Then singles by Skowron and Tracewski, a homer by Roseboro.

With an ordinary team, you figure trouble. But we had Mantle, Maris, and Elston Howard coming up to crush the figure on the mound.

First, the Mick.

Not on top of his game, as stated, but what there was, as Mr. Tracy said of Miss Hepburn, was "cherce." 172 at bats, 15 crunched.

Strike three. Looking. Four in a row.

Now we are all quiet in the room. Just watching the TV. Maris. Maris works the count to 2–2. He's fouled off a couple. And I know what he's doing: He's measuring Koufax; he's about to take him deep.

Strike three. Swinging.

"Somebody at least hit him," one of us said.

Elston Howard obeyed us. On the first pitch. Foul out. Inning over. And I guess we pretty much knew it then: We were looking at a legend.

There is a moment near the start of the fabulous barroom fight in *Shane*. I first saw it when it came out at Radio City Music Hall with 5,000 others and you know, going into the fight, that Shane is different. Nothing *bothers* him the way it does you and me. He has a certain confidence based on the fact, maybe, that he can, with his six-gun, kill[*] anyone else in the room.

But in the barroom brawl he's without his weapon. And he's outnumbered (it seemed like, oh, fifty to one) and he could have turned tail but he didn't, and the fight starts and he's doing great, clobbering this bigger guy—

—*and then he's hit.* A punch penetrates. He's not floored or anything, but the power registers and in that huge room, watching, everyone let out a cry of surprise: We didn't think anything could touch him.

And that's how it was with Koufax that day. Cruising with a five-nothing lead in the eighth, he gave up a grounder in the hole to Kubek, a home run to Tresh.

When Tresh hit it, we all in the room made the *Shane* sound: We didn't think anything could touch Koufax.

Not that many did. He struck out a (then) Series record of fifteen and started the Dodgers on an, admit it, deserved four-game sweep. Koufax won the fourth game too, beating Ford (who was never to win another Series game) again—2–1 this time, the "1" being a homer by Mantle, showing that some form of justice still existed in the world.

Koufax destroyed the Yankees. No one ever questioned that. When it mattered, he was *there*.

Gooden was elsewhere.

If Koufax was molded slowly, Gooden materialized full blown in 1984. (Why we were all so surprised I'm not sure; probably it was his age. Because in '83, when he was eighteen, in the minors, he struck out three hundred plus while compiling a 19–4 record and leading the league in ERA.)

Rookie of the year in '84. The greatest nineteen-year-old pitcher in the history of the game. And it wasn't just the seventeen wins. It was the strikeouts *plus* the control. No fireballer ever had his control at his age. And he was a fireballer, breaking the all-time major league mark of most strikeouts per nine-innings.

Rookie of the year, no contest. But could he do it again?

Nineteen eighty-five was one of those magic years. Like Carlton's '72. Gooden became, ho-hum, the greatest *twenty*-year-old pitcher in the history of the game. The Mets didn't win but he sure did. 24–4, an ERA of 1.53. Cy Young Award. Youngest ever. (Getting boring.) Dazzling and adored. But could he do it again?

He could not.

The season was okay. 17–6. And he pitched well in the playoffs. But in the Series, when it mattered, truly mattered, he was handed the ball twice, lost both games, gave up 17 hits in the 9 innings he managed to stagger through, his ERA a scary 8.00.

Of course the rumors were there all season long. Gooden was a druggie. Not possible. All the evidence pointed that way: He was simply too terrific a kid to fold, too mature, too much the quiet leader. The Mets were World Champions but he "overslept" the victory parade.

Not possible.

All the off-season escapades.

Not possible.

I didn't want it to be possible, don't you see? It was important to me that it not be possible. Because, on my death bed or, more happily, when I daydream, I don't think about Carlton or Seaver.

Koufax is my man.

And so are the others I've put on my pyramid. Legends are what keep sports alive inside us. Because they are different. Because they are strange. Because you can't two and two them and make them be four. I saw Willie Mays at twenty *and I knew.* If they let his body alone, he was going to make my pyramid. If a ball was hit to center field it was dead.

When I was twenty-two and so was he, I used to skip grad school and go sit in the bleachers of the Polo Grounds just hoping someone would club the ball to center. He was always there. Of course his glove is where triples went to die.

I cannot give my heart to Dwight Gooden anymore. I watched his wonderful comeback under all that pressure and he was, considering where he started the season, remarkable.

But I don't trust him.

He brought the Mets back, took the pressure off Darling, made him Darling again, kept the Mets in it as well as anyone could.

But I don't trust him.

He almost won me back the last inning he pitched in 1987. Against

Philly. Mike Schmidt was quoted the next day as saying something to the effect that he had never seen Gooden as overpowering as he was in that inning. What he did was strike out the side. Swinging strikes. One foul tick.

I sat there watching, aware he was Gooden again. The '84 and '85 Gooden. But he wasn't. The talent was the same talent. Then again, maybe *he* was the same.

But *I* wasn't.

Legends are everything to fanaticism. (Keep your list, I'll keep mine.) If the best baseball had to offer was just terrific players, it would be fighting indoor soccer for TV contracts by the year 2000. If Ivan Lendl was Bill Tilden, Ping-Pong players would earn more.

We need our senses of wonder. That's why we need our legends. They provide us with companionship at night, when we're young, drifting, fighting sleep. And as we age . . .

. . . and as we age. . . .

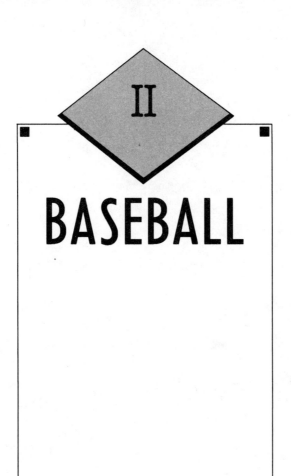

II

BASEBALL

THE
REPORTER'S NOTEBOOK

"GEORGE WAS WELL-MANICURED AS ALWAYS ..."

The New York Yankees had a history of legends—had been defined by legends since the team was owned by Colonel Jacob Ruppert.

You wanted to talk about legends, you started with the Yankees. They were the home office. There was Ruth and there was Gehrig, and later there was Joe DiMaggio, Mickey Mantle and Whitey Ford and Yogi Berra. Roger Maris. If Yankees did not have legendary careers, they did legendary things. Like Maris hitting 61. Or Don Larsen pitching the perfect game in the '56 World Series. Managing legends? Had them, too. Joe McCarthy, Miller Huggins, Casey Stengel.

But those were the *New York* Yankees, and they ceased operations on January 3, 1973, when a group headed by George M. Steinbrenner, chairman of a company called American Ship Building, purchased the team from CBS.

They have been Steinbrenner's Yankees ever since.

And in the mind of the principal owner, Steinbrenner, there has only been one true Yankee legend since 1973.

Steinbrenner.

The only connection between Steinbrenner's Yankees and the New York Yankees is in the team's nickname. And, as they say in real estate, location, location, location. The Yankees still play baseball at Yankee Stadium, Bronx, New York, 10451. To say that they are still the New York Yankees would be like a couple buying Pickfair and announcing they are Douglas Fairbanks and Mary Pickford.

In the fourteen seasons of Steinbrenner's ownership, the Yankees had again become the most famous baseball team in the known universe, as they had been before falling on hard times after the 1964 season. And

Steinbrenner became the most notorious owner in sports, the most flamboyant, the most relentless in his demand for attention and newspaper coverage, the highest roller in the game. He was the first to understand the possibilities of free agency, signing Catfish Hunter and Reggie Jackson and Rich Gossage in the middle seventies, watching the Yankees win the American League pennant in 1976, then the World Series in 1977 and 1978. Steinbrenner spent and bragged and yelled and fired manager Billy Martin and rehired Martin and kept signing free agents and kept going through other managers and general managers and team presidents and baseball players and pitching coaches and public relations men as though they were pistachio nuts.

I nicknamed him "Boss Steinbrenner" in the New York *Daily News*. He ran his team with the same bluster as the late Richard Daley had run Chicago. With about the same respect for his aldermen.

The Boss became an icon in sports, perhaps in America. Rare was the week during the season—or the off-season—when the back page of at least one of the New York tabloids didn't feature a headline that began with that nickname.

BOSS.

BOSS SAYS.

BOSS SIGNS.

BOSS HIRES.

BOSS FIRES.

BOSS THREATENS.

BOSS FUMES.

No owner since George Halas of the Bears had so dominated the public's perception of a team as Steinbrenner did. His posturing became more and more unattractive, his need to blame failures on underlings and grab all credit for himself became more obvious, he became, at times, the most well-known of all celebrity bullies; the Boss was this cartoon character Out There, away from New York, and frequently a cartoon character in New York.

But he was famous as any of the famous athletes to whom he paid millions of dollars, which may have been the point of the exercise all along. At the end of the seventies and then into the eighties, he became the symbol of the petulant boss much the way John McEnroe became the symbol of the spoiled brat.

Who do you think you are, *Steinbrenner?*

Shit, don't act like Steinbrenner.

And all of this would have suited Steinbrenner fine except that Steinbrenner's Yankees stopped winning the World Series after 1978. They lost the American League Championship Series to the Kansas City Royals in 1980. In 1981, benefitting greatly from a strike by the Major League Baseball Players Association that took a huge bite out of the season, the Yankees were able to clinch a playoff spot by having the best record in the AL East when the strike occurred. Then they made it into the World Series, and took a 2–0 lead in games over the Los Angeles Dodgers before the Dodgers swept the last four games and the championship of baseball. After that one, Steinbrenner issued a public apology to the city of New York; Reggie Jackson wondered at the time if Steinbrenner would issue a public apology to Fort Lauderdale the following spring if the Yankees lost their first exhibition game.

But after that World Series collapse in 1981 . . . nothing.

No divisional titles.

No pennants.

No World Series.

The parade of players continued through Yankee Stadium; it became like the Ramada Inn, South Bronx, players coming and going, checking in and out, all the time. Steinbrenner kept signing free agents, but none the caliber of Hunter or Jackson or Gossage. Martin would come and go as manager. Yogi Berra, a treasured hero from the New York Yankees, was given one season, then sixteen games the next. Lou Piniella, who had come along to play for Steinbrenner's Yankees and become perhaps the most popular player of his time, was given a chance. General managers were hired and fired or quit. Same with public relations men.

The Yankees just didn't finish first anymore.

Boss Steinbrenner kept making headlines, but more and more they were mean-spirited. Colorful as a winner, as a loser he was a whiner. And the Yankees were losers in Steinbrenner's mind, much as he defended his record. He still tried to dine out on the return to glory his ownership had brought to Yankee Stadium, and a lot of the fans still gave him that. But they were beginning to look at Steinbrenner as a big-time phony.

The whole philosophy of his ownership, touching the front office help and the managers and the players and the PR men and sometimes the secretaries, was simple:

What have you done for me, Boss Steinbrenner, lately?

So now the fans were saying to him:

What have you done for *us* lately, big-time?

If Steinbrenner could go through life thinking second place was garbage, so could they.

Only now that was all going to change. George Steinbrenner was going to sign Jack Morris, the most successful baseball pitcher of the 1980s, the same 1980s during which Steinbrenner's Yankees hadn't been able to win the World Series.

Morris had won 123 games for the Detroit Tigers in the previous seven seasons, 1980 through 1986. He had lost just 81 games. He was durable, he was a winner, he was an acknowledged baseball Boy Scout. Not counting the strike season, 1981, Morris had never made less than 35 starts in a season this decade. He had never pitched fewer than 240 innings. He was only thirty years old.

And he was available.

Jack Morris was a free agent.

Jack Morris wanted a new team. Steinbrenner needed pitching. A meeting was set up for December 19, at the Bay Harbor Inn in Tampa, Florida, which Steinbrenner owns. Steinbrenner, fittingly enough, would represent Steinbrenner's Yankees. The other two men would be Morris and his agent, Richard Moss.

There was obvious collusion going on between owners of major league baseball teams in the winter of 1986. They were ignoring free agents such as Morris, Andre Dawson, Tim Raines, Lance Parrish and Rich Gedman, trying to force them back to their original teams, drive down players' salaries (an arbitrator, Thomas Roberts, would rule during 1987 that the owners had already been guilty of collusion the year before, during the winter of 1985–86).

But those were the other owners. This was Boss Steinbrenner. The Mets had stolen New York from him in 1986, drawn nearly three million fans, won the World Series, become the sexy team in town. Steinbrenner could still make news by talking. The Mets made news by winning. The Yankees had Don Mattingly, Rickey Henderson, Dave Winfield. The Mets had more stars: Gooden, Darling, Strawberry, Hernandez, Carter. Steinbrenner had been neurotic about the Mets even in the seventies, when the Yankees were in first place and the Mets in last. He always, to his credit, saw them as a monster waiting to reclaim a National League City. Pity the manager of a Yankee team that lost to the Mets in spring training. After a while, there were no spring training games between the Mets and the Yankees. And the Mayor's Trophy Game, what had been an annual in-season charity game, that disappeared too.

Now, Steinbrenner couldn't ignore the Mets anymore. The thing he feared most—other than being ignored in the newspapers—had happened: The monster, freaking Mets were champions of the freaking world.

Steinbrenner had to sign Jack Morris.

The Minnesota Twins were at the top of Jack Morris's shopping list, first preference. He had been born in St. Paul. If he was going to leave Detroit after ten years, he would go home. Moss made the Twins three basic proposals:

1. A two-year contract for Morris. He would make $1.850 million the first year, then $2.050 the second year. Moss called it "The Valenzuela Proposal," since that is what Fernando Valenzuela, the top-paid pitcher in the game, was making for the Los Angeles Dodgers. It was merely logic on the part of Moss, one of the most successful agents in sports, and a man who had learned his bargaining as an assistant to Marvin Miller, during the time when Miller was executive director of the Major League Baseball Players Association and when the MLBPA became the most powerful union in the history of professional sports.

   Valenzuela's first full season was 1981. From 1981 through 1986, he had won 97 games. During the same time period, Jack Morris had won 107.

2. A three-year contract for $1.8 million a year.

3. Four years, $1.7 a year.

Moss also offered variations of each proposal, which included submitting them to arbitration.

Moss and Morris met with the Twins, and the Twins said they didn't want hometown boy Jack Morris, whether he was behind Door No. 1, Door No. 2, or Door No. 3.

Steinbrenner's Yankees were second on the Moss/Morris list. A meeting was set up in New York. Then there was an accident at Steinbrenner's American Ship Building plant in Tampa; Steinbrenner felt he should stay in Tampa. The meeting was shifted, with the approval of Moss and Morris, to the Bay Harbor Inn. Dick Moss said that would be fine.

He and Jack Morris flew to Tampa. By then, they were accumulating a press caravan, much as if it were covering a political campaign. Writers from Detroit who had made the trip to Minneapolis now continued on to Florida. A few writers from Minneapolis made the trip, to see how it would all turn out. And the New York papers were well represented at the Bay Harbor Inn.

Dick Moss said later, "It was quite a festive group."

Moss, Morris, and Steinbrenner met in the Bay Harbor suite Steinbrenner had designated. "George was well-manicured, as always," Moss said. Steinbrenner wore a blue blazer, gray slacks, blue shirt, tie. It was as basic a uniform for him as home pinstripes were for the Yankees.

He began by blowing smoke at Jack Morris. It was the come-on: Love you, baby.

Moss: "Never forget, George can be charming in person." Moss spoke the truth. For all of the bully-boy bluster, one-on-one, Steinbrenner was capable of schmooze the likes of which are not seen outside of Hollywood mogul meetings. So he told Jack Morris what a winner he was, what a credit to baseball, what a fine young man he, Steinbrenner, had heard that Jack Morris was, how lucky some team was going to be if it could get him.

Moss was thinking, Cut to the chase.

Morris smiled after every compliment and said, "Thank you, George."

Steinbrenner said, "I appreciate you changing your plans to come down here."

Morris said, "It was no problem, really."

Moss finally cut in.

"George," he said, "if you don't mind, I'd like to fill you in on what our proposals are. . . ."

Steinbrenner cut him off with a wave of the hand.

"No need, Dick. I'm pretty familiar with what the deals are. I've been reading the newspapers the last couple of days."

No copy editor in America read the newspapers more closely than George Steinbrenner. He was mostly searching for mentions about himself. When he was out of town, he would have one of his closest friends, New York limousine king Bill Fugazy, be his designated reader. If Fugazy saw something critical he thought should be brought to

Steinbrenner's attention, he would call American Ship Building. Then Steinbrenner would call the Yankee offices and ask for the story to be Xeroxed and filed. Or read to him over the phone. Or sent to Florida, immediately.

Stat, as they say in hospital emergencies.

"Two years, three years, four years, right?" Steinbrenner said to Moss.

Moss said that was right.

Then Moss surprised Steinbrenner.

"George, we also have a proposal that we didn't make in Minnesota," he said. "It's a one-year deal, and it's really predicated on a simple fact: We think that if Jack Morris is added to the Yankees, the Yankees can win this season. Then if you don't want to pay Jack after that, no hard feelings, we'll go someplace else. I honestly believe this is an offer you can't turn down."

The deal was simple. Morris would become a Yankee, and the two sides would let an arbitrator decide Morris's value. Steinbrenner would come in with one sum, Moss/Morris another, the arbitrator would decide. Morris would pitch for the Yankees for the one season, then be eligible to become a free agent again at the end of 1987.

The best pitcher in baseball across the 1980s was offering his services to Steinbrenner's Yankees in a one-time-only, let-an-independent-party-decide-how-much-I'm-worth deal.

It was the first-ever Jack Morris Sale.

"One year, contract arbitration is all we're asking," Richard Moss said. The proposal was, he thought, both creative and irresistible. Steinbrenner needed pitching. The other owners needed some sort of free agent signing, as a hedge against collusion charges. The charges had already been filed once by the MLBPA, because of the previous winter's chill toward free agents. Certainly they would be refiled over the even more dazzling array of free agents now being snubbed.

Steinbrenner said nothing.

Moss said, "What we're saying here is, just do what the Tigers are prepared to do. Go to arbitration with Jack Morris. Only the Tigers won't have Jack Morris. You will."

Steinbrenner said, "Geez, Dick, I hadn't expected this." He said, boy, Moss had surprised him, no question about that. He repeated that he hadn't expected any offer like this.

Steinbrenner: "This is very unusual. Interesting. I'm definitely going to have to think about this one." Then he reminded Moss that two of the Yankees' longtime stars, Ron Guidry and Willie Randolph, were also eligible for free agency, and Steinbrenner was presently negotiating with both of them, and Steinbrenner said he just didn't know for sure if he could afford Guidry and Randolph and Morris.

Moss thought that was funny, collusively speaking. If Jack Morris couldn't find a new team, how could Guidry and Randolph?

And: When had there been a time, at least before collusion, when George Steinbrenner couldn't afford somebody he really wanted?

Moss smiled, repeated the offer one last time: "One year, George. Arbitration."

Steinbrenner repeated what an intriguing offer it was, then said, "I will get back to you by noon tomorrow."

The three men shook hands. Moss later estimated the meeting took forty-five minutes, thirty of them taken up by small talk. Moss and Jack Morris took a cab to the Tampa airport, flew back to New York, had dinner. Morris spent the night as Moss's guest at the apartment.

At dinner, Morris asked, "Do you really think they'll let him sign me?"

By "they" he meant the other owners. There wasn't an agent, MLBPA lawyer, fan, writer, or player who didn't believe the owners were engaged in a conspiracy.

Moss said, "Maybe I'm naive, but I can't imagine how he can turn us down without looking foolish."

At noon the next day, as promised, George Steinbrenner called ... and turned them down.

"It wouldn't be fair to Guidry and Randolph," Steinbrenner said to Moss.

"George," Moss said, "this doesn't have anything to do with Guidry and Randolph, and you know it."

Steinbrenner stuck to his cover, that he had to settle with Guidry and Randolph before he could even *think* about signing any free agents.

"But it was a pleasure talking to both of you, and certainly a pleasure meeting Jack," Steinbrenner said. "Maybe we can talk sometime later?"

Steinbrenner ended up with Guidry and Randolph. Jack Morris went back to the Tigers. And for the first month of the season, it looked like Steinbrenner hadn't needed Jack Morris, that maybe the AL East hadn't been settled at the Bay Harbor Inn. The Yankees were in first place.

The Tigers were in sixth place, nine and a half games behind them, with a record of 11–19.

Without Morris, the ace of the staff, it was unlikely the Tigers could have righted themselves at that point.

But the Tigers still had Jack Morris, who had won $1.85 million from a baseball arbitrator.

One spring morning, March of 1988, Jack Morris stood in the Tigers' spring training clubhouse in Lakeland, Florida, and laughed at the memory of his negotiations with George Steinbrenner.

"The guy didn't sign me," Morris said. "But damn, he sure did love me."

POOR LITTLE RICH BOY

I am, and have been for years, a Yankee fan. I much prefer the Stadium to Shea. If you get there early there are those stores just across the street selling memorabilia—great time wasting. If you live in Manhattan, it's a quick tube trip to 161st. The hot dogs are better. The history is there, in the Bronx, not out in the sterile setting of Shea.

But George is there too, and for a Yankee fan, it's more than a puzzlement. The insults he hands out, the often lunatic rantings. He makes an ordeal out of rooting.

I think intentionally. (These notes are just personal gleanings from talking to a lot of people about the man. People he fired, people who quit, acquaintances, writers, TV guys, anyone who'd talk.)

You'll notice I didn't mention talking to any friends and there is a reason for that: He hasn't any. Toadies, yes. Many. But people who care?

None.

For all I know, he may do that intentionally, too. Because he is not without complications. There are, and this is crucial to any understanding, two Georges: the social animal and the Boss.

The social fellow is, when he wants to be, devastatingly charming. He is far from dumb, and is a great salesman. One of the reasons he's so good at getting people to work for him is they all think this: *It'll be different with me.*

It never is. Once he has you in his employ, forget it.

He hires talent—he just won't give the talent power. One baseball man put it like this: "After games? He'd like call his coaching staff up to his office and chew the crap out of them. They'd sit there quietly and eat the shit. If I were a social buddy of his, and I made a suggestion, even if I didn't know squat about the game, bet that his baseball people would hear the suggestion."

A social peer of his said this: "I don't understand the big deal about George. It's really very simple and very pure: He is first and foremost and forever just a bully. He never gets into arguments with equals. He's *never* in town when anyone gets fired. And he fires people in weird ways—he castrates them. Look at Piniella—for anyone else, going from manager to G.M. would be a step up. But Lou's just a joke now. All the old Yankees have jobs. They want his money and they want to stay in the game. He thinks it's because they like him—

—George wants to believe that. He's a very lonely guy. You'd be lonely too if nobody liked you."

A longtime follower said this: "I think the crucial thing to understand is this: It's pathologically impossible for *anything* to *ever* be his fault. The Nixon thing when he got nailed and found guilty—that was his lawyer's fault. Any goof-up with the Yankees? That's always his "baseball people's" fault. But there are no baseball people. There's only him. He runs the entire show. And even though he meddles less now than he used to since the press got on to it, he still meddles a lot more than the press has any idea.

"Here's how the fault thing operates and why he drives you so crazy. Sometime this year he'll call Piniella and Piniella will be out to a movie or to dinner with his wife and George'll go crazy. *He wasn't there.* But he won't come out and say it. What he'll do is look up Piniella's first assistant and call him instead. And he'll keep on calling him until that guy does something that ticks him off, when he'll drop down to the next guy. When he's run the ladder, he'll call Lou again, but without a word of why he hasn't been calling."

A baseball man: "He hates negative press. It tears him apart. But he's in trouble now with Dick Young dead. No mouthpiece. And I think the papers aren't as frightened of him now as they were—but maybe that's wrong. There's a newspaper war and he sells papers."

My own opinion of the man?

I don't think he's a bad owner. I just think he's a bad *baseball* owner. I think he'd be great with a football team. I wish he had the Jets. The public humiliations, the masterful castrations, those would work great, say I, once a week in an emotional game like football. But baseball is like the sunrise: Count on its arrival day after day after month. No one, not Pete Rose nor Ty Cobb, can get it up 162 games per season, not counting spring training and the playoffs. You're talking maybe two hundred games annually for a champion. Which is why George's style doesn't produce champions anymore. But give him the Jets? I think he'd have them foaming and cursing their way to the Super Bowl within three years.

And I don't think he's a bad person, either. Just a damaged one. So uncertain, so scared. This is all Psychology I, understand, but he had a very tough and very rich daddy. And in the dark night of his shredded soul, I believe Steinbrenner wonders, wonders fiercely, would he have made it had he not been born so rich and so privileged? And what rips at him, of course, is this: He'll never know.

I know, though. Not a chance.

THE
REPORTER'S NOTEBOOK
APRIL: "MY FRIEND WHO ISN'T HERE RIGHT NOW . . ."

As the 1987 season began, Darryl Strawberry was twenty-five years old, and the funny thing is, the Mets thought that if there was going to be a problem, it was going to be with him. Strawberry had been the Mets' No. 1 pick, and No. 1 pick in the country, when he came out of L.A.'s Crenshaw High School in 1980. He was the National League Rookie of the Year in 1983. In an age of statistical frenzy in baseball, Strawberry, entering the season, was the only player in the game to have had more than a hundred home runs and a hundred stolen bases over the previous four seasons. He was 6–6, whippet-thin, but strong as Michael Tyson with a bat in his hands, hitter of prodigious home runs, high, unforgettable home runs that tried to climb over the sky. There were already comparisons being made between Cincinnati's Eric Davis and Willie Mays—later in the spring, a front-page headline from *The Sporting News* would gush of Davis, GREATEST PLAYER EVER?—but among baseball people it was generally considered that Darryl Strawberry, Mets right fielder, was the sport's most physically gifted player, a combination of speed, bat strength, arm strength, grace.

Mets hitting coach Bill Robinson often said, "Someday Darryl Strawberry will hit a baseball farther than anyone has ever hit one."

Strawberry could make the game look ridiculously easy.

Sometimes he would even do it for three or four games in a row.

Starting his fifth season in the major leagues, he was lazy, inconsistent, moody—the only Met, really, who had come out of the championship season still dripping boos. The home fans had booed him frequently during 1986, even as the Mets ran away from the pack. He struck out 141 times in 136 games during the regular season, then 18 more times in 13 postseason games. There were three home runs in the postseason, including crucial ones against the Houston Astros in the third and fifth games of the National League Championship Series. And there had been a hot dog of a home run in Game 7 of the World Series against the Red Sox, after the Mets had taken the lead for good. Strawberry had done little with the bat during the Series, mostly had struck out while not offering a single run-batted-in. But he finally jerked a ball out of the park against Red Sox pitcher Al Nipper.

That wasn't the problem.

The problem was that Strawberry, in hot-dog baseball tradition, took so long to make his trip around the bases that it seemed at Shea as if he were making the trip on his hands and knees. This was two nights after he had complained loudly to reporters about being yanked by manager Davey Johnson in the eighth inning of Game 6.

Both gestures were like Strawberry autographs. Game 6 of the 1986 World Series had been one of the most improbably wonderful and bizarre and unforgettable games in the history of the Series, as the Mets came back from one strike away from losing and won when Mookie Wilson's innocent grounder up the first base line went through Bill Buckner's legs. It was the wrong time for Strawberry to bitch about anything, but he did. He was Darryl. Johnson and the Mets were used to him not knowing when to shut up.

And the hot-dog tour around the bases in Game 7? In the words of one of Strawberry's teammates, it was just "TDB ... Typical Darryl Bullshit." They didn't think it was such a hot idea to strut when the one home run of the Series comes when the Mets are turning off the lights, getting ready to lock the door.

Typical Darryl Bullshit.

More bullshit during the off-season. Strawberry's wife, Lisa, sued for divorce. Now, a New York ballplayer gets sued for divorce, the story is a lock for either Page Two or Page Three of the New York tabloids. Darryl and Lisa Strawberry, the story of their divorce, it made Page One. For one thing, Lisa Strawberry had hired Marvin Mitchelson to represent her.

The other thing was, she said that there were times when her husband physically abused her.

(It prompted an immediate New York response, which meant a joke started making the rounds as soon as newspapers were unloaded from trucks: "Lisa should have just told Darryl she was left-handed. Everybody knows Darryl can't hit left-handers.")

By the end of the season, Mr. and Mrs. Strawberry would again be a happy family, along with son Darryl, Jr. That was then, this was now. Strawberry was stung by the publicity his marital difficulties generated, humiliated by the allegations that he had even raised a threatening hand to his beautiful young wife. Once again, for perhaps the hundredth time in his Met career, he felt he was being picked on unfairly. Everything he did, "they" jumped on. "They" could be Mets management, teammates, fans, the press. Gooden skipped the parade, got himself arrested, got himself put on probation, *his* lady got picked up carrying a concealed freaking *weapon* through an airport. People kept forgiving Dwight and it was Darryl who was either causing the bullshit or being victimized by the bullshit, but the bottom line is that there was always this . . . well, Typical Darryl Bullshit.

Now "they" could even ask: When did you stop beating your wife, Darryl?

He was not a happy camper when he showed up in St. Petersburg for spring training, anyway. He was moody as ever. In his brief Mets career, he had been moody and overly sensitive in the best of times, but the breakup of his marriage had only made things worse. His teammates could see it. Management could see it. The reporters covering the team could see it.

"They" could definitely see it, no question.

"Let's be honest," said Keith Hernandez, the clear on-field leader of the Mets, on March 1. "I'm not saying he's going to fuck things up, but there's one guy everybody's sort of watching."

And nodded at Strawberry's locker.

March 1 is the official reporting day for the players, under the basic agreement between players and owners, and while pitchers and catchers have already reported to the camps by then, March 1 is the start of all ritual and ceremony associated with spring training by both players and fans, and the start of the sports year. It is New Year's Day in baseball, featuring the same resolve and resolutions and promise.

On March 3, at 9:45 in the morning, fifteen minutes before the Mets would take the field for their third official workout, Strawberry strode into the clubhouse and noticed Backman, Dykstra, and me sitting and drinking coffee, the three of us joking, looking at an early copy of

Dykstra's autobiography, *Nails*. It was one of the Mets books scheduled for release during March and April.

Gary Carter had written a book. Mets television broadcasters Tim McCarver and Ralph Kiner had both written books. And so had Dykstra. It was his book that showed both the pull and magnitude of a sports championship won by a New York team. Dykstra had hit a couple of dramatic home runs during the previous postseason, but his "autobiography" was arriving after 230 major league games and a lifetime batting average of .280, and seemed mostly to indulge his passion for the word "fuck."

Dykstra, on the morning of March 3, 1987, was twenty-four years and twenty-one days old, but his life was safely preserved now between the covers of a book.

"I got to drop a lot of f-bombs in it," Dykstra was saying.

Backman, coffee in one hand and ever-present Winston Light in the other, leaned over, grabbed *Nails* away from its author, grinned, said, "If you take out the fucks, this is an eighteen-page book."

All three of us noticed Strawberry then, standing and glaring.

At one point during the previous season, I had written, in response to a letter, "Darryl just needs to work a little harder." The day after Strawberry read it, he had said to Bob Klapisch, then the Mets beat writer for the *New York Post*, "Who's he to be saying I should work harder? I work as hard as anybody. How come nobody ever says Keith should work harder? I'm going to stuff that fucking weasel in a garbage can, see how he likes my work habits from inside there." Klapisch told him he didn't think that would be such a tremendous idea if you looked at the big picture.

Strawberry and I circled each other warily after that, from then until the end of the season. It showed how big or small a baseball clubhouse can be, depending on the size players and writers want it to be; it can be a confrontational place, but only if the player in question, or manager, wants it to be. When players want to make a man covering the team look bad, they get him right in the middle of their turf, in front of their mates, in the middle of the clubhouse or on the field during batting practice, and read him some kind of abusive riot act in a voice that can attract the attention of vendors.

So now it was early in the morning, early in the spring, it had been a long winter, Darryl was in a bad mood, and here I was and here was Darryl.

"I'm putting you on notice right now," Strawberry said. (Now, I'm about a foot shorter than Strawberry, so the players, who had heard the opening line and stopped with papers and coffee to watch, knew nothing much was going to happen, except hard words.

But it was going to be more of a show than they could have hoped for, third day, spring training, quarter to ten in the morning.)

"Something bothering you, Darryl?"

"I know you've been writing about my personal life, and I'm telling you right now, you write about my personal life, and I'll beat the fucking shit out of you."

"I don't know what you're talking about, Darryl, I really don't. I didn't write about your personal life all winter. I don't *care* about your personal life."

"I heard."

"You heard wrong."

Mets public relations man Jay Horwitz came around the corner of the lockers then. Horwitz's normal state is beleaguered. A big part of his job is acting as a buffer between players and reporters, and he is generally adequate at it. But this was already out of hand. Strawberry was talking too loudly, Horwitz had heard from the equipment room, where he was making a phone call. Horwitz had an expression on his face like he had discovered a corpse.

Even though Strawberry's presentation was winding down.

Strawberry said, "I heard."

"Darryl, we're going around in circles here. I honestly have no idea what you're talking about."

"You're on fucking notice. You write about my personal life, I promise, I will beat the shit out of you."

"Well, you know, I think you probably could."

Strawberry went down the row to get dressed for the workout. I went to get another cup of coffee. Two days later, I was standing at a back field at Payson, watching a kid second baseman named Keith Miller take ground balls. Joe McIlvaine came up next to me.

"I heard what happened between Darryl and you," McIlvaine said. "I know you don't need an apology from us, but I'll apologize anyway. We just don't condone that sort of scene."

Fine, Darryl was still just twenty-five years old. If I were his age it might have been a bigger deal, but I was older, no big deal.

I said, "Forget it."

McIlvaine said, "Can I ask you a couple of questions?"

"Sure."

"About what time did the thing happen?"

"Little before ten."

"In the morning?"

"Yeah, a little before ten in the morning. I'd just gotten to the clubhouse."

"How did Darryl seem?"

"Seem? Joe, he seemed pissed. He threatened to beat the shit out of me."

The same day, one Met official put the question to me this way, "Was Darryl drunk?"

I told him no.

A few weeks later, Strawberry was late showing up for a spring training game, was fined and sent home by manager Davey Johnson. It was not the first time this had happened in Strawberry's career. Darryl had somewhat of a problem with alarm clocks. And, his teammates thought, somewhat of a problem with the general responsibilities of making more than a million dollars a year and having all that God-given skill. The season before, it had become a running joke in the Mets clubhouse when Strawberry would beg out of a day game after the team had played a game the night before.

"For a guy his size," Wally Backman had said one day, "he sure gets crippled by an awful lot of sore thumbs and sore wrists."

The fine seemed to get Strawberry's attention, at least temporarily. He apologized to Johnson, said his on-time record would be better than TWA's, the beat writers gave him an alarm clock as a present. Smiles all around. No one was sure if Strawberry meant what he said, but everyone around the Mets hoped he did, because Hernandez's opinion was shared by others in the room:

Darryl was the one who could make the mess. With typical bullshit.

Then Dwight made the mess.

Dwight—the good one—turned out to be the problem Darryl was supposed to be.

And it seemed to wake Strawberry up as no alarm clock ever had. He would say, "What happened to Dwight made me realize how quickly you can lose what you have." He spoke of dedicating the season to his son, Darryl, Jr., and to Dwight, "my friend who isn't here right now." He would wear Gooden's uniform pants, with No. 16, Gooden's number, stenciled on the inside.

Then on April 7, Opening Day at Shea, after the world championship rings were presented in pregame ceremonies and the world championship flag had been raised, with Gooden in Manhattan at the Smithers Alcoholism Treatment Center going through what a spokesman would describe later as "a normal day in the rehabilitation program" and Bob Ojeda starting the game instead, Darryl Strawberry hit a majestic home run, good for all three runs in the Mets' 3–2 victory over the Pirates.

Jesse Orosco, the relief pitcher who had won three games against the Astros in the playoffs, had saved two against the Red Sox in the World Series, and had gotten the last out against both teams, pitched out of a bases-loaded trap in the ninth inning. Without Gooden and without McDowell and without Magadan, the Mets were 1–0 because Darryl Strawberry hit one over the wall.

"Just start the fucking season," Wally Backman said before the game. "The sharks are all out there circling the boat. Except the motor starts today, and the sharks are gonna be gone. You want to put more heat on us? Fine, do it. So we got dealt a different hand than we thought we were gonna get. Let's play it. We're still the best."

"You know what I was thinking in the last inning?" Cashen, the pessimist, said in his box on the press level after the game. "I was thinking, it's last season all over again. All of a sudden, this was like every game we played in October."

Maybe everything would be all right. Strawberry hit another home run in the second game of the season. Mets won. Strawberry hit his third home run in the third game. Mets won again. The record was 3–0.

They lost the fourth game, on a Saturday afternoon. Mookie Wilson, who was again platooning with Dykstra in center field, lost a fly ball in the sun. No problem, three wins, one loss.

Then on Sunday, April 12, the damn dove died.

On a Sunday afternoon at Shea, in front of a crowd of 37,019 people, which brought the attendance for the three-game series over 100,000, the Braves beat Ojeda and the Mets 12–4. During the game, Dion James hit what looked to be a routine fly ball in the direction of Mets left fielder Kevin McReynolds.

The ball never got there.

A dove—the sky above Shea is filled with both birds and planes; Flushing Bay is practically next door, and LaGuardia Airport sits at the end of Flushing Bay—intersected with the flight of the ball, fell to the ground dead. The baseball dropped with it, well in front of McReynolds, and Dion James got a double.

In the press box, Tom Verducci, the gifted young baseball writer from *Newsday,* turned to his friend Klapisch of the *Post,* sitting on his right as usual.

"That's it," Verducci said. "They're not going to win."

Klapisch, the product of a Columbia University education, said, "What are you talking about?"

Verducci was talking about the sign of the dove.

"Just remember when I told you," he said. Months later, Joe McIlvaine said, "You know when I got a bad feeling? When that bird got hit on April 12." McIlvaine had needed no prompting on the date. He was right there with April 12. "I said to myself, *that,* fella, is not a good omen."

A week later, the Mets went to St. Louis to play the Cardinals. Only this time, the Cardinals did the sweeping, not the Mets. John Tudor won the first game. The next night, Ron Darling—who was supposed to be the ace of the staff in Gooden's absence—could not hold a 5–0 lead. The Mets finally lost 12–8 in the tenth inning when Tom Herr hit a grand slam off Orosco. On Sunday afternoon, a kid left-hander named Greg Mathews beat Sid Fernandez, 4–2.

The Mets, who had come into St. Louis with a record of 6–2, left 6–5. Worse, they were now in second place instead of first for the first time in a year.

Another week later. The Cardinals came to Shea. The Mets were back in first place by one-half game. The Cardinals won two of three. The Mets went back to second place. Six games between the Mets and Cardinals. Five losses for the Mets. Notice had been served by the St. Louis team that it was a brand new year, brand new game.

St. Louis manager Whitey Herzog was already in full strut, and it wasn't even summer yet. "I'm fucking stunned by all this," Herzog said. "From what I read all winter, I was afraid we weren't even supposed to show up for the season."

Wally Backman tried to play down the significance of the five losses, saying, "We'll be fine. We just don't want to be six games behind somebody at the end of April."

They weren't. On April 30, Rick Aguilera gave up a two-run homer to John Stefero of the Montreal Expos, then no-hit the Expos over the final eight and one-third innings, and the Mets won, 11–3, bringing the April record to 11–9. Gooden was almost done with his month at

Smithers; with Ueberroth's approval, he would be pitching in the minor leagues by the second week of May.

And Roger McDowell was ahead of schedule, throwing on the sidelines, talking about pitching by the middle of May. He had been sent to New York before the end of spring training, to rest. He was back now, not a moment too soon. McDowell was the Mets' prankster, practical joker, hotfoot artist, wearer of funny masks, blithe spirit; his mere presence in the clubhouse now seemed as important as his presence on the mound would be later, lightening what had been a grim atmosphere since Gooden's departure from the team. Riding to Shea in his black jeep on Opening Day, McDowell had said, "I'm crazy, but when I'm around, it's like they think things are normal. Does that make sense?" He knew it did. McDowell would get laughs, then saves. The saves would take pressure off the rest of the bullpen.

The starters, particularly Darling, were struggling under the weight of Gooden's absence; and Ojeda, though not discussing it much (a pitcher's first response to arm pain is silent prayer), was feeling pain in his left elbow every time he took the mound. Orosco had started off with six saves in his first seven games, but now as April ended, he appeared tired. The men who generally preceded him in Johnson's bullpen parade—Doug Sisk, Randy Myers, Gene Walter—had also been overworked, and ineffective.

Still: One month down, and the Mets were only a game behind the Cardinals.

But there had been those omens.

Cardinals. And the damn dove.

Slice the month any way you wanted. Accentuate the positive, eliminate the negative. Say you got through April without your best starter and your best reliever; that the Cardinals were right there in front of you, all you had to do was reach out, touch them, with 142 baseball games left to play.

Do all that.

No getting around the fact that there had definitely been a couple of bad omens involving birds.

MAY: "WE STINK . . ."

The Prince of Darkness said, "We stink."

May 11, visitors clubhouse, Cincinnati's Riverfront Stadium. The

Reds had just beaten the Mets, 12–2. The record for the Mets was 13–16. They were only four games out of first. But they were in fourth place. A day before, the Mets record dropped two games below .500 for the first time since 1983.

The Prince reached down to the small ice bucket at his feet, grabbed a bottle of beer, drank some beer. The bucket, the beer, are always there for him as soon as a game is over, home or away, 162 times a season, not including playoffs. Sometimes The Prince did not always give proper attention to all the beers waiting for him in the bucket; if the night game had been at Shea and he was in a hurry to get back into Manhattan for a date or a show, he might only down one or two beers before heading off into the night, from whence his nickname had originally come.

But the bucket was always waiting for him.

"That's it in two words," he said. "We stink."

He dragged on a cigarette. The Prince only smokes during the baseball season, then quits until March. But during the season, he smokes like someone is about to hide all the cigarettes forever. Coffee and cigarettes before the game. Beer and cigarettes after the game. Get wired up before the game, settle down after.

The Prince of Darkness is Keith Hernandez, who had been the leader of the Mets since coming over in a trade from the Cardinals in 1983. Gooden may have been Mozart and the symbol of the Mets risen from the ashes, and Cashen may have been the architect. The manager, Davey Johnson, would soon have more wins than any manager in Mets history. Ron Darling, the handsome Yalie with a wife who had been a model? Darling was the cover boy. Gary Carter, with his own smiling looks and smiling disposition and almost relentless effervescence, was No. 1 in commercials. Radio, television, print.

But Hernandez, lifetime .300 hitter and perhaps the finest fielding first baseman in the history of baseball, was the leader, the intense and brooding soul of the team, the most fascinating personality in the room, a thirty-three-year-old man with leading-man looks and the insecurities of a fading actress. He was known as Mex to his teammates, but The Prince of Darkness to some of the writers covering the team.

The nickname was given in fun and almost with respect. Hernandez was a glamorous throwback star to a time when Babe Ruth owned Manhattan by night and baseball the rest of the time.

Hernandez was a fanatical on-field professional, seemingly running the game from his position at first base, and his No. 3 slot in the batting order. At the same time, he was a team gossip, master politician with the writers, constant source of information, at least off the record. The joke among the writers was that Hernandez was "gladiator off the record, puss on it." The description was relayed to him one night during batting practice and Hernandez just laughed at being called "puss," the crude and general clubhouse description of women.

"You're right," he said, and got into the batting cage for some swings.

He was quick to offer hard, even cruel analyses of the Mets anonymously, loathe to do it by name. To any remotely tough question, Hernandez had an immediate and automatic reply:

"For print?"

He was acutely aware of the way writers worked the clubhouse, passionately aware, obsessively aware. It was Hernandez who wanted to decide which comments, even the ones used without attribution, should find their way into the papers; it was this Machiavellian game with him, give and take, parry and thrust, sniping at teammates, playing one writer off against another. He would grab Klapisch or Verducci, his conversation with them long since over, and say, "And not 'one Met said.' " Or Hernandez would begin a conversation by saying, "This didn't come from me, boys." He knew the program, so did his teammates. When there was a story in the *Post* or *Newsday* or the *Daily News,* and some biting comment began, "One Met said," the Mets generally knew who the one Met was.

The Prince. As you walked into the Mets clubhouse, the first locker you passed, there on your left, was his. The writers knew where to find him and, an awful lot of the time, their stories.

Hernandez was a mass of contradictions, one of the noted clutch players of his generation, a man who had been Most Valuable Player in the National League in 1979 (he actually shared the award with Willie Stargell of the Pirates), and had been a key member of the Cardinals' world championship team in 1982. But he was also a thirty-three-year-old man who still called his father, John Hernandez, for batting help when he was in a slump. John Hernandez had been a fine Cardinals prospect until his own career was cut short by injury; the relationship ever since between father and son had been something right out of *Gypsy,* except with Show Biz Papa instead of Show Biz Mama. At home in San Francisco, John Hernandez stayed in touch with Keith's career via the satellite dish Keith had provided. And the telephone.

"Mex had to call Juan for some advice," Hernandez would say sheepishly, talking about himself and his father beyond the third person, in nicknames.

More contradictions: During the 1985 season, Hernandez was the man who had taken the stand in the celebrated Pittsburgh drug trial of caterer Curtis Strong and announced to the world that cocaine, for him, had been "a devil on this earth." And yet: There was the ice bucket and the beers, sometimes four or five, that would be consumed before he left the clubhouse; and all the ones that came after.

He was a student of the Civil War, having gone so far a to take a course at West Point one winter. He painted (Robert E. Lee, Stonewall Jackson) in his spare time. One of the things he loved best about living in New York, he said, was the access to museums and art galleries.

And yet: He was the Met, within the sacred jock confines of the clubhouse, who discussed women as if he were still a horny teenager.

Backman talked a lot. Carter talked. But Hernandez, even spending as much time off the record as he did, was the spokesman, the leader, the unofficial captain of the Mets, the player to whom younger Mets like Backman and Howard Johnson and McDowell looked for inspiration. The Prince was a flawed role model, since even the young Mets were aware of his demons. But he was a role model nonetheless. The Mets had first won 90 games in 1984, when Gooden showed up. But they first started to become professional again in 1983, when Hernandez came over from St. Louis with all his passions, good and bad.

"My wheel man," Davey Johnson said of him.

Wheel man. Mex. "One Met." Prince.

On May 11, just 29 games into the whole thing, The Prince said, "We stink."

May, in fact, was the month when the Mets who could still raise their arms without pain started pointing fingers.

Often in baseball, in sports really, you do not need to look at the standings to understand how a team is doing. You just use your senses around the clubhouse. You listen to the players talk. You see the fingers being pointed.

All of a sudden, you smell something rotten.

The year before, there had been nary a discouraging word said in the Mets clubhouse as the team danced and strutted and preened its way through the National League East. There were small brushfires, to be sure. George Foster was abruptly waived after suggesting his benching might have been racially motivated, and some of the black players spoke up about that. And there was a time near the end of the season when players began to choose sides when it became apparent that both Carter and Hernandez were MVP candidates (neither man won; Mike Schmidt of the Phillies did). But the incidents were exceptions. The rest of baseball might have hated the 1986 Mets, berated them for being hot dogs and showboats and the home office for high fives and curtain calls.

The Mets said, "Fight one of us, fight all of us." The Mets stood by the Mets.

That was then, this was now:

May 8, Atlanta. The Braves beat the Mets, 4–3 in 10 innings. The key playing was Dale Murphy of the Braves going from first to third on a steal attempt in the bottom of the tenth inning. Carter bounced the throw to second base, Howard Johnson—playing shortstop as he sometimes did when Davey Johnson wanted to get more offense into the game—could not come up with the throw. Murphy went to third. The Mets lost.

Afterward, the manager said, "I don't want to get on my shortstop, because he just moved there, but the ball should've been blocked."

The shortstop said, "It was a bad throw by Gary."

The catcher said, "That's what happens when you have to rush."

Stop, look, listen.

The manager was pointing at the shortstop and the shortstop was pointing at the catcher, so Carter, the catcher, pointed at the relief pitcher, Orosco, for not holding Murphy close enough to first base. "Murphy had the base stolen, anyway," Carter said.

May 10, Atlanta. The Mets scored six runs in the eighth inning to take a 7–6 lead. But in the bottom of the inning, with two outs and a runner on second for Atlanta, Albert Hall, a Braves outfielder, lifted a fly ball to shallow right field. Darryl Strawberry came in from his position. Tim Teufel, the second baseman, went out from his position.

At the last second, Teufel ducked away from Strawberry, giving way, but Strawberry wasn't in position, the ball fell. The score was now 7–7 and Hall was on second and the next hitter singled Hall home, and the Mets lost.

In the clubhouse, Teufel said, "Our communication was good." He meant: The outfielder can see the play all the way, it is his job to yell for the infielder to get out of the way. Strawberry yelled, Teufel was saying, and I got the hell out of the way.

"As soon as I heard Darryl call for the ball, I got out of there."

Down the row at Darryl Strawberry's locker, the story was a little different. *He* said, "There was no communication at all. I had to come a long way for it, and he broke away before I called for it."

And the manager talked in general about the mistakes his team had been making: "They're like a college team, a high school team, a Little League team." The manager stopped there because he had sort of run out of organized baseball; the next stop was going to be slow pitch softball, something like that, to describe the world champion New York Mets.

May 11, Cincinnati. Bobby Ojeda was finally put on the disabled list. Two days earlier, Ojeda had lasted just one inning against the Braves. From the first pitch, his arm was so inflamed he had told backup catcher Barry Lyons, "Don't call for any sliders or curveballs, okay? And not too many fastballs, either."

"We ended up going about eighty percent with changeups," Lyons would say afterward. "Obviously, it was something serious. I think Bobby knew it all along." Ojeda flew to New York after the game; X rays showed pressure on his ulnar nerve. No one said anything, but the feeling around the team was that surgery was inevitable, and that Ojeda would be lost for the season.

At this point, Gooden was three days away from his first training start in the minor leagues, but at least a month away from being ready to pitch in the majors. So now Davey Johnson did not have his ace, and did not have the No. 2 man in his rotation, the man who had won 19 games the season before, had two significant wins in the postseason, and had taken Gooden's place on Opening Day.

Cashen's response was to call up a twenty-one-year-old right-handed pitcher, John Mitchell, from the Mets Triple-A team at Tidewater, Virginia. Only Davey Johnson would rather have had Roger McDowell, who was ready to pitch. Mitchell had pitched the previous day at Tidewater, and would be unavailable to the Mets for three days, anyway.

The manager, as insecure in his own moody way as Hernandez, the man he would soon make captain of the team, reacted badly.

"They've had confidence in my judgment in the past," Davey

Johnson said. "But obviously they're losing that very quickly. This is the first time this has happened to me in four years. I guess that's what happens when your team is under .500."

So Johnson pointed at Cashen. Cashen said nothing, just filed the incident, the manager's words, away.

May 19, New York. Backman had three hits in five at-bats against the Padres, and the Mets won, 5–4. But Backman was unhappy. He had finished the 1986 season with a batting average of .320; now he was fighting to get it over .250. And this was eating at Backman, a prideful man who had never hit lower than .270 in his professional career. After the game, Backman said, "I looked at some tapes of myself from last year. My stance had completely changed. I had to notice it myself. But that's really Robby's job."

Robby was Mets' first base coach and hitting instructor, Bill Robinson. Even he was not immune from the fingers.

May 23, New York. Ron Darling lost again. The man who was supposed to be the ace while Gooden was away, who had been awarded a new million-dollar contract after taking the Mets to arbitration, had not won a game since April 22. Worse, Darling could not seem to get out of the first inning without the opponents scoring a run, or two, or three. Normally the most charming and aware of the Mets—in sports, "aware" frequently means being able to find the national or metropolitan section of the newspaper—Darling was becoming visibly frustrated, in the clubhouse, on the mound.

Mostly on the mound. In the clubhouse, Darling was rarely visible; he had taken to hiding out in the players-only room behind equipment man Charlie Samuels's office, across from the trainers room. Reporters were strictly forbidden from entering the room, unless they were cutting through it on the way to the elevator that took them up to the press box. Even when he was not pitching, Darling used the players-only room more and more as a sanctuary, at least until the clubhouse was cleared of writers before the game. "People want answers," Darling said. "I don't have any."

It was not an easy time in Ron Darling's life. His infant son, Tyler Christian, had been born to Toni Darling during spring training, nearly two months prematurely. You started with that in his private life. Publicly, with a baseball in his right hand, Darling was a holy mess. For two years, he had complained quietly, but pointedly, that he did not get the recognition he deserved because of Gooden—The Doc!—on the same team, in the same rotation; that it was not as wonderful as the world might think to look down the road knowing you were destined to play Drysdale to Gooden's Koufax. Now he had been given the opportunity, at least for a couple of months while Gooden went away to get his nose cleaned up, to step out of the line, sing the lead.

And Darling could not win.

It seemed he was behind in the count on every hitter, and when he got behind, the hitters knew he would be throwing a fastball. Not the split-fingered fastball with all the nasty break to it, the one that had earned him a million dollars for 1987. His regular fastball. The much straighter—more hittable—one. The hitters were knocking the cover off that one.

Plus, there was The Rumor.

Marv Albert, during a pregame show for NBC's *Game of the Week,* had suggested that another Met was about to enter rehabilitation for a drug problem. Albert later said he had "sources," though no one familiar with his work as a talented play-by-play man and New York nightly sportscaster had ever really confused him with Bob Woodward. The bottom line was that Albert, an entertainer taking a clumsy turn as a journalist, went on the air, to your United States of America, with the story without any real proof of information other than his "sources," and thus turned everyone on the team into a suspect. And before long, Darling became aware that people thought Marv Albert was talking about him.

Darling was in his Atlanta hotel room one night when I called.

I said, "You are aware people are talking about you, right?"

"Sure," Darling said. "People are even coming up to me on the street, in restaurants, and asking me right to my face. I was out the other night to dinner, and this well-dressed Arab-looking man came up to me and said, 'You're the Met they're talking about, right? The one who's supposed to be on drugs?' "

"But why you?"

"Because I'm the one who's going bad. First, it was supposed to be one guy, but he hit so great in April, so it wasn't him. Then I heard about another player when he was struggling a little bit, but then he got over .300. That left the rumor mill with me. I guess I fit the profile the best, anyway. I'm young, I'm making a lot of money now,

I'm fairly visible in the city. And I haven't won a game in a long time."

This Saturday was no different. From the time he walked Dodgers leadoff batter Steve Sax in the top of the first inning, Darling looked in physical pain on the mound, as if he had just taken a bullet; he walked around, he looked into the stands and into the sky and down at the ground, he rolled his eyes and seemed to want to do everything except try to throw an unhittable strike to the batter. The Dodgers got ahead in the first, and even though Darling settled down after that, the Mets lost again.

After the game, Hernandez said, "I wish Ronnie would stop rolling his damn eyes out there. If I'm a hitter and I see that, I know I've got the pitcher."

Understand: A baseball team, made up of twenty-four players, is really only a team of twenty-four when things are going well. Unity is a hallmark only in the good times. The rest of the time, it can be every man for himself; major league athletes are not given to searching and fearless moral inventories. Suddenly, in May of 1987, the Mets were looking around for Mets to blame. When things start to unravel, the instinct, even in the best of families, is to stand up, championship rings glinting, and yell, "He did it!"

So it was with the Mets. Davey Johnson forgot about pitching his starters with three days' rest in April, instead of the usual four, perhaps straining Ojeda's arm, and Darling's arm, and Aguilera's arm. He made noise about Frank Cashen instead.

Hernandez, whose batting average with runners in scoring position was under .200, talked about Darling, and a general stench in the room, saying "we" stink, but never really included himself in the presentation. Backman bitched about the hitting coach and Strawberry wouldn't admit he blew a play in Atlanta, and nobody would take the blame for that botched play on Dale Murphy's stolen base.

Later on, when the 1987 season would take one of its last turns for the Mets, Keith Hernandez would say, "The thing I'm proudest of was the way this team hung together."

It sounded fine in September.

Only The Prince was full of shit.

While the fingers were pointed, the problems with the arms weren't getting any better.

"It's important to remember one thing: In 1986, the Mets were not a great team," Tim McCarver was saying one night in the press room at Shea, preparing his notes for a broadcast. Thirty minutes before a game starts, McCarver can always be found at a table next to the bar, notes spread out in front of him, scribbling madly, generally cribbing as though preparing for a televised presidential debate. He bears a striking resemblance to the singer Huey Lewis, as if he were Lewis's older brother. Around 7:25, he would settle into the booth next to Ralph Kiner, put on his wire-rimmed glasses, light his first cigar of the night, and begin to sing his own, Memphis-hued brand of baseball music across the next three hours.

The Mets had dropped into fifth place, and McCarver was trying to explain why he thought that had happened.

"People look at what they did last season, 108 wins, finally the world championship, and they think, 'They *must* have been great," McCarver continued. "Well, they weren't. The Mets were a good team with great *pitching* last season. In fact, they had almost perfect pitching up and down the line, from the five starters, from McDowell and Orosco, from almost everybody. The pitching was so marvelous people now tend to forget that other than Dykstra and Backman, none of the hitters really had startling statistical years; at least, above and beyond what they'd done before. Now Dwight isn't here, Ojeda is gone, McDowell is back, but he doesn't have his strength yet [McCarver believed all season that McDowell's erratic pitching was due to being rushed back into action], and Darling isn't winning. You ask me why the Mets are where they are, and I think it's simple: The pitching has gone from perfect to mediocre."

Three days later, Ojeda had surgery on his pitching arm; the medical terminology was anterior transposition of the ulnar nerve. He was not expected to pick up a baseball for four or five months. Dr. James Parkes, the Mets team physician, said, "It's a common operation, something we've done numerous times. It's not career-threatening. We fully expect Ojeda to be back pitching in 1988."

But Frank Cashen spoke more realistically about the man he had brought over from the Boston Red Sox after the 1985 season, had watched become one of the top left-handers in the National League—a pitcher who saved the Mets after they had lost the first game of the National League playoffs, then saved them again after they had lost the first two games of the World Series. Ojeda, a pleasant, soft-spoken man from California, had quickly become one of the most popular Mets.

Cashen said, "Any time you cut a pitcher's arm, it becomes career-threatening."

It was May 23. Ojeda had the surgery in the morning, his girlfriend drove him home that night; no one except Ojeda knew it at the time, but he planned on pitching before the 1987 season concluded. The same day, Dwight Gooden made his third start in the minor leagues. Three days after that, Rick Aguilera was unable to pitch against the Giants in San Francisco because of pain in *his* elbow. Aguilera flew to Los Angeles, where he was examined by Frank Jobe, the famous surgeon who had first come to the attention of the baseball world in 1974, when he had effectively given then-Dodgers left-hander Tommy John a new arm by repairing John's left elbow with a tendon transplanted from John's right forearm.

Jobe's diagnosis of Aguilera: Sprained ligaments.

Aguilera went on the fifteen-day disabled list.

The New York Mets had played forty-three games. From the perfect pitching staff of the year before, Gooden had no wins, Darling had two wins, Ojeda had ended up on an operating table and now Rick Aguilera had sprained ligaments; his fifteen disabled days would actually extend into three disabled months. Sid Fernandez had become the rock of the staff, and even Fernandez had left a game during May, missed a start, when his left knee buckled on him. At the time, Hernandez said, "Let's face it, if we lose Sid, we're fucked."

So the starting rotation for the world champions was Fernandez, Darling, John Mitchell, a sidearming journeyman named Terry Leach.

And David Cone.

Or, more precisely: David Cone?

David Cone was a redheaded, right-handed pitcher whose existence was completely unknown to the Mets and their fans before he came over in a trade from the Kansas City Royals on March 27. The Mets traded a minor league right-hander named Rick Anderson and backup catcher Ed Hearn to the Royals for Cone and minor league catcher Chris Jelic. At the time, it was a meaningless transaction lost amid a hundred spring training transactions in Florida and Arizona. The Mets had picked up another pitcher. The pitching-rich Mets. Cone was pitching insurance for them, nothing more, nothing less. His acquisition was nothing to force the reporters covering the team to rush for phones, call offices, scream, "Get me rewrite!"

Exactly two months later, in a game between the Mets and Giants at Candlestick Park, David Cone had his right pinky broken by an Atlee Hammaker fastball; Cone was trying to bunt. The bone in the pinky, according to doctors, "just exploded upon impact." Cone, after surgery, would wear a cast until July.

Cone had a record of 2–2 at that point. He had nearly shut out the Reds two weeks before, pitching brilliantly, not losing his shutout until the eighth inning. The redheaded, right-handed pitcher from Kansas City about whom no one knew until March 27 had become, after Fernandez, the most reliable, healthy pitcher.

All of a sudden, the reaction around the Mets was this:

Oh my God. We've lost David Cone.

Wally Backman said,"We're fucked big time. We gotta pray a lot now. Pray and wait for the Doc."

On the last day of May, Ed Whitson of the San Diego Padres beat the Mets and John Mitchell, 1–0, in San Diego. The loss kept the Mets in fourth place, behind the Cardinals, Expos, Cubs.

The next day, Jack Lang, veteran baseball writer for the New York *Daily News,* broke the story that the Mets were about to reach almost as far back into their past as they could and sign a forty-two-year-old pitcher by the name of George Thomas Seaver.

JUNE: "EVERYBODY IN THE WORLD ALWAYS HAS ENOUGH PITCHING IN JANUARY . . ."

Tom Seaver, who wanted to be a New York Yankee, said something very prophetic about the New York Mets.

"Everybody in the world always has enough pitching in January," he said. "It's around the twenty-fifth of March that things change. Then everybody screams, 'What do we do for pitching?' "

And occasionally a team would just keep screaming.

It was the morning of February 10, in the study of Seaver's home in Greenwich, Connecticut. Jazz played softly on a transistor radio. Outside, the wind blew snow around his property, and sometimes built to a howl as it raced through the bare trees around Tom and Nancy Seaver's converted barn. Seaver looked thicker than the young man whose face adorned all the magazine covers surrounding him in the den, telling of a baseball life, the most splendid parts of which had been spent with the New York Mets. But his brown hair was still tousled, and the face was still more boy than man, and Seaver said he believed his right arm was fine as he told of waiting for the New York Yankees to give him a call.

Seaver had finished the previous season with the Boston Red Sox, but had been unable to pitch in the playoffs or World Series because of arthroscopic surgery performed on his right knee, surgery that repaired torn cartilage. The Red Sox had offered him another year, but Seaver had turned them down. Seaver wanted to pitch in New York for his last season, finish up where he started. Once, he had been Gooden for the Mets. He had been Tom Terrific—a symbol of triumph in the sixties the way Gooden would be a symbol of triumph in the eighties. The year the Mets had won the first world championship, had been the Miracle Mets, Seaver had won 25 games. He was good-looking, he had a beautiful wife. He was the first Mets superstar, pitching the way Gooden would later, getting the magazine covers Darling would get.

Seaver had left the Mets during the 1977 season, after an ugly, acrimonious contract dispute with then-Chairman of the Board M. Donald Grant. He pitched six seasons for the Cincinnati Reds, came back to the Mets for a grand homecoming in 1983, left again when the Mets gambled that no one would sign him if he were left off the forty-man roster during the winter. The White Sox signed Seaver, he won 31 games for them over the next two seasons, including No. 300 at Yankee Stadium. The Red Sox picked him up for the divisional race during the summer of 1986.

After twenty seasons as one of the premier pitchers of his time, part of an extraordinary generation of pitchers that included Steve Carlton, Jim Palmer, Gaylord Perry, Phil Niekro, and Don Sutton—all winners of 300 games—Seaver wanted one more summer. And he wanted it to be in New York. The Mets were out of the question; the Mets had a perfect pitching staff. The Yankees didn't. George Steinbrenner had not signed Jack Morris, and was still acknowledged throughout baseball to be pitching short. Seaver thought he would be perfect for the Yankees and the Yankees would be perfect for him; he would be able to commute for home games to Yankee Stadium, thirty minutes away.

"I'm just waiting for the phone to ring," Seaver said. "Woody

Woodward (Yankees general manager) has already called once, but he wanted me to go to spring training without a contract. I told him, "Woody, you either want me or you don't.' But I still expect to hear back from him."

Then he spoke of how every team in the world thought it had enough pitching in January.

"If I didn't think I could pitch I would already have announced my retirement," Seaver said. Outside, a tall young woman, blonde, walked briskly past Seaver's window, smiling and waving as she went.

I said, "Was that Nancy?"

Seaver shook his head.

"Sara," he said. His teenaged daughter. As much as anything in the room, Seaver himself or the magazine covers, it was Sara Seaver who represented most the passage of time; the little girl from his first Mets career was now a young woman, confused for her beautiful mother.

"Anyway," Tom Seaver said, "the option on my services belongs to me. There's no sense of urgency. I'm where I want to be. I'm just waiting to see what happens."

What happened was that the Yankees never called back. Not in February. Not in March.

But the Mets did in May.

It spoke of how desperate they had become. Baseball teams only want surprises on the field once the season begins. Teams do not want to have to make trades, do not want to have to dip into the minor leagues for help. That is the dream blueprint: Play the season with the twenty-four players they take out of spring training. Trades mean injuries, or failure, nothing less. Same with calling up kids from the minors. If the kid was good enough, he would have made the team in Florida, or Arizona. When a team has to start looking around, whether it is May or September, it points to one chilling fact.

Something Went Wrong.

Teams do not mind pleasant surprises on the field. In 1986, one of the most important Mets had turned out to be an all-purpose player named Kevin Mitchell, of whom little was expected when the Mets broke camp. Mitchell turned out to be one of the Mets' most valuable offensive weapons, and had been part of the two-out rally in the tenth inning of Game 6 of the World Series. Mitchell was gone, traded to San Diego as part of the McReynolds deal, but he was remembered as the kind of baseball surprise teams hope for.

Seaver was not. Seaver was the panic button. Already, the Mets had dipped into the minor leagues for pitchers like John Mitchell, Jeff Innis, Tom Edens. Seaver was something different altogether; the Mets had reached out of baseball and into the past for a forty-two-year-old man who had not thrown a baseball in competition since the previous August, and whose conditioning ever since had been on the squash courts of Greenwich, Connecticut.

There was a press conference on June 6, at Shea Stadium. Seaver and Cashen. It was announced that Seaver's signing was conditional. If his pitches still had any sting—Seaver would test his arm in an exhibition game against Tidewater, then in a series of simulated games before batting practice against some of the Mets—he would sign on for one last baseball ride, where his trip began.

If not, back to Greenwich, no hard feelings, the Mets had no obligations.

"This isn't a nostalgic thing," Seaver said. "I'm here to help this team win the division."

He retired, for good, sixteen days later. During that time, he was pasted by the Tidewater hitters, and by people from the Mets bench; in Seaver's last simulated game, on June 20, backup catcher Barry Lyons had six hits in six at-bats.

"I've used up all the competitive pitches in my arm," Tom Seaver said.

Back to the future hadn't worked.

Besides, the present was busy enough. By the end of the month, the seventeen-day comeback of Seaver, this ghost who showed up trying to throw fastballs, was barely a footnote with his old team.

Dwight was back.

And Darryl was back in the news.

It was the kind of media crowd reserved for a World Series, an All-Star Game anyway. There were the regular writers and the irregulars, and there were sportswriters from all over the country who were in New York to cover the Belmont Stakes horse race the next day. It was June 5, and Dwight Gooden was starting against the Pittsburgh Pirates. It was the season's fifty-first game. The Mets came into it with a record of 25–25, still stuck in fourth place. But the season was starting, that was what the atmosphere said at Shea. This was the Opening Day game Gooden did not get to pitch. The game had been sold out for weeks, from the time it was designated as Gooden's first start; Gooden's return even collided with a promotion scheduled long before the season began: the mock wedding of cartoon character Spiderman and his girlfriend.

So: After all the catastrophes, after 50 games that seemed like a season, with the imminent return of Seaver, the ghost and all that, suddenly, for this night, the ball park was filled with hope again. The Mets were five and a half games behind the Cardinals. What was that?

Doc was back.

During batting practice, the writers kept their distance. Only Klapisch and Verducci, the two writers he considered friends, ventured close to him.

Klapisch said, "The first fastball going to be a hundred and thirty miles per hour, or a hundred and sixty-five miles per hour?"

Gooden laughed.

"Nah," he said. "The first one is going to be eighty miles per hour. I expect Barry Bonds (Pirates leadoff hitter) to take it."

Gooden took some swings in the batting cage, came out, looked down at his hands, smiled. By June 5, even a pitcher's hands are calloused from holding a bat; the starters hit every five days, and the rest of the pitchers engage in a spirited hitting contest before almost every home game, before the official batting practice begins. Even after his month in the minor leagues, Dwight Gooden's hands were still soft.

Gooden said, "Don't want to wear them out. Better save them for the game."

Gooden took the mound at 7:36. The 51,402 people in the stands at Shea stood and gave him a standing ovation that went on for a couple of minutes. It was as if the noise were saying, "Well, hello, kid. Where you been?" Gooden, just like that, was forgiven, at least by the fans. When Hernandez had returned to Shea Stadium after his "devil on earth" courtroom speech in 1985, he had been cheered. Now Gooden, a month out of rehab, his team in fourth place at least partly because of that rehab, was cheered. Sports fans, when presented with a vehicle that can take them from fourth place back to first, reject Calvinism. They stand up and cheer. The kid made a mistake with dope? Well, who hasn't made mistakes? They would wipe the slate clean on the proviso that Gooden would commence throwing the living shit out of the ball. If he lost four or five games in a row later on, the same fans would probably wonder if the kid was back on the junk. But not on June 5, 1987. The Met had the Expos and the Cubs to pass and the Cardinals to catch. Gooden went fastball, curve, fastball, fastball on Barry Bonds and struck him out. The cheers exploded again. Gooden pitched into the seventh inning, struck out five men, gave up just four hits, and the Mets won, 5–1. Gooden's fastball was clocked by the radar gun at 92 mph; it was the same speed as always. It was as if he had not been away.

A good surprise.

But these were the 1987 Mets, so, of course, the dynamics of the season required a bad surprise, one from off the field, almost immediately.

Gooden had promised some of the writers that at some point during the summer, he would speak openly about all that had happened to him over the past year. On June 23, he opened the door a little bit for me in the New York *Daily News:*

"You know the stuff you're doing is wrong. When you're high, you realize how bad it is for you, for everybody around you. You're thinking, 'That ain't me.' Then, you know, you get high again. And you think you're being so clever, fooling everybody. But people know. And then finally you know that you've got a disease. At least if you're lucky, you finally realize you've got a disease. You aren't you anymore. It's in charge."

Gooden had a record of 3–1 as he spoke, his earned run average was 2.64 since his return, he had struck out 29 men in 30 innings, and he was generally singing a much different song about cocaine than he had sung in Frank Cashen's office at Huggins-Stengel Stadium on the morning of April 1, when he first cried that the EMIT Screen Test wasn't true, swear to God, and then he cried that he was just a couple-a-times-at-parties user of cocaine. Now he was 3–1 and he had his fastball back, and he was a grateful, recovering addict, faithful to his aftercare, living one day at a time like it said in all the books from Alcoholics Anonymous.

Or maybe he was, like Hernandez and other Mets in 1987, capable of self-deception.

When the *Daily News* came out the next day, Klapisch and Verducci, feeling betrayed that Gooden had broken his drug silence with someone else, went up to Gooden and said, "Hey, what's the deal?" Gooden said I had innocently asked some questions, he'd answered them, Klapisch and Verducci not being around.

A few minutes later, Gooden grabbed the two writers and said, "Let's go to the Jets locker room." It is the old football locker room down the hall from the Mets clubhouse, one the football New York Jets used when they played at Shea Stadium before moving over to the

Meadowlands. And for the next seventy-five minutes, the three men talked, Gooden doing most of the talking, the writers taking notes as fast as they could. Gooden said he had never been a "junkie." Said the twenty-eight days at Smithers had been one of the "scariest experiences of my life." Said he never used cocaine during the season, only during the off-season. Said he had been using cocaine once a week, and had planned to stop on Opening Day, before he got caught by the EMIT Screen Test. Said he was glad he got caught because his use of the drug was increasing, and that if the Mets had not requested he take the urine test when they did, "I might have ended up like Len Bias," referring to the former Maryland basketball star, and No. 1 draft choice of the Boston Celtics, who had died in the year before after a cocaine overdose.

Said he had experimented with cocaine as far back as Hillsborough High School.

When the *Post* and *Newsday* came out the next day, most of the Mets players were supportive of Gooden. Hernandez, ex-user himself, said, "I think it was a positive thing." Down the row of lockers from Hernandez, Howard Johnson, who drank nothing stronger than wine coolers, said, "It's obvious Dwight has taken control of his life."

Gooden had his fastball back. The players were as forgiving as the fans.

Not so the Mets front office. Joe McIlvaine said that the Mets would never have signed Gooden in the first place if he had known Gooden was fooling around with cocaine in high school. A week later, my paper, the *Daily News,* looking to catch up on the original Gooden confessional, published a copyrighted story that said that Gooden had been confronted by the Major League Baseball Players Association in the middle of the previous season; the MLBPA had been told by a Mets player that Gooden was indeed using cocaine during the season.

Gooden stood by his story, said he had never used drugs during the season. The *Daily News* stood by its story. And Frank Cashen, who had pounded his desk in anger at Huggins-Stengel on April 1 and was angry still, stood by the New York *Daily News,* and not his young star.

"I feel betrayed," Cashen said. "I feel like he has been lying to me all along."

On June 25, Gooden beat the Chicago Cubs and improved his record to 4–1 and said he was out of the business of answering drug questions for good.

He said, "I needed to let the public know I wasn't a junkie."
Swear to God. Swear to God. Swear to God.

It was eleven-thirty in the morning, June 9, the visitors' clubhouse at Wrigley Field. In twenty minutes, the Mets would take the field for batting practice.

All the Mets except Darryl Strawberry.

The day before, Strawberry had been a few minutes late for batting practice; Johnson let it pass. One of the things the Mets liked about their manager was that, for the most part, he treated them like adults. Didn't niggle them to death with rules. There were no enforced curfews on the road, no strict dress codes for team flights, no censorship of free speech in the Mets clubhouse. Johnson wasn't a warm man with the team, a backslapper, a hugger like Tommy Lasorda of the Los Angeles Dodgers; it hadn't been his nature during his playing career with the Orioles and Braves and Phillies, wasn't his nature as a manager. If anything, there were more and more times as things went wrong for the 1987 Mets when Johnson would go into his office and shut the door, withdraw from the team.

He did expect the players to get to the ball park on time.

And there were two things Darryl Strawberry had never done consistently in his major league career: hit left-handed pitching and get to the ball park on time.

Keith Hernandez saw that Strawberry had not yet walked into the clubhouse; so did the rest of the Mets. Hernandez went to a pay phone in the visitors' clubhouse and called the Westin Hotel, where the Mets were staying. He asked the operator to ring Strawberry's room.

No answer.

Strawberry showed up at Wrigley Field at 12:12 P.M., nearly a half hour after batting practice had begun. Johnson fined him $250, and announced Strawberry was being benched indefinitely. The fine was nothing; it was tipping money to someone like Strawberry, making in excess of a million dollars to play right field for the Mets in 1987. It was meant to be an insult, an embarrassment. And it worked.

The manager said, "I've got a lot of guys who want to play here. Apparently, Darryl isn't one of them." He was asked when Strawberry might return to the Mets lineup and said, "When it becomes important to him again."

Strawberry defended himself. Said the Westin had failed to give him his 10:00 A.M. wake-up call. Said he hadn't awakened until 11:45, realized how late it was, jumped into a cab, and got to the ball park. That done, he reacted with his usual catalogue of angers and resentments. He was, after that fine April start, with the 3 home runs in the first 3 games and the 10-game hitting streak, back to being Mr. Misunderstood.

"What does late have to do with not wanting to play? I've been busting my butt all year. And then he says he's not going to play me? It's not that I'm one of those crybabies on his team, who's always complaining of being hurt. Davey's always trying to bury me. Every time something goes wrong, he buries me in the papers. If I don't play tomorrow against the Cubs, I ain't suiting up in no exhibition game."

After the next day's game against the Cubs, the Mets were scheduled to fly to Virginia for an annual exhibition game against the Tidewater Tides.

"Fuck that," Darryl Strawberry said.

He got no sympathy in the clubhouse, not even from a noted reveler like Hernandez, Prince of Darkness, who knew Darryl was lying about waking up at 11:45 because Hernandez had tried to call him at 11:30.

"Rules are rules," Hernandez said. "I have had my four A.M. nights in this city, but I've always played the next day. You have to suck it up." The next day, the Chicago *Tribune* published a picture of Strawberry posing with the owner of Limelight, a Chicago disco. The owner said what Darryl Strawberry had been sucking up the morning before the game was vodka and cranberry juice, mixed together. The owner said Strawberry had not left Limelight until four in the morning.

Strawberry did not play the next day, while his buddy Gooden beat the Cubs, 13–2. And Strawberry did not back off on his threat to boycott the game against the Tidewater Tides. The Mets writers relayed Strawberry's position to Davey Johnson. Johnson curtly said, "Now you guys bring him a message from me: Tell him to reconsider."

There was still no sympathy for Strawberry in the Mets room, not even from Gooden, his best friend. "Darryl is crazy if he goes through with this," Gooden said. "He knows he has to play."

More than any incident of the season so far, the squabble between Johnson and Strawberry, one providing a picnic for the back pages of the New York tabloids, pointed to the difference a year made with the New York Mets. On June 10 of 1986, the Mets had a record of 38–16, and were 8 games ahead of the field. Now they were one game over

.500, just a part of the field chasing the Cardinals. Maybe if Strawberry had been late two days in a row in June of 1986, it would have been the stuff of fines and hard words and headlines. And maybe Johnson would have let him off with a warning, made a big production out of believing Darryl's excuse.

Again and again and again: That was then, this was now. You could have put it to music. The dynamics of the clubhouse had changed, the dynamics between manager and player. Johnson only had a few rules, but now he showed he could turn any one of them into a club when his team was one game over .500, and not 22.

Strawberry did not decide to play in the meaningless game until he got to the clubhouse at Tidewater, and his mother, Ruby Strawberry, called him from California. "Keep your head up and don't let the negative things get you down," Mrs. Strawberry said. It wasn't exactly Churchill's "fight them on the beaches" speech, but it did the trick. Strawberry played, while Seaver was pasted by minor league hitters and got the first inkling that his fastball had cobwebs all over it.

On the flight after the game from Tidewater to Pittsburgh, Strawberry and Gooden sat in the back of the plane.

"I'm sick of Davey," Strawberry said.

Gooden looked at him, finally said, "You're a time bomb, man. A time bomb."

A Fan's Notes

DICK YOUNG'S CHILDREN

*I*t might be argued that the job of contemporary baseball beat writer was invented by Dick Young, the remarkable (later embarrassing) reporter (later columnist) of the New York *Daily News* (later *Post*). In any case, he certainly redefined the position. Before Young, baseball writers often tended to be distant and lordly, didn't really dig. Young dug. He arrived at the game early, stayed late. He got to know the players in the clubhouse, was forever positioned behind the batting cage, listening, note-taking, talking, arguing.

The word "feisty" did not truly exist before Dick Young came along. And such was his energy, his lunatic passion, his unquestioned skill and knowledge, that all daily baseball writers after Young were, if not imitators, at least indebted.

Personally, I can't imagine many lifetime sports jobs worse than beat writing. It is many things, none of them glamorous. The hours, to begin, are dreadful. Writers get to the ball park around four in the afternoon for a seven-thirty start. They go to the clubhouse, chat with their contacts, go out on the field, see what's doing there. (I'll get to their writing in a moment—this is just about time.) Baseball games last over three hours now and by the time the writers reach the clubhouse and are allowed in after the game, it's maybe eleven. Then more talk, more interviews. Their game story has to be in usually before one in the morning. Which means they've spent nearly nine hours on the job when they're finished—

—and they're not finished at "21" either—they're either stuck at Shea, Yankee Stadium, or some park on the road. These are not the crossroads of any world known to cartographers. And they work these hours six days a week. Many beat writers are single. The life is tough on marriage. Bob Klapisch, now of the *Daily News,* says: "Either you spend all your time on the phone or you cheat on your wife."

As for the writing, they tend to do several stories per night. Often an early story summarizes the results of yesterday's events. Sometimes it will cover a later-breaking development, a trade rumor, an internecine spat. (Some papers also want what is called a "running story," which is essentially an expanded play-by-play of the contest.) The game story, the most important, has varying deadlines, all of them inconvenient.

All in all, then, maybe two or three distinct articles, maybe two thousand words. If you're saying, "What's so terrible?" you're welcome to your opinion. If you're saying, "Boo-hoo for them, they get to watch the game free," you're not as right as you think you are—because beat writers are working while the fans are chomping on their peanuts and beer—if they're watching, it's what might be called "selective viewing." Just sitting there enjoying the game unfold in all its gloriously simple intricacies (or intricate simplicities, if you like) is not what the job entails.

So the hours stink, there's a lot of brute work, and you don't get to enjoy the action. What else makes it a terrible job? Just this: You can't really write what you know. Not all you know.

Because beat writers come as close as any outsiders to living with the team. From March through October. Six days a week. And their job is not just to report the wins and the losses but, if they're good, the whys.

Let's say they know a certain player is drinking too much and it's affecting his play—

—can't write that.

Let's say they know a certain player is whoring around on his wife and it's affecting his play—

—can't write that, either.

Now these are rotten examples—baseball reporters don't work for *Confidential Magazine.* But a lot of what they know they can't write about because if they do—since they spend their lives with the players—they know the players will simply stop trusting them, stop talking to them, they won't get the job done properly and, more likely than not, they'll be gone next season—and even though I don't want to be a beat writer, there are a lot of people who do.

What these writers try to do is get the trust of the players. Let the players observe them. Let the players come to know they're not out to embarrass them. Don't be, as the trade has it, a "shit-stirrer." Then maybe the players will relax and talk openly, full in the knowledge that they'll be protected.

If not, you have situations such as early September when Michael Kay, the excellent young Yankee beat writer of the *Post,* was on the shit list of one David Allen Righetti. Why? Because in a story Kay suggested that Righetti, who was going badly, at least for a superb reliever, should be switched in jobs with Tim Stoddard, the setup man, who had been going brilliantly. Righetti didn't hit Kay. Or yell at him. They just weren't talking. Not a very big deal—there are a lot of other players in the locker room.

But if *all* the players stopped talking to him . . . not a career enhancer. So the beat writers are caught, trying to tell the truth, but not the whole of it.

One final point to be made about the job of the beat writer: There's not *that* much to tell.

Not that's relevant or interesting.

Still, the beat writer plunges stolidly (if you can do that) on. He must. Not only because it's his job but he knows something: Readers depend on him. (I know I do. I find a writer I like and trust and become a Kremlinologist of the man.) He is my heartline. *USA Today* gives me my stats. But the beat writer is the one who keeps my blood pumping.

I picked a day randomly—it happened to be the evening I interviewed Michael Kay—and decided to go through it as a beat writer might. Trying to find the story. Not the result, the story.

It happened to be the night of the thirty-first of August, the Yanks going against Oakland, the night before the stretch run in baseball unofficially begins. Both these teams were in the race, the Yankees five games out, the A's one behind, but dead even in the lost column, in the other division.

A reasonable amount of tension in the air. Some of it cut by the fact that the enemy managers, Piniella and Tony LaRussa, are not only both native Floridians, but also friends. I got to Yankee Stadium before four, clocked the clubhouse, the batting cage. All seemed normal—writers inside, talking to players, coaches, each other. Writers outside, talking to players, coaches, each other.

But two unusual things happened that night.

The first had to do with the game, which was won, incidentally by the Yankees, 4 to 1 with Guidry winning it, striking out 10 in 7-plus innings.

The Oakland "1" came about in a curious manner, and sent the night spinning slightly out of orbit. It was the fourth inning, a zip-zip ball game, two out, bases loaded, Guidry pitching to Steinbach, the Oakland catcher. As he's about to deliver, plate umpire Dave Phillips jumps out from behind the plate waving his arms: Guidry has balked, a run scores, the Yanks are now behind and Piniella is screaming out of the dugout, clearly not in total agreement with Phillips's decision. (Phillips may have been the only one in the stadium to see the crime: Guidry has balked perhaps half a dozen times in a career dating back to the mid-seventies.) Piniella and Phillips continue for a bit and guess who won? Piniella, still outraged, kicks a tennis ball that had been thrown from the stands. Guidry keeps his composure once he's allowed to toil again, whiffing Steinbach.

Bottom of the fourth. Curt Young has stifled the Bombers thus far. He opens the bottom of the fourth by throwing a ball to Winfield. Now here comes Piniella again, chugging from the dugout, pointing this time toward the pitcher's mound, pointing toward the rubber, with Phillips alongside. No one in the press box has the least notion what's happening on the field, but they know that eventually the crucial info will come trickling up to them. (What this actually turned out to involve was that the pitcher has to have his feet equal to or behind the rubber and Young was starting with his right foot slightly in front of the rubber. If Young was, and he probably was, he was not the first pitcher in major league history to commit such an egregious offense—most pitchers do it.)

Was Young upset by Piniella's sudden criticism? Impossible to answer. Certainly the ensuing meeting at the mound of all the umps plus LaRussa, who had rocketed out of his dugout, could not have done much to improve either his concentration or his timing. In any case, what happened was he shortly gave up a two run-homer to Ron Kittle, which put the Yankees ahead, where they would stay.

Now LaRussa, and it's good the TV audience couldn't lip-read, is out of his dugout again, demanding that Kittle's bat be confiscated and held for corking tests. Usually, corking charges are leveled against banjo hitters who have suddenly OD'd on spinach; so here's LaRussa claiming that Kittle, who has hit as many as fifty homers in one minor league season, is guilty. Seemed a bit thin.

When the game ended and the beat writers raced for their interviews, Piniella seemed sanguine. Contentedly he quoted that famous baseball rubber rule, "8.01," that every fan has tattooed behind his eyelids. Kittle, when asked if he corked his bat, laughed and admitted he did, "with the sausage we had in the clubhouse the other day. Much better than superballs."

LaRussa, in the visiting clubhouse, waited for all the press to assemble. "I'm only going to say this once," he said, his voice even and calm. He's a handsome Italianate man and very bright: a lawyer. Those who knew him well felt he was having difficulty controlling himself. I, of course, had never seen the man but I suspected something was amiss because these jets of steam kept coming from his ears. When we were all gathered around, he began: "This was bullshit baseball and if you want to play bullshit baseball, there are a lot of us can play bullshit baseball even though I hate bullshit baseball, I think bullshit baseball's bullshit, I think it was bullshit to ask for Kittle's bullshit bat, I never asked for a bullshit corked bat before and I bullshit won't ask for one again but if you want to not play baseball but bullshit baseball, then there's plenty of bullshit baseball we can play, you've got pitchers who pitch bullshit baseball and I will stop their bullshit tactics and as soon as any of those bullshit tactics are tried because if I haven't made it clear, I'm not much in favor of bullshit baseball, goodnight."

It was, all in all, a very enjoyable game for most of the beat writers to cover, the two friends going slightly berserk over the rule book, the invisible balk, on and on.

The second unusual thing that happened during the game was this: Dick Young died.

He'd been ill, been hospitalized, so it shouldn't have come as a shock. But it came as a shock.

At least to the old-timers. The ones who remembered when he was honest, forceful, important, battling against the intrusive television attempts to gain position, fighting the battles of the press.

The younger writers remembered only Young the management shill. And not a single one I asked felt remote regret. For his family, of course. For his friends, yes. But not for the man. He had become an embarrassment, Steinbrenner's mouthpiece.

A terrible R.I.P. for any man.

Call the game, "He Said, What Do *You* Say?"

Starting with spring training, the beat reporter who covers a major league baseball team spends two hundred days a year with his team. It means two hundred days with twenty-four players, the manager, a half-dozen coaches. It is a lot of people, over a long time. So diversions are required. The game of "He Said, What Do *You* Say?" is frequently the only thing to break the monotony of the long season: six and seven games a week from March through October. When played properly, "He Said" brings a sort of spontaneous combustion to the clubhouse. It gets the beat men to hustling, competing with each other. Occasionally, it gets them the best prize of all: A big headline that does not involve who won or lost the game.

Nowhere is the game played better than in New York City, where the Mets and Yankees have as many as ten men regularly covering each team for newspapers in the New York–New Jersey–Connecticut area. The Yankees used to be better at "He Said," back in Billy Martin's first tenure as manager in the middle seventies. In those days, the Yankees constantly had owner George Steinbrenner fighting with Martin, and with Martin's players. And the players, led by Reggie Jackson and Graig Nettles and the late Thurman Munson, were always at the ready to say unspeakably rotten things to and about each other. The Yankees made "He Said" seem effortless, an almost unconscious clubhouse thing, like spitting tobacco juice, or scratching themselves. In a lot of ways, the Yankees first elevated the game to an art form.

But as June ended for the 1987 season and July began, the Mets were as good at "He Said" as Steinbrenner's Yankees had ever been. The Mets were a team of talkers, uncommonly avid talkers, and they had the

audience of ten or more reporters there every day, and the local
television crews, and the usual battery of radio men. The Mets consistently filibustered to a fare-thee-well.

But it was for the newspapers that the Mets sparkled most. No
baseball team in history had ever been more aware of what was being
written about it in the papers than the 1987 New York Mets. When the
team was on the road, a stack of clips from the local papers was Federal
Expressed to PR man Jay Horwitz every day. There were game stories
and features and columns from the *Daily News, Post, Times, Newsday,*
Newark *Star-Ledger,* Bergen (N.J.) *Record,* the Gannett papers from
Westchester and Rockland counties. On and on. It was Horwitz's job to
bring the clips to the visiting clubhouse, where the Mets players would
fight over them like hungry dogs fighting at the back door for pork
chops.

It only made "He Said" better.

The game goes like this:

A reporter is sitting with a player at, say 4:30 in the afternoon before
a night game. There is not better time than 4:30 for the reporter to do
his work, and for the players to want to talk. It is the most relaxed
clubhouse time of the day. Crosswords are being done. Music is being
played. Papers are being read. Card games are being played. Coffee is
being drunk. Players are wandering in and out of the bathroom. Occasionally one of the clubhouse boys will show up with a take-out order
of food from a nearby deli. The players go through new boxes of
baseball shoes and baseball gloves. Mail is being opened. Day eases
toward night.

Now, if the reporter is lucky, Something Is Bothering this player. Or
the player knows why Something Is Bothering someone else. The
player is probably one of the reporter's "guys." Each reporter has one,
or two, or more. Klapisch and Verducci had Gooden; Gooden wouldn't
belch without alerting the two beat men closest to his age that he felt
some gas coming on. Dan Castellano of the *Star-Ledger,* he was tight
with Strawberry, and Jack O'Connell of the *Daily News,* he knew he
could always get usable quotes from Mazzilli. So on and so forth.

Anyway, the player suddenly says to the reporter, "You know, Lassie
has more heart than Darryl Strawberry."

An example, as a way of explaining the game.

The reporter puts the Lassie quote in the notebook, just nods, acting
like it's not a big deal, asks a few more questions, already seeing the
next morning's back page: MET TO DARRYL: YOU'RE A DOG!

The interview ends. The player wanders off to the bathroom, or to a card game, or to the field. The reporter waits. He gets Strawberry alone. He says, "So-and-so says Lassie has more heart than you. What do you say?"

The game is on. And the game is not just played in the newspapers. It is also played in the clubhouse. When New York developer Donald Trump calls New York Mayor Ed Koch a "moron," and Koch comes back and calls Trump "piggy, piggy, piggy," as both men were doing during the summer of 1987, it is big news. But there are different rules for Trump and Koch. Trump and Koch are rarely in each other's presence. When their silly name-calling is done, they don't have to sit in the same room, maybe twenty feet apart, and dress with each other, then ride on the bus with each other, then ride on the plane with each other.

Then sit in the dugout with each other the next day.

Rely on each other to win a baseball game.

When Trump and Koch play, or figures of government play "He Said," it is barely the same game. It works best with a team like the Mets because the game is played in a small, visible corner—the clubhouse—of a wonderful stage called New York City.

When played with the proper language and the proper stars, it is almost as silly as a Broadway farce.

On June 30, with the Cardinals in town to play the Mets, and the Cardinals having won the first game of the three-game series the night before, three things happened to the Mets.

In this order:

1. Darryl Strawberry spent the afternoon in a Queens recording studio, promoting a record called "Chocolate Strawberry." Photographers were there. Darryl put headsets on, like a real rap star. And made like he was rapping.

2. A few hours later, Darryl Strawberry showed up at Shea Stadium and said he was too sick to play against the Cardinals, even though it was the Mets' first crack at the Cardinals since April. And they would not see the Cardinals again for another six weeks.

   Strawberry said he had the flu.

3. Lee Mazzilli pulled aside Jack O'Connell of the *Daily News*—the game works both ways; O'Connell thought of Mazzilli as one of

his guys, and Mazzilli thought of O'Connell as one of *his* guys—and began a well-thought-out indictment of Strawberry.

Mazzilli began by saying, "I've been thinking about this for a month . . ." In the middle of his presentation, he said that Darryl was selfish and immature. Mazzilli ended by saying, "Darryl let everyone on this team down."

Fourth of July fireworks had started early for the Mets.

Lee said.

What do you say, Darryl?

The game was on.

The next day, the story all over the papers, Mazzilli did not back down, but also said he didn't want to talk about it anymore with the writers. But the beauty of "He Said" is that once it starts, it can be played with television reporters as well as newspaper reporters. So Mazzilli went on WWOR's television pregame show with Mets broadcaster Steve Zabriskie, and repeated what he had said to Jack O'Connell in the *Daily News*.

Strawberry went to his strength, a fighter on the ropes coming off swinging a left hook.

Darryl turned into . . . Mr. Misunderstood!

He said to a crowd of writers around his locker, "How can my own teammates say something like that about me? Especially when I'm sick?"

Strawberry's locker was on the left side of the clubhouse. Mazzilli's was diagonally across from Strawberry's. Seeing the crowd around Strawberry, Mazzilli crossed the room finally, spoke quietly with Strawberry for a few moments. Strawberry listened, nodded, listened, nodded.

The writers went to Hernandez's locker while Mazzilli's shuttle diplomacy took place across the room.

"I have no qualms about what Mazzilli said," Hernandez said.

Many of the beat men, veterans of Hernandez's media machinations, thought Hernandez himself had put Mazzilli up to the original statement. Hernandez, for all the character traits that made him The Prince, was a team man first. He thought the Mets needed to get Strawberry's attention, but did not want to confront Strawberry himself, on the record. It was not his style, confrontation in the middle of the room; he preferred to work the corners. So some writers thought he had sent Mazzilli, a veteran who had begun his career with the Mets and whose words would carry some weight, to do his bidding, even though Mazzilli said later it was his very own idea.

After the game that night, which the Mets won 9–6 to pull back to within five and a half games of the Cardinals, Strawberry's position had softened toward Mazzilli, hardened toward the reporters. It is a natural extension of "He Said." Ballplayers, when they want to stay mad, would rather fight with The Press than teammates.

The Mets were heading off on an eleven-game road trip to Cincinnati, Atlanta, and Houston before the All-Star Break. On the way to the team bus, Strawberry shouted, "Fuck the press."

Not "Fuck Mazzilli."

Fuck the press.

Strawberry did manage to conquer the summer flu; he slept fourteen hours in Cincinnati, hit two doubles the next night, the Mets won, 5–0. Now they were just five games out of first, picking up the half-game on the idle Cardinals. But then on Friday morning, the Cincinnati *Enquirer* got into the "He Said" game, picking up a wire service story from a few days before. The story featured quotes from Wally Backman.

Backman was talking about Darryl's bout with the summer flu.

"From what I heard in the trainer's room, Darryl should have been out there," Backman was quoted as saying. Then Backman went back to a familiar theme, one he had never taken all the way to a public airing before: "Nobody I know gets sick twenty-five times a year. There's only so much you can take."

Backman, as it turned out, had gone on to say that no one would be upset with Strawberry if the team didn't need him so damned much. But that part did not make the Cincinnati paper. Darryl did not see that part.

Darryl saw what he saw.

Before the game, the beat men approached him, trying to see if it was still "fuck the press," or if he wanted to talk about the Backman quote that had followed the Mets to Cincinnati.

Verducci said, "Well, at least you always seem to come back strong after there's been a controversy." It was true. Like Reggie Jackson before him, Strawberry somehow hit better when he was in the middle of trouble. It is a rare thing. Most ballplayers, when they take off-field problems into the game with them, see batting averages drop or, in the case of pitchers, earned run averages inflate like they had been injected with steroids.

Strawberry said, "I guess I do." He paused. "But I've been thinking, and I think it's best for me to get out of here when my contract is up. I can't play on a team of backstabbers, guys you thought were behind you and understood you. What I'm saying is, Fuck Backman." Today, anyway: with Darryl at this point, it always seemed to be, Fuck *somebody*. His voice was getting louder in the visitor's clubhouse at Riverfront Stadium.

Darryl was building to a big finish.

"And fuck Mazzilli. I don't want to talk to either one of them because they might get hurt."

There it was. Darryl was talking about a possible fistfight. A fight would have been, what? Somebody winning the million dollars in *Name That Tune*? The writers thought: How often does "He Said" ever get that far? And kept scribbling, burning up notebooks.

Strawberry walked away from the pack of writers and said, "I'll bust that little redneck in the face." He meant Wally Backman.

Strawberry left the clubhouse. Mazzilli came in. The writers went to Mazzilli, told him what had been going on. He said, "I'm sorry Straw feels that way. I meant it as a constructive thing." Then the writers went to Backman, told him that Strawberry had threatened to bust him, "that little redneck," in the face. Backman had just come out of the trainer's room. He laughed and said, "Guess I better put on my tennis shoes."

Then, seriously, Backman said, "What's a redneck?"

The writers looked at him.

Klapisch said, "You're kidding. You don't know what a redneck is?"

Backman said, "Is it like a red ass?" Red ass was the clubhouse nickname for quick temper.

He was told of redneck's racist connotation.

Backman looked honestly surprised. "I swear to God, we didn't have that expression in Oregon." Backman shook his head. "Darryl can't really think that."

He was asked about the prospect of actually fighting Strawberry. Backman dragged on a cigarette, Bogie-like, said, "If that's the way he wants it, do you think *I'm* going to be the one who backs down?"

By then, word had gotten into the manager's office that quotes were now flying around his team like bullets. Davey Johnson came walking out, said he was clearing the clubhouse of all the writers, told Hernandez to call a team meeting. The writers went outside the clubhouse door, stood there in a clump, like children at the door of the master bedroom, trying to hear exactly what was going on. They actually wondered if Mets were in there fighting with other Mets.

They heard nothing.

Fifteen minutes later, the door opened. They went back in, all of them heading for their guys. But all of a sudden, no one wanted to talk. It was a condition that never lasted long with the Mets; generally, a Met could only do it for about the same period of time as he could hold his breath. Hernandez, Strawberry, Backman, Mazzilli, none of them wanted to talk. "It's over," Mazzilli said. And Hernandez said, "It's all been taken care of." And Strawberry said, "The wounds are still fresh, but it's over."

O'Connell said, "Does that mean you've retracted the thing about wanting to bust Wally in the face?"

"It's over."

It was actually fine with the writers, exhausted after nearly a week of playing "He Said." They had Strawberry saying he wanted to leave the Mets when his contract was up. They had Strawberry saying "Fuck Backman" and "Fuck Mazzilli." They had Strawberry threatening to punch Backman.

That little redneck.

They had enough headline material—back page material for the tabloids—to last through the weekend. They didn't need anything else, with the baseball game between the Mets and Reds yet to be played.

Mookie Wilson decided right then to call the writers over to *his* locker and announce that he was sick and tired of being platooned with Lenny Dykstra in center field, and that he has asked the Mets to trade him.

The Mets lost the game. The Mets lost the next day. And the next, Sunday afternoon. They were back in third place, eight games behind the Cardinals, after being five games out on Thursday, primed to make a run. The loser on Sunday was Gooden, who had pitched so well since coming out of Smithers, but who was simply pasted in a 7–5 loss.

Johnson held another team meeting. It is what managers do when teams go bad. They call team meetings. It keeps them busy. When a team is in the midst of a winning streak, you cannot even see the manager if the light is bad in the clubhouse. He stays in his office, he makes out the lineup card. He stays out of the way. He would not think of calling a team meeting. But when a team goes bad, the manager wants to talk about it at some point. On Friday, Hernandez had done the talking. Now it was Johnson. The theme of the meeting was: For Chrissakes, stop playing "He Said."

"Cool it," Johnson told the Mets. "Okay? Cool it. The more you guys talk to *those* assholes"—he made a gesture to the clubhouse door, outside which the beat men were once again waiting—"the more you fan the flames. So be careful of what you say. All those guys out there are doing is their jobs. But they love shit like this."

So twice now in a week, the clubhouse had been cleared of writers. The year before, the thought of the writers being banished would have moved the New York Mets to crying jags. When writers tried to pass by a Met without talking to him in 1986, the Met would do everything short of tripping the writer to get his attention. The Mets were the toast of the sports world, they knew big endorsements would be coming their way in the off-season, everything was peachy around the team. They could not get their names in the newspaper enough.

Whip me, beat me, just don't ignore me.

Suddenly, the room was being cleared every other day. After the loss on Sunday, Hernandez, always the first stop for the writers, home and away, sat doing a crossword puzzle, shooing the writers without saying a word. Strawberry could not be found. Even Backman, who had to be muzzled to keep from yacking in the postgame setting, had nothing to say.

Only Dwight Gooden did. On this Sunday in Cincinnati, Gooden wasn't the Met fresh out of rehab. Wasn't the Met who had begun all the season's controversy with a dirty urine sample. Or the former baseball Mozart who had confessed to using cocaine all the way back to high school.

He was a voice of reason, pointing out an obvious fact in a quiet clubhouse.

"We," Dwight Gooden said, "are in trouble."

The next day in Atlanta, Dykstra announced that *he* was unhappy with being platooned, and that *he* wanted to be traded. It was raining outside at Fulton County Stadium; in a couple of hours, the Mets–Braves game would be postponed. Dykstra wore a T-shirt and sliding pads.

"Somebody's gotta be traded," he reiterated. Somebody sounded like thumb-body, because of Dykstra's mild lisp. But the message was clear. On this day, Dykstra was the perfect rainy day story. The writers crowded around his locker. Dykstra went on to say he was never going to be happy if he could not play every day.

Strawberry yelled, disdainfully, "Look at those guys."

He meant: Look at these guys trying to cause trouble again for us innocent ballplayers.

From somewhere in the visiting clubhouse, a roll of sanitary hose was fired at the head of Larry Schwartz, a writer for the Bergen *Record*. The writers didn't know who threw it, but a lot of the Mets were laughing when they wheeled around to face the room. The next day, the manager got into the spirit of throwing things, saying The Press was responsible for the Dykstra story.

In Cincinnati, the writers had just been doing their jobs. Now they were being charged with conspiring to incite the world champions.

Johnson said, "You guys know what questions to ask."

His solution to the problem?

"I'm closing my office to you guys before games from now on. And after the games, I'm only going to answer baseball-related questions."

Johnson did not appreciate the irony of the moment. The writers did. For most of the season, Johnson had been wearing them out talking about this fishing lodge he had bought in Florida, one he was turning into a celebrity fishing camp. He had gotten Whitey Herzog of the Cardinals to go in on it with him, and was trying to interest other managers from baseball, coaches from other sports. One day in his Shea Stadium office, Johnson asked one of the writers if he would mind contacting New York Giants coach Bill Parcells, see if Parcells was interested. When Johnson got wound up about his proposed celebrity fishing camp, he would draw maps and diagram the property for writers, talk and talk and talk, and the writers would have to beg to get back to the clubhouse, do some real work.

Now Johnson was apparently talked out about his own career as an entrepreneur, and would only discuss baseball-related matters. And only after games. It would not be the last time during the season that the manager of the Mets would open his mouth, then trip all over what came out of it.

But the damage was done. By drawing a hard line with the writers, putting up another barbed wire fence, he was openly contributing to the armed camp atmosphere around his baseball team. Because of the rainout on Monday, the Mets and Braves had a doubleheader Tuesday. Terry Leach won the first game, to move his record as a reliever and a starter to 8–0. Leach, a thirty-three-year-old sidearming right-hander, had become the Mets' unlikely pitching hero, a journeyman who did not get to the major leagues until he was twenty-seven, and had only won six major league games in his life. Leach had really waited eleven years in professional baseball to get his chance, and now all the pitching catastrophes around the Mets had given him his chance, and he was 3–0 as a reliever, 5–0 as a starter.

Leach was a quiet, mustachioed gent from Selma, Alabama, and one of the most popular Mets in the room. He described himself as a baseball "squidge." It turned out that when he first started out as a minor league pitcher, he had worked during the off-season at "7-Eleven-type stores back home," called Minute Shops. He said a squidge was a "gofer-type person." Now The Squidge had become the Mets ace, at least in May and June and into July. Not Darling, the Yalie. Or Sid Fernandez, who had been one of the World Series stars for the Mets. Or Aguilera, the injured right-hander with the good looks of a male model. The Squidge. He had an ERA of 2.70 in spring training, but Davey Johnson joked about Leach's 83-mile-per-hour fastball, and ended up sending him to the minor leagues. Again. Then Dwight Gooden's nose opened up a spot for another arm. Now Leach had found the one shining season he had always chased in minor league cities like Baton Rouge and Jackson, Mississippi, and Savannah; in winter league towns like Barranquilla, Colombia; in Puerto Rico and the Dominican Republic.

So on July 7, first game of the doubleheader, it was Mets 6, Braves 2, and The Squidge was 8–0, and between games, there are a dozen or so reporters talking to The Squidge once more about his baseball odyssey.

"Whatever happens," Leach said, "I think I deserve a shot to be in the big leagues. I've never been very high on the totem pole, wherever I've been. I've always had to take the leftovers. But I'll say this for myself: When I got the starts, I made the most of them."

Somebody asked a question about the All-Star Game. Johnson, as manager of the defending National League champions, was the manager. The manager was allowed to pick his own pitching staff. But Johnson had announced that Leach would not be on the team, despite the 8–0 record, because he did not have enough innings and enough starts. Sid Fernandez would represent the Mets instead.

Before Leach got the chance to answer, the firecracker went off at the feet of the reporters.

Real live firecracker, sounding like a gun going off in the armed camp.

The writers wheeled around. Obviously, it had been tossed at them by someone in the clubhouse. Probably it had been tossed by a Mets player. Halfway through the season, it had come to that. The manager wasn't talking. Strawberry said, Fuck the press.

Now the firecracker.

In the second game of the doubleheader, Ron Darling won his first game since April 22, and the Mets swept, and the clubhouse was a tomb, anyway. The Mets writers boycotted the office of the Mets manager after the game. The next day, Fernandez lost. In the space of six days, the Mets had gone from five games out of first to nine and a half games out of first.

Len Dykstra said, "The fucking All-Star Break can't come soon enough." It came out "thoon enough." But it was a lispy eloquence that spoke for everybody on Dykstra's fucking team.

Houston was the last stop on the last trip of the first half of the season. During the previous October, the Mets and Astros had staged perhaps the most gripping National League Championship Series in history, the Mets finally winning four games to two, winning the sixth game in Houston's Astrodome after sixteen unforgettable innings. But a lot had changed in the nine months since. Both the Mets and Astros were struggling teams, actors trying gamely to get to intermission with dignity intact after an ugly first act.

The Mets manager, he was starting to act like an actor, too. Before the first game of the Houston series, Johnson called the Mets writers into his office for a formal apology. The Bad Cop in Atlanta was playing Good Cop in Houston.

"This is a hard thing for me to do," Davey Johnson said, "because I usually don't think I make mistakes."

The writers just looked at him, waited. The previous October, they had all dripped champagne as they talked to Johnson in the same office.

"But I want to apologize for lashing out at people," Johnson continued. "I've let the frustration get to me, and I regret having done that. I'm going to talk to my team and tell them to take their frustrations out on the opposition and not each other, or the sportswriters."

Another pause.

"This is the most frustrating season I've had in baseball, and I've let it get to me." He went on after that to talk about his team's lack of desire: "We came back to win in thirty-nine games last year, and we haven't done that so far."

Then, to the amazement of everyone in the room—perhaps even Johnson himself—he took the rap for the Mets' ordinary play across the first half of the season.

"I've been responsible for my team's poor play."

Johnson spoke for fifteen minutes, then stood, came around his desk, and shook hands with each writer, and said Lieutenant Colonel Oliver North's testimony the previous few days before the Senate had helped him put baseball things in perspective.

Johnson said, "Lieutenant Colonel North made me realize my problems aren't much compared to everyone else's."

Oliver North couldn't help in the Astrodome. The Mets lost again.

Ten and a half games out.

Howard Johnson said, "That's a humongous lead. After a while, you start to turn the page quicker and quicker on losses like these. It's not a good thing to do, but you have to or you go insane. After a while, you start to think of yourself."

The Mets lost that night when Bill Doran of the Astros hit a ninth-inning home run off Randy Myers, the rookie left-handed reliever with the prodigious fastball. Myers had struggled earlier in the season, had been sent down to Tidewater to find his control, and his rhythm. Now he was back. Before Doran's home run that night, Myers's fastball had looked as intimidating as any reliever's in baseball.

The fastball certainly impressed The Prince of Darkness.

"If we fall out of this thing, Myers is going to get his chance," Hernandez said. "Then, we can trade Jesse. We can't have them both on this team. Trade Jesse and trade Teufel." Teufel, who was having a .340 season at the bat but who often fielded at second like a man with his hands on backwards. "Yeah, trade Jesse and Tim. Perfect."

In July, in the room where they had all dripped champagne, Hernandez spoke of next year.

Get rid of Jesse. Get rid of Teufel.

Perfect, he said.

July 16. Thursday. A pleasant midsummer afternoon, late afternoon, at Shea Stadium. In two hours, Dwight Gooden would begin to shut out the Cincinnati Reds, bring the Mets record to 48–40, eight and a half games behind the Cardinals. The Mets were beginning a stretch when they would play 30 of 44 games at home before September 1. It was obvious that this was their chance to get themselves together, seriously start chasing the Cardinals. It would be like a six-week season for the Mets.

If they did something with that six-week season, they would be real contenders on September 1, after everything that had happened.

If they did not, they would be looking at each other in September, not the Cardinals, wondering who was going to be around in 1988. And who wasn't.

On the field before the game, Frank Cashen sucked on a pipe, watched batting practice with me. Most general managers avoid the field once the season begins. Cashen isn't one of them. He likes the ball park, likes being in the clubhouse and around players, enjoys the give and take with the writers; seems to think the daily rituals of the sport, the hurly-burly of baseball *before* the game starts, is one of the best parts of his job.

On this night, the subject for Cashen was how much had changed around his baseball team since Gooden's urine turned up dirty.

"Nothing is given you in this game," Cashen said, "and nothing is owed you. If you are around this game long enough, you come to see that. You come to understand that the sort of things that have happened to us this year can happen." He smiled, took the pipe out of his mouth, emptied it. "But I never thought they would happen to me."

We moved out from behind the batting cage, walked past the dugout and then up along the right field line, away from home plate. Rock-and-roll music played on the sound system. Every few seconds there was the crack of a bat. It looked, sounded, like a normal day at Shea.

It was.

And it wasn't.

Cashen said he was looking at the team differently than he had in spring training, back when the only question was not if the Mets would win the National League East again, but how many games they would win it by.

"You start looking at things from different angles," Cashen said. "Nothing dramatic. It's just angles." He talked about how he would be watching Darling ("We do pay him a lot of money") a little more closely over the rest of the season, and Hernandez. Cashen didn't make threats, didn't say Darling or Hernandez were in danger of being traded. It was just angles, sharp or otherwise, he was talking about at twilight.

I asked him if there were any "untouchables" on the Mets, meaning players he would not consider trading.

Cashen said, "Darryl, actually."

"Really?"

Cashen put the unlit pipe in his mouth.

"Darryl Strawberry isn't going anywhere for at least two years," he said. He meant, the two years before Strawberry was eligible to become a free agent. "Look around this game. Is there the possibility that someone could come to me with an offer for Darryl, overwhelm me? Certainly there is. But I don't expect to be overwhelmed, and subsequently, I am not about to give up the production in home runs and RBI that Darryl can give me. Would I like to get more out of him? I would. The only thing that makes me angry with Darryl is that I do not believe, at least so far, he has gotten the most out of his God-given ability. But he will. And one of these days he's going to be the best player in baseball."

I said, "He does cause a lot of commotion in the clubhouse."

Cashen said, "That business sells newspapers. But it doesn't really concern me as much as you might think. I still believe, and will continue to believe until proven wrong, that Darryl's positives on the field greatly outweigh whatever negatives are involved in the clubhouse. Clubhouse chatter, frankly, doesn't get my blood racing."

I asked Frank Cashen if the manager, Davey Johnson, was a New York Met untouchable.

There was a long pause.

Finally Cashen sighed. "I don't really have any big problems with Davey." Another pause. "But I am getting a little tired of him going to the newspapers and saying we can't communicate every time there's a problem with this baseball team. He knows he can always reach me. And he knows when I'm not travelling with the team, I make sure Joe McIlvaine is."

The rituals of the day went on. The Mets left the field, the Reds took the field, the Reds left the field, the Mets came back, the batting cage was moved away, Cashen went back upstairs to have some dinner, everybody went about pregame business, Cashen and me and the Mets, but Cashen's words hung on the field at twilight. If the manager and the players Cashen had named did not know that the boss was unhappy, some of them sensed the change in the quality of the air anyway, a change in the atmosphere around the Mets. There isn't an animal in God's universe who can smell trouble the way a ballplayer can. Sometimes, ballplayers are just hypochondriacs: They go 0-for-5 and think they are dying. But generally, they have a sixth sense when it comes to self-preservation.

In the clubhouse a few minutes later, Wally Backman said, "Of course you have to start looking around. How many new guys do we have in this room right now? Ten? Something like that? And we *won* last year."

Sounds of summer at Shea.

A funny thing happened to the Mets at the end of July.

They swept the Cardinals in St. Louis.

The Mets had just come off the worst loss of the season. Jesse Orosco had served up a delicious ninth-inning fastball to Billy Hatcher of the Astros, Hatcher hit it for a three-run homer, and the Mets, leading 2–1 going into the ninth, lost 5–2. An 11-game homestand finished with the Mets having a 6–5 record, instead of the 7–4 record Orosco had in his glove. It was July 26. The Mets were in third place, eight and a half games back. It could have been much worse, but the Cardinals, slipping on banana peels for the first time all season, had just lost four straight games to the Giants in San Francisco.

"You guys are dead," I said to Lee Mazzilli in the Mets clubhouse. It was before the game, before the ninth-inning disaster wrought by Orosco.

"We've got six games this week with the Cardinals and Expos," Mazzilli said. He talked about the two teams ahead of the Mets. "You don't think we're capable of sweeping?"

"No."

"We don't even need to sweep. You don't think we can get ourselves together to win five of six?"

"No."

"I think you're wrong," Mazzilli said. "I think we can make a stand."

"You're dreaming."

Mazzilli wasn't dreaming. The Mets made a stand. The quality of the baseball they had been playing did not dramatically improve. The Mets still kicked the ball around in big moments, still tried to squander leads, still looked like a team trying to remember how to throw a big punch, knock an opponent out of the game. But they happened to find the Cardinals in the midst of their first real slump of the season. The Cardinals refused to let the Mets lose. If the Cardinals had swept the series, the Mets were finished; the Mets were probably finished if the Cardinals won two games out of three.

The Mets swept. The central figure of the sweep was Howard Johnson. Johnson had become the Mets' surprise batting star, indeed the surprise slugger of the National League.

Johnson, known as Hodge to his teammates (a bastardization of "HoJo"), was a twenty-six-year-old switch-hitting third baseman who had never hit more than 23 home runs in a season in the minor leagues, never more than 12 in his first three major league seasons; in fact, he had come into the 1987 season with 40 career home runs in the majors. He had played for the world champion Detroit Tigers in 1984, but had been kept out of the World Series by manager Sparky Anderson, who hinted that Johnson's nerves might not be able to stand World Series pressure. He had come over to the Mets in a trade after that season, and ever since had shared time at third base with Knight. Then Knight, the MVP of the 1986 World Series, left for Baltimore, and third base became the Mets' question-mark position in the spring. Johnson and Dave Magadan, it was assumed, would share third. But then Magadan had the lymph node problem, Johnson had a big spring, the job was his. For his major league life, he had been known as someone with some power batting left-handed, and an easy out batting right-handed. Johnson told anyone who wanted to listen in St. Petersburg that things had changed, that he had worked out at Shea all winter with batting coach Bill Robinson, working on his right-handed stroke; that he could hit left-handed pitchers, right-handed pitchers, he didn't care: He was ready to blossom.

The writers nodded, wrote the stories about Johnson's optimism, but everyone thought: big Florida talk. Johnson had never hit .250, for Detroit or the Mets. His big year had been 12 home runs, 50 runs batted in for the Tigers in '84.

It wasn't Florida talk. By the time the Mets got to St. Louis, Johnson was the team's most productive hitter, even batting seventh in the lineup. Hernandez was not knocking in runs from the No. 3 hole, Gary Carter was having a bad season. Carter, in fact, had finally been moved out of the cleanup position; Strawberry moved in to replace him on July

20. No one knew at the time that Strawberry, once settled into the No. 4 spot that he had privately craved for a long time, would begin a hitting spree that would last through the rest of the National League season.

Hodge had been the unlikely hero of the offense, the way The Squidge had been the unlikely pitching hero. In the second game of the Cardinals series, after Darling had struggled the night before but won 6–4, Johnson got the Mets in position for the sweep. He got four hits in the game, finally won it with a two-run homer off Pat Perry, a left-handed pitcher. It meant the home run was hit right-handed.

"Everybody thought I was full of shit in Florida," Johnson said. "But it's like everybody forgot that I'm still only twenty-six years old. Just because you're not a phenom in this game doesn't necessarily mean you're a dog."

The next night, Johnson hit another home run, left-handed this time, monstrous home run to right field off the Cardinals' Bill Dawley. Johnson silenced the Busch Stadium crowd with the shot, trotted around the bases, touched home plate, shook hands with Magadan, the next Mets hitter. Johnson noticed his bat was lying where he had dropped it, and picked the bat up.

Something funny happened then. Almost as funny as this sweep around which the Mets were actually tying a ribbon.

Cardinals catcher Tony Peña grabbed the other end of Howard Johnson's bat. So Johnson had one end, Peña had the other. Right there near home plate at Busch Stadium, Johnson and Peña suddenly looked, for all the world, like two kids getting ready to choose up sides for a sandlot game.

Johnson tugged.

Peña tugged.

Johnson gave Peña a little shove with the bat.

Peña shoved back.

Finally, home plate umpire Joe West came, took the bat himself, gave it to a member of the Cardinals ground crew, as a way of impounding it. It was the time during the 1987 season during which impounding bats would become all the rage, along with trying to catch pitchers disfiguring baseballs with sandpaper and Lord knows what else (to make the ball dip in a way other than Abner Doubleday intended). Bats were checked, for cork. A corked bat is cheating in baseball, the way a scuffed ball is cheating, but had been part of the game for years. A small hole was bored into the barrel end of the bat, a piece of cork was stuffed into the hole, the hole was sanded over. And it was believed that if a hitter caught a pitch really well, the effect of the cork would add distance to the ball, make it jump off the bat like one of those Superballs kids play with, turn routine fly balls into home runs.

Johnson's home run was No. 25 for the season. Two more than he had hit for Evansville of the American Association in 1982. Fifteen more than he had hit for the New York Mets in 1986. There had been talk in baseball for months that Johnson had cork in his bat. Whitey Herzog, the Cardinals manager, would say later that the Cardinals had stolen into the Mets clubhouse after the home run against Perry, taken Johnson's bat, X-rayed it, found cork in it, put it back, wanting to catch him red-handed next time he hit a home run.

After the game, which the Mets won, 5–3, West and his fellow umpires checked Johnson's bat without use of an X-ray machine, decided it was legal and corkless, returned it.

In the Cardinals clubhouse, Herzog was like Peña, his catcher. Would not let go of the bat. "HoJo ain't that good," the Cardinals manager said. "He ain't Babe Ruth."

Peña said, "You hear something funny when a bat is corked. And the bat sounded funny when he hit that home run."

Johnson, a pleasant man with thinning brown hair and a Fu Manchu mustache, said in the Mets clubhouse, "There's nothing wrong with the bat. It's perfectly normal. And it's an insult to my talent for them to say there's cork in it. That ball was right down the middle of the plate. How else did Whitey expect me to hit it?"

In the spring, he was a man fighting for a job. Now, they were insulting his talent. The home run off Dawley finished the sweep. The night before, Mookie Wilson and Jack Clark, the main man of the Cardinals offense all season, collided at first base, injuring Clark's right elbow. Clark would not be healthy again for three weeks. The lead was back under six games, and the Cardinals had lost seven in a row.

There were still 61 games to play.

"They can be beaten," Strawberry said.

Maybe it was the first time since April the Mets believed that.

"Sonofabitch," the Met known as Hodge said to Backman on the flight from St. Louis to Montreal, "we're going to get out of this yet."

Sonofabitch.

AUGUST:
"I'M ONLY HUMAN . . ."

The Prince, he was ready to talk on the record now. Goddamn, he was *pumped.* Kent Tekulve, skinny sidearming reliever from the Phillies they used to call Stork, had tried to run a fastball past him inside, but The Prince grabbed it with his bat like a batting practice pitcher had thrown it, and tried to hit the ball over the night of August 3. It was the bottom of the eleventh at Shea Stadium, and when the ball landed over the right field wall, it was Mets 3, Phillies 2. The Cardinals had won up in Montreal, but now the Mets had won too, were still six and a half behind. But that wasn't the news. You kidding? The Prince was back. He had a twelve-game hitting streak now, and he was hitting the ball *hard.* Let's see them write some of that shit now about The Prince being too old, or not being able to hit in the clutch anymore, or not hit No. 3, or move aside, make way for the kid, Magadan, at first.

In the clubhouse afterward, Hernandez was even more wired than usual. James Brown was performing at the Lone Star Cafe, down on lower Fifth Avenue in Manhattan, and Brown knew Hernandez and some Mets were coming in after the game, so he was holding his last set. So Hernandez, dressing in a hurry, swigging a beer as he went, reaching down every so often to take a puff on his cigarette, needed to get out of the clubhouse, but not without talking about the home run, and the criticism—first criticism he had seen in New York, really—about his low RBI production of the first four months of the season.

Hernandez wasn't going to strut and crow, it wasn't his style. But he wanted it clear that he was hurt that the assholes had turned on him, were trying to bury him.

"For the first time in his whole career he felt like people were losing respect for him," Backman said from the next locker while Hernandez quickly showered. Backman, perhaps more than any other Met, idolized Hernandez the player. "And it's hurt him, you can see it."

Darling said, "See it? It's in his eyes. It's killing him. Talk that he might be traded kills Keith." Darling had told Klapisch once, "I honestly don't know what's going to happen to Keith when he doesn't have baseball as an outlet."

Hernandez came out of the shower. There were twenty writers and radio men waiting for him. This was his moment for the season; as dramatic a moment as his team had had.

"It is not a ninety-game season," Hernandez said. He yelled across the room, "Darryl, we're out of here in fifteen." Then to McDowell, "You hear that? Gone in fifteen. My man James awaits." Butted out a cigarette, lit another, turned back to the media, especially the assholes who had been doing the burying: "When the season is over, pass judgment, but not after ninety games." Swig of beer. "Hell, I knew I was miserable with men on base. [His batting average with runners on base was under .200, after a career when it had consistently been over .300.] The stuff that was written about me could have been written two months ago."

Hernandez never lost his head completely, never lost his sense of politics.

"But I kept telling myself I was a second-half hitter. Then I turned things around in St. Louis." He called his father in St. Louis, is what he did. His father had watched the first game of the Mets–Cardinals series on the satellite, and noticed something. He told Keith to widen his stance. Keith widened his stance; Mex always listened to Juan, even if it sometimes burned him to still be so dependent on him. And he started to hit in St. Louis, like he said. In the last game of the previous series in Montreal (where the Mets had won two of three to finish their little road trip at 5–1, as Lee Mazzilli had predicted they would), Hernandez had spanked two doubles into the outfield gaps, had three RBI. For the first time all season, he looked like something more than a pesky singles hitter.

He was dressed now, in sweater and pleated slacks, and the fifteen minutes he'd yelled to Strawberry and McDowell about were gone, but Hernandez wasn't done. Now the words were pouring out of him, like he couldn't control them. He was off the home run now, talking on the record—The Prince, on the record!—about his own insecurities. "I began to doubt myself," he said.

"I'm only human," he said.

Then, out of nowhere, this: "I don't want to be traded. I don't want to leave the Mets or New York. I love New York. I love what this organization has done for me, I love my teammates. I want to finish my career here. I'd never want to play anywhere else. This is a team that is going to be good for years to come, and I want to be a part of it. The Mets haven't just been good to me, they've been *damn* good. I consider this my home. I stay around in the off-season. I've come to revel in all the things the city has to offer."

Most of the writers left. A few radio men stayed around. Hernandez answered their questions. Strawberry and McDowell were ready to go, but they knew this was Hernandez's night, so they waited patiently. I waited for Hernandez. I was the one who had first suggested that Hernandez be moved out of the No. 3 spot in the batting order occasionally, and once pointed out that Hernandez ranked eighty-eighth in major league baseball in runs batted in.

Hernandez said, "This season has been a bitch for me. I usually don't let things get to me. Even when the Pittsburgh trial was going on, I was able to block that shit out, get to the ball park and just *play*. It's been harder for me this year. There are days when I'll spend eight hours at my lawyer's office, getting ready for this divorce case. [Keith and Susan Hernandez were nearing the end of a drawn-out proceeding.] And to top things off, my girlfriend left me, and I've been trying to get back together with her, and it's driving me crazy. It's all been going on, and I haven't been able to respond the way I did in the past. At least not until now."

He took one last swig of his beer, and headed off into the night. The Prince of Darkness, feeling like a king.

"I'm not mad at you," Hernandez said to me. "Really, I'm not. Some of those other fucking assholes have pissed me off, but you've always been good to me, so I've got to respect your opinion."

We shook hands. It was a touching scene. Except that there would be a December night four months later at the Hard Rock Cafe, a trendy Manhattan club on West 57th Street. Hernandez was drinking with some people. My name came up.

"Lupica got on my ass," Hernandez said. "But I buried him with my bat."

He is a beauty, my most unforgettable Met, on the record, off the record, summer and winter, great player, great subject, champion and poseur. The Prince.

But as August began, Hernandez became a symbol of baseball's long season. Hernandez could struggle for four months, and still have two months to redeem himself. Same with his team. The Mets had spent four months trying to patch one leak after another in the boat Wally Backman had spoken of on Opening Day, back in April. But there were still two months to go. Darling had begun to win. Gooden was pitching brilliantly. Aguilera was about to come off the disabled list. So was David Cone.

The Mets, in August, decided they were still the Mets. If hard feelings and hard looks and harsh words are infectious on a baseball team—as the Mets had proven with great brio—so was confidence. If a player can go 0-for-4 and decide he is dying, he can also go 4-for-4 and decide that he is the second coming of Ted Williams. Baseball players, because of the long season, alternate between dark clouds and silver linings. They are the authentic, no-fooling manic-depressives of sports.

August was all about silver linings. There were bad omens as far back in March. Fuck bad omens. Look at August, sucker:

Hernandez hit his home run to beat the Phillies.

The next night Gooden struck out 11 men in eight innings, the first time he had gotten 11 strikeouts in nobody-could-remember-when. Mets won again.

On August 5, the Mets won 13–3, and moved to within four and a half games of the Cardinals, who lost in Montreal. The Cardinals' loss, in fact, provided the backdrop to the Mets victory, because of two long rain delays while the Mets played the Phillies. One was eighty-one minutes, the other was forty-five minutes, and during the delays, because of the wonders of the satellite dish outside Shea Stadium, and the huge Diamond-Vision screen out in center field, the rain-drenched crowd was able to watch the Cardinals eventually lose to the Expos in the thirteenth inning. It was as if the whole National League East was right there in the rain at Shea, for everybody to watch. The Cardinals were losing and the Mets were pasting the Phillies and so the crowd, whooping over the Expos victory, was of a mood to say, Fuck all the bad omens. Just like the players.

In the clubhouse after the game, Gary Carter sat in his corner of the room and said, "I'm sure the Cardinals can hear us coming. They have to be a little afraid of us now." And Howard Johnson said, "There's no doubt in my mind we're going to win this thing now. Two weeks ago, I might've said maybe. Now I'm certain."

The Mets, a lot of them, had sat in the dugout during the rain and watched the Cardinals play the Expos. Ron Darling was one.

"You know what I realized, watching them on the screen?" Darling said. "Those aren't the Cardinals we saw a month ago. I get the feeling they're a little scared. They can fold."

Ballplayers assume that other ballplayers are as paranoid as they are when things are going to shit.

The Mets won two more games, stretching the winning streak to seven, cutting the Cardinals' lead to three and a half. The Mets, after everything, had a record of 63–46, 17 games over .500, the most they had been all season.

There were still 53 games left to play.

But these were the 1987 Mets, and so even in the best of months— the team had a record of 18–11 for August, which was just under the winning percentage it had had for all of 1986—there were headlines and off-the-record stabs in the back.

It was as if they couldn't help themselves.

Gooden, who for the most part was pitching brilliantly, was in the newspapers for drinking an occasional beer. Now, a ballplayer drinking a beer is hardly news; most of them think beer-drinking was spelled out for baseball players in some kind of amendment to the Constitution: They are supposed to drink beer, chase women, scratch, cuss, and spit. But Gooden wasn't just any ballplayer. He was the ballplayer who was three months out of rehab for chemical dependency. And Gooden himself had admitted that his problem started with beer-drinking in the first place.

Now he would have an occasional beer. The *Daily News* reported it, Gooden didn't deny it. The *Times* reported it after the *Daily News* did.

And people saw him out in public, having a beer with his teammates. John Filippelli, an NBC network baseball producer, was walking through the Galleria bar in Houston the Friday night before the All-Star Game when he saw Gooden and Lee Mazzilli and Darryl Strawberry seated at a table. Filippelli was invited to join them, offered to buy a round. The Mets agreed. It is also part of being a ballplayer: A free round of drinks is almost as stimulating as a late-inning rally.

Mazzilli ordered beer.

Strawberry ordered beer.

Gooden ordered beer.

Filippelli said later, "It didn't really occur to me what had happened until I started reading about Gooden again in the papers. You know: 'Gooden Drinks A Beer.' "

"It's no big deal," Gooden would later say for the newspapers. "I watch myself, and I never have more than one or two."

It fit into the general context of drinking being a part of sports, drugs being a menace. Generally, the people who run professional sports are so worried about drugs they have to have three or four drinks, settle their nerves. Sports has never really worried much about cross-addiction. The beers, particularly Budweiser and Miller Lite, dominate baseball advertising. The message of the brilliant Miller Lite commercials with the ex-athletes is this: Once the game is over, get your ass to the bar, let the good times roll. Baseball Commissioner Peter Ueberroth talks all the time about stamping out the drug menace and policing ball parks for excessive drinkers, but allows all the beer money into his sport; after the 1987 season, at the annual baseball Winter Meetings in Dallas, Ueberroth described Busch Stadium in St. Louis as being the best "ball park experience." People laughed. Busch Stadium in St. Louis, everyone knew, was the world's largest outdoor beer hall, dominated by Budweiser billboards and billboards for Busch beer and the Budweiser Clydesdales. It is the only baseball park in the world where the Budweiser theme song is played during the seventh-inning stretch instead of "Take Me Out to the Ball Game."

Beer and baseball are inextricably linked. Beer started the problem with Gooden, but cocaine *was* the problem, that's what baseball decided. So three months out of Smithers, Gooden could have a beer and nobody said a word. He was being tested regularly and, more importantly, he was throwing the seams off his fastball and striking people out again.

Gooden didn't drink in front of the writers in the clubhouse. But he drank.

And found a predictable defender in Hernandez, The Prince, who had had his own problems with cocaine, and liked his beer the way he liked his cigarettes and his coffee; loved the nightlife, loved to boogie.

He thought boys should be boys.

"What's the big deal?" Hernandez said one August night, after there had been another mention of Gooden drinking in the papers. "So he likes to have a beer once in a while. He's a kid. Is that a crime?"

He reached down to where he knew the ice bucket was, got his beer without even looking.

It was also during August that Gooden, in the context of being depressed over blowing a 5–0 lead to the Cubs in Chicago (the Mets finally lost 7–5), started angling for a long-term contract.

Again, the timing: He was three months or so out of Smithers. He had been back in the rotation for two months. All of the Mets' problems had started with the urine sample; there wasn't a Mets player, fan, writer, front-office official who thought the Mets would be behind the Cardinals if Gooden had been around for those eleven starts between April and June 5.

Now he wanted job security, because he'd been such a good scout.

"That's it," he said in the Wrigley Field clubhouse. "I'm going to quit. I'm getting my ass kicked, and if I can't be successful at this, what's the point? I'll go back home and play softball. I've never blown a lead like that. I had absolutely nothing out there. Couple of times, I didn't even want to throw the ball, because I didn't think I could throw it by anyone."

It was only the overture. When Gooden was twenty years old, and the Mets were protecting him from the press as much as possible—one mass interview before the game, all other interview requests filtered through Jay Horwitz—the world wondered if Gooden would ever open up. Now, no one could get him to shut up. Before the Mets leave Chicago, Gooden played a slightly different melody than the one about going home to Tampa, playing softball the rest of his life.

"You know," Gooden said, "if the Mets ever traded me, I'd quit. What I'd really like, right now, is a long-term contract. No kidding. Something like twelve years, fifteen million. Think of it: That's less than what I'm making now."

By November, Gooden had scaled down the request considerably, but was still looking for job security, seven months after the scene in Cashen's office. The Mets were offering another one-year contract for 1988. Gooden said he wanted three years. Said if the Mets didn't come across with more than one year, he would remember when he became eligible for free agency after the 1989 season.

Al Harazin, under orders from Frank Cashen, basically told Dwight Gooden the team hoped Gooden had an even longer marriage than Ozzie and Harriet, but there was nothing to discuss on the contract.

The Mets told Mozart: One year, take it or leave it.

If he didn't like it, he could always go back to Tampa, play softball with the boys. It was like Cashen had said in July.

Nothing is promised you, nothing is owed.

Finally in August, Rick Aguilera came back to pitch. By the time he did, his elbow was fine, but there were a few knife wounds to the back still healing.

Mets will be Mets.

As early as two weeks after Aguilera went on the disabled list, Wally Backman had said in Los Angeles, "I really don't think Aggie's hurt all that bad. If what happened to Bobby O [Ojeda] hadn't happened, with the surgery and all, I don't think Aggie would have even missed a start. I just think what happened to Bobby scared the piss out of him."

Maybe. But Aguilera had been away for three months. When it looked like the Mets were going to fall out of the race in July, his absence was nothing to cause tremors in the clubhouse. But now the Mets were in the race. There were concerns about Sid Fernandez's shoulder every time he took the mound. There had been a couple of occasions when Fernandez said he couldn't make it, and his replacement was a refugee from the Cleveland Indians by way of Tidewater named Don Schulze. After Schulze gave up eight hits and four runs in just three and a third innings of a start against the Cubs—a game the Mets would lose 5–3. An anonymous Met showed up talking in the New York *Post*.

The Met said, "If Aguilera's hurt, he should've had surgery by now. If he isn't hurt, then why isn't he pitching?"

Aguilera let the quote go, at least for the time being. A week later, as part of the rehabilitation for his arm, he pitched seven shutout innings for Tidewater, and pronounced himself fit and eager for a return to the big leagues.

"The rumors that I imagined this injury are a bunch of shit," Aguilera said. "Why would I fake an injury? Why wouldn't I want to be out there? I'm only hurting myself. It pissed me off to hear stories that I was faking it."

On August 24, Aguilera pitched what catcher Carter called "the game of his life" in his return, giving up just four hits before leaving in the eighth inning. The Mets, to a man, celebrate Aguilera's fastball, control.

And true grit.

Across the summer, Backman had questioned the seriousness of Aguilera's injury, and so had Len Dykstra, and so had Darryl Strawberry. Even pitching coach Mel Stottlemyre had wondered a couple of weeks earlier if Aguilera might not be "magnifying" the pain.

Now they all came up, patted him on the back, said luv-ya-baby over and over again.

Keith Hernandez, in a wonderful move, told Aguilera, "Whatever was said didn't come from this clubhouse."

And through it all—somehow—after Gooden and the hernia and Ojeda and Aguilera and oh-my-God-we've-lost-David-Cone and I'll-bust-that-little-redneck and Gooden's cocaine confessional and confiscated bats and the manager's big mouth and Frank Cashen's ominous July words, they were in this big race with the Cardinals and Expos in the National League East, even if not one member of the Mets organization thought the Expos had it in them to win.

It was the Mets against the Cardinals, everybody knew that. The Mets had played their best baseball in August, and had only picked up another game on the Cardinals. But the Mets were as healthy as they were going to get. They felt, as all contenders did, that a new season started on September 1. There is a saying in golf that there are two Masters golf tournaments: the one played over the first sixty-three holes, and the one that begins Sunday on the back nine.

The Mets had Aguilera back. Ojeda was even making noises about pitching in the stretch run. Hernandez was hitting. Johnson had never stopped. Strawberry, who had slumped a little at the end of August, promised he would be all right in September; happy at last in the cleanup spot, he had already shown he was capable of carrying the team with his bat.

"When I hit," Darryl said privately, "we win."

So there they were. Ready to play the back nine of the season, five and a half out, but knowing there were still six games on the schedule with the St. Louis Cardinals.

The boat Wally Backman talked about on Opening Day, it wasn't the "Love Boat." But there they were.

A
Fan's
Notes

A LIFE IN THE DAY

*A*nd I am Out There. It is September eleventh, a day that will live in infamy. Some people feel that Los Angeles is plastic, coreless, that Pia Zadora serves them right. Personally, I feel some people are way too kind.

But—and this is important to any True Believer—no place in the continental United States is as good for sports results. In New York when you pick up the *Times* sports section, they are giving you the day before yesterday's box scores. That's with luck.

But L.A. If it happened last night, you know it. And with your Cracklin' Oat Bran too. (I do not call Sportsphone or their clones. Not because I believe them to be inaccurate. But when I am on my game, when I am controlling major events around the country, which I can do, I just don't know when, phoning in can either break my power or piss off the gods, neither good for the Jews.)

The above preamble is only noted because finding out the results of the Mets–Cards battle to go on that night was not my difficulty. It started at four-thirty in L.A., I'd know the result by suppertime.

But how to find it out? Such was my quandary.

I am, at heart, a Yankee rooter, but things had been going badly and I felt the best thing I could do for them was pretend I didn't care. They were six behind Detroit. I thought if I acted blasé over the weekend, they had a good chance of getting back in it by Monday next.

Besides, the Mets were really in a spectacular chase with the hated Cards. (Problem: I like the Cardinals. When I was a kid, since none of the Chicago teams had much chance to be in it by the All-Star break, the Cards took over my heart. And why not? With Musial. And Marty "Slats" Marion, his era's Ozzie Smith and the man who to this minute made the greatest infield play I've ever seen, and "Country" Slaughter and Brock and Gibson, surely the greatest pressure pitcher in the history of western civilization. No, I didn't hate the Cards, I hated Herzog, their white rat manager. (Problem: I like Herzog, too; I wish to Christ he was managing the Mets.)

What the above should show is simply this: On the morning of September 11, I was in Los Angeles in turmoil.

The biggest game of the year was taking place that evening and I had to decide how best to hear about it. I had a good feeling that my power was on. That if I didn't anger the gods, if I just acted hubris-free, the Mets were a shoo-in.

I don't know a lot of Angelinos but one of them I did know not only had a big screen TV, he had cable—he could get the game *live*.

Great. Because he was, in the normal course of events, going to watch it. So that I, casually, would keep in occasional contact with him, nothing pestery, and find out the score. Understand, I would never be such a fool as to call and go, "What inning, who's ahead?" You don't do that. So I had figured various other things to call him about, which would give him the chance to say, "Oh, since you're on the phone, do you want the Mets score, it's so and so."

The gods could only smile at that.

Then he called and informed me on the morning of this day that would live in infamy, that his TV was on the fritz. "FIX THE FUCKER," I didn't say when he phoned to tell me, because that would have been uncool, might have made Them decide to punish me for wanting something too much. "Not working?" I said. Calmly. "Gee, you might call a repairman." "Oh I have, this is a big game." I relaxed. "Good," I said. "No," he said. "He can't come till Tuesday." "TIP HIM FIFTY BUCKS HE'LL COME RUNNING," I didn't say. Same logic as before. Then I added, "But you'll be listening to it, won't you?" "Nothing to listen to, it's all blown. No sound, no picture, but I'm checking out the hotels in town to see if any of them have cable, I'll take a room for the night."

Deep inside me, warning signals. Taking a hotel room for a ball game was pushing it. I didn't mind that *he* did it. I just felt it was wrong for me to call in.

"We'll talk tomorrow," I said.

He was a fellow nut. "You think it's wrong for me to take the room, don't you? Think I'm pushing it?"

I knew I had to get off the phone. I didn't want to screw with his power any more than I wanted him messing with mine. "You do what you think's best," and I hung up.

And started pacing my room in the Four Seasons Hotel. (Note to any travelers: If you have to go to L.A. on an expense account, do yourself a favor and stay at the Four Seasons.) I'm still pacing, trying to show no arrogance, because I know as soon as I hear that the tube man can't come till Tuesday that I am being Tested and the reason for that can only be this: My power is working.

If—big if—I don't screw it up.

I decided I must ignore the game. It was not happening.

Not an easy decision. Consider: The Mets, once ten and a half down, had cut the margin to one and a half. And they were hot—two in a row, eight out of their last ten. While the hated Cards were swan diving magnificently—they'd been stomped three in a row by Montreal, and won only four out of ten.

And now, weak and humiliated, they were tippy-toeing into Shea to be faced by none other than Ron Darling, the cerebral one, among the hotter pitchers of the year. (Once his record was 2 and 6—now it was 12 and 8.) And not only did the Mets have Darling primed, they had the Doc ready for tomorrow.

The Mets had not been this close to first place since May seventh. With ordinary luck, Darling and Gooden should have us on top in thirty-six more hours. But they had more than ordinary luck—they had *me*. And I had my power.

Could I ignore the game?

Difficult to promise. I had meetings all day and the people I was meeting with were transplanted New Yorkers, all of them frothing about the coming conflict. Clearly, I could not say, "We must not talk about the Mets and the Cards." The reason is obvious. They would ask why. And then I would have to lie—"No reason, I'm bored with baseball"—which I knew would go over with the gods like a turd in a punch bowl. Or I would have to be honest and explain because of the busted TV set I knew it didn't matter what moves Herzog or Davey Johnson made, it was of no consequence who slugged what where or what pitcher punched out what batter. *The game was mine.*

But you can't say that. The minute you say that, you lose it. (There may be some people reading this soon-to-become-a-cry-of-pain who think I'm horseshitting. But any Believer knows that it *does* happen. It's like flying saucers—everyone knows they exist but until some drooler from NASA admits it, we have to keep our opinions quiet. Aside: The greatest World Series of the Fifties was played not between the Yanks and the Dodgers but between four of us in my apartment on West 72nd because all four of us, at various times, had power, and two of us were for the Yanks while the other idiots wanted the Dodgers, so every time you'd get a good winning position someone would shout, "He's got his legs and his right-hand fingers crossed" and then there would be movement and my power would be taken from me. I was never so tired after baseball games as then, four nuts in a room, moving, jinxing, trying to control events taking place uptown.)

No, I could not ignore the game. If others wanted to talk about it, let them. If they asked me about it, I would answer, but dispassionately. And then change the subject as quickly as possible.

I did that. The morning went smoothly. Lunch was not hard—Lori McNeil was playing Steffi Graf at Flushing Meadow, having upset Chris Evert, and it was an easy segue whenever the subject of the Mets became too intense. The afternoon went just fine. It was after four-thirty. The game had started. I turned my mind away. It was essential that I know nothing until it was over. The final victorious score would be the first news. If I could hang tough enough, we were in.

Then a crisis came up. Some discussions on the ads for the movie *The Princess Bride* (based on a novel and screenplay of mine) became essential. A bunch of us hurried across Century City to Norman Lear's office.

Norman Lear, who put up the money for the movie, has a lovely office. And in his lovely office is a nice television set. It was far across the room. And it was off. Then somebody turned it on and the next thing I heard was this: "Hey, he gets the Mets game."

The turn of the screw.

We're in this meeting but some guys are watching the tube—with the sound off—and they're clocking the game. I hadn't expected this. Being in the same room with the game. Carefully standing out of sight lines so I couldn't see the picture. Keeping my eyes averted so I couldn't tell from the expressions of the people watching whether we were winning.

Talk about your Chinese water torture.

Surely, I was being tested. There was a meaning in all of this, some overall plan. I concentrated on the desk in Lear's office while Rob Reiner and Lear talked about switching this to that, thus to so.

In truth, I wasn't really sure what they were saying. What I was trying to figure was this: Should I take two quick steps forward, grab a quick glance at the set, try to catch the score?

Risk all that.

What if I did and Vince Coleman, the little pecker, was stealing third. What if I did and Ozzie was robbing Keith of a double. What if I did and—

—and I realized I had to take the chance. Because if I didn't, They might think I was being arrogant in over ignoring the game. Not blabbing on about it is one thing. But not even taking a quick peek when it's in the room there with you is something quite again. I knew I had the power. Or had had it early in the day. I mean, taking away the TV set with cable was a sure sign. Did I still have it? Could I lose it by glancing toward the set? They were playing with me—if this sudden meeting doesn't happen I can go home to my hotel room without ever being anywhere with the game on and just wait until someone calls me from New York with the happy outcome.

I did a brave thing then—I took the steps, faced the set, figuring if they were going to destroy me for a glance, then I didn't really have the power anymore and as I watched—

—as I watched, Darryl Strawberry hit one off John Tudor. Crunched one off John Tudor. The others watching shouted and jumped but I knew not to do that. I dared to watch the replay and then I daintily went back to the advertising meeting.

WE WERE UP 3–0.

The meeting went on a long time. I did not return to the set. News reached me, but I couldn't stop that. I had gotten Strawberry the homer. If I hadn't turned to watch just when I did, he might have whiffed or flied to right. Time went on. The Cards scored: 3–1. The Mets scored right back, 4–1.

It was 4–1 when we left the meeting.

I assumed it was still 4–1 when I reached my hotel. I was having dinner with some married couple friends at eight. Carefully timed. The game would likely be over shortly before eight. And with such craftsmen as Darling and Tudor, probably much sooner.

Still, it was a pistol being alone in the room. I knew the Cards were dangerous—I knew they'd come from behind 45 times already this year to win. Around quarter past seven I began to fidget. Not precisely true, I had fidgeted all day, now it was out of control.

I thought I might shave again, that would take five minutes if I was careful. I ran the hot water. Then I realized I never shave twice in one day. They might get pissed if I shaved twice in one day. I turned off the water. My TV set got ESPN. I played with the clicker but never turned it on. That would be rushing things. I had faith someone would call from New York as soon as the victory was ours. I started dressing for dinner. I was eating downstairs in the hotel restaurant, The Gardens. Was it a necktie place? Probably not. L.A. doesn't have many necktie places. (I think it has two and one of them is rumored to be going under.) I put on a necktie anyway. It took time to get the knot right because my hands were out of control—

—twenty of eight. Twenty of eleven in New York. The game has lasted three hours now. *Why?* How many runs could the Mets have scored? Six more, maybe. How long would that take? Depends. Hard to figure, Herzog switches pitchers so often and that takes time.

A quarter of and the phone rang. I answered. And heard among the happiest words of the year: "They're partying at Shea." Only said with such joy, the voice soaring, the last word dragged into two wondrous syllables:

"They're . . .

      partying . . .

           at . . .

                Shay-yay . . ."

"Thank God," I said, though I of all people should not have been surprised. (But you can never be too confident of your power, sometimes They think it's snooty of you.)

"What score?"

"Four to one."

I just nodded gratefully over the phone.

"And there's more. HoJo stole his thirtieth—eighth guy, all time, to do it."

I really liked the guy who was calling. Not only was he a real fan, not only was he thinking of me as soon as the game was over, he also had the kind of stats I love hearing.

"Only eight guys in history," I said. "Really an achievement." And it was. To steal 30 bases and hit 30 home runs in the same season is a legitimate rarity—very few players in history have that power/speed combination. And for Howard Johnson to do it, a player most experts felt was at best a part-timer, made it even more unusual.

"And there's more," the guy went on—"Howard's the first full-time infielder *ever* to do it."

That's such a happy moment for me, hearing about Howard Johnson, knowing we were only half a game back, knowing the Cards had folded, lost four in a row, knowing they wouldn't sleep that night, not with Dwight Gooden going tomorrow, knowing that at last, after all the injuries and bad luck and bad behavior, the Mets were going to be in first place, and rightfully, tomorrow by sunset.

"They're dancing in the aisles at Shea," he said, bubbling.

"They're . . .
        dancing . . .
             in . . .
                  the . . .
                      aisles . . .
                         at . . .
                           Shay-yay . . ."

"They just won't leave the ball park," I said. I know that feeling. An event is done, gone, but the texture of the air is so splendid, you just linger.

"Not till Willie McGee makes the last out," the guy said.

You know how people of a certain age always know where they were when they heard the Japanese attacked Pearl Harbor? Or where they were when they heard that Kennedy was shot? Well, this person will always remember where he was when he found out the game wasn't over. On my deathbed, if I have grandchildren and they ask, "Grampa, what does Willie McGee make you think of?" I would answer that Willie McGee makes me think of this asshole who called me to gloat *before the game was over.* I really hated the guy who was calling. Not only did he know nothing about sports, he was always out to get me, to take away my power.

As calm as Chamberlain at Munich I said, "Uh, you mean the game isn't quite over?"

"As good as. Two outs, two strikes, top of the ninth, Roger McDowell with stuff on the mound. I can't quite see the set from here, I'm across the room, I thought that I'd share the news."

"There really isn't quite news yet, is there?" I said. "It's really more of an interim report than news."

The fool must have sensed some of my disapproval because he said, "Hey, Lori gave Steffi all she wanted today, lost in three but she had the break in the third on her racquet and blew the volley."

I muttered something.

He went on about Lori and Steffi.

Finally I said, "Is Willie McGee still up?"

I heard the phone being put down. Steps. I hear the phone being picked up. "No big deal, he singled, Pendleton's up, no power, four–two, two out, two strikes—"

I screamed, "Get the fuck off the phone!" and slammed my receiver down.

Agony.

I rushed to my desk for my copy of *Who's Who in Baseball.* I rarely travel without my copy of *Who's Who in Baseball.* Sometimes I forget my toothbrush. Neckties are fifty-fifty. But never *Who's Who in Baseball.*

"Pendleton, Terry Pendleton" I said out loud, envisioning the sparkplug-like third baseman Herzog likes for defensive purposes. I checked his record. We were safe. Not a home run threat. Last year, '86, in 578 times at bat he'd managed all of one homer. So the worst he could do was triple in a run (he'd hit five triples the year before) which meant we were still up 4–3 and Johnson would bring in Orosco, who would punch out Herzog's best. 4–3 was close. Too close when you go into the ninth 4–1. But a W is a W and the Doc still goes tomorrow just like the sun still rises in the East and we'd be in first before it set tomorrow night.

The phone rang again.

I was dressed, my guests were probably already in the lobby where I said I'd meet them. And I knew it was this same putz, this schmuck, this fool of all the world calling with news. Logically, the news could have been good or bad. Except he knew he was risking death if he called with something of a negative nature.

Should I answer? If I did, would I lose my power? Or had he taken it away by his, to put a fine point on it, ill-timed call? If I didn't answer, by the time dinner was done the game would clearly be over and I could turn on ESPN. But if I didn't answer, and the Mets had won, I would have ruined a glorious dinner with truly unnecessary fretting.

And the Mets *had* to have won. Because not enough time had elapsed for anything else. Make the worst possible scenario: Pendleton doubles or triples and McGee makes it 4–3. He wouldn't call with that news. The only possible news was that Pendleton had made the third out and the game was over. There wasn't time for anything else.

I picked up the phone.

"Pendleton homered to center, four-four tie."

I said nothing. No need to. I hung up. Had I misread my *Who's Who in Baseball?* I checked again. One fucking homer all of last year. And now, in the most important game of the year, he puts it over the center field wall? Four hundred and ten feet? I went out to the little terrace of my room, stared at the sky. They really had no limits when it came to testing me.

I wanted to cancel dinner but my guests were assuredly down there. I went down there. They were there. I explained the events of the previous minutes. The man wasn't a nut but he commiserated, said they'd probably pull it out in the bottom of the ninth. I was grateful to him. His wife said, "Oh cheer up, Bill, it's just a baseball game, aren't they playing another one tomorrow?" I nodded that they were. "Well, there," she said. "You see?"

And on that we went to the Gardens for dinner.

We were seated in the lovely hotel restaurant. The husband and wife, both wine lovers as am I, said they would wait, Perrier for now. I ordered Perrier, for now, too. And the wine list. And a double Finlandia on the rocks with a twist. Some nights you know early on the size of tomorrow's hangover. Not that I was giving up—there's not an ounce of quit in me when it matters. And God, this mattered. Because if the Mets somehow didn't win, the loss would be so devastating I doubted that even the Good Doctor could compensate tomorrow. So instead of having our anointed (rightfully so) lead, we would be two and a half back and staggering.

I needed the Finlandia as a hedge. If, by some absurd cosmic blunder, we lost, I could chug it and forget my torment. When we won (note the "when," please) I could simply toast the Fates for giving me a little nudge of anguish, knowing I was of sufficiently stern stuff to smile.

Now, to the wine list. My male guest, like me, unstuffy about wine (none of that "it's an amusing little bottle but you'll be amused by its presumption" shit) said he'd had a super Chardonnay recently, the '85 Matanzas Creek. I'd never tasted it so I ordered it along with a victory celebration bottle of Heitz Martha's Vineyard, I forget the year because I was squiffed when I chugged it.

The Perrier came along with my double vodka, I ordered the wines, we chatted in this lovely spacious restaurant about what one always chats about in L.A. Which studio executive was next to be fired, how bad was Michael Cimino's next film *The Sicilian,* were television bosses dumber than their movie counterparts and was such a thing possible, and then—

—and then, two words, muted, from the table behind me.

". . . six . . .

. . . four . . ."

Sometimes you know things. Those words could have referred to a man's height, a tennis result (the Open was still very much on), a mathematical sequence (six, four, two, zero), part of a telephone number, any number of items.

Except I knew. It was the Mets–Cardinals baseball score. What I didn't know was who had the six. Should I turn and inquire? Would They think it pushy? And maybe the guy at the next table was a liar. Maybe he'd say the Cards won six-four just to piss me off.

L.A. sports fans do that kind of thing.

The Matanzas Creek '85 arrived. Was opened. Poured. Sipped. Many California whites are what they used to call "monster" wines. The grape flavoring blended to such intensity that they score wonderfully in blind tastings against French burgundies but are overpowering when combined with food.

Such was not the case here. On my deathbed I will say it was the finest California white I ever tasted. I finished my glass, poured another, turned to the guy behind me. He was maybe mid-thirties, Howie Long–looking, big, crew-cutted. A neck-load full of gold chains. Shirt open to the navel to show all the good work his undoubtedly personal trainer had done.

"Sorry to interrupt, but was that six-four the Mets?"

Big smile. Slow nod. Then he said it: "They did their usual fold."

A guy declares war, if you're uncivilized, you wound him. I turned back silently to my table and my guests; another Chardonnay sip. I had to keep my mind clear—I couldn't chug the vodka. Because, *because,* I told myself, he hadn't actually said the game was over. The "usual fold" line could have referred to the Pendleton homer.

Hating him, I turned back. "Final?"

Big smile. "Fuckin' A. Cards wiped their asses in the tenth." Then a very, very long pause. Then he said it, in a playgroundish nyah-nyah tone. "Fernando won." He smiled still, leaned back in his chair.

"Fer-nan-do won."

I took one more sip of the white, turned in my chair. My hands were out of control. FOUR-ONE IN THE NINTH AND THEY BREAK THE TV SET AND TAUNT ME WITH DARRYL'S HOMER AND SEND THIS SCHMUCK VIA THE PHONE WIRES (It was Lupica) TO DESTROY MY POWER BEFORE THE GAME'S OVER AND THEN THE FINAL NEWS IS SENT BY AN ANGELINO ASSHOLE.

It was too much. My mind, troubled by reality all day long, veered over the line into fantasy. . . .

I kicked the chair out from under him. He fell hard. I was on him like a cat, pulling him to his feet, backhanding him across the table. Customers started to shriek and scream. The maître d' hurried over going "Gentlemen, gentlemen" —and I said, "He intentionally humiliated a New York sports fan," and the maître d', his heavily Brooklyn accent obvious, said, "Kick the shit out of him for me, the son of a bitch," so I grabbed the guy off the table and punched him into a corner where we weren't causing that much disturbance and like all L.A. sports guys, he was gutless and I hit him a few more, not even my best stuff and he went to his knees sobbing, begging me to stop and I grabbed him by the collar and said, "Admit what you are, you're a goddamn thief, you stole the Lakers from Minneapolis and the Rams from Cleveland and the Dodgers from New York, you're nothing but a bunch of sneaks in the night—"

"—it's true," he sobbed. "It's all true, I'm so ashamed."

"And you hate us because you know New Yorkers are the only True Believers, the only ones who understand passion, who know the true depth of suffering, you hate us but you want to be us only God left out courage when he made you."

"—it's true," he sobbed. "We're all gutless thieves, and our hearts are filled with envy, we want to be you so badly, only we lack character."

I cold-cocked him then and left him slobbering on the floor.

I went back to my table, apologized to my guests, chugged my double vodka, ordered another.

How did I feel? Well, it's always fun beating up on bad guys. And there were a lot of New Yorkers in the restaurant that night and they all came over to thank me, shook my hand in gratitude. And the wine was great, the food glorious.

But reality set in. I'm a Fan, and I knew the long-range truth: Terry Pendleton was my Titanic. After that liner sank, no one ever felt quite as confident again, not in deep water. And I was in deep water now. . . .

THE
REPORTER'S NOTEBOOK

"A FUNNY THING HAPPENED TO ROGER MCDOWELL'S RIGHT ARM...."

The tool belt wasn't the only prop in the locker. There were also fright masks; McDowell was a collector of them too. He had Nixon, he had a Freddy mask from the *Nightmare on Elm Street* movies, and one he referred to as his "Jay mask." He said that one reminded him of Jay Horwitz, the team's PR man. There were also piles of blue Adidas baseball shoes and sneakers and boxes of bubble gum (McDowell had incessantly chewed tobacco in the minor leagues until Karen, his wife, made him switch to bubble gum; it was what McDowell did all the time, to the point of blowing bubbles while he was delivering his sinker to the batters), and Adidas sneakers and whatever toys McDowell had picked up on road-trip forays into Toys R Us. Other ballplayers might go to bars, or discos, or chase women.

McDowell, he liked Toys R Us, that was his idea of a big day on the road.

Roger McDowell, for all the backbiting and sniping that went on around him, went through the season the way he went through every season, even if it had started out with a hernia: He threw nasty sinkers and laughed a lot.

"I'll tell you why," he was fond of saying. "I feel like I'm here on a pass. If you think about it, I probably shouldn't be here at all. So I'm not going to waste one day."

He had been a five-foot-six, 115-pound high school pitcher in Cincinnati, Colerain High, when he first tried to impress the scouts at a Cincinnati Reds tryout camp. When it was time for him to take his turn on the mound, McDowell threw as hard as he could.

The scout said, "Okay, now let us see your fastball."

The kid said, "That was my fastball."

He went back to high school, grew up, got a baseball scholarship to Bowling Green, signed with the Mets as a starting pitcher after his junior year, pitched his way to Jackson of Double-A ball, met his future wife, was second in the Texas League in complete games and innings pitched, and blew out his right elbow. He was twenty-three years old when Dr. James Parkes cleared out the elbow of bone chips and bone spurs in January of 1984. He was supposed to miss the entire 1984 season. McDowell was back with Jackson by the playoffs.

And a funny thing happened to Roger McDowell's right arm.

It was a better arm than he'd taken into surgery. It was stronger. It was more durable. And it was already producing a sinker that started out around the batter's midsection and then tried to burrow into the dirt behind home plate like a mole.

Arm surgery ends careers. Or arm surgery changes fastball pitchers into junkball pitchers. Star pitchers who have arm surgery become meat-and-potatoes middle relievers.

The baseball gods gave McDowell, the Sunshine Boy, a better arm. The next spring, the sinker got out so many hitters in spring training, Davey Johnson had no choice but to keep McDowell. By the end of that season, during which the earned run average was 2.83 and he had 17 saves, McDowell was an equal in the Mets bullpen to Jesse Orosco. By the championship season of 1986, he was the Mets bullpen ace, even if Orosco did end up with more wins and saves in the postseason.

"My arm," McDowell said all the time, "never gets tired. If I had to pitch every day, I could pitch every day."

After coming back from the hernia, McDowell had struggled. The key for him, the reason he was in the big leagues, was that he could keep the ball low in the strike zone almost all the time. Now he was getting the ball up as often as it was breaking down with old-fashioned mystery. One day he would get a save with a ground ball, the next he would leave the mound amid a rainstorm of line drives.

"My whole career hinges on six inches, one way or the other," McDowell said blithely. He is handsome, open-faced, smiling most of the time, never one to duck the press after a bad outing. When he did it was unusual.

He said, "If I get the ball six inches higher than I want it, it never makes it into the catcher's mitt. It ends up in a mitt out there." He gestured vaguely through the clubhouse wall to the general area where the outfield is at Shea Stadium. "Sometimes, it doesn't go into the mitt at all." He was talking about a home run for the other guys.

But McDowell, like his teammates, seemed ready for the Cardinals, either on or off the record. He seemed, toward the end of August, to finally have found the consistent form for which he'd searched since he ended up on the bathroom floor in St. Petersburg with the hernia in the area of the left groin. Between August 23 and September 6, he had not allowed the opposition a single run in eight straight appearances. He had six saves during the period, five in five games he pitched between August 23 and September 1. On the thirty-first of August, he was awarded his twenty-second save, tying his career best.

Davey Johnson was using him almost every night, and McDowell was responding, and it was why on September 9 he made his prophecy about the race in the National League East. He knew, the way the rest of the baseball world knew, that the Mets and Cardinals would conclude the regular season with three games at Busch Memorial Stadium.

The last time into St. Louis, when the Mets had swept, McDowell had pitched in all three games, getting two saves, one win.

Roger McDowell was keeping the ball down. When Roger McDowell kept the ball down, 1987 looked an awful lot like 1986.

"It's going to be me," he said. "Me against the Cardinals. I figure the moment of truth will come in one of those three games in October."

McDowell was right about everything except the month.

McDowell ate like a condemned man the morning of September 11, but then he ate breakfast that way every day: heaping plate of scrambled eggs smothered in American cheese, bacon "dripping grease, the way I like it," stack of toasted bread, the bread smothered in Smuckers blackberry preserves, pot of coffee.

"I knew I was going to get the ball that night," he said later. "I knew before the game was over, Davey was going to give me the ball. And we were gonna go about the business of getting into first place by the end of the weekend."

It meant the Mets would have to sweep.

But: Why the hell not? The Friday morning papers were filled with stories about Clark's injured ankle; he had been seen limping badly at the Cardinals' Manhattan hotel, the Grand Hyatt. The official Cardinals' line was that he might be available for pinchhitting sometime during the weekend, but no one believed that. The Cardinals had been swept in Montreal, they didn't have their big gun, a lead that had once been ten and a half was now one and a half. The Cardinals would have to face Darling and Gooden the first two games of the series, then David Cone on Sunday.

"I just wanted it to be two o'clock," McDowell said of September 11. "That meant it was time to take the 2:19 train to Woodside, then take the subway from Woodside to Shea and get to the ball park about three-thirty."

When he was done with breakfast, he drove into Amityville, to Melville's Delicatessen, to buy the morning papers. He knew all the help at Melville's and they all knew him, of course. McDowell would joke later that Friday was the last day he got to take the newspapers for free at Melville's Deli.

The papers were full of stories about the Mets and the Cardinals. The Yankees were dead in the American League East; it was as if they had left town. The sports pages were filled with Mets stories. Even when both teams were in divisional races, the Mets dominated the baseball coverage. It had been that way for a few years. Even with the Dodgers and Giants thirty years gone to the West Coast, New York was a National League town. Shea had become a ghost town at the end of the seventies, but now the fans were back with a vengeance, and the Mets were back to being the sexy, controversial, glamorous National League kings of the town. And they were ready to kick the Cardinals' asses all the way back to the Mississippi.

McDowell: "All season long, people said we couldn't. Couldn't do it. We were supposed to be dead in July. We were all those games out for all that time. We were bums. *Everybody* had been on our ass. But now here we were. By Sunday night, we were going to be in first, not them."

He took the papers home, read them, watched some game shows, took a nap, took the 2:19 to Woodside and the subway to Shea, and walked into a playoff atmosphere at Shea. It was 1986 again. It was October of 1986. That kind of atmosphere. More writers, more photographers, more television cameras. The Mets had become baseball's under-the-big-top team. McDowell was right. They *had* been dead. Now it was September 11, and there were all these hands wearing baseball gloves pushing up the top of the coffin and saying, "Surprise." If they pulled this off, if they ended up in first, they would be bigger than ever. It would be a better story than 108 wins and the rest in '86.

"It was gonna be like the end of *The Sting*," McDowell said. "Newman and Redford, you're sure they're dead. then Redford smiles and you say, 'Holy *Shit!*' "

Holy Shit.

Baseball is a sport of rituals, whether it is a meaningless game between Texas and Cleveland in July, or a no-holds-barred September showdown between the Mets and the Cardinals. There is an orderliness to the day, every day, from the time you get to the ball park until "Play Ball." So McDowell was on the field early for the normal batting competition the pitchers staged, and then he was shagging fly balls in the outfield, and there was some running with the other pitchers in the outfield, and some mugging in the dugout. The usual card games were played. Darling, that night's starter, repaired to the private players' room next to Charlie Samuels's office. Hernandez did a crossword. Rafael Santana ended up in front of his locker, smoking. Mel Stottlemyre, the pitching coach, looked over charts on the Cardinals hitters.

Shea was jumping by seven o'clock. The games, all three of them, had been sold out for weeks. Jay Horwitz had even told the writers three days before, "No comps. I'm completely busted."

Which is the way the Cardinals looked after the second inning. In the bottom of the first, Tim Teufel singled and Hernandez doubled him home and then Strawberry hit a monstrous home run to right, and it was 3–0. The Cardinals got a run off Darling without benefit of a base hit in the second, but the Mets came back with another run, and it was 4–1. The score would stay the same until the ninth. The Cardinals not having a base hit, that would stay the same until the sixth.

Not only were the Mets winning 4–1, not only was Shea the sound of New Year's Eve . . . Ron Darling was pitching a *no-hitter*.

McDowell began to wonder if he would get the ball. "I still thought I'd get in," he said. "I kept thinking about pitching all three games in St. Louis. But not if Ronnie was gonna insist on pitching a damn no-hitter." McDowell was in the bull pen, passing the time with the rest of his bull pen mates, idly toying with the notion of having one of the ushers go and buy him a burrito from the concession stands. Randy Myers occasionally leafed through a magazine. Vern Hoscheit, the ornery, ancient bull pen coach, watched the game and seemed constantly on the verge of nodding off. Doug Sisk and Jesse Orosco groused to each other and wondered if they would be Mets the following season.

Then, in the top of the sixth, the bull pen stirred. Vince Coleman dragged a bunt between the pitchers' mound and first base, a superb bunt, and Darling dove trying to field it, and landed on his right thumb. Coleman had the first hit for his team. Darling then got three outs to end the inning, but when he walked Dan Driessen to open the seventh, he realized there was so much pain in his thumb, he could not continue.

(With good reason. Darling found out the next day he had torn ligaments in the thumb. His season was over. He went from the near no-hitter on Friday night to the news of the torn ligaments on Saturday to surgery on Sunday at Roosevelt Hospital.)

The bull pen phone had rung in the sixth, as soon as Darling dove. Myers and McDowell got up. After Driessen walked, Myers came on to pitch the rest of the seventh, showing the Cardinals a venomous fastball, striking out one.

When the seventh ended, the phone rang in the bull pen and McDowell was told he would be the one to finish the game, bring the Mets to within a half game of first.

He was getting the ball, just as he had planned.

"Six outs," he said.

He got three of them in the eighth, no problem.

It was still 4–1, Mets. It was still New Year's Eve at Shea, had been since the very first inning, really. They would have liked a no-hitter, and there was some concern about Darling, but how badly could he be hurt if he got up and pitched after he fell down? Davey was just playing it safe.

McDowell walked Ozzie Smith, who led off the top of the ninth for the Cardinals.

Roger McDowell: "I'm pissed, but not that pissed. Hell, I've got a three-run lead. Clark's not waiting for me at cleanup. I'm just thinking, bear down and get (Tom) Herr."

Herr grounded to Hernandez. Smith advanced to second.

Two outs to go.

McDowell struck out Dan Driessen, the veteran left-handed hitter the Cardinals had rescued from the minors to replace Clark, swinging.

One out to go.

The 50,000-plus at Shea Stadium were up on their feet. The ball park is close to LaGuardia, it is in a LaGuardia flight path, the planes make a

God-awful racket, there was the same kind of God-awful racket now—only no planes.

Just Mets fans.

Willie McGee was at the plate for the Cardinals. Ozzie Smith was on second base.

One strike away.

McDowell: "I got two strikes on nasty sliders. I mean *nasty*. Then I threw a ball outside. Then he fouled off another slider. So the count is one-two, and I figure he's looking for another slider. The crowd's up. They're cheering like crazy. I felt like I was in the middle of a war, only we were winning. We're gonna be a half game back. Anyway, I figure McGee's looking for the slider, so I throw him a fastball. And for like the first time in three weeks in that kind of situation, I get it up."

McGee bounced a single up the middle, scoring Ozzie Smith, making the score 4–2, Mets.

McDowell: "Everybody later on would want to talk about what happened next, but the pitch to McGee, *that* was the pitch right there. That was the damn pitch."

Still, McDowell had a two-run lead. Still two outs. Terry Pendleton, the Cardinals' third baseman, was the next batter. Pendleton who had hit one home run for all of 1986.

Pendleton stepped into the batter's box, a pudgy switchhitter batting left-handed against McDowell.

Roger McDowell didn't know it, but this was the one-pitch season he had predicted. September eleventh.

This was the moment of truth. . . .

A Fan's Notes

LAST STAND

The final home stand for the Mets began on Wednesday, the twenty-third of September. Under circumstances that could have been heartier. The Cardinals, winners of four straight, were four up on the Mets in the loss column, with but a dozen left to play.

All, however, was not remotely lost. Because the Cards' final seven games were against the Mets (three) and the surging Expos of Montreal, (four, including a double-header). More than that, Montreal had been pasting the Cards constantly, so although a sweep was probably wishful thinking, three out of four seemed almost likely, a split a lock. So if the Mets swept their final three, and they were only three down in the loss column when the series began, and then won the playoff, which they surely would (it was to be played, if played, at Shea) they had only to stay close to the Cards to repeat as National League Champions.

Skip all that; the fact that mattered was this: After a hundred and fifty games of stumbling and bumbling and drugging and broken limbs, the Mets were, as they say, in it.

This final stand had more than the Cardinal battle riding. It was to be a five-gamer, two against the Expos themselves, the final trio against the remarkable Pirates, no longer objects of scorn. For the month they were as hot a team as baseball had to offer.

Although all fans, this one among them, gather the bulk of their amazing perceptions from the print media or the tube, I thought it might be of some interest to actually attend the two series the way real writers do. (I had much earlier secured, through the kindness of two genuinely fine gentlemen, Harvey Greene of the Yankees and Frank Cashen of the Mets, press passes for the season.)

Real writers always begin their sojourns at the press gate where you show your credentials to a guard positioned there. (Not always, though—once I got to Shea very early, say two-thirty for a seven-thirty game, and the press gate was open, yes, but there was no one there. I wandered in. No big deal. Except *anybody* could have wandered in. And gone on the field or into offices or whatever. I remember thinking then, even though I'd just done it, that you could never write such a moment in a movie. Even the fans of *Nightmare on Elm Street, Part XXXI, Freddy Visits the Manicurist,* would never believe it.)

To properly cover a game, a reporter basically needs four things:

1. Somewhere to watch the game (the press box)

2. Somewhere to write about the game (the press room)

3. Somewhere to interview the players (the clubhouse)

4. Somewhere to eat (often, though not at Shea, the pits)

At Shea, once you've left the press guard behind, you walk straight ahead down a corridor, take a right down another corridor, and you're eventually at the clubhouse door where another guard waits. Across the corridor from the clubhouse is a tunnel that leads to the playing field.

An elevator ride up to the fourth floor takes you to the press box, the press room, and the restaurant. Many reporters head up to the press room first, dump their debris, their briefcases, personal computers, etc., and head on back down either to the playing field, if batting practice is going on, or the clubhouse.

The clubhouse, any number of baseball people feel, is the single greatest unknown factor in the ultimate quality of a ball team. Most players, as has been noted, spend more time in the clubhouse than they do with their wives. A seven-thirty night game, for example, requires the athletes to be present by four-thirty. But they're almost all there well before then. And if the game runs three hours plus and after that comes the showering and changing and God knows what else, you're talking about a long day. Or night.

One of the shocking things about a baseball clubhouse (or, by extension, the field during batting practice) is this: accessibility. The athletes, no matter how famous, are all there.

At, if you will, the media's mercy.

Now, most of us have never been on a movie set, but probably we've seen enough movies about movies or documentaries about the making of movies to know what a sound stage looks like and one word pretty much sums it up: *private.*

There's the cast. With the stars usually off in their trailers. And there's the crew, busying itself for the next shot. And that is pretty much that. Of course, there are exceptions but for the most part, it's a cut-off little enclave.

Well, imagine if you will, a Rambo picture. There's the special effects guy over there, fussing with his arsenal of explosives. And just to his left, that's the blood guy, surgically mixing his batch of red goo, getting it just the proper shade and thickness. And behind them is the man himself, old Sly, pumping iron or taking vitamins or whatever the hell he does to have so remarkably remolded his body the way he has—

—and now, imagine, if you will, anywhere from fifty to a hundred reporters with note pads or microphones or TV cameras, all wandering wherever they want when they want except for the few minutes when they're herded away and the camera's actually rolling. No trailer for Sylvester to hide in. No place to run as one guy after another comes up and says, "Sly, is it true your ex-wife's a dyke, like they're hinting in the magazines?" or "Sly, did you know your ex-wife Brigitte bought new breasts for Kelly Sahnger, her, you should pardon the expression, 'physical fitness instructor,' like I read?" or "Sly, did she really stiff you for six million plus jewels and furs in the settlement?"

An extreme example, perhaps, but substitute drug questions and that's what Dwight Gooden got on occasion. That's what a clubhouse is like. Any fool with a credential, such as your correspondent, can go to any athlete and ask anything and the poor guy has to answer something. (He can take refuge in the off-limits trainer's room but that's not a place that's a whole heap of fun because, being filled with healing equipment, it brings to mind an athlete's greatest fear: injury. The athlete can also, as was the case with Steve Carlton, simply refuse to talk to the media. But those exceptions aside, the jock is fair game.)

It's not like this in other sports. Not nearly to this degree, anyway. But baseball players are purely and simply prey, and with the paper wars going on now, they have to watch *everything* they say so carefully or tomorrow's headlines will read STRAW BLASTS WALLY. MAZ BLASTS STRAW. STRAW BLASTS DAVY. To the end of time.

Some athletes handle this remarkably well. Some just can't handle it at all. And the continual pressure from the large number of media people that are always around is one of the reasons some guys can't perform in New York. These masses of intruders don't exist in Cleveland. Or any other city. Even L.A. has less media and their reporters (not Jim Murray) tend to come from the "Gee-Whiz" (or ass-kissing) School of Journalism.

Of the Mets, just from my observing, Roger McDowell handles the mob wonderfully—no matter how his performance was during a game, he *never* hides afterward. He may have given up the Pendleton shot, but he's there telling you about it afterward. (McDowell had a marvelous comment to the effect that he was never bothered about getting batters out because he always knew he'd get them out—what he didn't know was would they score five runs off him before he did. No one has ever better capsulized the mentality of the successful relief pitcher.)

Hernandez does well, once he knows who you are. But no one does it as well as Gary Carter. I saw Carter about to leave the field during this home stand, tired, in pain as always, needing to get ready for the game—

—but there were about half a dozen TV crews waiting for interviews. These were not locals, but the Montreal series had brought them in from all over. The first guy asked for a minute's time. That's what they all wanted, just a minute's time. Maybe two. Carter took a deep breath, nodded, and started to do them all. The question they all wanted an answer to was the same: Could the Mets catch the Cards? Carter gave a different coherent answer to each group. Smiling, laughing. Nothing bothered him. Just before one interview the interviewer said, "Gary, my name's Steve," and the camera rolled and halfway through Carter said, "I'll tell you, Steve, we're going to need breaks but this team can do it," as if old Gary and Steve had just had lunch together.

Interestingly, many of the other players don't like Carter's facility with the press. "Why do they always ask *him* stuff?" they grumble. The reason is because he's pleasant and accessible. Those players that have trouble with the press wouldn't have it to the degree they do if they'd just answer the boring questions with boring answers. Innocuous. God knows there's enough media at Shea for everybody.

Personally, my favorite place in the ball park is standing behind the batting cage quietly watching and listening. Sometimes you hear conversations:

FIRST COACH
*(Watching a long home run disappearing
into the upper deck)*
Wow, that's way up in there.

SECOND COACH
(Nodding)
That's what *she* said.

But mostly what I listened to was the sound of the bat connecting with the ball. You can tell, even with a little experience, the power behind the swing. (I had a stopwatch and only Strawberry could hit the ball hard enough to keep it airborne for over six seconds.) With your eyes closed, you can't, of course, judge the trajectory, but the degree of murderous intent is there even for the beginner.

I watched Strawberry hit one before the first game. Not over the fence. He was just beginning BP and was taking it easy. But he swung with such grace and ease. Not the remotest bit of strain visible. And the ball bounced on the warning track. Of the five-game series, that moment, that swing, is one of the two things I'll remember. (The other involves Davey Johnson coming apart at the seams, but we'll get to that.)

After batting practice, when the clubhouse is closed to outsiders, the media heads up to eat. The food is free but you tip a couple of bucks in a basket. It's cafeteria-style and really pretty decent. (Much better than the food at Yankee Stadium. There, you can't see what you're getting, selections are far fewer, not as tasty and most importantly, you can't go back for seconds.)

By now it's after seven, and the media crosses the corridor, bypassing the press room for now, heading, instead, to the press box where many of them have assigned seats.

When the game is about over—two outs in the ninth—the beat writers all bunch by the exit door, waiting for the last out. Then they charge to a waiting elevator that takes them down to the clubhouse, which is usually opened quickly, and they stream in, again usually first to Davey Johnson's office for his perceptions, then out into the clubhouse proper for chats with the individual athletes.

If there is a star or important performer, Mets' P.R. chief Jay Horwitz will usually escort him to a table where a lot of people can crowd around and fire questions.

And where the radio people drive you mad.

If, say, a pitcher has given up a crucial hit, when he sits down the print people start slowly. Maybe a "tough night" will bring forth a grunt and maybe a next "he hit the curve, didn't he?" will start the actual give and take. The print people move in slowly, notebooks at the ready.

The radio guys shove their mikes into the player's face and say, for example, "You must feel you really let the team down giving up that hit" or "Was this a disaster for you or just a disappointment?"

More often than not, the player will say, because he's been given the words, "It was a disappointment" and with that the radio guy scurries off to the next player because he's got what he needs. Those few words are it. The rest will be edited out and the announcer will say, later on the air, Orosco admitted after the game that it was a disappointment to him, giving up the winning run and then you'll hear Orosco saying "It was a disappointment" and then back to the announcer.

All these interviews are done while the players undress, shower, dress (you don't follow them into the shower) and leave. And the players, experienced at this, don't do what you or I would do if asked a question by a group: raise our voices so the group can hear.

They mumble. It's definitely louder than a whisper but not much. And it's conversational. Have you ever been in a radio cab where you have this constant farting sound from the dispatcher and the driver doesn't notice, he's used to it, he's trained? Well, the reporters are trained. I've stood a yard from a guy talking and I couldn't make out boo while all around me reporters are scratching down his wisdom.

When they're done gathering info, the reporters march upstairs and file, the players depart, the clubhouse boys clean up. They reminded me of the guys who paint the George Washington Bridge, in that the bridge is never finished because by the time you're done with the far end the near end needs a new coat. Clubhouses seemed like that to me, too. People moving out, others coming in, new towels, dirty uniforms, always work to be done.

(One aside here, before the series starts: I'm excited, of course, to be here. But not as excited as I would be if this were going on across the river. I am a Yankee fan. If this had been at the Stadium, and Montreal had been Detroit, the excitement would have, say, trebled. I like the Mets, have since Stengel—except when they shafted Seaver—but the Bronx is where I hang my baseball hat.)

The game began at seven-thirty, I was there by four, wandered around the clubhouse, spent a lot of time behind the batting cage, chatted with a few people, eventually, as the crowd filed in, went up for a little nosh, then took a seat in the press box armed with something that sportswriters get before every game and don't think much of, but for us True Believers is a little bit of heaven: *stats.*

I mean pages of them. All neatly mimeoed. How many pages? The number varies from game to game but for the Montreal opener, I was flipping through close to *thirty* pages of single-spaced, legal-sized, fact-filled stuff. (I think the Mets—and all home teams for that matter—should put a paper clip on them, call them "Stats for Nuts" or something Madison Avenue-ish, and sell them at the park for a buck; make a fortune.)

Do you want to know what Tim Raines is batting left-handed vs. righty? It's there: .301 vs. .393. Do you want to know who is ninth in on-base percentage? It's there: Strawberry, .398. Are you wondering the record of the Dodgers on grass vs. artificial surfaces? Coming right up: 56–55 vs. 10–30. Are you concerned about average attendance for the season between the two leagues? Easy: 24,581 American, 26,031 National. Galarraga—how many four-hit games thus far this season? Two. The Expos' bull pen's ERA? 3.39. How does Montreal do when they're leading after eight? Not bad: 69–2.

But, of course, our true interest lies with the home team. You want their '87 winter instructional roster? Forty-two players listed by position complete with height, weight, dates of birth, etc. Tonight's starter, John Candelaria; it's his second time out for the Mets. Last time, he didn't do so hot. "1.1 in, 8 h, 5 r, 5 er, 0 w, 1 k." The last time he beat Montreal was September 24, 1983, when he went "5 in" in a combined shutout (a 1–0 shutout, if you want to know it all; the other four innings, for the passionate among you, were thrown by Guante). Every game between the two teams this season is skimmed over. Everything is skimmed over. From how many of their last 22 games the Mets have won (14) to who has the most pinch-hit homers for them (Magadan, 2).

If you are a baseball nut and a statistics fan, and you cannot be one without being the other, you don't care if the game ever starts or not.

This one eventually did, and the Mets emerged victorious, as the late great Harry Balough used to say, 4–3. Raines tripled in the first and scored. Raines doubled in the third and scored. Raines singled in the fifth to keep a rally alive and somebody else scored, making it 3–1 against. (Carter had brought in Strawberry in the fourth. Then, in the sixth, Carter struck again, a two-run job this time which, following as it did a run-scoring McReynolds double, accounted for the totals.)

In other words, an ordinary game between contenders. Tight. Well enough played. But a couple of things happened that explain why baseball is the most fascinating of games long before you get to the playoffs.

1. In the ninth inning, Raines, who is not a famous star like, say, Reggie or Darryl, came to the plate. Two out. Runner on second. First base empty. And suddenly from the crowd of 41,000-plus comes this weird chant that doesn't make sense until you've heard it several times.

   "WALK HIM," they're shouting. "WALK HIM." Now these are knowledgeable fans and they know you don't walk the winning run on intentionally. But Raines had tattooed us with two singles, a double, and a triple so far and nobody wanted much to give him a chance to beat us with a dinger, something he'd done already this season, a grand-slam job off Orosco his first game back after his free agent bid was spurned. (Raines was hitting .333 by this point and is on any list one of the half dozen best everyday players in the game, but no team was interested in gainfully employing the man.)

   No one had heard a chant like that at Shea before. In fact, no one could remember ever hearing a chant like that before, except one very old guy who thought that maybe the Dodger fans used to do it in Brooklyn when Musial came up. But Musial was famous, Raines isn't, and I was surprised at the close attention the fans were paying here in the top of the ninth.

2. In the eighth inning, something even more unusual happened. Something I'd not only never seen, I never knew was possible. I'll try to get it straight for you but don't bet on it. Winningham is batting for Nichols. Leach is pitching. The count goes to 2–2. At this point, Randy Myers comes in to pitch for Leach. At this

point, Engle comes in to bat for Winningham. Myers strikes out Engle.

So?

Well, according to baseball rule 10–18–h (I'm serious), you can't penalize the pinch hitter for the earlier hitter who got the two strikes on him. So although Myers fired the ball at Engle, who he strikes out, the record book records it differently. Myers gets credit for the strikeout. But Engle is *not* the victim. Winningham is.

In other words, according to history henceforth, Myers struck out Winningham—

—who he never faced.

After the game, all the press charged to the elevator and then, once on the main floor, down the corridor where they divided, some going to Montreal's locker room, most to the Mets' clubhouse. And once the door was open, into Davey Johnson's office.

Davey Johnson was already a controversial man, though before the week was over he would be enormously more so. Six-one, with a playing weight of 170, he probably went over two hundred as he sat behind his desk. A successful second baseman (four All-Star games), a good fielder (three Gold Gloves), with power (a record-tying, for second basemen, 42 home runs), he had managed in the minors, played with Sadaharu Oh in Japan.

Tough and bright (a math degree from Trinity University in San Antonio, Texas), he seems like a quintessential Texan. There is a swagger about him even when he's sitting down. You always expect to see him in cowboy boots. Mustachioed and cold-eyed, he seems to say, "You don't want me mad at you."

In his first three seasons with the Mets he had never won less than 90 games, had piloted a world champion, was doing his damnedest to get them through this difficult year.

But he was not liked. Not much by the players and not much by the media. (Which matters not one bit in terms of either what kind of a man he is or what kind of a managing job he does.) But the arrogance of the man is clear. As is his distrust of the media. He's not at ease with them, at least in groups.

The most irritating thing about him is this: After four years in the minors, twelve in the majors, two in Japan, after close to ten more managing, he has yet to make his first baseball mistake. Not only that, but he gets more than riled when any move, no matter how stupid, is queried.

His press conferences after ball games are, to be brief, brief.

"I thought Candy had real good stuff, it was good to see Gary come through for the team that way, no, I didn't think about putting Raines on in the ninth, I'm not fond of that."

A few more questions. But he was not happy answering them. Behind him, blocked by the reporters, was a TV set with the Cardinals on. They were losing (and eventually lost) and it was clear that Johnson was infinitely more interested in that outcome than anything the dozens of men in the room wanted to know. If the Cards lost, the Mets were alive.

Soon he was alone.

Tough. Bright. Invulnerable. (How that was to change.)

Thursday was tense for me. We are only two and a half back, the Cards having been shut out the night before. We are three back in the loss column but that's okay with me if we can just stay there, since I am convinced we'll sweep the Cards, if need be, in the last series of the season.

We just can't afford to slip back a game, down to four.

I read the papers and read the papers. All the papers. The *Times, News, Post, Newsday, USA Today*. The Cards have got to be shaky at the shutout. And Pittsburgh, who they play again, is, as Marv Albert likes to say, on fire.

And so is the Mets starter, Rick Aguilera. One of the seemingly infinite number of injured Mets pitchers, he did not work in the majors between May twentieth and August twenty-fourth.

Ah, but since his return. Six starts, six wins. An overall string of seven straight. (One more and he ties Seaver for the club record.) An overall record of 10–2. A cinch to win, I say.

Well, almost a cinch. Because the opposing starter is also having a non-sub-par season. Dennis Martinez is 10–3. Not only is he unbeaten for September (4–0), he is unbeaten against the Mets for the year (3–0).

Sort of a maybe off-beat classic confrontation shaping up at Shea.

It is a classic confrontation all right. But it isn't between the Mets and the Expos at Shea, it is between the Mets at Shea and the Cardinals in

St. Louis. Because as eleven-thirty nears, the Mets are about to win and the Cards are about to lose.

Twelve hundred miles apart, the enemies are locked in death grips. Both teams can scoreboard-watch. The Cards are down by a run in the ninth. The Mets are down by two, but Mookie singles, there is a steal, Timmy Teufel's fourth hit, a few more zigs and zags and suddenly the bases are full up, and Carter (four hits, three ribbies last night) is at the plate. And there is a *lot* of noise from the forty thousand plus faithful. (What we don't know is the Cards are making their move at the same time. Well, not entirely true—in the press box it was known, there was a TV tuned to the Cardinal game—but the fans were, for the moment, ignorant.)

Bases loaded in New York, one run down, Carter up.

Bases loaded in St. Loo, score tied now, Lance Johnson up.

Hysteria, I know, at Shea. Hysteria (must be) at Busch. If the Mets and the Cards both lose, well, sort of okay, we're still only three down in the lost column. But if the Mets win and the Cards lose, we're two down and confident, they're two up and panicking. (They know the Expos are coming, us right behind.) If the Mets lose and the Cards luck out, though, not good. Twelve hundred miles apart, two batters swing.

Not good.

Davey's eyes are dangerously bright. "Bad day at Black Rock," he mutters. The reporters write that down. He makes a few more quiet comments. The reporters take those down, too. It's poison in the manager's office because the TV set is on and the Cardinals' win is visible for all to see. "They tried to give it to us." (Montreal made five errors.) "We just didn't get the big hit." (The Mets left eleven men on base.)

Outside in the clubhouse, it's like the plague has struck. Hernandez, who has the key locker (first left as you enter the room) and who always puts the games in perspective, does not talk. (He has a world-class head cold and has had a nightmare night, whiffing his hundredth time for the season, leaving more men on base than any major leaguer ought to.) Most of the others flee.

Carter faces it, though. Iced, looking like a misshapen warrior with the taped icepacks all over his body, he answers whatever is asked. "I tried as hard as I could. Don't you think I'd like to give back one of last night's hits for just one tonight?" Shrug. "Baseball just doesn't work that way." The press, grateful that anyone would speak to them, murmurs thanks as Carter limps away through the quiet room.

And seated alone, watching the media, quietly eating, a cheshire cat look on his face, sits Roger McDowell. Impossible to tell what he is thinking. But he must know what everyone else in the room knows. After this craziest of seasons, it was done.

The Mets are dead.

That was the consensus in the papers the next day—write it up and print it, it's over. The injuries undid them maybe, maybe lots of other things undid them. It didn't matter, from the perspective of history. They were undone.

(I alone knew the truth: They were still in it.) We had not suffered this much, come this far, to lose. To Montreal, maybe. I could see Fate in that. But not to those whining clutch artists from the City on the River.

Friday the twenty-fifth was an exceptionally tense day for me. Not only did I read the sports sections of all the papers, I also read the entertainment sections of all the papers—

—because *The Princess Bride* was opening that day. Not only that, it was a project close to fifteen years in the making. Not only that, it was the movie of mine I was most desperate to see because it's by far my favorite piece of my own writing, my only favorite piece.

And I loved the resulting film.

Would the critics cream us?

I peeked.

They didn't. Almost the reverse. Four stars in *Newsday,* four stars in the *Post,* good everywhere else.

Which had to reflect well for the Mets; I was obviously—just look at the goddamn reviews, for chrissakes—on a streak.

I have a bad back. (This, believe me, relates to baseball.) And one of the things I do for it, along with stretches and other exercising, is walk in water. (I haven't mastered *on* yet.) There is a large (for New York, huge) pool in the basement of my office building and at two-thirty, I am there, walking around and around in waist-high water. You feel like a jerk and clearly are to anyone looking at you, but my chiropractor says it helps. I figure it can't hurt.

So I'm walking. And I'm thinking. About how the reviews for *Princess Bride* were really all I could have hoped for and could Sid Fernandez win his twelfth against the Pirates tonight. Some typo was going for them—Bielecki; he should be candy. I was so pleased with the *Princess Bride* reaction, it meant so much to me, and could Sanderson of the Cubs beat St. Louis? It was at Wrigley and the Cubbies were tough there. Mr. Dawson, another unwanted Expo, was murder there.

I'm still walking. And I'm still thinking. Just getting those *Princess Bride* reviews didn't mean the people would come, and would they? The movie had tested amazingly well, the best of any flick since *E.T.* (true) but you could only test people already *in* the theaters. Would the public outside venture in so we could please them, because no movie I've ever been connected with has ever had the emotional impact on me as this one did.

And right then—

—right then in the pool—

—I had, at 2:42 P.M. on Friday, the twenty-fifth of September, 1987—an epiphany.

Do you remember a few pages back when I put in my little aside about me being a Yankee fan?

Well, I wasn't anymore. For the first time in forty-five years I had switched allegiances not for a geographical reason. Sure, your team moves or you move and you change.

Nothing had moved.

The teams were still the teams, in the same stadiums, I was still me. But everything was suddenly different. Would Winfield get his 100 RBI's this year? I hoped he would. A week ago I was anxious, worried, fretting. All that was gone now. Would Mattingly hit thirty homers? I hoped he would. But somehow, I didn't really deep-down-sports-fan *care*.

I stopped in the water, thunderstruck. Nothing in my adult life like this had ever happened before and I didn't know why it had happened.

Only, as I stood there stunned, I guessed I really did. I'd been Steinbrennered to death. (The papers were full of Billy coming back to manage and I dreaded that so—the headlines when the booze started, the macho challenges, the overall *tackiness* ahead in the Yankees' path.) I'd slogged through it before, telling myself I liked the team but detested the owner, loathed everything about the bullying rich man's son.

He'd beaten the passion out of me. The Yankees were just the Yankees now. No more hand-sweating over them.

The Mets were mine now.

And I had to get them home.

The first order of afternoon business was the Cardinals, who were playing in the daylight of Chicago. Should I check up on them? Remembering *l'affaire Terry Pendleton* I decided, in order to insure the Cards losing, I must know *nothing* about their struggle. So I did not answer phones, totally insulating myself. I left for the game early, being careful to pick a cab without a radio on.

Safe.

Then, just before the Triborough Bridge, stalled in traffic, from the *next cab* I hear "and that's the fifth hit for the Cubs"—

—I screamed—

—right there in the traffic jam, making my driver spin his head pretty good. Because not only was I supposed to know nothing, what I did know was bad—five hits was not enough to insure victory.

I sink back, close my eyes, put my hands over my ears, and pay no attention to anything until I hit Shea. I walk onto the playing field, take a breath, raise my eyes to the scoreboard: Cubs win, 2–1. When we win tonight—no "if's" for me, not on this *Princess-Bride*-opening-team-changing day—we'll be three back again.

The Pirates scored a puny two in the top of the first. Some were concerned. I was not. A brave attempt to show spunkiness. We would rock them.

And so we did, scoring ten runs in the first five innings.

Johnson was smiling in his office. "You guys write such boring stories—we're dead, we're alive, dead, alive. Well, we're alive and we're primed to make that run."

He was, I knew, understating the case. Because Gooden was going tomorrow and he didn't like Pittsburgh, openly said so, openly predicted a victory. And the Doc don't mess around.

Hell, we weren't alive, we were blooming.

Two Saturday stunners.

Gooden gives up a run in the first, four in the second, is gone after the third, as the Mets lose, the Cards win, and suddenly it's four back in the see-sawing loss column.

That was the smaller of the two, because in, would you believe, the *Times* that morning was an article headlined MANAGER AND METS IN CONTRACT DISPUTE. In Joseph Durso's article was the news that Johnson was threatening to quit unless his contract, already signed through the end of '88, was extended still further. And thus far, management was not complying.

Inexcusable behavior. Unacceptable.

Here they were, in the midst of the death throes of a pennant race and the manager picks this time to leak to the press that he wants more bread. If Darryl had done it, they'd have booed him out of the state, in spite of the career year he was having.

Before the game, a bunch of old pro writers were standing in the clubhouse, discussing Koppett's law, a commandment bequeathed to the fraternity by the great Leonard Koppett, once a major sports writer in New York, now gone straight, working on real news in California. Roughly, Koppett's law states that the World Series will always be played by the two teams who will cause the greatest inconvenience for the greatest number of sportswriters covering the event.

After the game, these guys were just shaking their heads.

The news had not spread far yet. Gooden, who took his postgame press conference wonderfully, was clearly unaware of Johnson's stand.

And Johnson, in his office, wasn't talking about it because there were other things he felt of more importance, such as that Bob Klapisch of the *Post* had written that Gooden didn't like Pittsburgh. Referring to the Pirates he said, "A weary ball club can get picked up by derogatory remarks."

Or destroyed by greedy managers.

On Sunday, the last home game, the Mets went over the 3 million mark in attendance. Remarkable. Because that meant there were 3 million fannies actually in the seats, not just tickets sold. And since the early season weather is so unpredictable, they can never get off to a great attendance start.

In Chicago, Andre got his forty-seventh and the Cubs beat the Cards again. In New York, everybody clubbed the ball and the Mets beat the Pirates again, 12–3. It was a joyous crowd. The Mets scored six in the fourth and from then on, it was party time. Sixteen hits including a homer and five doubles.

Joy pretty much unconfined.

Except in the manager's office after the game.

Before the game, I saw a bunch of players going into Johnson's office and wondered what it was about. "It's nothing," a beat writer told me. "They do it every Sunday. It's voluntary prayers."

The bulk of the praying was done, apparently, by Johnson. He had called some players in to apologize.

After the game he explained why he'd called it: "I didn't want the players to think I was looking for an extension when we're in second place. I didn't ask for an extension and I didn't ask to negotiate."

All sound and solid. But it was startling if you were there because of the man doing the talking. The tough Texan was gone now. This guy rambled, and you could see that he couldn't control the trembling of his hands.

"I stayed out of baseball for one year and I was miserable. I made a lot of money in real estate, but I was miserable." That was how what he said looked. What it sounded like was this:

"I made ... a lot of money in ... real ... estate ... but I was ... miserable. ... "

Obviously, his end run to the press for a fatter contract hadn't worked and now the reality of not managing at all was hitting home. In all the other press conferences of his, you sensed how unwelcome you were, how badly and quickly he wanted you gone.

No strutting now. All swagger gone.

"... I'd like ...

  I'd like to be here ..."

"... my priority ...

  is to win ball games ..."

"... when I got up ...

  this morning ...

  I figured I was fired ..."

"... why did everyone ...

  assume I was trying to

  extend ... ?"

"... I'm getting traded ...
     abandoned ...
     and I was king of the
     hill ..."
"I don't ...
     need the glory ...
          I've had enough glory ..."
"... and I don't ...
     need the money ...
          I've got enough money ..."
Now some reporters began asking some quiet questions.
"... You're just getting me ...
     deeper and deeper
     in shit ..."
Now some more quiet questions.

And suddenly he's whirling on two columnists, one from the *News,* the other from the *Times,* and accuses them of being in collusion in their columns that came out this morning. They are stunned and ask, "Davey, do you think we actually show each other our stuff?"

He sinks deeper in his chair. Now he's quiet again. Quiet and pale and frightened. I keep expecting him to get a couple of metal balls out of his pocket and start rolling them around in his hand. Someone says, "Davey, you look like a man who's already been fired."

Not much of a reaction.

Someone else says, "Davey, this is what it's like every day working for Steinbrenner." All the reporters laugh.

Not much of a reaction.

He just sits there, knowing his money grab has failed, knowing he had blown maybe the best managing job in baseball, a club with young replacements already available, a club that wins 90-plus games in the media center of the world.

"... I was king of the hill ..." he says.

"... I've had enough glory ..." he says.

He talks for close to an hour. Saying, "I can't talk anymore," and then talking some more.

"... I'm the one who keeps opening his mouth ..."

"... I'm the one who says enough to get things screwed up ..."

"... my priority is to win ball games ..."
"... just to win ball games ..."

The Mets were three down in the loss column and still alive.
Davey Johnson was who was dying. . . .

OCTOBER:
"... IF WHITEY WERE MANAGING ..."

The last week of the season, in Philadelphia, Keith Hernandez took to whispering in writers' ears.

"Bobby Valentine," he would say, and then wander off, winking, grinning a rakish grin.

Earlier in the year, Davey Johnson had made Keith Hernandez the first captain of the Mets. Now Johnson's job was in trouble and Hernandez figured it was time to start looking ahead. Hey, it was all part of being a good wheel man. He wasn't saying he wanted Johnson fired. Far from it. He liked Johnson, and liked playing for him. Besides, it wasn't his style, picking a fight. . . .

He was nominating somebody in case Davey Johnson couldn't serve anymore.

So he whispered, "Valentine."

Bobby Valentine was the ex–third base coach for the Mets who had gone on to become the dynamic young manager of the Texas Rangers, but who made no secrets about his New York ties. Valentine's wife was the daughter of ex-Dodger pitcher Ralph Branca. Valentine owned restaurants in Stamford, Connecticut.

"If Davey's not coming back," The Prince whispered, "start writing up Bobby in the papers."

It had come to that for the 1987 Mets. Forty-eight weeks from the seventh game against the Red Sox, it looked like the manager might not make it. The Mets were legally dead on September 11, soon as Pendleton's home run got over the wall in center. They would never recover. Starting with the Pendleton game, the Mets would have a record of 12-11 down the stretch. Win one, lose one, win one, lose one. The defending champions, missing only Ron Darling—they even had Ojeda back—stumbled toward the finish line like drunks. It was as if the combination of real injuries and the ones inflicted by all the fussing and feuding off the record and through the newspapers had robbed them of the heart that had made them so great in October the year before.

Now maybe the manager was dead, too.

On September 26, Joseph Durso, the veteran Mets writer for *The New York Times,* had broken the story that Davey Johnson wanted an extension of his contract, and that Frank Cashen had turned him down. Johnson denied the story.

Cashen believed it.

Cashen kept saying "no comment," but privately he was incensed that the story would break during a divisional race. Observers of the team were not so much incensed as amused, wondering what Johnson's reaction would have been if one of his whipping boys—Darryl, say —had been the subject of a *New York Times* story about a contract extension.

Cashen felt that Johnson had been doing so much talking about wanting an extension, to friends and other managers, that it was inevitable the issue would be raised in some newspaper. Cashen's information had Johnson telling Tommy Lasorda of the Dodgers he wanted an extension; to Cashen's mind, it was the same as calling the Associated Press, since Lasorda not only had one of the biggest mouths in baseball, but one of the biggest mouths in the history of professional sports. Cashen felt that Johnson was singing a show tune he had sung before:

Tell me you love me.

And, while you're at it, give me more money.

Cashen called the episode "unconscionable."

The Johnson version of the story: There was a late-August meeting with Cashen. The topic of 1989 came up casually. Johnson expected Cashen to say, "What's on your mind for the future? You've got one more year left on your contract. What would you like to do within the organization?"

Instead, according to Johnson, Cashen said stiffly, "I'm not extending your contract, Davey."

That would be the version to which Johnson would stick from the time Durso's story broke until the end of the season. He was, he said, stunned by Cashen's reaction. Stunned again by Durso's story, which, according to Johnson, never accurately represented the conversation.

"I'll take a lie detector test," Johnson said at lunch in Philadelphia to Klapisch and Verducci.

Once the *Times* story broke, Johnson issued denial upon denial. Cashen issued one "no comment" after another.

Privately, Johnson said he would never forgive Cashen for letting him—Johnson's words—"twist in the wind." He said he had never been able to read Cashen, that it was impossible to have "heart-to-heart" talks with Cashen, and that he would "never work for the man again." The Mets were still mathematically alive when Johnson made the last statement, trying to get into St. Louis for the last three games with a chance.

Johnson: "If we somehow win the World Series, I might just quit."

That was his side.

Here was the Mets' side:

The previous October, within weeks of the Mets winning the World Series, Johnson invoked, publicly, a clause in his contract that said he would make as much money as Yankees manager Lou Piniella. It was not a great sum of money, and Cashen was not all that reluctant to part with it, but he fumed that Johnson would make an issue of it in the glow of his, Cashen's, greatest baseball triumph: the rebuilding of the Mets that had culminated with the championship.

There was a meeting.

Cashen told Johnson at the time, "I'm giving you this money, but that's the last I ever want to hear about this contract. I mean it. You and I will not discuss money for the length of this contract. Do you understand?"

Johnson: "Yes."

Cashen: "Fine."

Later, Cashen would say of Johnson, "He is more obsessed by money than anything else in his life." But after the October '86 meeting, Cashen considered the issue resolved. Cashen's story was that he remembered and Johnson forgot, and that when Johnson indeed broached the subject of his contract in August of '87, that is when Cashen said, "Davey, we had this conversation already. You know my position. There won't be an extension, a raise, or any more talk about it."

Johnson said Cashen's reaction stunned him. Cashen was stunned that Johnson could forget the admonition of general manager to manager, in quite specific terms, the previous October. Cashen understood Johnson's insecurities but still he was angry that Johnson, after what everyone in New York deemed an ordinary season in the dugout, would even want to talk about money. Cashen had begun to wonder where the Mets fit into Johnson's priorities, how important it was to Davey Johnson to be a baseball manager. Cashen, too, had read and heard about the celebrity fishing camp, and Davey's passion for real estate and business in general.

Finally, on October 1 in St. Louis, Cashen and Johnson met at the Mets' downtown hotel, the Marriott. Later, it was announced that Johnson would manage the team in 1988, then become a superscout within the organization.

Cashen said that's the way Davey wanted it.

Johnson sort of nodded, like he was playing Charlie McCarthy to Cashen's Edgar Bergen.

It was generally agreed that both men were full of shit, that Cashen was firing Johnson but, for some reason, giving him a year to clear out his office.

(By spring training, 1988, there had been another little twist in the Cashen–Johnson soap opera. On the day the Mets pitchers and catchers reported to Port St. Lucie, Cashen up and announced that how long Davey wanted to manage the Mets would be up to him after the '88 season. Johnson said, "No comment." And it was generally agreed that both men were *still* full of shit. Cashen was giving Johnson one more chance to prove he wanted to be manager first and mogul second. The noose was still around Johnson's neck, just a little looser than the previous October. If the manager won, and kept his mouth shut, he could keep his job. Any deviation and he wasn't going to be a superscout in 1989, just gone.)

So there was that bullshit from Cashen and Johnson in St. Louis as the 1987 season ended. The Mets, from top to bottom, were being the Mets. Once the announcement about Johnson's future was made, the players lined up in the clubhouse and saluted Davey Johnson.

They did it in true Mets fashion, like they were singing a college song.

More bullshit.

Bullshit so thick it started to choke everybody.

Strawberry: "No way Davey deserves to be fired. Look at the job he's done for four years. It's not his fault we didn't win. I hope Frank can change Davey's mind about coming back [after 1988]. I want Davey to manage here for a long time. You bring in a new guy, he'll try to change the rules. He won't be able to handle us. That could destroy the club."

That was in October. In January, after hitting in the indoor batting cage in right field, Strawberry would say, "Nobody could figure out some of the stuff Davey was doing all season. We could never figure out why this guy was playing, why this pitcher was coming out and why that pitcher was staying in. We just used to watch Davey and shake our heads. He'd talk about strategy and double switches, and we wouldn't know what the hell he was talking about. We're hoping that Mel (Stottlemyre, the Mets pitching coach) will make a lot more decisions in '88, because *Mel* knows the staff better than anyone."

Strawberry also said, "Man, I wonder all the time how many games this team would win if Whitey were managing it."

Bobby Ojeda was a Met who defended Johnson honestly, talking about how much the Mets could get away with under Johnson, how open his door actually was.

Then, in the visitors clubhouse at Busch Stadium, Ojeda uttered the most honest assessment of the 1987 New York Mets season:

"Players here say things no one would dare say in other cities."

Well, goddamn. At least one Met finally cracked the case.

The series with the Cardinals, the one to which the Mets had pointed across the summer, became meaningless thanks to the managing of Johnson and the pitching of Jesse Orosco.

In the last game of the Mets–Phillies series in Philadelphia, the 159th game of the season, Gooden pitched for the Mets. He had a rocky start, giving up three runs early, but then found dazzling '85 form the rest of the way. In the eighth and ninth innings, he struck out five of the six Phillies batters he faced. In the ninth, he struck out the heart of the Phillies order, Mike Schmidt included. Schmidt described Gooden as being "unhittable" later. Gooden said, "It was my best fastball of the year." Probably in two years. The Cardinals were losing to the Expos in St. Louis. The Mets would have still been two and a half games behind, with the Cardinals having one more game against the Expos before the Mets go to St. Louis.

If the Cardinals won the game against the Expos the next night, they would have had a three-game lead with three to play, meaning the Mets would have to sweep the series to tie the Cardinals for the National League East, then win a one-game playoff.

But they would have had a chance, anyway.

They lost to the Phillies in the tenth.

Gooden didn't lose.

Johnson and Orosco, the playoff and World Series hero whose record would go to 3–9 on this night, did.

For some inexplicable reason, Johnson pinch hit for Gooden in the top of the tenth inning. He did not pinch hit Babe Ruth. He pinch hit Billy Almon, the thirty-four-year-old utility infielder who was hitting .230 for the season. He pinch hit Billy Almon with two out, nobody on. Almon made an out, Orosco came on for the bottom of the tenth, a little-known Phillies shortstop named Luis Aguayo hit a game-winning home run, probably the longest home run of Aguayo's life, and the Cardinals could eliminate the Mets the next night against the Expos, which they did. It was the fourth game-winning home run Orosco had given up in 1987, a huge number for a star reliever.

Worse, it was the twenty-second time the defending baseball champions of the world had been beaten in the other team's last at-bat.

In his office after the Aguayo home run, Johnson offered prattle but not one excuse that made any sense.

"I didn't want to Tommy Lasorda him (Gooden)," he said. Lasorda, in Johnson's opinion, tried to get too many innings out of his starting pitchers as he tried to compensate for a Dodgers bull pen that had been weak for years. "I didn't want to ask Dwight to pitch to the end, win or

lose. If I need him again Sunday in St. Louis, it wouldn't be fair
to ask him to throw a hundred and forty or hundred and fifty
pitches."

Gooden was furious, saying he didn't even watch the tenth inning
from the dugout. "How could he have been thinking about Sunday
when we have to win today?" Gooden said.

All that was left was for the Mets to fly to St. Louis, sit in the
press box on Thursday night, and watch the Cardinals wrap up the
division by beating the Expos. Across the '87 season, the Cardinals
had had their injuries too, to ace pitcher John Tudor, and Danny
Cox, another frontline starter, and catcher Tony Peña, and Tom
Herr, and Jack Clark. Shortstop Ozzie Smith had played most of the
season with a sore shoulder, but continued to be the sport's Fred
Astaire at shortstop. But the Cardinals endured. The Cardinals had
Herzog. The Cardinals had this idea to fight everybody else, instead
of each other.

The Cardinals had heart.

By the eighth inning of the Cardinals–Expos game, only three Mets—
Hernandez, Carter, Dykstra—remained in the Busch press box, as the
sellout crowd waited to explode in celebration by taunting Hernandez,
the ex-Cardinal who became a villain in St. Louis after admitting to his
cocaine problems.

The Prince of Darkness, who had been drinking beers throughout
the game, waved to the crowd.

"These people hate me," he said. "I know it. But so what? The
Cardinals deserve to be congratulated."

Hernandez was asked about his own season. He had finished
with a .290 batting average, 18 home runs (career high), and 89
RBI. It was the second consecutive season that Hernandez, hitting
No. 3 every day, had failed to reach 90 RBI. He had only reached
100 RBI once in his major league career. His one significant
streak of the season—22 RBI in 23 games between August 11 and
September 5—had saved The Prince from having an embarrassingly
low RBI count for the "wheel man" in Davey Johnson's scheme of
things.

The Prince didn't see his season as being soft, but then he wouldn't
have been expected to.

"It was an A-minus until three weeks ago," Hernandez said. "Now it's a B-plus." As the Mets were stumbling down the stretch, winning one then losing one, Hernandez had been able to produce only 8 hits in 54 at-bats.

As the crowd shouted abuse at him in the press box, Hernandez said, "As a team, we have nothing to be ashamed of."

Not as a team. Only individual Mets. Howard Johnson, who never did stop being the slugging surprise of baseball, finished with 36 home runs, 32 stolen bases, 99 RBI. McReynolds, who had been brought over from the Padres to hit 30 home runs and knock in 100, nearly did both; he had 29 home runs, 95 RBI. McReynolds, a taciturn man from Arkansas, was practically an alien in the Mets clubhouse. Not only did he keep quiet about his teammates, he kept quiet about everything. McReynolds saved most of his emotion for the afternoon card games.

Strawberry? He became a star, one of the most charismatic hitters in baseball, once he moved to the cleanup spot. He ended up with 39 home runs, 104 RBI, a .284 batting average, 36 stolen bases. The man who was supposed to be trouble, the one who was supposed to end up traded or something, became the best player on the team, the true wheel man of the New York Mets. Strawberry showed that he was the only Met capable of carrying the team offensively. Carter couldn't do it, Hernandez certainly couldn't do it, neither McReynolds nor Howard Johnson were expected to do it. At the age of twenty-five, Strawberry finished his fifth major league season with 147 home runs. In all likelihood, if he stayed healthy and serious, he would have 300 by the time he was thirty, a prodigious number. He never got fined again after Chicago. He never uttered a discouraging word about his teammates. He reconciled with wife Lisa on the Mets' second West Coast trip, at the end of August. He seemed, at the end of the '87 season, on the verge of being an irresistible New York star: great name, great stroke, big mouth, good looks.

"Next year," Strawberry promised, "all performance, no bullshit."

Gooden ended up 15–7, with a 3.21 earned run average, 148 strikeouts in 180 innings. Darling scratched back to a 12–8 record, same as Sid Fernandez. Aguilera was 11–3. David Cone was 5–6, but had an ERA of just 3.71. At the end of the 1986 season, the Mets were generally conceded to have the best young arms in baseball, even after the events of the intervening twelve months. Even Ojeda got into a handful of games, and seemed completely recovered from his surgery. Only Orosco had been a true failure. He would be traded to the Dodgers during baseball's winter meetings in December.

The Squidge, Leach, finished at 11–1.

And the Mets finished with a 92–70 record, three games behind the Cardinals.

Sixteen games behind the 1986 Mets.

"We gave it our best shot," Keith Hernandez said.

With that last little piece of bullshit, The Prince got up to leave the press box at Busch Stadium. The Cardinals–Expos game was over now. The celebration had begun outside. The streets around Busch were immediately choked with cars and fans and noise. A group of police officers led Gary Carter, Len Dykstra, and Hernandez out of Busch, through the crowd, across the street to the Mets hotel. There were three games left for the 1987 Mets.

No one cared.

THE YANKEES

APRIL/MAY/JUNE:
"DOES HE DO IT TO YOUR FACE . . . ?"

GEORGE (jorj), *v.*, GEORGED, GEORGING. 1: *To insult, verbally abuse, taunt members of the New York Yankees in the newspapers.* 2: *To threaten with demotion to the minor leagues, usually Columbus of the International League; or threaten with trade to another major league team.* 3: *To actually bully Yankees to the point where they are unable to perform at previous levels of baseball skill, specifically, levels exhibited before becoming Yankees.* USAGE: *Exclusively relating to the principal owner of the Yankees, George Steinbrenner; i.e., to be* Georged *by Mr. Steinbrenner.*

The Brewers had a fast start. The Blue Jays looked to be as solid a team, top to bottom, as there was in the American League. The Tigers, after May 11, began to turn their season around.

The Yankees—manager and players—weren't losing sleep over the Brewers, or Blue Jays, or Tigers.

See, across the first half of the 1987 season, the Yankees seemed to have a team that couldn't be Georged.

The Yankees understood that if you could somehow beat your own boss, keep him out of your face, the rest of the American League East was like sitting on the living room floor, playing with Lincoln Logs.

You knew you were going to be Georged if you played for the Yankees. Some handled it better than others. Reggie Jackson, when he was in his prime with the Yankees, was immune to being Georged, even though Steinbrenner kept trying; no matter how many times Steinbrenner spit at Reggie and Reggie spit back, Reggie always seemed to hit balls into the parking lot. The late Thurman Munson used to bitch when he'd get Georged, but he mostly played through it, because Munson, even when he was acting like the orneriest sonofabitch in history with the writers, was one of the great Yankees, a catcher never really replaced after his death (piloting his own plane) in 1979.

Graig Nettles, the former Yankee third baseman, had his own methods for dealing with Georging. Nettles, the owner of a devilish, cutting wit, used to deflect Georging with humor.

One time Nettles said, "There's two things George doesn't know anything about: Baseball and weight control."

Another time, Steinbrenner had insulted Nettles because of *Nettles's* weight. One night after a game at Yankee Stadium, Nettles came out of the shower and found Steinbrenner entertaining a crowd of reporters in front of Nettles's locker.

Nettles poked his head over the crowd, looked at Steinbrenner sitting there on his stool, said, "You know, Steinbrenner's right. Nettles *is* too fat," wandered off.

If Steinbrenner yelled at Lou Piniella, Piniella would yell right back. More than one time in Piniella's playing days, his teammates heard Piniella snap, "Well, fuck *you*" into the clubhouse phone, slam it down. Piniella's teammates knew it wasn't *The Sporting News* calling about Piniella's subscription.

And there were a few selected Yankees who never got Georged. Ron Guidry never got Georged. Willie Randolph never did, either. Catfish Hunter avoided it, and so, for the most part, did Goose Gossage in his Yankee days.

But they were the exceptions.

Dave Winfield had been intermittently Georged ever since he batted just .045 (one hit in 22 at-bats) in the 1981 World Series. Dave Righetti—the Yankees' star reliever, successor to Gossage, and the man who had broken the all-time record for saves during the 1986 season— got Georged all the time.

In the middle of the 1986 season, the season during which he would break that record for saves, Righetti picked up the papers one day and found the Yankees' principal owner saying, "Righetti is *killing* us."

Righetti was having the sort of slump all relievers have from time to time.

Wasn't allowed.

Righetti got Georged, but good.

No one knew who brought the verb to the Yankee clubhouse, made it part of the club's oral tradition; it was probably Nettles. It might have been Reggie. There was a period when the Yankees referred to the results of being Georged as "Soderholm's Disease." Eric Soderholm was a pleasant man brought over to the Yankees in 1980 to be a part-time DH; the Yankees thought he could give them some pop from the right side of the plate. Soderholm managed to hit .287 in 1980, but his teammates, across the season, saw him wilt under the pressures of being Georged, or waiting to be Georged when he had a hitless game, or left runners on base in crucial situations.

Hence, Soderholm's Disease.

In 1981, the Yankees roster featured a utility infielder named Larry Milbourne. There was a game against the Indians early in the '81 season, and Milbourne made two errors, and the Yankees lost. Milbourne, new to the team, was perfectly aware that Yankees were likely as not to be Georged after such a performance. Bucky Dent and Nettles found Milbourne after the game, sitting in front of his locker, engaging in a rambling stream-of-consciousness monologue. It didn't seem to matter to Milbourne whether he had an audience or not. He just kept talking.

"What's it gonna be like?" Milbourne said. "Does he do it to your face? Do I have to wait until the papers to read what he's gonna say about me? Is there a chance he wasn't watching the game?"

On and on.

Dent and Nettles listened to Larry Milbourne, as though they were doctors making rounds. Then, as if on cue, they turned to each other, nodded gravely, said at the same moment, "Soderholm's Disease."

There were other demanding owners in sports. None of them, not one, was as demanding as Steinbrenner. There were others who went to the papers with criticism. They didn't do it with the alarming frequency. Steinbrenner did. Steinbrenner wouldn't even bother to pick up the phone sometimes, or dictate a release to the Yankee public relations man (of the moment). He would wander into the press box and begin insulting his own players.

That was how Winfield became Mr. May during a Yankees–Blue Jays game in 1985.

Once you took George Steinbrenner's money, you opened yourself up to the Georging. It was part of the deal. There was a lot of money. You wore pinstripes at home. You played the home games at Yankee Stadium, the most famous sports arena in the United States. You had access to the endorsement potential of New York City, the media center of the frigging world.

And you knew that you would get punished, publicly and relentlessly and in the most common sort of language, for failures, great and small.

You would get your ass Georged.

Sometimes with a red-hot poker.

The Yankees of 1977 and 1978, world champion Yankees, had enough tough guys who ultimately didn't give a shit about getting Georged. But the makeup of the team had dramatically changed over the years. Munson had died. Reggie had left to free agency. So had Gossage. Nettles had gone to San Diego, then Atlanta. Piniella had become a coach, then the manager.

Problem? The Yankees were still a team of stars, but now the stars were gentlemen instead of SOBs.

Mr. Mattingly.

Mr. Winfield.

Mr. Righetti.

Sure, Steinbrenner would George them. But they really wouldn't respond. They didn't relish the fight the way Reggie had; didn't relish finding the proper comeback, the way Nettles had. Winfield had signed a ten-year, $25 million contract with the Yankees in 1980; mostly his answer to being Georged was to say, "I'm not going anywhere, so Mr. Steinbrenner better get used to me, or he's going to be upsetting himself all the way into 1990." And Winfield never relished the infighting the way Reggie did; Reggie used to bitch and whine about Steinbrenner all the time, but the truth was, Reggie *loved* it, because Reggie loved seeing his name in the paper the way Steinbrenner loved seeing his name in the paper.

Righetti, a sensitive man, would occasionally indulge himself in a media outburst when he thought Steinbrenner went too far with him, but mostly he just took the Georging and burned inside. Righetti loved New York, loved being a Yankee, and would pay any pound of flesh, or ton of flesh, Steinbrenner demanded.

Mattingly took some newspaper abuse, but rarely; Mattingly knew Steinbrenner would never go too far with *him*, because Mattingly was the new Lou Gehrig at first base, the most beloved Yankee since Mickey Mantle, and one who carried himself with the quiet, off-field grace of DiMaggio. Mattingly was a taciturn Hoosier. He wasn't built for pissing contests.

Winfield. Righetti. Mattingly. None of them had the pit bull personalities that had distinguished the old Yankees. The personality of the team had changed, and maybe it was a coincidence and maybe it wasn't, but the Yankees had not won a world championship since Munson died, Reggie and Nettles and the others left.

The superstars were a lot nicer in the middle 1980s; you couldn't find three nicer men in sports than Winfield and Righetti and Mattingly.

It's just that the Yankees didn't win.

And the longer the Yankees went without winning, the more Steinbrenner kept Georging them. And people began to wonder if the Georging wasn't wearing the Yankees down, each and every season, to the point where the Yankees always died in the end.

Death, by George.

Until, it seemed, the 1987 season.

There seemed to be lots of reasons why 1987 was different, as April became May and May became June. Winfield, for the first time since the 1981 World Series, didn't seem to be Steinbrenner's favorite whipping post anymore. Mattingly had won nearly $2 million from the Yankees in an off-season arbitration hearing, and Steinbrenner had gone on television and into the newspapers to say that it was now Mattingly's responsibility to lead the Yankees to the division title, the pennant, the World Series.

(It was a ludicrous argument. The arbitrator had simply decided Mattingly's proper worth. But Steinbrenner lit into Mattingly anyway, even announcing to the world that Mattingly couldn't play "Jack Armstrong" anymore, as if Mattingly had robbed Steinbrenner, somehow, of not only the $2 million, but also a color TV and VCR.)

Righetti, it seemed, had finally proved to Steinbrenner in 1986 that he was one of the premier relievers in the game.

Rickey Henderson got off to a wonderful start in the leadoff position, hitting home runs, stealing bases, causing a commotion on the bases, being called the best leadoff man in history and perhaps the No. 1 all-around star in the game.

Willie Randolph, one of the Yankees co-captains (along with Ron Guidry), got off the best start of *his* career, hitting the ball harder than he ever had from the No. 2 position, knocking in more runs than he ever had; by June, Randolph was on a pace to have 100 RBI.

Only Mattingly started slowly. He was hitting just .239 on May 9. But then Mattingly began to raise his average, home runs, RBI from that point on, and just went back to being Mattingly.

The stars at the top of the lineup were backed up by tough veteran journeymen named Gary Ward and Claudell Washington. Washington, in particular, seemed a perfect addition to the chemistry of the Yankee clubhouse. He had played on a world championship team with the Oakland A's; he had worked for Charles O. Finley, Steinbrenner's obvious role model in running a ball club; he was full of sass and wit. It was Washington, in spring training, who had made the theme of the 1987 Yankees, "The Quest for the Ninety G's."

Washington was talking about the $90,000 he figured the winning team would get for winning the World Series. Whenever a Yankee would make a mistake on the field, or cost the team a run, or leave runners in scoring position, Washington would joke in the dugout, "Don't fuck with my money, boys." Washington kept the Yankees loose, became the flip side to the Georging.

If the Yankees heard one refrain again and again in the spring of '87, it was that sassy one from Claudell: "Don't fuck with my money, boys."

The Brewers began the season 13–0, but the Yankees never believed the Brewers were going to win the American League East. Steinbrenner did. Steinbrenner is always looking for hobgoblins, demons, ghosts, and teams other than his own who were somehow more capable of winning the American League East. There was the time early in the 1987 season when Steinbrenner stormed through the Yankee offices, saying that the Brewers "are running away with the damn division."

His office employees just looked at him.

"I told Lou (Piniella) we had to get off to a good start," Steinbrenner said. "I told him how important that was going to be."

The Yankees had played nine games at that point.

They were in second place, three and a half games behind the Brewers.

Six of the nine Yankee games had been played on the road.

But the players knew that Piniella, perhaps Steinbrenner's favorite Yankee during his playing days, was acting as a buffer, at least early in the season. So did the Yankee coaches. Piniella was keeping as much of the Georging off the players as possible. The players knew. They knew from hints Piniella would drop, or things the writers told them, or things the coaches told them. They knew Piniella could count on late-night or early-morning phone calls if the Yankees lost. They knew how fast Steinbrenner was to second-guess the most insignificant tactical error on the part of his manager. Piniella, Steinbrenner's pet, was finding out that things changed when you became Yankee manager.

Nobody gets Georged like a Yankee manager gets Georged.

"I was a Yankee player, I was a Yankee coach, I was a scout, I was general manager," Gene Michael, then manager of the Chicago Cubs, said. "The only time I had a real problem with George was when I was manager."

But Piniella took the phone calls, took them every time the Yankees lost, kept Steinbrenner off his players, waited for the Brewers to come crashing back to earth, and saw the Yankees go into first place on May 14.

Piniella figured if he could keep Steinbrenner off the players, he would take his chances with the AL East. It is a funny way to look at a baseball season.

But then, these were Steinbrenner's Yankees.

In a city of stars—Mattingly, Winfield, Gooden, Strawberry, Carter, Hernandez—the most electrifying across the first quarter of the season was Rickey Henderson, the twenty-eight-year-old outfielder who had come over to the Yankees two years before from Oakland. By 1987, he'd had two roller-coaster seasons for the Yankees—big starts, slow finishes (.262 batting average as a Yankee after July 1)—and he seemed to wear down because of the way he threw himself into each game, each trip around the bases. But Henderson, without doing a lot of talking, had become, in the spring of '87, the most theatrical Yankee since Reggie.

Henderson strutted down to first after a pitcher walked him. He swaggered around the bases after home runs. Without ever saying a word, he taunted opposing pitchers with his leads off the bases, glared them into balks and wild pitches and lousy control; glared them to distraction just by being over there on first. In the outfield, he made a catch he called The Snatch: Henderson used his glove, but the motion he made evoked a man trying to catch flies with his bare hand; when the ball was safely in the glove, Henderson would whirl the glove behind his back.

He seemed to have a lot of Reggie's act.

Just not his rap.

"Well," Don Mattingly said on the afternoon of May 14, "Rickey's got the rap, he just chooses not to use it." Then Mattingly—who in a players' poll conducted by *The New York Times* has been called baseball's top player—said, "When Rickey's going, we're going. It's as simple as that." Mattingly made his remarks on what had been a routine day for Henderson: He led off the Yankee first with his eighth home run (the fourth time in 34 games he'd done it; every time he did, the Yankees won). He would end up scoring three runs against the Texas Rangers, getting hit by a pitch, stealing a base, jumping over the wall in left to take a home run away from Texas's Larry Parrish. It was a familiar Henderson show involving speed, strength, extraordinary athletic skill. The Yankees won 9–1, moved the season's record to 22–12, one of the best Yankee starts in thirty years. Mattingly had broken out of a slump with a grand slam—the first of his career (and, as it turned out, the first of six he would hit in '87)—but the day belonged to Henderson, the way a lot of them had in April and May.

"If I was a fan, and I knew Rickey was coming to town," Willie Randolph said, "I'd get *excited*. You just never know with him. Is he gonna hit a home run five hundred feet? Is he gonna steal three bases? I just don't know, he should be a lot bigger around here than he is."

Randolph, like a lot of Henderson's Yankee teammates, thought one of the reasons Henderson wasn't a bigger celebrity in New York—lots of athletes are New York stars, not all of them are *celebs,* there's a world of difference—was because of the color of Henderson's skin. I said to Randolph, "You think it's because Rickey's black?" And he said, "What do you think?"

In New York, it has been historically more useful to be a white star than a black star; the opportunities for endorsements and commercials and billboards and all the rest that comes with being a celeb are more readily available to you. With the Mets, Gary Carter and Ron Darling were infinitely more appealing to Madison Avenue than Darryl Strawberry and Dwight Gooden, even before Gooden's difficulty getting the passing grade on the urine test.

This sort of racism is not specific to New York, or baseball; it is part of professional sports now. There was just more conversation about it around the Yankees early in 1987 because Henderson was having such an electrifying start, the Yankees were in first place, the Mets were in trouble, and Henderson still wasn't the toast of the town. A lot of people thought it was a combination of the normal racism of sports, and perception—the way players were presented to the world in the newspapers. Henderson had the image of being cocky. Lenny Dykstra, the white center fielder for the Mets, strutted and swaggered just as much at Shea Stadium as Henderson did at Yankee Stadium. But Dykstra, who had traded mightily on the Mets' World Series championship during the off-season, had a reputation as being tough.

Henderson was a hot dog.

Dykstra was his nickname: "Nails."

It was a subtle distinction, but a distinction nonetheless. Henderson, the black man, was cocky.

Dykstra, the white man, was tough.

Henderson had an image problem, Dykstra didn't. That day at Yankee Stadium, the crowd kept cheering after Mattingly's grand slam, wanting Mattingly to come out and take a curtain call. Mattingly, a shy man who thinks curtain calls are silly displays, didn't want to go. Henderson, laughing, ran up the dugout steps, waved, got Mattingly's cheer.

In the clubhouse, Willie Randolph said, "It's the only way Rickey can get one."

And there was more than racism going on. Henderson simply refused to sell himself to the writers; he simply was not one of the kings of clubhouse schmooze. He would not, or could not, make himself available to writers before games. Rickey had his own way of doing things, and his reluctance to promote himself in any way just seemed to fit into the tapestry of being Rickey. He was a game player. He did not enjoy the running and drills of spring training; did not like rules of any kind; he would hide in a corner of the dugout in Fort Lauderdale when the Yankees ran laps early in spring training, then jump out when Piniella and the coaches weren't looking, join his mates for the final lap. He did not like getting to the ball park any earlier than he had to; it was obvious to teammates and writers covering the team that he had terrible work habits. The slightest injury sent him to the bench; it was a problem that would become more and more acute for Henderson, and his team, and his image, and Yankee fans.

And there was "Don't need no press now, man."

The writers had never forgotten those first words Henderson spoke in the Yankee clubhouse, in April of 1985. Henderson had injured an ankle in Florida, had needed extra time to recuperate, and the regular season had started without him. When he did show up, the writers were waiting for him.

Henderson shooed them away from his locker, saying, "Don't need no press now, man."

He hadn't gotten a lot of press since. He would hit a hot streak, and there would be a rush of Rickey features in the newspapers, but generally he took a back seat to the other baseball stars of a baseball-rich time in New York. Without much visible anxiety Henderson would say, when asked why he wasn't a bigger name in New York, "I'm sharing the limelight with some of the biggest players in the game." He would leave it at that.

His black teammates, they had more to say.

One day a writer said to Dave Winfield, "Why isn't Rickey bigger around here than he is?"

And Winfield, voice dripping sarcasm, said, "You mean like I am?"

Claudell Washington was more vocal and belligerent about the issue, especially at the end of May, when Dennis Rodman and Isiah Thomas of the Detroit Pistons would create a national sensation with some remarks about Larry Bird, and the fact that he might not be as big a star as he was if he wasn't white. Thomas, when given the chance to explain himself by columnist Ira Berkow in the *Times,* said "Magic (Johnson) and Michael Jordan and me, we're playing on God-given talent, like we're animals, lions and tigers who run wild in the jungle, while Larry's success is due to intelligence and hard work."

Washington, dressing in the Yankee clubhouse before a home game, said, "Don't get me started."

He started anyway.

Washington: "You think Rickey Henderson doesn't understand what we're talking about with this whole black–white deal? You think he doesn't know? That man Rickey is a legend. He should be on every billboard in town, on every commercial. Rickey Henderson is the best."

Henderson didn't get any commercials with his great start in April and May, into June. He just kept hitting the ball over the fence, grabbing balls back from over the fence, getting on base, running, and the Yankees kept winning while they waited for Mattingly to get hot.

Rickey Henderson pulled his right hamstring on June 4, during a Yankees–Brewers game in Milwaukee.

The same night, Don Mattingly hurt his back.

The original story was that Mattingly hurt his lower back bending for a ground ball during infield practice before a game the Yankees lost, 9–3.

Then came the story, never substantiated, that Mattingly had hurt his back during a clubhouse wrestling match with pitcher Bob Shirley. MATTINGLY MYSTERY was the back-page headline for the *New York Post.*

The Yankees were still in first place. But now they had trouble for the first time all season. Henderson was hurt. And Mattingly was hurt. The injury to Mattingly was more surprising. The innings he missed on June 4 were the first innings he had missed since August of 1986 (Mattingly, in fact, had missed just six innings total during the '86 season). Mattingly flew back to New York, tests were taken, it was discovered he had a slight disc problem, a problem more painful than career-threatening, and the only thing the doctors could recommend was rest. Rest, then stretching exercises.

Perhaps somewhere other than New York, and with an owner other than George Steinbrenner, that would have been the end of the story:

Man hurts back.

Man has tests taken.

Man gets better.

Man rejoins team.

But these were the Yankees and George was George, so all of a sudden, the whole thing became, well, Backscam.

Steinbrenner puffed out his chest, said he was going to conduct an investigation, find out whether Mattingly was telling the truth about how he hurt his back.

The players heard—and this was never substantiated either, no matter how firmly the players believed it—that Steinbrenner was having the Yankee coaches take lie detector tests as a way of finding out whether there was a cover-up about Mattingly and Shirley. And Steinbrenner was quoted in the papers as saying he was going to have a meeting with Don Mattingly, look him in the eye, make sure Mattingly wasn't covering up for Shirley, either. Like it was *The Caine Mutiny Court-Martial.*

"You hear anything about lie detector tests?" Claudell Washington asked me, a week after the Mattingly injury.

"Lie detector tests?"

"I heard some of the coaches had to take them about whether Mattingly was fucking around with Shirley."

"No kidding?"

"No kidding."

The coaches, as fearful of Steinbrenner as anyone else in the man's employ, said, Lie detectors? Us? Haw, haw, haw. And since the writers couldn't give lie detector tests *about* the lie detector tests, that was the end of that.

Except that Bob Shirley, with a record of 1–0 and an ERA of 4.50 and no saves, was put on waivers June 5.

The waivers were for the purpose of giving Shirley his unconditional release from Steinbrenner's Yankees.

Henderson was hurt (he would miss 22 games), Mattingly was hurt (he would miss 18 games), and the Yankees stayed in first place and kept winning anyway.

The reason was David Winfield.

Mr. May kicked some ass in June.

The man who had been Georged more than any Yankee of the Steinbrenner era, the man who had become, for Steinbrenner, the symbol of all the Yankee failures of the 1980s, took over the leadership of the Yankee offense to the point where even Steinbrenner himself said, "He's making a lie out of everything I ever said about him."

It was a Reverse George.

An Un-George, something like that.

Steinbrenner would rather eat cat food than his own words, but Winfield made him do it, June 1987.

Winfield's performance in June may have been a surprise to Steinbrenner, but not to real students of the game. Nowhere was Winfield described better than in *The 1987 Elias Baseball Analyst,* the Bible of baseball statistics written by Seymour Siwoff, Steve Hirdt, and Peter Hirdt:

> Despite fourteen outstanding seasons, the last six under the scrutiny of the New York media microscope, Winfield still lacks the general acceptance that most great players have received in the late stages of their careers. Everywhere they go, Pete Rose, Reggie Jackson, and Tom Seaver hear only applause from fans who treat them like grandfathers in need of tender loving care. Winfield's ears ring with boos, even at Yankee Stadium. Winfield has vocal detractors among fans, writers, and his team's own calm, dispassionate owner. Perhaps because of his enormous contract . . . or his futile performance in the 1981 World Series . . . Winfield has become that rarest of baseball commodities: A superstar disrespected in his own home town.

He was all of that. Steinbrenner, through his public flogging of Winfield over the years, had painted Winfield as a loser. It was bullshit, of course. It was the Georging that had kept the Yankees out of the World Series after 1981. It was Georging, and mediocre starting pitching, and the usual chaos about the manager's job, and the fact that at least one team was better than the Yankees every season. But George himself, incapable of ever admitting that he was wrong about anything, blamed Winfield. Winfield, entering the 1987 season, was the only major league hitter to have five consecutive seasons over 100 RBI. He was trying to become the first Yankee since Joe DiMaggio to have six consecutive 100-RBI seasons. He was perhaps the singular right fielder of his generation, providing breathtaking plays at the outfield wall time and again, using all of his six-foot-six height and grace and a wondrous jumping ability remembered from his basketball days at the University of Minnesota.

But Steinbrenner made him out to be Mr. May, in his relentless way, and eventually turned a significant number of Yankee fans against Winfield.

Except now it was June, and Winfield was keeping the Yankees in the race. Between June 5 and June 23, with Henderson and Mattingly both out of the lineup, Winfield hit .355 with 4 home runs, 6 doubles, 15 RBI, and the Yankees, who had fallen to second place a few days after the two injuries, were able to stay in second, not lose sight of the Toronto Blue Jays. The Yankees had taken first from the Brewers, and the Blue Jays took first from the Yankees, but because of Winfield's bat, the Yankees never fell more than three games behind.

Winfield, a striking man because of the combination of size and looks and baritone, responded to his own heroics as he usually did, wit fronting for ego.

"You saw it, boys," he would joke with the writers. "Write it. I'm the best."

Privately, he was enjoying the season. For the first time in years, he felt free to just play his game. Steinbrenner had given Mattingly some Winfield-type abuse for the first time in Mattingly's career, really, and if Winfield felt anything about that, it was relief. Winfield felt that he had never gotten the respect he deserved in New York, and not just because of Steinbrenner, because he was competing for the affections of the fans with Mattingly. White superstar. It was why Winfield thought it so ironic that everybody suddenly thought Henderson was the victim of racism.

Winfield thought: *Now* everybody wants to wake up, smell the coffee?

One June day, Winfield sat in front of his locker, talking about the dynamics of the Yankee team. Because of Henderson's fast start—before the hamstring injury—there had been a lot of conversation around New York about which player you'd rather have to start a team, Henderson or Mattingly.

Winfield didn't want to be included in the debate. He would be thirty-six years old by the end of the season, and you didn't build ball clubs around thirty-six-year-old ballplayers. But he found it amusing, he said, when people put Mattingly in Henderson's class, or Dave Winfield's class, as a baseball player.

"Donnie's the best hitter, no question," Winfield said. "But I have to laugh when people talk about him as an all-around *ballplayer*. I mean, to be all-around, you've got to be able to hit, hit for power, field your position, and run. Donnie can do all of them, except run. *I* do all of them. And Rickey does all of them. But it's never quite enough." Winfield had never forgotten the end of the 1984 season, when he and Mattingly had chased the American League batting championship like two great racehorses in the stretch. Mattingly finally won on the last day of the season. Winfield felt that Mattingly had been the favorite with Yankee fans because he was white, had left the ball park that October afternoon without sharing his insights on the race for the batting championship.

But this was another season, and Winfield had quietly become part of the core of veteran leaders on the Yankees, a core of leaders that seemed to make this Yankee team tougher than the others of the 1980s, immune to the Georging. Piniella was juggling his shabby pitching staff and the Yankees, no matter what the injuries, kept taking punches.

On June 26, Friday night at Yankee Stadium, the Yankees fell behind Roger Clemens and the Boston Red Sox, 9–0. Clemens had started the season late because of a protracted contract negotiation with the Red Sox, but he was still, along with Jack Morris, the pitching class of the league. Clemens would end up with seven shutouts for the 1987 season, and his second consecutive Cy Young Award.

Except he couldn't hold 9–0 against the Yankees. Winfield hit a three-run homer in the third inning, and before the inning was over, the Yankees had 11 runs.

The game ended Yankees 12, Red Sox 11.

Three nights later, the Yankees went to Toronto, and now first place was on the line. The Yankees went out to an 8–3 lead. But then the Blue Jays were ahead 14–11 in the eighth inning.

The Yankees came back to win, 15–14.

The Yankees won the game, on June 29, on a grand slam home run in the eighth inning by Dave Winfield, Mr. May.

You want to talk about omens in baseball? How about coming back from 9–love to Roger Clemens, then taking first place *at Toronto* with a grand slam home run? Forget about it, these were the kinds of games you talked about in October. The Mets were having all those bad omens, with doves and all the rest of it?

Winfield hand-carried the Yankees to first place with two extra special good omens.

The Yankees would stay in first place until August 7, through the 109th game of the 1987 season. They would lose a game to the Tigers on August 7, fall back to second. But then Tommy John shut the Tigers out on August 8, Saturday, and the Yankees were back in first place with a 66–45 record.

It was then that, well, you never saw such Georging. . . .

JULY/AUGUST/SEPTEMBER: "THE MAN IS IN TOWN . . ."

The Tigers had charged into the race, joining the Yankees and the Blue Jays.

Rickey Henderson's hamstring wasn't getting better, was starting to look so serious people were wondering if anybody ever got *cancer* of the hamstring.

Winfield stopped hitting.

Gary Ward, first-half RBI star (61), stopped hitting.

Charles Hudson, the early-season starting pitcher phenom, stopped getting people out and ended up in Columbus, then the bull pen.

Willie Randolph had to have surgery on his knee. Randolph played in the All-Star Game because it meant a lot to him, being picked to start, and then he went away.

Steinbrenner made a trade for this left-handed pitcher from the Cubs, guy named Steve Trout, then Steinbrenner called up Lou Piniella and said, "I just won you the division," except there was this problem, and the problem was that Trout put on a Yankee uniform and came down with a case of Soderholm's Disease so bad he couldn't find the strike zone if he ran down from the mound and *placed* the frigging ball in the catcher's mitt.

More?

Steinbrenner was in a frenzy, making deals, sending players to Columbus, calling players up from Columbus, having players checking in and checking out almost daily, trying to make up for Henderson's hammy (Henderson called his hamstring "my hammy," like it was his pet hamster). And then there was Randolph's knee and this dismal pitching staff he'd given Piniella to work with, and injuries to a lot of his bit players, guys in the chorus.

It was amusing, unless you were a Yankee. Steinbrenner liked to accuse his players of choking, but the truth of the matter was, when the race got tight, it was Steinbrenner's balls that ached the most.

From the *1987 New York Yankees Post-Season Guide,* pages 28 and 29, from the section headed "1987 New York Yankees Regular Season Transactions":

July   ... Bobby Meacham placed on 15-day disabled list with sprained
             right ankle.
             Jeff Moronko purchased from Columbus.
        ... Rich Bordi outrighted to Columbus.
             Charles Hudson recalled from Columbus.
        ... Ron Kittle placed on 15-day disabled list with inflamed neck
             musculature (retroactive to July 6).
             Henry Cotto purchased from Columbus.
             Lenn Sakaka transferred to 21-day disabled list.
        ... Bob Tewksbury optioned to Columbus.
             Pete Filson recalled from Columbus.
        ... Bob Tewksbury, Rich Schied, and Dean Wilkins traded to
             Chicago Cubs in exchange for Steve Trout and an undisclosed
             amount of cash.

. . . Jeff Moronko optioned to Columbus.

Willie Randolph placed on 21-day disabled list with torn cartilage in his left knee.

. . . Jeff Moronko recalled from Columbus.

Pete Filson optioned to Columbus.

Rich Bordi purchased from Columbus.

. . . Willie Randolph underwent successful arthroscopic surgery to repair torn cartilage in left knee.

Cecilio Guante placed on 21-day disabled list with strained right shoulder.

Bobby Meacham activated from 15-day disabled list.

. . . Dennis Rasmussen optioned to Columbus.

Dan Pasqua recalled from Columbus.

. . . Jeff Moronko optioned to Columbus.

Juan Bonilla purchased from Columbus.

. . . Rich Bordi outrighted to Columbus.

Brad Arnsberg recalled from Columbus.

. . . Ron Kittle assigned to Columbus for injury rehabilitation.

. . . Paul Zuvella outrighted to Columbus.

Roberto Kelly recalled from Columbus.

Aug.   . . . Rickey Henderson placed on 15-day disabled list with sore right hamstring.

Dennis Rasmussen recalled from Columbus.

. . . Pat Clements optioned to Columbus.

Al Holland purchased from Columbus.

. . . Joel Skinner purchased from Columbus.

Pat Clements recalled from Columbus.

Mark Salas optioned to Columbus.

Al Holland placed on 30-day special disabled list with ligament damage of left elbow.

. . . Willie Randolph activated from 21-day disabled list.

Roberto Kelly optioned to Columbus.

Ron Kittle again assigned to Columbus for injury rehabilitation.

. . . Ron Kittle activated from 15-day disabled list.

Henry Cotto outrighted to Columbus.

. . . Al Holland underwent surgical procedure to repair torn ligaments and muscles in left elbow; placed on 60-day emergency disabled list.

Lenn Sakata assigned to Columbus for injury rehabilitation.

... Wayne Tolleson placed on 15-day disabled list (retroactive
to August 19) with a sore right shoulder.
Randy Velarde purchased from Columbus.
... Dennis Rasmussen traded to Cincinnati Reds in exchange for
Bill Gullickson.
Jerry Royster obtained from Chicago White Sox along with
Mike Soper in exchange for minor league pitcher, Ken Patter-
son, and a minor league player to be named later.
... Juan Bonilla optioned to Columbus.
Brad Arnsberg placed on the 15-day disabled list with strained
right elbow.
Mark Salas recalled from Columbus.
... Randy Velarde optioned to Prince-William.
Pete Filson recalled from Columbus.

And as all this was going on, with bit players coming and going and
No. 1 in the batting order, Henderson, nursing that hammy and No. 2,
Randolph, trying to hurry back from knee surgery, and the pitching
going all to hell, it still looked like the Yankees were going to survive.

Mattingly was hitting.

On July 8, against the Twins, Don Mattingly hit two home runs, one
off Mike Smithson, a three-run homer, another off Juan Berenguer, a
solo homer, no one on base.

On July 9, he hit a solo home run off Richard Dotson of the White
Sox.

On July 10, he hit a grand slam off Joel McKeon of the White Sox.

On July 11, he hit a solo homer off Jose DeLeon of the White Sox.

Home runs in four consecutive games. Plenty of guys had done that.
It wasn't as if the baseball world was being set on its ear.

Call me when he gets to seven straight games, okay?

On July 12, Mattingly hit another solo job against Jim Winn of the
White Sox. The season was interrupted for the All-Star Game. When
the season resumed, Mattingly kept hitting home runs. On July 16, in
Texas, Mattingly hit two more: *another* grand slam, off knuckleballer
Charlie Hough, and a two-run shot off Mitch Williams. The next night,
Mattingly had a solo homer off Paul Kilgus.

Home runs in seven straight games.

Now people had noticed, because the major league record for home runs in consecutive games was eight, set by Dale Long of the Pittsburgh Pirates in 1956.

Mattingly tied Dale Long on a Saturday night in Arlington, Texas, with a fourth-inning solo home run off a pitcher named José Guzman.

At the age of twenty-six, Mattingly had already had three marvelous years at the plate (1984: .343 batting average [batting champion], 207 hits, 44 doubles, 23 home runs, 110 RBI. In 1985: .324 batting average, 48 doubles, 35 home runs, 145 RBI. In 1986: .352 batting average, 53 doubles, 31 home runs, 113 RBI). He had been known as a singles hitter when he first came up to the Yankees, then a singles/doubles hitter. But then there had been 66 home runs the previous two seasons, and now people were wondering if there was anything Mattingly couldn't do at the plate, any numbers out of his reach. He seemed to be the only active hitter thinking about accomplishing an extraordinary double: 4,000 hits (only Pete Rose and Ty Cobb had done that) and 2,000 RBI (Babe Ruth, Hank Aaron). He had a funny-looking, peekaboo batting stance that reminded people of Stan Musial. And Dave Winfield was right, he sure wasn't a sprinter. And Mattingly seemed to play smaller than six feet, 175 pounds; looked to be too much of a runt to hit as many home runs as he did.

Mattingly is modest, polite to a fault, reluctant to sing his own praises, a tireless worker, inspiration to his teammates because of the work habits, and a mad scientist on the subject of hitting a baseball. Even if Mattingly got two hits the night before, or three, or four, he was out the next afternoon at four o'clock, three and a half hours before the next game, setting baseballs on a tee about waist-high, digging in, talking to himself, checking hands and stance, knocking the ball off the tee and into the net in front of him, doing this a hundred times or more, the way he had been doing it since Evansville Memorial High School.

"He is," Lou Piniella said, "obsessed with hitting a baseball. He was obsessed in the minor leagues, and I assume he was obsessed in high school, and American Legion ball."

Here was Mattingly himself, speaking in his Texas hotel room before the seventh game of his streak:

"I missed three weeks [with the bad back]. So my numbers for the season really aren't where they oughta be. But I don't worry about stuff like that. I don't think that way. I *can't* think that way. I try not to put any limitations on what I can do. Why would you want to do that? Why limit yourself? I don't think in terms of streaks. I don't look back,

I really don't. I don't want to talk about what I did last Saturday, because that doesn't help me tonight. I only care about tonight. Or *today,* man. That's the whole deal.

"I want to help this team every day. I can't be worrying about what's already past. I'm gonna help the Yankees win tonight. I'm gonna hit it hard tonight. How can I do that? Who's pitching? I just worry about a one-game streak, then a one-game streak, then another one-game streak. I don't think about being hot for six or seven days. I just want to be hot *tonight.*

"With the home run thing, well, you know I haven't been trying to hit them. Not once. You don't try to take Charlie Hough deep, for example. It's just the same old story for me. One at-bat after another. Take 'em one at a time. Knock in some runs. Try to get us a lead. Get up again, try to knock in more."

Mattingly did not hit a home run in the game of July 19, a game the Yankees lost by the embarrassing score of 20–3. (By the end, the game was such a rout that Piniella sent in a catcher, Rick Cerone, to pitch the last inning, rather than waste another relief pitcher.) Mattingly, in fact, had felt something grab in his right wrist on his last at-bat the previous night, against a Texas pitcher named Mitch Williams. He would say later that it was the type of thing he felt several times a year, had never kept him out of the lineup. Plus, he was going for the record. So he played Sunday night in Texas. And Monday night against the Twins in Minneapolis. Mattingly set no home run records against the Twins, but tied a fielding record instead, making 22 putouts in one game as Yankee starter Tommy John recorded ground ball out after ground ball out.

The Yankees won the game, 7–1. The team's record was 58–36, and the team's lead in the American League East was three games. Mattingly's wrist still hurt. He had his wrist X-rayed. The injury was diagnosed as a slight sprain. No problem. Piniella rested him in the Tuesday night game against the Twins, said he would rest him again Wednesday, but that Mattingly would probably be ready for the weekend series against the White Sox in Chicago.

Even after the Tuesday night loss in the Metrodome, the Yankees were still three games ahead in the American League East.

But George Steinbrenner was in town.

And George, he was worried about the Tigers now (even if he hadn't been worried a bit back in December, when he had the chance to sign Jack Morris, take him away from the Tigers), and the divisional race in general—even if it had nearly seventy games to go—was already making his balls ache as if they were in a vise.

After the 2–1 loss, Steinbrenner stood outside the door to Piniella's office, arms folded, staring at the Yankee players as they showered and dressed. Sometimes he would pace in front of Piniella's office door, situated next to the trainer's room in the visiting clubhouse. Then he would go back to glaring.

"The Man is in town," Claudell Washington whispered to Michael Kay of the *New York Post*. "Now you know why it seems like death in here."

Remember: It was July 21. The Yankees had just completed their ninety-fifth game of the season, out of 162. They had been in first place for nearly a month. Piniella had done wonders with his pitching staff, holding it together around one ace starter, Rick Rhoden, one forty-four-year-old man (John), and Righetti. Henderson had come back from the disabled list, but he was just another player, still favoring his hammy, a .250 hitter afraid to run all-out. Randolph was recovering from the arthroscopic surgery. They had lost, 2–1, but Mattingly had been on the bench. Winfield, who had played all thirteen innings of the All-Star Game, looked to be swinging the most tired bat in baseball all of a sudden. Ward's bat wasn't so perky, either.

But the Yankees were ... in ... first ... place.

And ... got ... Georged ... anyway.

Steinbrenner was treating the ninety-fifth game like it was No. 162, or the last game of the American League Championship Series, or the deciding game of a World Series, if he could remember what the hell *that* was like.

Every few minutes in the visiting clubhouse, Steinbrenner would dispatch an aide to make a call, get a Tigers score and a Blue Jays score.

The aide would come back with the scores, tell Steinbrenner, Steinbrenner would nod grimly.

The Blue Jays were in the process of losing to the Texas Rangers. They would stay three games behind the Yankees.

The Tigers were playing the Oakland A's, a game the Tigers would eventually win, 6–5, in ten innings.

The Tigers would move into a second-place tie with the Blue Jays. Three games behind.

"I was worried about this," Steinbrenner snapped when he found out the Tigers had won. "I've been watching the Tigers come on. I *knew* this was going to happen." The way he *knew* the Brewers were a lock to win back in April.

Then he stalked out of the visiting clubhouse in the Metrodome, owner with a first-place team who acted like all his ships had sunk. And no one knew it at the time, but one season, a ninety-five-game season, was ending for the Yankees, and another one was beginning.

It was Georging season.

Some things happened to Steinbrenner's Yankees over the next couple of weeks.

The small losing streak that began against the Twins would extend to four games. But the streak stopped with a victory that belonged in the omen class, right there with the June comebacks against the Red Sox and the Blue Jays. In the last game of the White Sox series, the Yankees held on to first place by coming back to win, 5–2, after being no-hit by Richard Dotson in the eighth inning.

That Saturday in Chicago, on NBC's *Game of the Week,* Steinbrenner spent some time in the broadcasting booth with Bob Costas and Tony Kubek, and stated at one point that the Yankees were spending too much time worrying about home run records. Since Mattingly was the only Yankee who had been involved in any home run records lately, it was obvious about whom the principal owner was speaking.

So Mattingly, who was back to getting base hits, even with the sore wrist, got Georged on national TV.

Behind the scenes, Steinbrenner was growing more and more impatient with Rickey Henderson's hamstring injury. There were, at the end of July, daily discussions between Steinbrenner and team doctor John Bonamo about the condition of Henderson's hammy.

Steinbrenner wanted to know if Henderson was 100 percent.

Bonamo told him no.

Steinbrenner wanted to go public, say that Henderson was fit enough to play, but wouldn't play, at which point Steinbrenner planned to suspend Henderson.

He wanted Bonamo to back him up.

Bonamo told him he didn't care to do that. Hamstring injuries are hard to verify.

Finally, on August 1, Henderson was put back on the disabled list, retroactive to July 26 (and maybe it was a coincidence, sports fans,

maybe it wasn't, but Dr. John Bonamo resigned as Yankee team doctor
after the season was over).

Then, on August fourth, at the Stouffer Inn on the Square, a Cleveland hotel, Lou Piniella wasn't in his room to take a phone call from
George Steinbrenner. And that—more than Henderson's hammy, Randolph's knee, Mattingly's wrist, or all the rag arms Piniella had on his
pitching staff—became the turning point for the '87 Yankees.

The Yankees had just taken two out of three games from the Tigers
at Yankee Stadium. They were still in first place. They went to Cleveland. Tom Candiotti, a knuckleball pitcher, shut the Yankees out, 2–0.
Mark Salas, a catcher picked up from the Twins earlier in the season,
had a passed ball in the game.

When the game was over, Steinbrenner sent word to Piniella that he
wanted Salas to come out the next afternoon, in full gear, to practice
catching.

He also sent word that Piniella was to be in his room the next
afternoon—before Salas's catching practice—to take a phone call from
Steinbrenner.

But Lou Piniella, on the third of August, 1987, was tired of being a
dog. Tired of being told to roll over, sit up, beg, every time Steinbrenner
said roll over, sit up, beg.

He was tired of answering the fucking phone.

So that afternoon in Cleveland, at the Stouffer Inn on the Square, the
phone kept ringing and ringing, and nobody answered it, because Lou
Piniella had gone out.

The next day, Piniella said he called Woody Woodward, the Yankees
general manager, to talk about Joel Skinner. Skinner was the Yankees'
best defensive catcher, but, alas, a man unable to hit even .200 in the big
leagues. Skinner had been demoted to Columbus on June 10, to work
on his hitting. But now Piniella didn't give a shit about his hitting, he
needed a catcher who could catch the ball. After the one passed ball in
the loss to Candiotti, Salas had had three more in a 15–3 loss.

Woodward (he would move on to the Phillies after the season) said,
"I'm not allowed to talk to you, Lou."

This was a manager calling a general manager about an important
roster move as the manager's team tried to stay in first place.

Piniella said, "Huh?"

And Woodward repeated that he was under instructions not to talk to
Lou Piniella. And that night Piniella told the writers that Woody
Woodward wasn't allowed to talk to him, and how, call him silly, but

he didn't think that was such hot communication with the front office in the middle of a divisional race, and he didn't know what the hell was happening with Rickey Henderson. The Yankees beat the Indians in the last game of the three-game series, 5–2.

Still in first, by half a game.

The next day, the New York newspapers included stories about Lou Piniella talking about lousy communication between him and the Yankees' front office.

The Yankees lost that night in Detroit, 12–5.

Still in first. Half a game.

The Yankees lost to the Tigers again the next night, dropped to second place for the first time since June 29.

The next morning, before another NBC *Game of the Week,* George Steinbrenner dictated the following statement through Yankees publicity man Harvey Greene:

Reacting calmly to what he termed "inaccurate newspaper reports aimed at creating sensationalism rather than reporting the facts," New York Yankees owner George M. Steinbrenner confirmed that he had not planned to talk with Yankee Manager Lou Piniella in the near future and that he did not forbid Yankee General Manager Woody Woodward to speak with Piniella except on the matter of bringing up a new catcher and then only until he personally had talked to Piniella himself.

"The fact is that Lou Piniella failed to be available to his boss at a preset time on Tuesday afternoon in Cleveland," said Steinbrenner. "The accurate facts are that Piniella was told by Harvey Greene that I would call him at two P.M. at the hotel and to be sure to be there at that time. If there was a problem, he should have contacted me. I told Greene I never heard from him, and that was not acceptable. I told Greene I didn't want to disturb him after Cleveland shut us out two-oh because I knew he would be upset—second, I had an early board meeting in Cleveland and I didn't want to bother him early in case he was sleeping in, so I could call him at two P.M., at which time the board meeting would be over. The simple fact is that Piniella didn't even bother to 'come back from lunch,' if that is where he really was, to get a call from his boss at two P.M. He didn't even bother to call me to get word to me that the time was inconvenient for him. I don't know of too many guys—even sportswriters—who if their boss told them to be available for a call at a certain time, wouldn't be there! That type of behavior I'm sure wouldn't be tolerated by any major newspaper, and it won't be tolerated by the Yankees, either! The facts are that Piniella was all for the Salas–(Joe) Niekro trade. I opposed it—but I let Woody and Lou make the deal. Just several months ago, Piniella told us that Skinner was not going to help us, that he couldn't get the job done—Salas was the left-handed bat we needed. Now all of a sudden, Skinner is the answer to our problems and that Salas is a 'bum.'

"In answer to Lou's request I told Woody to put the plan to bring Skinner up to full action. Everything was set, but I wanted a chance to talk with Lou briefly before the move was consummated. That was the purpose of the call. If Lou didn't have the intelligence to adhere to his boss's request and be present for the call, instead of just saying he was 'late getting back from lunch,' or whatever, I just assume it was not that important to him. It's as simple as that and it's not going to change.

"Now, as far as the Rickey Henderson matter is concerned, I was leaving that in the hands of our team doctor and trainer and general manager until Woody called and told me that Piniella wanted to disable Henderson right away because he was 'jaking it,' his teammates were mad at him and he (Piniella) wanted guys who wanted to play and he would win it all without Henderson. I told Woody to get me the doctor's report—that I wouldn't want to disable a man as punishment—and despite what Piniella thinks, I don't think we can win it all without Rickey Henderson. Woodward agreed on all counts. I said we should talk to Lou. We did, and Piniella told us he wanted Henderson traded as soon as possible. Both Woody and I agreed 'no way.' We told him we were going to be sure Rickey was okay and if not, then we were going to disable him. Woody said he would not affix his signature to any disabling papers as punishment. Dr. John Bonamo told us Thursday that Rickey might be ready for the weekend series in Detroit by Saturday or Sunday. Then on Saturday he reversed that completely and said Rickey's leg was sore with some swelling and told us the prognosis was not good. I went to the training room personally—told Rickey of our plans—patted him on the back and then told some writers that Rickey was indeed hurt, that he was not jaking it, and that we would disable him, but for the right reason. End of that chapter. That is the story, factual, and the only reason for the release is that some of you guys might get it straight for a change.

"As for me not talking to Piniella, that's pure horseshit—ask Woody. He didn't think it was important enough to talk to me because he couldn't get back from lunch in time or wherever—so what the hell is so important about me rushing to the phone to call him? Woody will get him the catcher he wants or the catcher he wanted shipped out because 'the kid can't help us,' and the left-handed hitter he wanted will take the first plane to Columbus or whenever Woody thinks it's time.

"*Me*—the manager says the manager 'doesn't need to talk to me.' A couple of the players think I should not get involved as much as I have been all year to this point—fine. That's okay with me. I've got enough other things to do. We'll just try it that way, and we'll see how well they do. They think they can do better that way, that's just fine. I'll keep the whole month of October open, anxiously awaiting the World Series at Yankee Stadium. They can put up or shut up. Maybe it's about time for it."

It was a landmark, even in the Georging category.

George Steinbrenner had suggested his manager was a liar, with the "lunch in time or wherever" business.

He quoted the manager as saying one of his catchers, Skinner, couldn't do the job and that another catcher, Salas, was a "bum."

He had Piniella accusing Henderson, one of his stars, of "jaking it," meaning dogging it, meaning not trying, one of the worst athletic slurs there is.

The rest of it needed a surgical team from the English department, but the message was quite clear: The noose was around Piniella's neck.

General tone of the statement, by George? The general tone was that the principal owner of the team didn't give a shit, one way or another, whether his manager brought the team home in first place.

Harvey Greene showed Piniella the statement before the game. Piniella decided the players wouldn't be told until after the game. Greene released the statement to the writers in the press box, and NBC released chunks of it over the air. Tommy John shut the Tigers out, 7–0. The Yankees went back into first place.

After the game, Steinbrenner's statement, typed on two long pieces of Yankee stationery, was given to Randolph and Guidry, the Yankee co-captains.

Then there was a crowd of Yankees, all reading the statement.

Then, in perhaps the most bizarre scene in the history of Steinbrenner's Yankees, half the players crowded into the trainer's room, visiting clubhouse, Tiger Stadium, and some of them held the papers and some of them passed the lit matches around, and the New York Yankees burned George Steinbrenner's statement.

It was like the murder scene in Agatha Christie's *Murder on the Orient Express*. They were *all* burning the statement.

They were all Georging the boss, on the last day they would spend in first place.

The Yankees' billboard slogan for the 1987 season was "The Yankees: Where Traditions Are Born." The next day, Gannett columnist Barry Stanton amended the slogan to "The Yankees: Where Traditions Are Burned."

That day, August 9, the Tigers beat the Yankees, 15–4, and the Yankees went to second place. The Yankees went to Kansas City, and lost three games; each night, the players waited for word that Piniella had been fired. They played baseball like a team on Death Row.

"A lot of things happened to us before that and after that," Lou Piniella confided to a friend. "But that statement took the heart out of my baseball team."

The second loss in the Royals series dropped the Yankees to third place, behind both the Tigers and the Blue Jays.

The Yankees would eventually drop to fourth place, seven games out of first, on September 12, when they lost to the Blue Jays, 13–1. Now the Yankees were back behind the Milwaukee Brewers, just where they were in April, after nine games, when Steinbrenner proclaimed that all was lost.

They would end up in fourth, with a record of 89–73, nine games behind the Tigers, Jack Morris's Tigers, who had been nearly twenty games better than Steinbrenner's Yankees after May 11.

After Steinbrenner's statement on August 8, the Yankees' record was 23 wins, 28 losses.

There was no September.

Death, by George. . . .

"BILLY WAS BORN TO MANAGE . . ."

The first manager of Steinbrenner's Yankees was Ralph Houk.

Houk was replaced in 1974 by Bill Virdon.

Virdon was fired during the 1975 season, replaced by Billy Martin, who had been fired from the Texas Rangers earlier in the season.

Under Martin, the Yankees won the American League pennant in 1976, and the World Series in 1977.

Martin was replaced in July of 1978 by Bob Lemon; the Yankees went on to win another world championship under Lemon.

Lemon was replaced by Martin during the 1979 season.

After the 1979 season, Martin was replaced by Dick Howser.

The Yankees won 103 games in 1980, won the American League East, but lost the American League Championship Series to the Kansas City Royals. So by the 1981 season, Howser was gone. The Yankees had two more managers in 1981, Gene Michael and Bob Lemon.

In 1982, the Yankees had three managers: Bob Lemon, Gene Michael, Clyde King.

Martin managed in 1983.

He was replaced after that season, and Yogi Berra became the manager for the 1984 season, and 16 games of the 1985 season.

At which point, Yogi Berra was replaced by Billy Martin.

On the afternoon of the seventh game of the 1985 World Series between the Kansas City Royals and the St. Louis Cardinals, Clyde King (who had gone from being manager to general manager) announced that Lou Piniella had succeeded Billy Martin as Yankee manager. When asked what role Martin (whose contract still had plenty of time to run, the contracts of Yankee managers always had plenty of time to run) now played in the Yankee organization, King said, "I have no idea." Martin, as it turned out, became part of the Yankees broadcasting team on WPIX, Channel 11.

Now, in October of '87, Piniella had been kicked upstairs, and Martin was back to manage the Yankees in what the New York tabloids simply referred to as "Billy V." The *New York Post* even ran a photograph in its October 20 editions showing Martin holding the *New York Post* (Front page: BILLY'S HOME! Back Page: BILLY'S BACK!) on the day when he was hired for Billy III back in 1983.

Martin had resigned under fire in 1978, after a speech at Chicago's O'Hare Airport, during which he said of Reggie Jackson and Steinbrenner, "one's a born liar, the other's convicted." Martin, with the convicted part, was referring to Steinbrenner's long-ago felony conviction for illegal contributions to Richard Nixon's 1972 reelection campaign. Billy was no Alistair Cooke, but this was a particularly clumsy verbal gambit. The mere newspaper mention of the felony was enough to send Steinbrenner into an office rage. For his manager to insult him publicly about it meant the manager had to go away, quite soon.

He did. Martin said he was resigning. Anyone who spoke English knew he had been fired.

But, well, stay tuned with the principal owner of the Yankees. Five days later, in Steinbrenner's favorite Barnum play as Yankee owner, Martin appeared at Oldtimers Day at Yankee Stadium, where it was announced he would be returning to manage the team in 1980.

Martin came back early. After the first 65 games of the 1979 season, the Yankees had a 34–31 record. Martin replaced Lemon. The Yankees finished fourth anyway, and Martin was accused of punching out a Minnesota marshmallow salesman in the off-season, and went away again. And kept going away and kept coming back, and giving Steinbrenner plenty of opportunities for Georging him, and providing Steinbrenner almost constant access to the back pages of the tabloids, especially the *Post,* which had become a shameless arm of Steinbrenner's public relations machine, celebrating his every belch and snort, even hiring him as a guest columnist during the 1986 World Series between the Mets and the Red Sox.

Steinbrenner believed you could never count on ballplayers. Billy, you could count on him. No matter what, Steinbrenner was mesmerized by Billy Martin, convinced he was the one manager who could get the most of any one Yankee team, and provide shitstorms like they were coming off an assembly line. Martin would feud with players. He would feud with writers.

And, with almost frightening regularity, Billy Martin would find difficulties in places where whiskey was served.

It didn't matter to Steinbrenner. "Billy was born to manage," he would say time and again. And between regimes, Steinbrenner would develop amnesia about Martin, and again begin to think of him as a combination of Miller Huggins, Joe McCarthy, Casey Stengel. He even put his plaque out there in the legends section of Yankee Stadium, with Ruth and Gehrig and DiMaggio and Mantle.

Martin had been dismissed from the Billy IV regime after the Yankees finished second to the Blue Jays in 1985. An ugly, late-September brawl with pitcher Ed Whitson at the Cross Keys Inn in Baltimore sealed his doom. The fight started in the Cross Keys bar, continued into the parking lot, and would have continued in the hall of the Cross Keys' third floor, where the Yankees were staying, if Whitson would have accepted Martin's screaming invitation to come out to fight some more. Martin was in his underwear by then, broken arm at his side.

Now ... Billy was back! Again! And his hiring, and the shifting of Piniella to the general manager's job, and the timing of the whole thing, was Steinbrenner at his Machiavellian best.

Or Rasputin-like worst.

It sort of depended on where you were sitting, actually.

"I will never work for that man again."
SPEAKER: Lou Piniella.
SUBJECT: George Steinbrenner.
(Who else?)

Lou Piniella said it over and over again during the last days of the 1987 regular season. He said it privately, both to beat writers he trusted and to friends, but he kept saying it: He would never work for the sonofabitch again. He told Bill Madden of the New York *Daily News* and he told Moss Klein of the Newark *Star-Ledger*.

It was generally acknowledged around the American League that Piniella had done a brilliant managerial job with the '87 Yankees, at least until Steinbrenner cut his legs off in August.

Henderson had played only 95 games, and had been a shell when he came back from the disabled list the last time.

Dan Pasqua, the young left-handed slugger who had excited Steinbrenner, Piniella, and everyone else with tape-measure home runs in spring training, batted just .233 with 17 home runs and 42 RBI, spent part of the season in Columbus, and was traded to the White Sox in November.

Rick Rhoden won 16 games, but ended the season with a sore shoulder. Tommy John won 13. Ron Guidry, whom Steinbrenner just had to sign instead of Jack Morris, won five games, and ended up with a bad shoulder. Dennis Rasmussen, the ace of the Yankee staff in 1986 with 18 wins, was traded to the Cincinnati Reds. The earned run average of the starters was 4.37 (fifth in the American League) and the earned run average of the relievers was 4.43 (ninth in the American League).

Trout, the man who was going to win Piniella the division?

His ERA was 6.60.

His record was 0–4.

He pitched 46.1 innings and gave up 51 hits and 36 runs and walked 37 men and had 9 wild pitches.

One wild pitch every five innings, if you're scoring at home.

In December, General Manager Piniella dispatched Trout to the Seattle Mariners. Seattle wasn't far enough away to suit Piniella, but was the best he could do.

Mattingly missed 21 games. Randolph missed 42 games. Winfield never really hit his way out of the post-All-Star-Game slump, and did not have his sixth consecutive 100 RBI season. Randolph, on his way to the best season of his career, missed a month because of the knee surgery. The catching was woeful all year long. The Yankees were painfully thin in the infield. Gary Ward had just 17 RBI after the All-Star Break.

The Yankees used more players, 48, than at any time in the history of either the New York Yankees or Steinbrenner's Yankees.

And as late as September 9, the Yankees were still only five games behind the Tigers and Blue Jays.

Wasn't worth a bag of balls.

Piniella was gone at around 2:05 P.M., August 4, when he wasn't there to take the phone call at the Stouffer Inn on the Square. Like Billy had been gone from the moment he said the f-word (felony) at O'Hare Airport in 1978. There was what was billed as a peace-pipe meeting between Steinbrenner and Piniella in September, at which time Piniella apologized, and the two men were supposed to have worked out their differences.

Once again: Wasn't worth shit.

Piniella was done. He had been Steinbrenner's favorite Yankee, he was from Tampa, Steinbrenner's adopted hometown, the two men had owned racehorses together, socialized together. As far back as the late 1970s, Reggie Jackson said Piniella was being groomed to be either president of the Yankees or manager, everyone on the team knew it. And it had finally happened. And Piniella had done fine with two Yankee teams not good enough to win. And had found out that managing the Yankees was managing in hell.

He was out of there. All during the month of September and into the first week of October, Lou Piniella bitched and bitched about how he had come to the end of the line with George Steinbrenner.

"George," he told Steinbrenner when the season was over, "I've only got a year to go on my contract. Fire me."

This was during the American League playoffs. Piniella and Steinbrenner met in Steinbrenner's office. Steinbrenner danced the way he had danced with Dick Moss and Jack Morris, said he didn't know what he was going to do about the manager's job. As much of a bully as Steinbrenner is from a safe distance, or through press releases, he can't load up and throw a punch to a man's face.

Piniella knew.

"George," he said. "Like I said, let me make it easy for you. Get rid of me. I can't manage for you, I realize that now. We've known each other for fifteen years. Our families know each other. Fire me as manager so we can go back to being friends."

Steinbrenner said he didn't know what he wanted to do.

Actually, he did.

He wanted to bring back Billy Martin. He had already met with Martin and his lawyer, Edward Sapir, the last weekend of September, at the Bay Harbor Inn. Bill Madden, a bulldog of a reporter who had been predicting all year that Martin would replace Piniella, broke the story. Steinbrenner called Madden, demanding to know how he found out. Madden said, None of your business, George. Steinbrenner denied that he was talking to Martin about Billy V.

"Billy and Eddie were just passing through town on their way to a golf tournament," Steinbrenner told Madden.

Madden said, yeah, he wanted to take that down to the bank before the tellers closed all the windows.

So Steinbrenner was getting ready to make the same old play with Billy. But he didn't know how to make the play without Yankee fans forming a lynch mob. As popular as Martin had been through all the shitstorms, the Steinbrenner-Martin act had become this tired, oft-told dirty joke. Steinbrenner-and-Martin jokes are what Liz-and-Dick jokes used to be.

There was that problem.

And that problem was all tied up with another one involving Lou Piniella:

Fans loved Lou.

Players loved him.

Media loved him.

How to get rid of Lou, get rolling with Billy V, and not look like, well, an All-American, born-on-the-Fourth-of-July (George was) jack-ass sonofabitch?

Then George had what passes for a brainstorm:

He would . . . keep them both!

He offered Piniella the job of general manager.

Piniella—"I'll never work for that man again"—took the job.

Steinbrenner didn't care about the media. Let those assholes say what they wanted, they were always after him anyway. There wasn't a Yankee fan living who was going to piss on George and Billy with Sweet Lou Piniella standing there in front of them.

Friends of Piniella were amazed. He tried to explain. He told them he simply wasn't going to quit, no matter how badly he had been Georged, that if he quit, he would blow his $300,000 salary for 1988. He had a son starting college at Villanova; the Piniella family lived in New Jersey, and he had urged his kid to stay close to home. There were no other managing jobs he felt were available to him. And he wasn't all that crazy about moving; he had been in the New York area for fifteen years.

He told Madden, a friend, "I know how bad I look, but it's something I feel like I have to do for my family." So he took the job, knowing he was a front man for Steinbrenner and Martin, knowing it looked to all the world as if he had sold out.

Piniella temporarily sold his good name—hell, his soul—for the $300,000, and immediately joined a television dog-and-pony show with Martin. As soon as the announcement was made, Steinbrenner ordered his PR man, Harvey Greene, to book Piniella and Martin on any show, local or national, he could; after a while, people in the metropolitan New York area expected Piniella and Martin to show up at supermarket openings.

On Wednesday, October 28, for example, Lou and Billy began the day in New York on WABC's *The Morning Show,* starring Regis Philbin and Kathie Lee Gifford, Frank Gifford's wife. The interview was about as hard-hitting as Bill Mazer's; if everybody had gotten any cozier, they would have had to be in their jammies.

Kathie Lee Gifford ended things by saying, "Can I ask one question before you go?"

Lou and Billy nodded. Sure, honey.

Kathie Lee Gifford said, "Why do ballplayers have to scratch and spit so much?"

Then Lou and Billy stopped at City Hall, where New York Mayor Ed Koch honored Baseball Commissioner Peter Ueberroth for baseball's antidrug campaign. It wasn't exactly a network shot, but there were television cameras present.

From there, Lou and Billy traveled to Madison Square Garden, where they appeared on the Madison Square Garden network's *Sportsnight* program.

By then, the Yankees' new general manager and the Yankees' new (again) manager had also appeared on *Good Morning America,* ESPN's *Sports Look,* Bill Mazer's show on Channel Five, WNBC's *Live at Five,* and the entire list of Sunday night sports anthology shows, ones that wrapped up the weekend's highlights. On each show, Piniella and Martin tried to appear closer than Robert and Elizabeth Dole.

If the 1987 season had begun, and perhaps ended, with Steinbrenner turning down Richard Moss and Jack Morris in December of 1986, the 1988 season was beginning, and perhaps ending, with the dog-and-pony show. There would be the Pasqua trade after that, bringing the Yankees a much-needed starter, Richard Dotson. The Yankees got rid of Trout, and picked up Mets shortstop Rafael Santana in another trade. The trade was effected at baseball's Winter Meetings, at Dallas's Loews Anatole Hotel, in December.

By then, things were settling into place. Piniella thought he had made a deal for A's shortstop Alfredo Griffin, but found out Steinbrenner had gone ahead and made the Pasqua deal himself. Piniella just shrugged and headed for the hospitality suite; hell, he had already stormed around the Yankee offices threatening to quit, and had already told friends he had no plans to sign the contract extension that supposedly came with the new job. He was already that fed up with Steinbrenner, after two months in the front office with him.

It was quite a surprise to his friends.

Billy V?

There was a bit of a storm cloud in Dallas.

Michael Kay of the *New York Post* is the one who spotted it. He came down to the Anatole lobby one morning about nine o'clock to buy a newspaper. And in one of the Anatole bars, he saw the manager of the New York Yankees, treating himself to the breakfast of champions.

Budweiser beers.

III

BASKETBALL

THE KNICKS

REVOLUTION COMES TO MADISON SQUARE

*I*f you're a performer, and your agent calls and tells you he's got it all locked up for you to sing the National Anthem before a Knicks game, a lot of thoughts go through your head. You know it's not a big deal—but then you also know you're not The Boss, filling the Meadowlands with eighty thousand plus. And you know you're not going to get rich—maybe a pair of freebies, maybe a little more.

But it's a job—and a singer's nothing without people to listen. And it's exposure; a lot of media people go to Knick games. Or used to.

The real reason you decide to sing, though, is because, if you're a performer, you know the legends. Lana Turner . . . Lana Turner sitting . . . sitting on a stool in a drug store . . . Schwab's drug store . . . Lana Turner just *sitting* there at the right time and before you know it, fame, fortune, and Johnny Stompanato were all hers.

Or Shirley the Gypsy. Understudying. And just like in the movies, the star gets sick. So Shirley goes on. And just like in the movies, a big Hollywood producer is in that matinee audience. And he offers her a shot. And she takes it. And thirty-five years after *The Pajama Game,* Shirley MacLaine is still a very famous lady.

So singing the "Star Spangled Banner" at Madison Square Garden before a New York Knickerbocker basketball game may not be a *big* deal. But it's still a deal.

And *ohhhh*, the possibilities.

So you relearn the words and maybe you take an extra voice lesson, and you try to figure what's best in the way of attire, and then the day comes, 7:35 arrives, you're announced as a "famous recording artist," which could mean you may once actually have been inside a studio, and you're on. Standing alone. Mid-court.

Oh, say can you see,
By the dawn's early light . . .

Not bad so far. Not the best you've ever sung, but now you're over your nerves, the fear of getting the words wrong, and you begin to relax.

What so proudly we hailed
At the twilight's last gleaming.
Whose broad stripes and bright stars,
Through the perilous—

"YOU SUCK."

You're standing there and suddenly you find yourself entering a nightmare. Did someone actually think you were so bad they shouted "You suck" in the middle of America's anthem? Could it be true? No. No. Maybe you're not great but you don't *suck*. Sure you've been in better voice but who anywhere does a decent job with this turkey of a song?

But what if that voice was right? What if you do suck? What kind of a future can you have when a stranger who didn't sound drunk could be such a quick and violent critic? Now—

"GO TO HELL."

A different voice. From a different part of the arena. High, high up, this one came from. And that's good and that's bad. Bad because who tells a stranger doing his best to "go to hell"? Good because at least, being high, high up, he can't physically assault you.

And the rocket's red—

"YOU STINK."

Not terrific, this new voice's sentiment, but not as bad maybe as "Go to hell" and a lot better than "You suck." *What's going on at the Garden?*

And finally, finally you understand, as the next malediction comes first from in front of you, then is picked up by another voice to the side. Then a third joins in, all of them going:

"FUCK YOU, HUBIE."

"FUCK YOU, YOU SONOFABITCH, HUBIE."

"HUBEEEE, FOKKKKKKKKKKK YOU!"

They weren't hating you—you can still be the next Sinatra. It was

Hubie Brown, the Knick's coach, they were addressing their sentiments toward.

And indeed they were. For the above is a not unreasonable Xerox of what it was like sitting there before a game near the end of Hubie's reign of error.

Hubie Brown gives great press, so for years he was able to fight clear of corners with his remarkable knowledge of basketball statistics. For if any of you have heard him on the networks, you know you are listening to no dummy.

Nor is he a terrible coach. He's just a terrible *professional* coach—I think he'd be sensational in college, where his teaming of knowledge and abuse would work for the four years of a scholarship.

To understand the dental-like pain of sitting through a Hubie Brown–coached team season after season, let me posit two questions:

1. Who would you rather have as your point guard, Magic or Isiah? Tough question, and there is no wrong answer. They are both among the greatest passers in history, Isiah is a better scorer, Magic has his size. My guess would be, because of the Lakers' success and exposure, if you asked a thousand people, Magic would win eight hundred votes.

2. Who would you rather have as your point guard, Magic Johnson or Rory Sparrow? (And no, this is not a shaggy dog story.) Obviously I can't be sure, but as long as I'm making up the poll, I'm going to make up the result. If you asked a thousand people, Magic would win, nine hundred and ninety-nine to one.

Well, Hubie Brown is that one.

Why? Because in the first place, Magic wouldn't take Hubie's shit, the constant insulting, the obvious contempt in which he holds his athletes. (They're all so stupid.) The real reason is this: Sparrow, an absolutely adequate guard, was willing to totally follow orders. To strip himself of creativity of any kind.

This is a totally creative game. If Hubie were casting *Hamlet,* he wouldn't want Olivier, no, give him Maria Ouspenskaya for the lead. She'd be grateful.

Hubie, you must understand, called the Knick plays. I suppose the standard memory of watching Hubie's Knicks would be when the Knicks would get a defensive rebound, kick it out to Sparrow on the break—

—only he wouldn't break. He'd slow, look over at the bench where Hubie would be standing—his right hand in a fist, or his arms crossed at the wrist—signaling the play.

Just like Tom Landry.

The Knick "play"—there was really only one and it consisted of dumping the ball into whichever big man near the basket seemed most open—worked okay when he had a truly great scorer like Bernard King to take the shot. But when Bernard went down, and the other scorers too, Hubie didn't change his system. Same old shitty play only now it was being executed by a CBA refugee.

Agony.

Masterson, my fellow masochist who I attend the games with, had been among the first to go mad. The year before, in a game against Cleveland, he suddenly started shrieking for them to beat us, humiliate us, stomp us mercilessly. "It just came over me," he remembers now, not smiling. "I didn't go to the game intending to root for the damn Cavaliers. But I realized if they destroyed us, and then if *everyone* destroyed us, maybe they'd do something about that asshole."

When the Knicks breezed to four wins in their first sixteen games with the media at last blessedly merciless, Gulf+Western circled the wagons, decided on decapitation: Hubie was gone.

Such joy.

He was replaced by Bob Hill, who did a decent enough job with what he inherited. For Hill was faced with this one weeny problem: Most of the players he inherited from Hubie were ploughhorses—and Hill wanted an up-tempo game, to pitch the shackles, to run. So Hubie was gone, and such wonderful riddance, but the Knicks were now bifurcated. (Just trying to keep you on your toes.)

The fans, thrilled with the enemy banished, began to realize that, banished or not, Hubie's presence was still felt. The Knicks were now just a different shade of horrendous.

March 17, 1987.

One of the great ones in the "World's Most Famous Arena." Patrick Ewing night. Ten thousand-plus fans were given posters of the Knicks' fine young center. *Biiiiig* posters. Patrick sized. Actually, the ten thousand strong were not fans at all; rather they were as revolution conscious as any Bastille stormer. And in the second half, they struck.

Ewing proved a perfect catalyst that night. In twenty-six minutes of play, he scored all of 11 points. Couple that with his 3 rebounds and you've got a genuine smeller on your hands.

In the second half, the attack came. (A Gulf + Western spokesperson said later that "Not *that* many posters were thrown.")

Knick fans simply went mad. And started hurling their Patrick Ewing posters onto the court. Others ran to courtside, threw, screamed, and ran back to their seats. One spectacular achievement was done by a fellow who ran to courtside and just stood there, past hope, ripping his poster to shreds.

Glory.

These tend to be good folk, Knick attendees. They don't drink much, know their game, punch-outs are rare.

But sometimes a man's gotta do what a man's gotta do.

Because Hubie had turned the Garden into a bomb shelter. He had made us cowards, expecting to be beaten. Our faces were haunted. We slipped surreptitiously into our seats as night fell. We sat until the carnage was complete. We had, at the end, no hope. Our job was to suffer.

To try and quell the poster attack, the Garden announcer asked people to refrain from throwing their posters because, so he said, "There are ten excellent athletes on the floor."

Alas, few of them in Knicks costumes.

So why do I go? If a deli opened near my apartment that had food that gave me heartburn, would I eat there forty-one times a year?

The Knicks give me heartburn.

If *Howard the Duck* was playing at my local movie theater, would I go and sit there forty-one times a year, knowing the thing turned me into a lesser human being?

I'm a lot lesser after Knick games.

I guess I go because I've been. And saw such wonders. Bradley running onto the court in the old Garden for his first pro game. DeBusschere in the fifth game of the first championship year, with Willis down, successfully guarding Chamberlain, looking all the while like a small, muscular child hiding behind a giant. I was there in the seventh game when Reed, shot so full of painkiller that if he'd been a horse he would have been disqualified, limped out onto the court while many in the crowd, at least the hard-bitten ones like myself, could not stop our tears. I was there for Frazier's steals, Barnett's fall-backs, The

Pearl's impossible spins into the paint. And some of those moments—especially Reed's—are among the greatest pleasures of my life and I know how ridiculous that sounds if you don't understand; I'm fifty-six, why should it still matter that Reed gimped us to the championship?

Of course there's no logic to passion. The Knicks owned my heart. It was once a blissful marriage; now it was filling with bile. Still I was hooked. Maybe it could be again what it was.

We needed a lot. Talented players wouldn't have hurt. Decent management could only be a plus. But of course the most immediate need was apparent: a coach who understood glory.

THE
REPORTER'S NOTEBOOK

"I WANT THEM TO BE WINNERS
AS SOON AS POSSIBLE. . . ."

$\mathbf{A}$h, glory. There was nothing definite yet, but Larry Brown was going to coach the New York Knicks, he just knew it in his bones.

Brown figured it was a natural. At the age of forty-seven, after a gypsy basketball life and a reputation for flying to more cities than United, Brown was ready to come home to New York. Everything about the move felt right. Or as right as anything feels to Larry Brown, who often is happiest when unhappy.

Brown was a New Yorker, born in Brooklyn, raised in Long Beach, a basketball gym rat who had used a General Organization (G.O.) card as a teenager, bought 60-cent tickets to basketball games, college and pro, at the old Madison Square Garden on 49th Street, and had come to think of the Garden as the only sports arena in the world worth talking about. To Brown, to *all* basketball dreamers of his generation, playing the Garden was the basketball equivalent of playing the Palace.

Brown left the New York area after high school. A New York basketball legend named Frank McGuire had recruited Brown for the University of North Carolina, at the time in the fifties when McGuire was raiding New York and Long Island for the best high school talent, bringing it down to Tobacco Road. But Larry Brown never forgot the view from the cheap seats at the old Garden, never stopped wondering what it would be like to work the sidelines.

Brown had a brief career as a player in the American Basketball Association, making stops with teams in North Carolina and New Orleans and Oakland; then he had coached in the ABA. He later coached Denver and New Jersey in the National Basketball Association. He had 448 pro wins and a lifetime winning percentage in the pros of .625. He had coached in college at UCLA, going to the NCAA finals his first season there. Now he was at Kansas, finishing the fourth year of a four-year contract, and he had also taken Kansas to college basketball's Final Four the season before. The stop at Kansas was the longest for Brown since Denver. He had left UCLA after two seasons to coach the New Jersey Nets, thinking East Rutherford, New Jersey, was the same as coming back to New York. It wasn't. Amid controversy and criticism he richly deserved, Brown bolted the Nets at the end of his second season—as the team was preparing for the playoffs—to take the Kansas job.

"I've made mistakes," Brown said at Kansas. "I've moved."

But the Kansas experience had been good for Brown. Better for Kansas. As he did with every job he took, Brown turned a faltering program around immediately, made the Jayhawks into a basketball power again, became the most popular sports figure in the state. Brown felt it was important to show not just the Kansas people, but everyone in the basketball world, that he could fulfill the requirements of a contract. He had. "I didn't say I was going to stay at Kansas forever," he said in New Orleans, where he was attending the coaches convention always held at the Final Four (national semifinals, then final). "But I told them I would give them four years, and I've given them four great years."

He had. Now his star player, forward Danny Manning, was a junior considering leaving school for the NBA draft. Manning—whose father, Ed, was one of Brown's assistant coaches—had made it clear that he would wait to see what Brown did. It had become public knowledge by the Final Four that the Knicks were interested in Brown.

Again: natural move. The Knicks were finishing out a 24–58 season, the end of three seasons during which they had lost more games (175) than any team in pro basketball. Most nights, the Garden was half full, if that, for Knicks games; fewer and fewer New Yorkers chose to make the trip to what was still billed as "the world's most famous arena," to watch the Knicks lie in state. In the late sixties and early seventies, the Knicks had been the most glamorous team in sports, had won two NBA championships, had become a big-city symbol of elegance and style; no New York team is remembered with quite the same romance, even today. A ticket to a Knicks game in those days was the toughest to find in New York. Now the Knicks had become a joke under the ownership of Gulf+Western. They were finishing out another disastrous season with interim coach Bob Hill, who had replaced Hubie Brown earlier in the season.

And the best news? The Knicks' general manager, Scotty Stirling, had a friendship with Larry Brown dating back to Oakland of the ABA. Stirling needed to bring in a dynamic coach who could turn the Knicks around, get them headed toward the playoffs, and old glory, at the same time.

Brown was his man. Stirling had made that quite clear. They had already talked a couple of times during the season. After Kansas was eliminated by Georgetown in the NCAA tournament, Stirling told Brown, "Don't do anything, *say* anything, until you hear from me. And for God's sake, don't sign a new contract at Kansas. We'll talk as soon as our season is over (April 18)."

By the time he got to New Orleans for the Final Four, Brown was already musing about possible trades for the Knicks, the kinds of players he wanted to bring in, wondering if he was ready to deal with the New York/New Jersey media, which had been a problem for him when he was with the Nets. Brown admitted readily that he was sensitive to the extreme, always had been, unable to deal properly with either negative press or the intense scrutiny to which the New York market submits its sports celebrities.

"It's a big thing for me," Brown was saying one morning during his daily one-hour walk (he was unable to run, even at the age of forty-seven, having undergone hip replacement surgery the previous summer). "I know I can coach. There's nobody better than me. I wouldn't say that publicly, but it's a fact. I don't worry about getting there, doing the job. That part excites me. It's just going to be dealing with the press again, certain guys. I haven't changed, and I know they haven't."

But the more he walked each day, the more Brown talked himself into the Knicks job. Three more weeks, and he would have made the trip, finally, a thirty-year trip, from the 60-cent seats at the old Garden to the Knicks bench at the new Garden, the one at Penn Station.

He just had to give reporters the dodge for three more weeks, wait for Scotty to call.

Scotty never called.

Scotty had reasons.

On April 20, two days after the NBA regular season ended, Richard Evans—president and CEO of the Madison Square Garden Corporation—fired Bob Hill as Knicks coach.

He also fired Scotty Stirling.

*   *   *

Larry Brown still figured he was a natural, even as Evans began seriously courting Providence College coach Rick Pitino (ex-Knicks assistant) almost as soon as Stirling and Hill had cleared out their desks.

"Let me ask you something," Brown said to a friend one day as a story headlined RICK'S THE PICK adorned the back page of the *New York Post.* "If that kid from Austin Peay makes the one-and-one, does Pitino even get offered the job?"

Brown knew before he asked the question that the answer was probably no.

Now back up:

Pitino, thirty-four years old, a basketball Sammy Glick from the East Side of Manhattan, was the current Hot Boy of college coaching. His unlikely Providence College team had made it to the Final Four before losing to Syracuse in the semifinals. Pitino had become coaching star and tragic hero all at the same time; his infant son, Daniel, died just before the NCAA tournament began. The child was six months old, and had spent very little time outside a hospital in his brief life. Pitino and his players banded together and made it all the way to New Orleans.

Had help, too.

The help came in Providence's second tournament game, Southeast Regional, Birmingham, Alabama. The score was Austin Peay 82, Providence 82. Two seconds left. An Austin Peay player, Bob Thomas, was fouled. He stepped to the foul line for a one-and-one. One-and-one simply meant this: If Bob Thomas made the first foul shot, made the score 83–82 in favor of his team, he got a second, and the chance to make it 84–82. If he missed the first (which meant no automatic second shot) and Providence got the rebound, Providence would have the chance to win the game with a desperation shot, at the very least send the game into overtime, maybe win there and advance in the NCAA tournament.

If Thomas made both foul shots, Austin Peay would lead by two points with two seconds left. Austin Peay almost certainly would win the game. Even if Thomas made only the first, it would take some kind of miracle shot from Providence in the last two seconds of the game.

So Providence wouldn't be the Cinderella story of March 1987. Providence would be out of the tournament.

And Rick Pitino wouldn't be the Hot Boy.

And Richard Evans wouldn't be cooing at him to become the new coach of the Knicks a few weeks later. Evans, who had come to his job as president and CEO of the Garden from Radio City Music Hall—*that* cradle of basketball minds—probably would not have known Rick Pitino's name.

If Bob Thomas of Austin Peay had made a free throw, Evans, of the Rockettes, frankly wouldn't have known Rick Pitino if Pitino had high-kicked his way into Evans's office like one of the girls in the line.

(Big decisions in sports are rarely made for the most sophisticated reasons.)

But Bob Thomas missed the front end of the one-and-one, clanged the ball so hard off the back rim that the rebound ended up fifteen feet away from the basket. The game went into overtime, Providence won, kept winning until it got to New Orleans. Pitino did, in fact, become the Hot Boy, pushed along by this wave of circumstance that carried him along, Evans along, the New York Knicks, and even Larry Brown.

What Pitino didn't become, at least in those first few days after the firing of Stirling and Hill, was the Knicks coach. Pitino, after meeting with Evans, flew to Phoenix to be interviewed for the coaching vacancy with the Phoenix Suns, and suddenly Richard Evans cooled on the Hot Boy.

Larry Brown was back in the game, that's the way it looked. Pitino had been to the Final Four once? Brown had been twice, with two different programs. Pitino had never been a head coach in the pros? Brown had won those 448 games.

Jack Diller, executive vice-president of the Garden and Evans's right-hand man, called Joe Glass, Brown's Long Island–based agent, and said that he, Diller, and Evans would like to meet Larry Brown.

"I made it clear that this wasn't going to be a case where they were interviewing Larry Brown," Glass said. "I told them Larry Brown was far too respected a coach to have to come in like an actor and read for the part. I told them I wasn't going to have Larry fly in from Lawrence, Kansas, if they weren't prepared to offer him the job once they got to know him, heard what he had to say. It wasn't going to be the type of thing where Larry came and read his resume."

Glass also told Diller about the time constraints on Brown. Danny Manning had two more weeks to decide whether he would file for entry into the NBA draft. If he went past the deadline, he would play his senior year at Kansas. If he filed, his college career was over. Manning would stay if Brown stayed, leave if Brown left. Manning needed a quick answer from Larry Brown and Larry Brown needed a quick answer from the Knicks.

Diller told Glass to tell Brown to come ahead.

Glass took it to mean that the Knicks were prepared to offer his man the job.

Diller would say, much later, "There was a misunderstanding. We weren't prepared to offer anyone the job at that point."

Evans, Diller, Glass, and Brown would meet at the Waldorf-Astoria Hotel on April 29. Brown took a TWA flight to LaGuardia Airport from Kansas City. Glass picked him up at the airport, they drove to the Waldorf, on 50th Street and Park Avenue. Glass and Brown went up to the room Diller had reserved. Knocked on the door. Knocked again. No answer. Evans and Diller hadn't arrived yet. Glass and Brown were about to return to the lobby, find someplace to have a cup of coffee, when Evans and Diller got out of the elevator, saw them standing there in the hall. The four men went into the room to talk about Larry Brown becoming coach of the Knicks.

Or so Glass and Brown thought.

For half a minute, according to Larry Brown.

"Thirty seconds," he said later. "After thirty seconds, it was apparent they weren't going to offer the job to me."

It was as if Brown were a consultant, brought in, at the Knicks' expense, to analyze the Knicks.

"What do you think of the team?" Evans asked.

Brown went through the Knicks players, from center Patrick Ewing to free agent Bernard King, the veteran forward who had played the last six games of the season for the Knicks after missing more than two seasons because of a devastating knee injury. Brown talked about the kids he would keep, the veterans he would release, players he had heard were available around the National Basketball Association.

Diller was on the telephone while this was going on.

Evans said, "What style of ball do you like to play?"

Brown, after 448 pro wins and coaching the Nets about seven miles away in New Jersey and two trips to the Final Four, thought to himself, Now *there* is an interesting question.

Brown told Evans anyway. About his passing offense, and theories about unselfishness, and how you had to adapt your system to your talent and not the other way around.

"It's a players' game," Brown told Richard Evans at the Waldorf-Astoria. "It's not supposed to be a coach's game."

Joe Glass sat there wanting to smoke a cigar, squirming and angry, knowing Brown's trip had been a waste of time. Glass, a father figure to Brown from the time Larry and his mother and brother had moved to Long Beach from Brooklyn, had just assumed that there would be an exchange of philosophies, then his man would be offered the job, wasn't that the point?

But only Larry Brown had brought a philosophy into the room, and neither Evans nor Diller, who got off the phone finally, had brought an offer.

Brown turned to Evans. "What do *you* think of the Knicks?"

Evans, from a show business background that included not only Radio City, but also Walt Disney Productions and Ringling Bros.–Barnum and Bailey Combined Shows, said, "I know that I want them to be winners as soon as possible."

Brown said, "That's what I do."

Joe Glass thought: They haven't done their homework. All they knew was a name, Larry Brown, they kept reading in the papers.

"Here's a guy that had won more games than anybody, that was supposed to be in contention for the job," Glass said later, "and they never really wanted to talk about the job."

At the Waldorf, Richard Evans said, "I want something to happen right away with this team. I don't expect the Knicks to win the championship next year, but I want a different atmosphere around this team, a completely different aura than what we've had the last few seasons. I want a winning climate established."

"I can do that," Larry Brown repeated politely. "I've done that wherever I've been."

There was more small talk from both sides. Evans and Diller thanked Brown for coming. On the way to the elevator, Glass told Brown what he had been thinking for the whole meeting.

"Waste of time," he said. "I don't know who they're after, but it's not us."

Larry Brown, from the cheap seats, said, "I had to come. I had to satisfy myself what it was like around here now, who these people are who're running the Knicks."

Brown went to the apartment of his wife, Barbara, who had been working in New York City for TWA, commuting when she could to

Lawrence, Kansas. (It was another reason why the Knicks job appealed to Brown: His wife's new career and the commute from New York to Kansas had put a strain on his marriage.) Glass went back to Long Island. He had told Evans and Diller that one way or another, Brown needed an answer by the following Friday, for Danny Manning's sake. The call didn't come. Manning decided to stay at Kansas. Glass called Jack Diller and said, "I don't know if you're still considering Larry Brown for the job, but if you are, forget it, he's not interested anymore."

Over two months later, on July 8, Evans hired Al Bianchi as the Knicks vice-president and general manager, ending the 79 days during which the Knicks were without both a general manager and a coach.

Bianchi, who had coached in the NBA in the 1960s and the ABA in the early 1970s, had been an assistant coach with the Phoenix Suns for the past twelve seasons. The most important part of the resume, as it turned out, was the ABA part. It was during his ABA years that he had struck up a friendship and developed an admiration for the coaching ability of Larry Brown.

Al Bianchi confided to friends that Larry Brown was his choice to coach the Knicks, even though Danny Manning was staying at Kansas and so, according to Larry Brown, was Larry Brown. Bianchi, like everyone else in basketball who knew Larry Brown, knew how much Brown wanted to coach the Knicks.

Bianchi called Brown and told him to keep quiet, stay by the phone, he might have something to tell him in a couple of days, sounding the same way Scotty Stirling had back in March.

And Al Bianchi was true to his word.

He called Brown back and told him Richard Evans, after waiting seventy-nine days to pick a new general manager, was picking the new coach himself.

It wasn't Larry Brown.

Rick was the pick. After all.

Rick Pitino. First coach Evans had interviewed in April. Same Hot Boy, still hot to Evans. Bianchi found out the day of his own press conference at Madison Square Garden. When the press conference was over, Bianchi was escorted by a Knicks employee to a waiting cab. Evans and Diller were already in it. Bianchi said, "Can someone tell me where we're going?"

They were going to Providence. The tide of circumstances that had begun with a missed free throw in Birmingham, Alabama, was carrying Evans, Diller, and Bianchi back to the Hot Boy.

"One missed free throw," Jim Valvano, the North Carolina State coach, said. "One missed free throw and Pitino became the greatest basketball mind of our time."

Valvano had been the Hot Boy once, back in 1983, when *his* Cinderella team had won the NCAA championship, not just made it to the Final Four. Valvano was another New York City product, raised under subway tracks in Corona, Queens, son of a famous New York high school basketball coach, Rocco Valvano. Valvano also wanted to be Knicks coach. He was also interviewed by Evans and Diller. He was also turned down.

But Valvano was right about the free throw that Bob Thomas missed in March. All it did was start to make the most important coaching decision in the history of the New York Knicks.

Guy clangs one off the back of the rim, and all of a sudden, he might as well be president and chief executive officer of the Madison Square Garden Corporation. . . .

A Fan's Notes

THE KNICKS HELD HOSTAGE

*A*s has been stated, the day after the Knick season ended, Richard Evans, the whiz of Radio City Music Hall who had failed sideways to become the president of Madison Square Garden, fired both the coach and the general manager.

The day of the firing, the name of Providence College coach Rick Pitino, an ex-Knick assistant, was in all the papers. Although nothing was official, the articles indicated Pitino had the job.

Evans indicated that although he liked Pitino, he would not be stampeded into replacement decisions; he just wanted to be sure he had a coach by the time of the college draft.

Ludicrous, that—the draft was sixty days away. It shouldn't take *half* that long to get a coach. Ever.

And Alysheba won the Kentucky Derby. General Richard Secord was leadoff man in the Iran-Contra hearings. Donna Rice flew from Florida to D.C., where Gary was. The jobless rate fell and so did Hart, withdrawing from the race for the presidency. Bernhard Goetz went on trial. Michael Reagan was reported to have revealed in an outline for a book that he had been sexually molested by a day-camp counselor for almost a year. His father seemed unmoved by the news. Debra Winger had a boy. McFarlane followed Secord on the hottish seat. Mrs. Thatcher announced that in a month she would hold a general election. Klaus Barbie went on trial in Lyon. Steffi Graf won the Italian Open. Alysheba won the Preakness. Steffi Graf won the Ladies Championship of West Germany—

—and the Knicks could not land a coach.

Sacramento could: They hired Bill Russell. Phoenix found somebody. The L.A. Clippers fired Don Chaney, hired Gene Shue.

And Tom Cruise got married. Sir Rudolph Bing, 85, with his forty-seven-year-old bride, hotfooted it about Britain. After months of denying he knew specifics about private affairs to aid the Nicaraguan rebels, President Reagan said not only did he know, it was his idea to begin with. Owen, Calero, and Singlaub (not a law firm) sang at the Iran-Contra bash. Paul Simon (not the singer) announced he was running for president; banner headlines were not forthcoming. Joan Rivers was out as host of her talk show. The Dow Jones Average dropped 52.97 points in one day. The Dow Jones Average increased 54.74 points in one day. *Ishtar,* for one frail week, was the top-grossing film in America. Larry Bethea, once of the Cowboys, blew himself away. Gus Johnson lost to brain cancer. William Casey died, they say. No doubt about Rita Cansino, turned Hayworth. Or the great Segovia.

All these things happened and the Knicks could not find anyone to take the goddamn coaching job. Probably the highest profile job in the NBA and though names kept appearing and reappearing in the press, the Knicks management, expert though they undoubtedly were in clocking Rockette kicks, was slipping and sliding and falling foolishly down and a West Coast basketball figure who likes the Knicks said, with sadness: "They used to be just bad; now they're the laughingstock of the sport."

Little did he know that by the end of May, the search wouldn't even be half over.

OCTOBER:
PITTINO'S [SIC] KNICKS

For a starter, Masterson chose the white bean soup. I had the *carpaccio de poissons* with vinaigrette sauce. A fish lover, he chose the cold poached salmon with sliced cucumber and homemade mayonnaise. I had the mustard chicken, a specialty of the Bistro Bordeaux, where we were eating on the night of the twenty-seventh of October, where we usually eat before Knick games. It's a terrific small place, on 8th between 30th and 31st, hard by the Garden. The Bistro does a solid business at lunch from the nearby office buildings.

Evenings, they are at the mercy of the attraction. They are packed Ranger nights. They do turnaway business for Neil Diamond. They don't even do so badly during the dog shows.

They were doing badly this particular Tuesday. Very badly, the chef, Gerard, admitted. He follows the Knicks from his particular position. "Theese is their first gamm, yes?"

We nodded.

"Bott eet dozz not count."

We nodded again, explaining that it was their first home exhibition.

He looked around at all the white tablecloths. "They weeel be bettair theese year. They have to be." He looked at us almost beseechingly. "Don't they have to be . . . ?"

The crowd was cheering before the players hit the floor. It was 8:21 when suddenly the noise began. No Knicks to be seen but passion was audible from those seated across the floor from the tunnel where the players make their entrance.

Tonight's enemy, Houston, was already well into their pregame rituals, had been for eight minutes. The lithe Ralph Sampson was moving gracefully through his shot repertoire, all eighty-eight inches of him. The remarkable Akeem Olajuwon, basketball's single most valuable commodity, looked as unstoppably quick as last year, a claimed seven-footer, though I suspect reality would have it closer to six-ten. The famed Twin Towers of the Rockets, resplendent in their fire-engine red pregame uniforms.

Ho-hum.

Through Houston's feeble eight minutes of posturing, the Faithful waited. Because this was a different day's dawning for us. The new Knicks, Rick Pitino's Knicks, the-winners-of-three-straight-exhibitions-Knicks (and of course everyone knows about exhibitions, that coaches are judging talent for cuts, that the established players don't put out, but when you've lost 175 games in three years, A WIN IS A WIN) were (please, God) coming home at last with but one thought on their minds: seduction.

They're on the far end of the court from us (Masterson and I sit in the corner of the end zone—*front row,* close to the carnage. He peers down toward where we are making brilliant lay-up after brilliant lay-up. "Hey look," Masterson says to a bunch of us. "We've still got Bob Thornton." Then he paused, his timing perfect as he said it: "And guess what, he's starting."

We all, as the English say, fell about.

Bob Thornton is a big, handsome twenty-five-year-old Angelino. He first attended Saddleback Community College in Mission Viejo, California, where he averaged a trifle over six points per game. He then transferred to the University of California at Irvine where he upped his average, ending his three years there with a boffo 9.6 points per game.

Few players work harder. He throws his six-ten, 225-pound body around with no fear. You've heard about players who give you 110 percent every time out? Thornton gives you 110 percent every time out. And he's a relentless practice player, pounding and chugging and clawing every second he's on the floor.

There's only one knock you can lay against the guy, but it has to be mentioned: He has absolutely no talent for the game of basketball. He might make a great stockbroker or a world-class veterinarian, but in two years with the Knicks, rarely taking shots more than four feet from the basket, he has a shooting average of 45 percent. This, coupled with his 54 percent free throw average is why he scores less than, for his career, 4 points a game. He's not much on quickness either: Last year, in 33 games, 282 minutes, he managed 4 steals and 3 blocked shots.

But to give him his due, he's got fabulous skin: it's all white. If he weren't Caucasian, I doubt he could make it past halftime in the Continental League. And as much as any player, he symbolized our anguish over the recent seasons. I don't know of any teams in the couple of decades I've been watching that were so knuckle-bitingly bad as to have a spot for a Robert George Thornton.

After the laugh, people wandered around, saying hello for the first time since the old season ended. We all asked each other how many we thought we'd win this year after only 24 the year preceding. (I thought 30.) Most thought at least 35, the most optimistic thought 40.

I could live with 40. Hell, I could live with 30 if it was fun.

8:36 and Anthem Grading time. A stocky low tenor. A cappella. A ringing "free" on "land of the free." Cheers. Definitely a B-plus anthem.

8:39 and John Condon, the announcer, said the magic words: "And here they are, your New York Knickerbockers." Big cheers. (Houston had already been introduced; no one could bring themselves to boo Akeem but we pasted the others pretty good.)

Still 8:39 when Condon said it: "STARTING AT ONE FORWARD, BOB THORNTON."

A gasp, truly, from the huddled masses. Garment District executives went pale. Housewives turned to each other in astonishment. But there it was: This year was last year: Lucy had pulled the football out from under Charlie Brown.

Booooooooooo.

Quickly the rest of the team was introduced: Kenny Walker (boos and cheers), Gerald Henderson (cheers and boos), Gerald Wilkins (cheers), and Patrick Ewing (*Biiig* cheers).

Ewing wins the tipoff against Sampson but the ball bounces off Kenny Walker's head and out of bounds. But the Rockets have fouled so it's our ball—

—and Bob Thornton scores on an offensive rebound, 2–0 *us.*

There were those who might consider that the high point. (I am not among them.) But from a basketball point of view, perhaps it was. We were down 12–6 when Billy Cartwright came in for Ewing. In a blink we were down 18–6. Half the first quarter gone and we had come up with a point a minute.

The "We want Bernard" chants began to boom.

Flashback.

Bernard King had returned and scored ninety points in the final three games of the preceding season. After the season there was a moratorium for many months, so no players were signed until the fall.

Bernard was up for a new contract. A very dicey affair. If you are management you are facing the demands of one of the great forwards. Who is thirty years old. Who has come off a devastating injury. Who can predict how long the knee will survive the pounding? Two years? Five years? Five games?

I was for keeping King. (It's easy, it's not my money.) It's a risk, God knows. And I would not have thought management stupid if they had signed Bernard and traded him for some younger, healthier, if less talented, bodies.

But the Knicks, at least as I write this the week of the Houston debacle, have done something so extraordinary that it will go down in the history of sports negotiations: They are going to lose Bernard King and get *nothing* in return.

The new Knicks management, to cover this Krakatoan gaffe, have used the mighty New York basketball press to badmouth King. When he was scoring champion, in '84–'85, how many games did the Knicks win? Answer, 24. And last year, when he managed a big-deal 6, how many games did they win? Answer, 24. Ergo, said all the press, where can it be shown that he is a plus to the team?

What no one said was that when he was scoring champion, he was hurt—he only played fifty-five games, and in some of those he was clearly not one hundred percent. So you could argue and not be far wrong that with *only* King, the Knicks were a .500 ball club.

And the year before he got hurt, when he barely averaged a shade over 26, with not much help besides Cartwright, the Knicks had won 47 and carried Boston to a seventh game in the playoffs.

The press also wrote at length about King's defensive deficiencies. True, he is not Bobby Jones. Or Michael Cooper. But Magic sucks on defense and nobody writes about that. Doesn't matter, he's a great player. And he gets a lot of steals not because he's a capable straight-up defensive player, he gets them because he very likely knows he isn't and, always playing within his limitations, guards the passing lanes, knowing when he's beaten that Kareem will cover for him.

But suddenly, Bernard King, who we had seen work miracles, was a loser, a defensive liability, and worse, worthless.

Suddenly I was on my feet (I don't do this often) screaming along with the others: "We want Bernard. We Want Bernard! *We Want Bernard!*" Then, a bit embarrassed, I sat back and watched the game go on.

A couple of first-half oddities worth mentioning:

1. At one point, Chris McNealy, a minor league forward and, believe it, the best rebounder we have, was sitting on the bench after a time-out. We had but four men on the floor. Everyone looked around in some confusion. Finally, McNealy realized his boo-boo, charged on court to even the numbers, if not the talent.

2. And this was something I'd never seen before. Houston has the ball out of bounds. A high, delicate pass to Steve Harris, who skies, just missing a spectacular alley-oop stuff. What's so special? you're wondering. This: He was trying it *on his own basket.* I turned to Masterson and wondered how dumb Harris could be. "He's not dumb," Masterson replied. "He noticed his mistake right away."

Halftime was mostly taken up with us regulars trying to figure out specifically how long the team had been horrid. When was the year, or better yet *month,* when it all turned sour? (We were down 63–43, it might be noted.)

The third quarter brought a dazzling moment. Not from the Knicks, from the crowd. Behind me, a group began, I thought with some inspiration, chanting *"We want the scab Knicks—we want the scabs!"*

In the blessedly fourth quarter, a moment of hope. The Knicks had slimed to within 12 when both Sampson and Akeem fouled out. And with plenty of time to go.

Ever a team to seize fortune by the throat, the Knicks were soon down by 20, losing eventually, 117–101. The crowd, which had begun at probably close to the announced twelve thousand-plus, was by my count down to five *hundred* by the final buzzer. It was like the Garden had turned into L.A. when they did the real version of *Long Day's Journey Into Night.*

And were the Knicks executives upset about this less-than-splendid display of roundball? I think not. Because along with getting rid of Bernard for nothing, they were also, according to the papers, in the act of getting us a Savior.

Probably you all saw the poll about who was the greatest basketball player of all time. If you didn't, the winner wasn't Wilt, not arrogant Russ, not the regal Abdul-Jabbar.

It was Sidney Green.

In their munificent wisdom, they had paid $2.2 million for three years of his services. As a steal, Manhattan Island pales. (Green was paid with the money that could have gotten King.)

Just as the papers were full of how rotten King was *and always had been,* now the Garden was feeding them and they were printing raves about Sidney Green, who, in case some of you are so dumb you don't know, is the *third-string* power forward for Detroit. Green, a rebounder of dubious quality (he's never done it when anything meant anything), is from the Manute Bol school of passing. (He had 62 assists in close to 1,800 minutes with the Pistons last year.) The press was trumpeting the potential of the suddenly young Knick starting line of Walker, Ewing, and Green. They are certainly young. (Average age twenty-five.) But Patrick has bad knees. Green has an attitude problem. And Walker has lost confidence in the poor shot he once had. (This night he shot 0 for 7 and didn't damage his average all that much.)

To sum up my feelings about the coming year (trying to ignore what well may be the budding of my very first ulcer):

1. Al Bianchi, the new Knicks general manager, is a neat guy, fun, a genuinely stand-up fellow who has spent the last eleven years as an assistant coach in Phoenix, which is the worst, at present, drug-beset franchise in sports. It is doubtful that he could have gotten any job in the league above assistant coach until rescued by Evans, the genius of Madison Square. Bianchi is there to keep the press happy. A gofer.

2. Pitino is cute. And not dumb. (You don't get to where he is at his tender thirty-five years by being dumb.) But he has never head-coached in the pros and his system, say I, of constant pressure on defense will only break bodies. It may be effective in college where the games are fewer and shorter. But the casualty list by December I feel will be awesome.

3. Richard Evans knows less about basketball than he professes to know and he professes to know nothing.

4. The Knicks, as presently constituted, have no one who can score. Or shoot the ball accurately. I predict these shortcomings will someday haunt them.

5. Thirty wins is a fantasy.

6. Importantly, since Pitino was commandeered after the most intense beauty contest since Scarlett O'Hara, the Garden score-board should really learn to spell his name properly. They had it this way: Pittino. (Maybe we could trade the extra "t" for the second-round pick we didn't get for Bernard.)

7. This, being the beginning of a new regime, is going to be worse than the shards of months past. At least then we had hope. We knew Hubie would go. We knew Bernard would come back. We knew after so many humiliations, the Garden would get solid experienced professionals.

8. Please bring back last year....

HONK

The following article appeared in *The New York Times* sports section dated October 29, 1987:

BULLS FINE JORDAN

The Chicago Bulls fined MICHAEL JORDAN an undisclosed amount yesterday for conduct detrimental to the team. Jordan, last year's National Basketball Association scoring leader, drew the fine a day after he stormed out of a practice session, accusing Coach DOUG COLLINS of failing to keep the correct score during a scrimmage. "People may think this to be so trivial," Jordan said after the incident. "But when you're a competitor and want to win, nothing is trivial. I know the score was 4-4. Doug said it was 4-3, my team losing. I know after a long, tough practice, the losing team has to run. I felt like he was stacking the odds against me on purpose." Admitting he was right to be fined, Jordan explained why he walked out of the practice: "I was afraid I would say something I would regret later." Collins refused to talk about the incident.

Let's be Kremlinologists. No. Let's not be. It won't hold water to say, "That kid is some competitor." It's dumb to think that Collins would go to war with Jordan. (Call Paul Westhead and ask him what happens to coaches in the NBA who clash with their superstars.) Jordan, by the way, happens to be perhaps *the* outstanding superstar in all of sports.

Look, there's no law that says we have to be sports fans. Not so long ago, if you were a singer/actor, the best thing to be was a Broadway star. Next down the line, a movie star. Not yet in existence: a rock star. Today, the rock stars have it all, Steve Martin, who cannot really sing or dance better than thee or me, stars in $20 million movie musicals, and there are no Broadway stars. (Liza Minnelli was the last, but after *The Rink*, when she crashed and burned, she extinguished the occupation.)

The subtext of the *Times* article in these times can only be this: Watch it! That's problem behavior. That's the glowing paranoia these days, even when I know Jordan is an exemplary young man.

I shall go out of my way—wrong, I've already been doing that—

what I mean is I shall break my ass, in the future, to see every Chicago Bulls game. Michael Jordan is so special. And I must watch him extra carefully, put his glorious moves in my memory bank. And I must start now.

In the event he crashes and burns.

When Walter O'Malley, the brilliant Walter O'Malley, his little pumping heart full of Uriah Heapean greed, moved the Bums, he began to rip the fabric of modern sports. Before that, the dance between fan and owner was sort of like the old ditty, "I love you and you love me and we'll be as happy as we can be." Many New York fans haven't remotely recovered from that 1957 day. And many fans around the country couldn't have cared less; they hated us then, they hate us now. And besides, *their* home team would never move.

There is a wonderful character in a fabulous, almost unknown Tennessee Williams play, *Camino Real,* a gypsy's daughter who screws around a lot but that's okay, because every moonrise makes her a virgin.

Well, the moonrises aren't working so hot for us Followers anymore. We all know that modern owners make a piker of O'Malley. So we don't give our love quite so freely to a team.

And free agency, among other things, has dampened our passion for players. Why dream of Mattingly when soon he might be gone?

I am, and I suspect always will be, hooked. Fanaticism is half a century inside me. But if I were a kid now, and I read about Lawrence Taylor and Gooden and M. R. Richardson and David Thompson—if I got rejected enough times, I might begin to think about putting my passion somewhere besides sports. I know that seems unlikely, probably is.

It's just a bitch being a Fan. Caring makes us so vulnerable. Probably we would have all been better off being used car salesmen. How many of them give a shit?

If you know any, honk.

BEWARE OF THE CREEPING PHILOSOPHY

The three main American team sports have achieved their popularity for one and only one reason: even Jo-Jo the Dog Faced Boy can understand them. Let me put them on their simplest (and truest) levels.

Football: All it is is this: blocking and tackling.

Baseball: It comes down to one word: "stuff."

Basketball: It's just putting the ball in the hole.

That's really it, folks. You can rave all you want about how great Eric Dickerson is, but when the Bear tacklers were better than the Ram blockers, as they were in their Super Bowl year, he's just another big fast guy who fumbles a lot. Dan Marino has a great arm. But last week Buffalo forced Shula to remove him from a lost-cause game, thereby shattering his chance at Unitas's amazing (think about it, it really is) record of throwing at least one touchdown pass in forty-seven consecutive games. If his blockers can't handle the enemy tacklers, Marino is no different than Marc Wilson.

You can argue whether Bo Jackson is this or Jerry Rice is that, but it's all horseshit. Football games are won in the trenches.

Baseball games are won on the mound. If a quality pitcher has his mysterious inexplicable "stuff," his team is going to win. If both starters have their "stuff," whoever has better "stuff" will prevail.

Basketball, gloriously improvisational, works like this: Whichever team with the ball feels most comfortable and can therefore create offensive instants, will score. When that team is on defense, what it tries to do is minimize the strength of the enemy, make him do something he doesn't want to do. If you can make the other team take ten additional shots to score its allotted points, you'll win, because you get the ball back fairly frequently after they shoot.

Blocking and tackling, stuff, putting the ball in the hole. That is all ye need know or ever need to know.

Things, however, are changing. Paul Brown may have incepted it all back in the forties when he began shuttling in his guards on alternate downs, each puffing lineman bringing with him the news of the next play. Why did he do this? Because Brown, like all owners, coaches, and managers thinks he knows best and wants more control. And if he can control his team's mistakes, well, he'll maybe keep his job longer. Now every idiot owner, coach, and manager wants control—

—and the creeping philosophy (often called a "system") slithered out of primeval soil. And nothing has gotten better since, because these men have forgotten one crucial aspect about all sports: They're played by the players.

You cannot have a system unless you happen to have fallen into the precise players that can make, however briefly, your system work. But the coaching brains won't change when their players change—they insist their system will, given time (don't fire me, boss) prevail.

Example: The Oakland Raiders were known for years as a bunch of big guys who needed deodorant and whose philosophy was this: Stretch the field.

Go, in other words, for the bomb.

Super, if you've got Cliff Branch chasing his tail across the greensward and Stabler or Plunkett uncorking. But if you try and do that without the personnel, you end up where Oakland is now: Irwindale.

Basketball is in the most trouble. Philosophy is creeping out of all control. With the Knicks now, for example, young Pitino has installed what the media hopefully refers to as "the motion offense."

Among other tenets, it holds this to be true: The ball moves faster than the man on defense can react, so eventually, if the passes are crisp enough, one Knick or another will be free to shoot and you know what that means?

With the Knicks this year it means this: airball.

I recently saw a game where Seattle's slumping forward, Tom Chambers, scored an easy 32. And the Knicks' forwards? Well, Sidney Green played twenty heart-stopping minutes before he fouled out, took three shots, came home with none. Kenny Walker was better: He averaged .125. Our starting forwards took eleven shots, made one biggie. But ah, the Knick bench, so crucial to Rick Baby's system. Chris McNealy played eight minutes, had the wisdom not to hoist up a clanger. Pat Cummings, playing to continuous boos, made one of three in nine minutes. Our star forward of the night was Ray Tolbert, three for four, mainly stuffs.

Five for eighteen. (Chambers alone was eleven for seventeen.) Now two of our stellar group were always on the floor and I ask you this: what's the point in passing the ball around if at least forty percent of the team cannot, cannot, cannot shoot the thing.

Look, during the championship Knick years, the starting five, alphabetically the first time, were Dick Barnett, Bill Bradley, Dave DeBusschere, Walter Frazier, and Willis Reed, with Cazzie Russell coming off the bench. The second time they won, Earl Monroe had replaced Barnett and Jerry Lucas was Cazzie.

And what did Holzman tell his chargers? "Hit the open man." Well, that made pretty good sense because we are talking about twelve of the greatest shooters you'd want on your ball club.

But you don't "hit the open man" if the open man is so frozen with fear because he can't shoot that he won't shoot. And is Pitino going to change his motion offense? 'Course not; 'cause it'll work if you just give it time. (Don't fire me, boss.)

What is happening in sports that is so terrible is that coaches are becoming more and more important with their insidious systems. I don't think Pat Riley of the Lakers or K.C. of the Celts could come near Hubie Brown in a test of arcane basketball minutiae. What they both do know and what makes them so successful is this: They let the players play.

Never forget that Bill Fitch, before he was fired from Boston, made Larry Bird the sixth man. Great idea, that. Would have worked, too. All part of Fitch's philosophy. Fortunately he was stopped before he could make Kevin McHale his point guard. . . .

THE ENTERTAINER

Masterson, perhaps feeling traditional, began with chilled asparagus. Followed by one of the genuinely marvelous house specialties, chicken with raspberries. I joined him in the main course, struck gold with my appetizer: *frisée aux lardons*. What it is, is chicory and hot, cut-up bacon bits and a poached egg, all with a special vinaigrette sauce. What you do is mushel the egg so it mixes with the vinaigrette, and the combination of tastes makes for one of the finest dishes served at the Bistro Bordeaux, which on this Monday night was packed. At 6:15.

Jammed.

Alan, the partner of Gerard the chef, usually just seats customers and chats and busies himself being charming. Tonight he was chasing all over, taking orders, serving dishes, clearing tables, bringing wine. It was the home opener for the '87–'88 Knicks. But that was not the reason for the crowd. The enemy was the Celtics; but that wasn't why even the bar area of the place was stuffed with diners. We all knew why we were there. You could hear his name spoken again and again at every table.

Larry Joe Bird was coming to town.

*   *   *

Some say he is the greatest forward ever. Some say he isn't. Others say he is the greatest *player* ever. Still others disagree. What seems to me beyond dispute is this: No history of the sport can be written without examining his skills and contributions.

Bird began this Monday up in Massachusetts; Brookline, to be more specific. At 7:30. He had breakfast, caught the news, then drove to Logan Airport, met the team, got on the ten o'clock shuttle.

At ll:45 K.C. enters the revolving door of the Summit Hotel, 51st and Lexington. Red is with him. Cousy too. Then a bunch of players, and there he is in the midst of them. He gets the key to his room, elevators up with some other Celtics. "See you later, Birdie," an assistant coach calls.

The maid has not finished cleaning his room. "Just my luck," he mutters. "Larry Bird," she says, hurrying now, starting the vacuum cleaner going. He sits in a chair patiently till she's done.

He looks better at thirty (thirty-one in December) than he ever has. His hair is cut short, he's lost a good bit of weight. He does not wear jeans and sneakers, but rather gray loafers and matching slacks, a yellow sports shirt, a blue pullover sweater.

"I don't do much on the road," he says. "The Celtics pay me to play well. I can't do autograph sessions or business things then. They pay my way down here. I've got to be at my best for them.

"I don't like making new friends on the road. It can get to be a hassle. When you have friends, it's only the one time for them and they think, 'Great, I get to stay up all night.' But *you've* got to get your rest because you're probably playing tomorrow.

"I found out in high school that game day can be total confusion. A hundred people will call you asking for tickets." He pauses. "If someone wants them, they'll have to get them on their own—I am now completely out of the ticket business."

He eases himself back into the chair. The subject of the Washington game two nights before is mentioned. This is what the papers said about it:

CELTICS 140, BULLETS 139

Larry Bird hit a 20-foot jump shot at the buzzer ending the second overtime to give the Celtics the victory.

Bird, who finished with 47 points, scored 19 in the fourth period, including a running one-hander from 24 feet with 4 seconds remaining in regulation to force overtime. His two free throws with 4 seconds left in the first overtime put Boston ahead, 131–129, but Darrell Walker forced a second extra session with a jumper from the left corner with a second left.

This is what Bird says about it: "I had a terrible game. People keep saying I was wonderful. But I had eight turnovers and I made some bad decisions on the break and I made some passes where I thought someone would roll to the basket and I anticipated wrong. I played fifty-three minutes and only had eight rebounds. All I was doing was shooting well. Except for my shooting, everything else was terrible.

"But there was one thing I liked about the game. Ninety-nine percent of the players in this league will take the final shot at the buzzer if the game is tied. But be down one or two and no one will. And my teammates, they *wanted* me to take those shots. That means a lot. We'd set up a play with a bunch of options and they'd be waiting for me to come get the ball after the first couple of options. Knowing my teammates want me to take it: That's worth everything."

Special problems posed by playing in New York?

He shakes his head. "To tell you the truth, the Celtic–Knick rivalry never happened but one year since I've been here. When Bernard King took us to seven in the playoffs. I can see how it would be a wonderful thing for the fans and the league, a rivalry like that, and I've heard about how it used to be, but the Knicks never gave us that many problems.

"But I enjoy playing on the road. I get more out of it. It's fun going in there, playing for a packed house, and you know it's just the fifteen of you against everybody. And when you win, it's wonderful.

"A lot of guys don't like playing on the road. Everybody in this league can play at home. A lot of guys can play if they're petted and flattered. But maybe only fifty percent are good on the road.

"The road gives people an excuse to lose. You say 'I don't feel that great' or 'Well, we're on the road, everybody in the league loses on the road.' They don't like getting booed. It's an excuse is all."

And how will he prepare for tonight's road game?

"Well, I'll go down and have lunch. Then I'll come back up here and try and sleep for two or three hours. The bus leaves at five and I'll be shooting at five-twenty. I never worry about my shooting. I keep telling myself that if I keep putting enough effort into it, it'll happen. In high school, our coach made us shoot an hour of free throws a day. I'd start at six A.M. I got up to seventy-five percent by my senior year. In college I was seventy-eight to eighty. I'm in the high eighties now.

"Shooting drives you crazy, though. Sometimes, before, you can't miss, and in the game you can't hit. Sometimes it's the other way around. You just have to do it enough. Even though it drives you crazy. It's a mystery.

"I like to be the first one out there. And I like to have someone to retrieve the ball so I can get off twice as many shots. If I'm there first there aren't a lot of things flying around. You can really concentrate. You learn things. Like if you have an injury, a sore elbow maybe, you learn what shooting adjustments you have to make.

"In the summers, I'll try and see how many free throws I can make in a row. Summer before last I broke a hundred, I hit a hundred and five. This past summer I got up to a hundred and sixty-three. Now, when I go to the line I figure, 'If I can hit a hundred and sixty-three in a row, I can make these two.' Next summer I plan on going past a hundred and sixty-three.

"Today, if I'm hitting, I'll practice less. If I feel loose. When I shoot and it goes in but it hits the rim, that's not good. I judge it all by net. If I'm just hitting net I'll try some bank shots. I hate to bank but if I can make those, I figure my touch must be good that night.

"After that I go in and look at film for twenty, twenty-five minutes. You can tell some stuff from film. Like is the man I'm guarding using one move more than the others to score with—if he is, I'll try and make him do something else. And is Ewing trying to block every shot or is he trying to play good defense? Once I've done that, I figure I'm ready for the game. After the game I don't do much—go have a sandwich and a beer with my teammates. Then I'll go to sleep because I imagine we're getting up early tomorrow morning to catch a plane.

"When I'm on the road I stick around the team."

The media?

"In college I used to get upset if they had it wrong, but not so much anymore. I don't like it when they get on a teammate. But say like Ryan—(Bob Ryan, the *Boston Globe* reporter; probably the best basketball writer today—) Ryan knows our plays. When we run something and if we mess up, he'll write exactly how we messed up in the paper. I think that's fine. But when someone comes in once a month, they can't know that much. Things don't bother me so much anymore."

*　　*　　*

On that rainy Monday, 19,591 souls came out to watch him play. Garden sellouts used to be common. Now they happen only when Bird or Magic or Michael are on the floor. Bird was introduced just before 7:40 to by far the loudest cheer for any player, Celtic or Knick.

But before the introduction of the players something happened that was so remarkable it made it tough for any game to top. Because at 7:35, after a big buildup, the "Star Spangled Banner" singer was announced—

—it was Pia Zadora.

Shock in the arena. It is very hard not to have heard Pia Zadora jokes. (Steve Allen, I think it was, said, during one of those *Night of a Thousand Stars* galas, something to the effect that if a bomb hit the place, Pia Zadora would be the biggest star in Hollywood.) "Is it going to be like this all year?" somebody asked. "I don't suffer enough?" Frankly, I was delighted because I knew something few others did: Pia Zadora can really *sing*. I've heard her belt, I've heard her croon. The lady can bring it.

What she cannot do, alas, is sing the Anthem.

Do you remember how when you were a little kid and you took music lessons, when you'd have a recital coming up or you'd have to play in front of your folks or something your teacher would touch her hair net (my piano teachers all had hair nets) and say this: "Whatever you do, if you make a mistake, *don't stop*. Just go right on as if nothing had happened because no one will know the difference."

Well, Pia starts out okay—a little shaky, but okay. Frankly, I'm disappointed because I wanted her to knock 'em dead since it would be funny seeing everybody turn and say, "Hey, was that Pia Zadora? I didn't know she could sing like that." But it's an unsingable song as we all know, and besides, there's brass playing somewhere, I don't know if her husband, Riklis, had brought in musicians to play just for her or if it's a different arrangement but anyway, there are trumpets blaring as she goes through the start and then—

—*and then*—

—just as she's into "What so proudly we hailed"—she stops. Dead. The music is blasting on and there's this tiny girl in a gray suit looking around the Garden saying, "I can't hear it."

Boooooooooo.

We are not, we weary faithful, as tough a crowd as some. In Philly, they boo the Pope. We're willing to suffer. Just give us something entertaining to suffer through. I mean shit, it wasn't La Scala opposite Pavarotti, it was the dumb "Star Spangled Banner" at the Garden and if you goof, you goof, *but you don't stop.* Don't make a big thing out of it, just don't bump into the furniture and get off stage.

Boooooooooooooooo!

Now she's turning back and she realizes she's in the quagmire because the music has kept on and so she recovers nicely, jumping to "bombs bursting in air." And by that time the crowd was into its usual "let's drown out the singer" cheer and you couldn't hear her anymore.

It may not make the *Guinness Book of World Records* but no veteran of any age could recall a singer getting booed in the Anthem before.

She's a tough kid, she'll survive. (I think she can act too, who else admits things like that?) Besides, as one old guy warned a booer, "If you're not careful, her husband will buy the whole goddamn Garden."

We win the tip and by now everyone is talking about Bird's new look. He looks like an athlete more than ever, having worked out with weights for the first time over the summer. His eating habits changed, too. "But I didn't give up beer and french fries."

It's really a remarkable thing—a world famous athlete at his peak going into an entirely new physical regime to make himself still better. (Ryan thinks this year he will make his other three MVP seasons look like CBA years.)

"I weigh two-eighteen, two-seventeen now. Before, in the summers, I'd usually get up to two-forty, two-forty-five. I worked out ninety minutes a day. I did my running and my ball-handling work, but this was in addition to that. If I did it, I wanted it to be successful so I cut out the junk food. I did it because I thought if I was stronger, I'd be stronger as the season went on, the little nagging things wouldn't crop up. You hope that, anyway. I guess I can do some things better now. I'll never be quick but since I've lost the weight I think I'm quicker so I'll probably make more moves to the basket."

He was making no moves to the basket as the game began. He wasn't looking to shoot, period. But in the first few minutes he made four dazzling passes and the Celtics were soon up 21–13. They led by 11 at the quarter, 14 at the half.

In the third quarter they broke it open: 69–44 halfway through. The crowd was anguished. The loudspeaker kept asking for a Doctor Fenster Cosgrove over and over. Would Doctor Fenster Cosgrove please report someplace.

Then the Knicks made their run. In the fourth quarter they cut the
Celtic lead to 7 with four minutes to go. It was still that with three left.
The Celtics had scored 10 points in ten minutes.

Then Bird, who had a poor (5-for-18) shooting night, made the
play of the game, blocking a Knick guard's jumper, resulting in a fast
break that got the lead up to 10.

The fans filed out. It was a loss, 96–87, but not an embarrassment. No
boos at the end. We shuffled silently home, our work done.

Bird was beginning what surely must be the most trying work for
him. At 9:55 the visitors' locker room opened and the media poured
in, maybe thirty, forty of them in all. And they all, or as many as
could crowd around, zeroed in on Bird. It's a small, cheerless place, the
visitors' locker room. There was no escape.

In Boston, the home team has an off-limits trainer's room, and after a
win Bird is known to hide in there. And he doesn't come out until the
media has talked to all of his teammates, making sure they get coverage. But after a loss he sits waiting, in front of his locker.

Now he sat waiting, icing his feet. He wore a shirt; a towel covered
his lower body. The tub of ice and water was not very large. Large
enough for three feet. Jerry Sichting, the Celtic reserve guard, was icing
a foot, too. It made for a splendid loony scene. Here is Sichting, sharing
the small tub with Bird, sitting next to Bird, and floods of people are
shoving microphones in Bird's face as if Sichting doesn't exist. He's
right there, their heads can't be more than a yard apart, and people are
all around Sichting to get to Bird and no one even says "Excuse me."
Sichting stares straight ahead.

So does Bird. There's a kind of tunnel vision that's taking place now,
you can see it on his face, I've seen it on the faces of movie stars when
they're trapped on a junket. Because when you are very famous, there
is truly nothing you haven't been asked and asked and asked before. I
once inquired of one of the most famous forwards who ever lived, and a
notoriously bad interview, if he'd ever been asked a really interesting
question. This was a bright man, truly, and he considered before
shaking his head. Then he was asked what would he do if that had
happened—and his eyes lit up with genuine animation as he said,
"Oh, I'd answer it."

They came at Bird in waves. When one group would be done,
another would arrive. And when they would be finished, there were
more, always more. For a solid half hour, unrelenting: "Larry, what

would you want the young people of America to know?"—"Larry, who were your heroes?"—"Larry, what's the secret to rebounding?"—"Larry, how much do the Celtics miss Kevin McHale?"—"Larry, how important is good position in rebounding?"—"Larry, do you think you can win without McHale?"—"Larry, do you think the Knicks can play this way for eighty games?"—"Larry, when did you decide to lose weight?" —"Larry, what's your diet?"—"Larry, were you worried when the Knicks came back?"—"Larry, is jumping high essential for rebounding?"— "Larry, when did you think the game was over?"—"Larry, have you changed your offense to compensate for McHale's being injured?"— "Larry, how much did McHale's absence affect the Knicks coming back in the fourth quarter?"—"Larry, is this a different team without McHale?"—"Larry, was it the pressure defense of the Knicks that made you miss your shots?"—"Larry, are you faster, Larry, are you quicker, Larry, are you stronger, Larry, about your shooting, Larry, about your haircut, Larry, about your diet, *Larry, Larry, Larry*—"

Finally, the room was pretty much empty. He dried his feet, finished dressing. He thought his defense on the whole was pretty good. He had no idea why his shot was off. "I hit everything in practice." Shake of the head. "Shooting drives you crazy." The films he's watched before the game, he'd seen so many open men when the Knicks pressed. That was why he passed so much at the start. Later, when he went into the offense more, he thought too much about it: "I should have just shot."

We said good-bye. "I'm going to put it all together one of these days," he said.

He was in good humor. It was a road win. And although he had an average evening for him, he still ended up one rebound short of a triple double (9 rebounds, 10 assists, 16 points). And he had made the crucial play of the game.

Now a sandwich with teammates, a couple of beers, and bed. (The blackboard in the locker room said: "Wake up 7:30. Depart 8:30.") Seventy-nine games until the playoffs. He had such hopes for the team—"I think we're one average player away from being a great team, like '86."

These are good times for him. But he's worked for them. Worked on his shooting and his ball handling and his rebounding and his passing and now his body and who knows what surprises he'll have in store next year. He adores the game of basketball and that translates to the masses. Earlier he had said, "I really do believe that people enjoy watching me play."

Only the sighted—and I wouldn't bet against the blind. . . .

"CAN'T REPEAT THE PAST?
WHY, OF COURSE YOU CAN."

I could not watch the first half of the Knicks–Celtics affair going on one Wednesday in Boston. It might have been reasonable to think that missing a bit of carnage wouldn't be all that terrible, since we were 1-and-5 while they were 6-and-1.

But Bird wasn't playing. Tendinitis. McHale was absent too. The game was very much, I figured, in contest.

Setting up my trusty VCR, I went about my business. It was shortly after nine before I was free to catch up on the game. Turning on my aging Advent, I kept the tape running, sat back. It was the third quarter.

The score was 64–36. *Us.*

The relief. I cannot venture a description. But if you follow a team and that team for the past three years has been six steps below vomitous, has lost a shattering 175 games in that time, the notion of being able to lounge and watch the Celtics wriggle and die was so overpowering, so seductive, I only wished I could bottle my mood.

More than that, I could watch Danny Ainge self-destruct.

Although I'm told he's a genuinely terrific person, I can't help it: I hate Danny Ainge. If you were to ask me who is the most detestable figure in team sports, no other names leaps to my lips. I've hated him since college and when he struggled to hit the curve as a putrid baseball player, I beamed.

Why do I hate him?

If you're a sports fan, I think you have to. He's got that angelic face and he's secretly dirty and he whines more than anyone since Rick Barry.

More than these reasons, though, is his rarity: He is one of the few overrated/underrated players in sports.

This gets a bit arcane, but I'll be brief. We all know there are overrated players—Brian Bosworth—and underrated players—Alex English. We make up all-underrated teams or the reverse, it's part of being a Believer.

But there are some players—few, but they exist—who go a step beyond. If you're a Celtic writer, you blab about Bird. And then you skip to McHale. Then DJ and Parish. Well, as the months go on, you hunger for something a little different. So you start writing about Danny Ainge—

—and how he is underrated.

Logic dictates you write that—he's a starting guard on a team that's won championships, he must be underrated. So that's how the hype goes.

The fact is, Danny Ainge, and this is a personal intellectual judgment, stinks. He is lucky to be in the league and blessed that he is on a team where his infinite weaknesses are covered and his one strength—he can, if unguarded, shoot—is allowed to show. But if he were on the L.A. Clippers or Sacramento you would never, repeat never, hear his name.

If I'd been an Englishman at my club, I'd have ordered some '63 Dow and let the world bliss by.

64–36. Us.

I did not expect the margin to swell, by the by. The Knicks are unused to victory, let alone blowouts. Pitino would pull some moronic substitutions, I knew that.

But I didn't care. We were winning big in Boston and we were playing so well, Bird or not, we would have triumphed. Although I doubted we would have held them again to *zero* for *nineteen* scoreless from the floor in the second quarter, as my man Marv Albert amazingly reported was true. Had any team since the 24-second clock ever gone zip for twelve minutes? Not very often. At the least, they had to have tied a record, the evil Celts.

Boston ran off 10 straight.

Yawn.

(Why do they say, announcers, 10 "unanswered" points. How many points do you have to get to be allowed to call them unanswered? Can you say the Knicks have just scored 2 unanswered points? Don't think so.)

The third quarter went along. We were up by 20, then 18, then 20, then 18, time was joyously passing.

Then Ainge hit a 3-pointer.

Then Ainge hit another 3-pointer.

And even though we were ahead, far ahead, I knew at that moment, that we were going to die and he was going to kill me. . . .

I had almost died earlier that week in the Caribbean. A gorgeous day. I have, more often than I wish, bad knees. So this morn I wandered out into the water and let the waves have a go at the swelling. Chiropractors have a wonderful word, when you're in pain and they come to help you. They touch your back or your hip or wherever it hurts and it still hurts but God are you glad they're there, and they ask, "Is this, what I'm doing now, is where I'm touching now, is it *gratifying?*"

If you have the kind of pain chiropractic helps, there is no word more adroitly chosen.

And the Caribbean waves now, as they rolled in against my knees, they felt just the same: gratifying. I was standing in water lower than my waist and just above the knee. The waves worked their therapy. It was so perfect I lay back in the water and took some strokes, letting the sun paint my stomach warm. After a few moments of this, it couldn't have been more than a few moments I don't believe, I stood—

and the tips of one foot only could barely make the sand.

Odd, I remember thinking. I hadn't swum that far and this was not a part of the sea that had sheer drops—

—a wave washed over me—

—I wasn't ready for it, took a lot of water in the mouth, coughed and spit—

—now another wave—

—only this time I was ready and when the wave came I pushed off from my single tippy-toe position and timed it well and went into my best crawl, holding my breath with my arms working like pistons and a good solid flutter kick and after a while, when it was becoming a bit hard to breathe, I stopped, stood in the waist-high water—

—only it wasn't waist-high—all that effort and I could still barely touch the sand with the tips of the toes of one foot, only now I was panting and it was during that moment of heavy breathing that I realized I was caught in the undertow.

I bolted for shore. I knew that was an error, knew you were supposed to go sideways—I understood you could also drift out to sea gently—but to hell with that, I was in an undertow and I was *scared*. I flailed at the water and turned on my back and kicked and backstroked and then turned over and flutterkicked and crawled.

(On the shore, the lifeguard had spotted me, had already gone to get his rope and life preserver.)

But I didn't know that. I only knew that my air was going and my arms ached and my heart would not let my rib cage alone and more waves were coming, all of them for me. And surely they were going to kill me, surely I would die. . . .

*   *   *

Such were my merry thoughts as I watched the rest of the game. Ainge hits his fourth 3-pointer, and the lead is four. A bit later he tries another 3-pointer but they won't give him room so he lunges off-balance, knocks down an impossible pressure packed 2-pointer and the Celts are down by one.

A minute to go. The Knicks have the lead back up to 3. It didn't matter. (My mind was on the Caribbean. The waves would never leave me in peace, not this night.) Three points is nothing. Not with that little shit on a roll. I wait in my chair, almost screaming for him to stick it into my heart and twist it and then bitch that I'd fouled him.

Seconds ticking away.

Knicks up by 3.

Ainge has the ball.

Death.

From what looks like thirty feet he lets fire.

The net barely whispered.

Overtime.

We went ahead by 6 with three minutes to go.

The waves were pounding at me.

Double overtime.

A tip in at the buzzer.

111–109 . . . t . . . h . . . e . . . m . . .

I sat in my chair. Wiped out. There had been a lot of time-outs the last minutes and there were a lot of commercials for a Buster Keaton special upcoming.

Probably the stone-faced wonder would have laughed at me—

—*no!*

I would not would not *would not* wallow in self-pity—

—didn't have to—

—I had my VCR.

I put it on rewind, went to open a bottle of Moulin-A-Vent. By the time I was done the tape was back to the beginning.

Screw the beginning.

I wanted the second quarter.

Fast forwarded.

33–26, the Knicks only up by 7. Ainge shoots—

—a clanger.

I sip my wine.
Ainge shoots again.
Clang.
Parish misses a three-footer—*a three-footer*—
Amazing.
D.J. doesn't even come close.
We're up by 16 now.
They bench Ainge.
He sulks. Always was a rotten loser, always will be.
Parish misses again.
D.J. misses again.
D.J. misses again again, a lay-up this time.
Ainge is back in.
Clang.
We're up by 20.
Ainge sends up a ten-foot prayer.
The Moulin-A-Vent has a lovely flavor. Truly.
At least the first half of the bottle did.
We're up by 21.
Ainge, poor, pathetic, feeble clutch artist, tries a three-footer.
CLANG CLANG CLANG.
Halftime.
We're up by 25.
Rewind.
Second quarter starts. It's 33–26, Knicks. I watch it all.
Again.
I open another bottle of wine.
Smiling now.
So happy.
Ainge shoots—
—laughter.
Ainge shoots—
—guffaws.
You can tell a pressure player. I can, anyway. And I know a clutch
artist.
Clang.
Going on to two o'clock now.
I've watched the second quarter four times.
Eventually, I'm going to have it bronzed. . . .

HISTORY LESSON

I have a memory of a once-famous *New Yorker* cartoon, which was in many panels. In each, a sort of snooty guy in tails was railing against various things that ticked him off. When he was in his thirties, it might have been modern music. In his forties, modern art. In his fifties, modern fashion. In the last panel, when he was in his eighties, it was "modern anything."

I hope I'm not a prototype of that gentleman, but as I write this I'm not so sure, having come across the following snippet in the press this A.M., in an article about the splendid Denver guard, Lafayette Lever, cognomen "Fats." I quote:

> He became the master of the triple double last season. He recorded double figures in scoring, rebounds and assists 16 times, which led the league and was two short of Magic Johnson's modern-day record.

Guess why I am steaming. Got it? I'll make it easy for you by doing the paragraph again, this time with a hint involved. You have but to ferret out the hint.

> He became the master of the triple double last season. He recorded double figures in scoring, rebounds and assists 16 times, which led the league and was two short of Magic Johnson's *MODERN*!!! *DAY*!!! record.

I am not a member of the "Yesterday Was Better" club, but I would be remiss in not mentioning the Big O, Mister Robertson, who *averaged* a triple double the first five *years* of his matchless career. The fifth year of that stretch was the 1964–65 season. That may seem like the Mesopotamian Era to some of you but please believe me on this: It wasn't that long ago.

Or else Jack Kennedy was pre modern-day. Malcolm X. And *Psycho*. And Hemingway, Faulkner, *Catch-22*. Hammarskjöld. Eichmann. (These are just a precious few of the people who died or works that were born just prior to Robertson's fifth season.)

The point of all this is not to talk about how occasional dumb writing gets into the papers. That we know already. But it's not just the press—just before the Heisman award was won by an athlete from the University of Notre Dame, a TV sports reporter, realizing that the second favorite this year went to Syracuse, discovered that Ernie Davis had won and also attended that university. So he went to the PR guy at Syracuse, this TV sports reporter did, and he requested an interview be set up with Davis.

But it's not just TV, either. A couple of quick movie stories. A producer I know was having a meeting with a bunch of honchos at a studio and was trying to describe a project and they interrupted, told him to high-concept it. (A Hollywood phrase meaning, "comic-strip it for me.") And this producer said that the tone of the piece would be like a Preston Sturges movie.

None of the honchos knew who Sturges was.

This year, Fred Zinnemann supposedly had a meeting with a powerful Baby Mogul at a studio. (Zinnemann won the Oscar twice, for *A Man For All Seasons* and *From Here to Eternity,* but among his nominations were *High Noon, The Nun's Story,* and *Julia.*) The meeting was brief. The Baby Mogul said, "What have you done, Mister Zinnemann?" Zinnemann replied, "After you," stood, and left.

But it's always easy to come up with Hollywood stories. What I'm fumbling for is this: Nobody knows shit about history anymore. An Ivy League school gives a course in American History since 1945. And it's packed. An acquaintance of mine, who forced his daughter to take the course, met the teacher and wondered why the course was so popular. The teacher said, "It isn't popular—they're only there because parents make them take it. Otherwise, it'd be empty."

Are people dumber today?

I think not. Smarter? Nope. Just like always.

Are teachers worse today? Same as above. Just like always.

Why, then? Why this really extraordinary arrogance about what must be retained in the old bean, what safely jettisoned?

I'll give you my answer: It's the thundering hoofbeats of the media. There is such irising in on stories, there is such intensity given an event, which is then replaced by the next night's event, people have come to think if it didn't happen today, it didn't happen.

Remember the joke of the teenage girls looking at the record album and one of them saying, "Gee, Paul McCartney had a band before Wings."

Not only is that not funny anymore, I'll bet most of you can't figure out why it was *ever* funny. Because you're not trained to. Maybe I am like that *New Yorker* curmudgeon ticked about "modern anything."

But I have a deep fear that before too long, MODERN!!! DAY!!! will be what begins tomorrow. . . .

GRANT TINKER'S WAY

Masterson, absorbed in work (he'd just seen a first rough cut of *Full Moon in Blue Water*) went with the specials, asparagus vinaigrette, salmon with shrimp sauce. I joined him in the appetizer, chose the sliced filet in peppercorn sauce, crisp french fries, plus, this being that time of year, Beaujolais Nouveau. The Bistro was doing adequate business. Masterson spoke of possible changes in the movie—editing is similar to screen-writing, only on the far side of shooting. It was an interesting enough meal, with only occasional intrusions: From a nearby table one fan said, "I hope he scores forty," to be answered with, "Forty? *Only forty?* I want eighty. Eighty would be good."

Bernard was returning for the first time this season, as a Washington Bullet. Bernard King—in other words, our Bernard—was the enemy. The Knicks didn't even mention his name when they were hyping the game the week preceding. "The Washington Bullets with Moses Malone and Tyrone Bogues will be in town," the announcer read. Not just an enemy now, worse—not even a worthwhile one.

But we knew. Knick fans need bullshit detectors to survive, and we knew they were *afraid* to mention his name. We might riot. They gave him away to D.C.; not even a draft choice. Those of us who cared will never forgive Garden management for that. Eighty would indeed be good. We were ready to cheer his introduction till our throats begged for mercy—

—but he wasn't even introduced.

The Bullets, under the panicked coaching of Kevin Loughery, were off to at least as rotten a start as we were—42–40 last year, 4–11 now. (A prediction: Loughery will never see February.) Bernard King had been reduced to the second team. Loughery, in his wisdom, went with Charles Jones, who scored absolutely zip in the minutes he played. The Faithful were denied the chance to scream for the fallen hero. You could bottle the anger in the World's Most Famous Arena. . . .

And just the April past, it had all been so different. For, at 8:37, the standing ovation began.

The handsome, slender black raised his left hand briefly, thumb up, in acknowledgment. He tried not to smile, succeeded. He was famous for his game face, the scowl that terrorized opponents. He kept it on now.

8:38. The ovation was louder.

8:39. The sound was beginning to hurt.

And still it built. By this time, he was jumping up and down on the Garden floor, clapping his hands quietly. He must have been nervous, must have been moved.

Nothing showed. The game face was still on.

At 8:40 it became clear that the screaming might never stop, so the announcer went on with the rest of the names and the crowd eventually quieted. But not totally. This was too important to us all. April 10, 1987, and Bernard King was returning to the Garden.

In October of '82, when Dave DeBusschere stole him from Golden State for Micheal Ray Richardson, King was just another fine forward. Certain things stood out—he was a local, Brooklyn born, and he was a recovering alcoholic. His first year with the Knicks he played well, scored 21.9 points a game. The year after that, his average was over 26 and he was first team all-pro.

It was the year following that, '84–'85, that it became clear the Knicks had a Hall of Famer. That year he became one of the three highest scoring forwards of all time (only Rick Barry and Elgin Baylor had higher season averages than King's 32.9). King was voted by his peers the most valuable player in the league, over Larry Bird.

Then in March, toward the end of an absolutely meaningless loss when Hubie shouldn't have even been playing him, he tried to block a Reggie Theus breakaway and destroyed his right knee. The anterior cruciate ligament was ripped. Surgery was done the next week, pronounced successful. (All sports surgery is pronounced "successful" by the way.)

Immediately, there were doubts that King would ever play again. And even if he did manage somehow, what manner of Bernard King would take the floor? Until that terrible March night, he was blinding.

What followed the injury was two years and seventeen days of mystery. Because King insisted on rehabilitating himself totally in private. Not only did the papers know nothing, the Knicks knew nothing. But there were constant rumors. He'd given up, it was hopeless; he was doing incredibly well; the doctors were forlorn, the doctors were jubilant.

Six months after the operation, he was secretly working out on his own at a college in Jersey. A year after the rumor, the Knicks announced he had reinjured the reconstructed knee working out on a weight machine. A year after that, October 17, 1986, he at last returned to Knick workouts. Two days after that, he reinjured the knee jogging near his home, partially tearing another ligament. Then in February, he announced he would return by April.

This was April.

And the Knicks were playing Milwaukee. Brilliantly coached by Don Nelson, they had destroyed the Knicks by 39 points earlier in the season. And were clearly a far superior team.

But you could tell during warm-ups that the Knicks with King back were flying. They were all loosey-goosey, doing outrageous stuffs, laughing, confident. Sure, Milwaukee was better, sure, Milwaukee was tough, but you could sense that a Knick victory was assured.

But we wanted more. We'd waited too long. We wanted a rout. Stomp the bastards. Give—us—some—*joy*. The most points ever scored in a regulation game was 173 by the Celtics in 1959. Well, 173 was a nice number.

But against Milwaukee? With just one new man, albeit a great player. Could he inspire a team to salvage a season with one outrageous effort? Not at the start. The Knicks quickly fell behind 11–4, with King on the bench.

"We want Bernard. We want Bernard." Louder and louder.

He entered the game early in the first quarter, got the ball immediately, shot, and missed but it didn't matter. Because he moved so quickly, the defense couldn't remotely adjust. The ball just didn't fall for him. But it would later. (And it did.) Even though he missed the shot, that miss was still, for most of us, the high point of the season thus far.

But a much higher point was soon to come. Because in the third quarter, with precisely 7:47 to go, the fans stared in silent astonishment and with very good reason.

Because the scoreboard read as follows:

KNICKS: 171
BUCKS: 112

That's 171 to 112 with more than a quarter and a half to go. Two points shy of the all-time NBA scoring record with more than a quarter and a half to go. The largest margin of victory in NBA history was 63 points, and here the scoreboard showed the Knicks already up by 59 with more than a quarter and a half to go. Did even the most passionate of us think that such a slaughter might happen on Bernard King's return with still more than a quarter and a half to go?

Was it really, *really* happening?

Alas, no, what it was was a scoreboard fuck-up: the actual score was 112 to 71 Milwaukee. The Knicks were down by an amazing 41 points with more than a quarter and a half to go. (They eventually lost by 39 again.)

And the fans were in a frenzy. Whatever the reverse of a standing ovation is, that's what they were giving now. Because Bernard was back—he scored 7 points—*but we still stunk.* For all the games he missed, as bashing followed humiliation, we thought, okay you bastards, do it to us while you can, because when we get Bernard back, we're going to do it to you.

The booing subsided eventually and we sat sullen, watching our future, knowing it was going to be like our past. Sometimes there's God so quickly—and sometimes there isn't.

What's the color of glum?

Now, in his first return as an enemy, he sat on the bench watching as the Bullets, helpless, let us get off to a 9–0 lead. We were still up by that amount when Bernard was at last allowed to play, 6:04 to go in the first.

And in the remainder of that quarter?

Twelve points!

Twelve points in six minutes from a player we didn't even ask a draft pick for.

Were we exulted?

We were not.

Why?

Because our passion was gone. Replaced by an ache. He was in the wrong color uniform now. And would be. Forever. All our fantasies crushed. He wasn't our Bernard any longer. Just another good pro forward, getting on in years. Another foreigner who could creep into town, labor, leave.

In the first 16 games (of which they'd won 4) Pitino's Knicks had made four subtractions, added one guy on.

The addition, Sidney Green, had proved himself a $2.2 million wipe-out. He was shooting 43 percent, averaging slightly over 6 points and 6 rebounds a game.

The four subtractions:

1. Rory Sparrow, gone to Chicago where he became their starting point guard.

2. Gerald Henderson, who this same night was leading the Sixers to a win over the Michael Jordans in Chicago. Henderson scored 13 points in the last quarter alone to ice the upset.

3. Again this same night, Jawann Oldham, playing for Sacramento in Houston, held Akeem even. Oldham, now the starter for Bill Russell, who isn't entirely ignorant of center play, had 19 points, 14 rebounds, and 4 blocked shots.

4. Bernard. Nineteen in the Bullet loss to the Knicks. Nineteen is not perhaps world class, but coming off the bench he still scored as much alone as our two starting forwards did together.

A famous television figure once said to me. "When you get really desperate, you do it Grant Tinker's way."

I didn't understand and said so.

He explained: "Everyone has all kinds of bullshit theories. And sometimes you get lucky and do okay for a while. But when it goes bad, and it always will, when you get really, *really* desperate, you do what Grant Tinker does—it's very simple—you hire talent you have faith in and you leave it alone."

It's not hard, looked at from that perspective, to run a sports franchise. All you do is hire, whatever his title, the best general manager available. And the general manager then chooses that man who he thinks will best run his team.

They *must* be in synch. If you're a baseball team and the general manager believes in home runs and the manager lives and dies with speed, you may luck out for a while but disaster is smiling, waiting for you.

It's the same in basketball.

The Knicks started going bad with Sonny Werblin. He hired Hubie Brown as his coach before he hired Dave DeBusschere as his head of basketball. There is no way DeBusschere hires Brown—not because they like each other or don't, but because they see different games. Hubie likes to walk it up and control the game; DeBusschere believes in letting the players play.

But as a team they did okay. Taking over a franchise that had won 33 games, they won 44, then 47.

Then they were killed by injuries. But that 47-game team, headed by Bernard King and Billy Cartwright, was clearly on the come. The ensuing injuries brought the losses. DeBusschere was fired. Brown should have been at the same time. I asked a Garden executive why they didn't and the answer was, "He's still got too much left on his contract, we'll fire him then."

By waiting, by allowing the Knicks to start 4–12 the year preceding, they had to fire Brown under duress. Had they done it sooner, well, Jack Ramsey, among others, was available.

This year, for the first time since the end of the '81–'82 season, they were starting from scratch again.

And made the same mistakes, only worse.

The president and chief executive officer of Madison Square Garden Corporation, which means he is, among other things, the president of the Knicks, is this guy Richard Evans. Who is titanically inexperienced, although theoretically not dumb, but you can't tell that from me, and has given the store to Pitino, a thirty-five-year-old hustler who is a protégé of Hubie Brown—you know, walk it up, I'll call the plays, forget you might once have been an athlete. In the first 16 games, the Knicks were ripping the league apart in number of fouls per game. That is part of Pitino's philosophy—don't give away any easy baskets, make them pay, foul them. The Knicks are 10 percent ahead of the old record— *over 33 fouls per game.* Which means a procession to the free throw line.

Which means snooze.

Agony sitting there.

Worst of all, though, is if we'd just done nothing but go with what we had, we'd have been all right.

> BACKCOURT: Mark Jackson
> Trent Tucker
> Gerald Henderson
> Rory Sparrow
> Gerald Wilkins

FRONTCOURT: Patrick Ewing
Billy Cartwright
Jawann Oldham
Bernard King
Pat Cummings
Louis Orr
Kenny Walker

I'm sorry, but to me that's a playoff team. It's not going to win, but it'll get there. You may argue and say that Ewing and King can't play together. I think you're full of it. The point is, *no one knows.*

King was hurt during Ewing's first two years except for the last six games, and in those, Ewing was not 100 percent. He wanted to play, management wouldn't let him. I think Ewing and King might have been sensational together. Throw a rookie like Jackson in there, with Wilkins or Tucker shooting and Oldham coming in to block, that's a basketball team.

What we have now is not. Pitino is already sniping at Bianchi in the papers.

What this is really about, to 'fess up, isn't the Knicks, it's me. I know what's going to happen. From experience. The Knicks will stink and lose and stink and lose and Bianchi will get fired when it gets really awful and then Pitino will join his god Hubie somewhere in Jersey.

But what about me?

I have been mad for this team for twenty-plus years now. I have won and I have lost. I have endured injuries, suffered pain, humiliation, comebacks, joy.

And always I have *cared.* Ask anyone who knows me. Boy, do I care. And the terrible truth is, I'm starting not to. The Knicks won the other night and I was sour afterward. I'm starting to live with bile bubbling constantly. I don't tape every out-of-town game anymore.

It's bad, a bad team, a bad dumb team run by assistant coaches presided over by a guy who helped bring Liberace to Radio City. Put that on Evans's tombstone.

But that's his job. I'm talking about my *life.* If I stop caring, tell me, pray, how do I survive the winters . . . ?

THE NETS:
REBUILDING A FRANCHISE

49.
45.
42.
39.
24.

What could those numbers mean? Let's be optimistic. Say you were a
fat person who suddenly was confronted with true love, went not on a
crash but a sensible diet. And those beautifully diminishing numbers
represented your waistline. Cause for cheer.

Let's be realistic. Suppose you were the nomads of the NBA, the
New Jersey Nets basketball team, and those numbers represented your
total wins over each of the past five years. (On an 82-game schedule,
remember. So when you won 49, you only lost 32. But when you won
24, you lost 58.) Even Mister Micawber wouldn't find much to smile
about.

The Nets, in this week's hour of need, turned for help to Harry
Weltman, and made him vice president and general manager of the
club. Not a stupid move. Because if those numbers seemed daunting to
thee and me, and Lord knows they should, they weren't to Weltman.
Not because he is an optimist by nature. It's because he's seen a lot
worse.

Cleveland, the year before he took them over in '82, had won but 15,
one of the worst records ever. (Not to mention no first-round draft
picks for the next several years.) Three years later, Weltman had
them in the playoffs, and attendance had come close to tripling.

Weltman, fifty-three, is a slender, charming guy, quick to smile, who
often seems to be repressing the need to giggle when things get just
this side of murderous.

What sustains him just might be an eye for talent. His first pro team
was the ABA St. Louis Spirits. A new franchise when he began with
them in '74, they folded with the league in 1976. But in that time
Weltman had assembled one of the most talented squads in history:
Don Chaney, Ron Boone, Freddie Lewis, M. L. Carr, Marvin Barnes,
Caldwell Jones, Maurice Lucas, Moses Malone.

So he knew a player when he saw one, and he'd seen clubs in more dreadful condition. Still, rebuilding the Nets was going to be brutal. Not only were they a crumbling franchise, he was without four of the next eight first and second round draft choices. And sure you can build with rejects and trades and European players and CBA players, but the best way to stabilize is through the college draft.

This year the Nets picked third. David Robinson had to be taken first, and the odds favored Phoenix plucking Armon Gilliam, the power forward from Las Vegas U. (Phoenix indeed did take him.) The Nets had so many needs—everything but power forward, where Buck Williams anchors the franchise. But Williams, a splendid player, and the most unknown (to the world, not to his peers) star of his time, is not, except by example, a team leader. He does not, in the locker room, grab the job by the throat. And as much as anything, the Nets needed a team leader.

Alas, none were thought to be available for the No. 3 slot in this draft. Drafting, by the way, is about as reliable as phrenology. But there are at least a few fumbling rules of thumb.

1. The first thing you look for is the player himself.

2. The second thing you look for is the most pressing immediate needs of the team.

3. The size of the player. Teams tend to talk small and pick big. Everyone always says they're going after the legendary "best player available" and ends up taking size.

4. The color of the player. But this is, tra-la, diminishing. Primarily because older people, who remember when the game was white, resented the dominance of the black athlete. But the younger fans are used to black stars, expect black stars, and aren't remotely as bothered by black dominance.

And beyond these are gut feelings. Teams call players in for lunches, dinners, breakfasts. They talk to them, test them, give them physicals. G.M.'s talk to them, coaches talk to them, groups of people talk to them. You ask the kid the toughest guy he's played. You ask him his strong points, his weaknesses. You probe and you push and you do your very damndest.

Still, it's at best an odds-against crap shoot.

And even though there were thought to be no team leaders up for grabs, there were some terrific players to be had and the media felt the Nets were most interested in three. The scouting reports, when put into English, more or less follow:

DENNIS HOPSON	REGGIE WILLIAMS	DERRICK MCKEY
Born: 4/22/65	Born: 3/5/64	Born: 10/10/66
Ohio State	Georgetown	Alabama
6'5", 200	6'7", 190	6'9", 205
All-American, First Team	All-American, First Team	All-American Second Team

GOOD	GOOD	GOOD
Speed	Almost a carbon	Big
Quick	of Hopson	Runs
Ballhandling	Can go 6 for 18	Shoots
Passing	and still help you	Shotblocker
Competitive	Wants to win *badly*	Good free throw
Good kid	Hard as nails	percentage: 86%
Liked by teammates		Wants to please
Led US in scoring		Good team player
Can rebound		
Got better in college		
Coachable		

BAD	BAD	BAD
Not a leader	Lateral quickness?	*Very* quiet
Defense?	Defense only within	Not assertive
	a structure	Not as good a rebounder as he should be

The draft, to repeat, is so important to a team, and so many things can screw up. (Last year, many of the early picks had drug-related incidents.) Teams nowadays try very hard to check the backgrounds of the players. Weltman also uses an hour and a half psychological written test to be used as a personality guide; he'd also done this in Cleveland.

There are three main predraft basketball tournaments each year, in Portsmouth, Virginia; Hawaii; and Chicago.

1. Portsmouth: Mainly for prospective second- and third-round players looking to move up.

2. Hawaii: Many potential first-round players, minus the super top guys.

3. Chicago: For top guys who screwed up in Hawaii and others who did well in Portsmouth and are looking to move up even more.

This year, for example, Scottie Pippen went from being a total unknown to being very hot (taken fifth by Seattle). Ken Norman, a projected lottery pick, did poorly in Hawaii and needed Chicago to vindicate himself (taken nineteenth by the L.A. Clippers). Muggsy Bogues, all sixty-three inches of him, was thought by many to be the best player, not the best prospect (taken twelfth, by Washington, I think a gutsy, terrific pick).

The three players Weltman was most interested in might not be of interest to a different club. But the Nets needed, most desperately, help up front and a shooting guard.

They took Hopson. (Williams went next, fourth, to the Clippers, while McKey, an undergraduate, was taken ninth, by Seattle, another terrific pick, say I.)

(Aside: Any predictions or feelings I write down are not written with hindsight. This is being done before the season gets under way. I'm a lot of things, but not a second guesser. Except sometimes.

For example, I stopped writing about the Knicks when they were 14-and-28 this season, before their thumping, Jackson-led drive to the playoffs.)

Weltman's theory is simple: The players are the team. And the coach's job is to maximize results with the players he's been given. Play the hand you're dealt. You try to lower the age of your team. You hire strength coaches.

But there is no quick fix. Not for a franchise in deep trouble. You pray for a good spot in the draft. Hope you select well for your needs.

But there simply is no easy solution. You have to dig in and be willing to suffer. (Weltman suffered in Cleveland—one year they started 2-and-19.)

After the draft, this was Weltman's team:

POWER FORWARD	SMALL FORWARD
CHARLES LINWOOD (BUCK) WILLIAMS	ORLANDO WOOLRIDGE
The best.	20 points per game.
Superb rebounder.	A wonderful runner.
17-plus points per game.	Can explode on any night.

Not a great passer.
An attitude you want to
     bottle.
Amazingly durable—had
     never missed a pro game
     because of injury.
     Almost 500 games.

Fair passer.
Not a trench warrior.
Reasonably durable.

CENTER

DARRYL DAWKINS
All body.
Wonderfully talented.
Has been wonderfully talented since '75.
A consistent disappointment.
Fragile—in the Nets' last 246 games,
     he has missed 150.

MIKE GMINSKI
A wonderful backup center.
A wonderful free-throw shooter.
Smart.
Durable enough—but only for a
     backup. In trouble when he's
     starter.

POINT GUARD

DWAYNE (PEARL) WASHINGTON
A playground legend.
A high school superstar.
A college starter.
A pro disappointment.
     Overweight, inconsistent.
     Which way would the graph
go this year?

SHOOTING GUARD

OTIS BIRDSONG
Super shooter.
Thirty-two.
Fragile—missed 75 games
     last year.

DENNIS HOPSON
Rookie.

Not enough to send the Celtics into shock, but with a lot of luck, not an embarrassment either. Williams is a franchise player, Woolridge can score, and with Williams flanking him his rebounding deficiencies are bearable.

Dawkins, though, is a problem. Arguably, the most disappointing player of all time. A breaker of coaches' hearts from coast to coast.

Should always be remembered as perhaps the dumbest young center ever—if it weren't for Dawkins's stupidity on the court, Magic Johnson, in his rookie year playing out of position at center, wouldn't have become famous while still in puberty.

If Dawkins is problem *A*, Washington is *A*-prime. He'd been on a weight program over the summer and his attitude was said to be much improved. But he was a local kid and the pressure on him to duplicate his childhood years was unending.

So Weltman makes a trade.

A terrific trade, thought I. He sent Dawkins and another thirty-year-old physical specimen/disappointment to Cleveland, in return for point guard John Bagley and the enigmatic forward Keith Lee.

Bagley, twenty-seven and chunky, is never going to be a scorer. But he can penetrate, can really rebound for a man his size, is a top pressure free-throw shooter.

And he takes the pressure off Washington. The Nets now have two point guards potentially capable of leading the team.

But Keith is the key. A double All-American at Memphis State, Lee is twenty-four, six-foot-ten, 220 pounds. Weltman is enamored of his talents. Lee can pass, shoot, score, block, rebound in traffic, has a strong desire to win.

He also has these knees.

He also has these knees.

They will never be compared in durability with Walter Payton's. Not only that, Lee has played for Weltman before. If any single personnel decision led to Weltman's firing from Cleveland, it was when he traded for Lee on draft day of '85, getting him from Chicago essentially for Charles Oakley, who turned into a rebounding monster. (And is leading the league as I write this now in late '87.)

Still, Weltman took the gamble and now this was his starting eight:

POWER FORWARD	SMALL FORWARD
BUCK WILLIAMS	ORLANDO WOOLRIDGE

CENTER

MIKE GMINSKI

And KEITH LEE spelling them all.

POINT GUARD	SHOOTING GUARD
PEARL WASHINGTON	OTIS BIRDSONG
JOHN BAGLEY	DENNIS HOPSON

Still not a powerhouse, but all in all, a competitive team. Young, quick, a good rebounding bunch. Weltman hoped to get 30 points a game out of the shooting guard position. Pressure off at point guard. Sure they were small—the up-front guys only went from six-foot-eight to six-foot-ten, but they were good enough to give you trouble at the other end.

If only they stayed healthy.

Something Weltman did not do. On the Fourth of July, while casually volleying a tennis ball with his wife, Weltman got his feet tangled (though he was an excellent athlete), went down, and decimated his Achilles tendon. He could feel it scooting up his leg.

Most of the rest of the month is a blur. He's in the hospital, he's out of the hospital. He's in a huge cast, toe to thigh, can't sleep, is ill all the time until it's realized the cast is what's making him ill by unbalancing him in bed. A smaller cast is put on. He's still taking medication for the pain while trying to stay in touch with his New Jersey team from Cleveland, where he was when the accident happened, getting ready to move.

Eventually, he goes onto crutches, then just one crutch, finally a cane. He is trying desperately to be able to walk to his seat for the home opener. It's against Cleveland, the team that fired him. (He won't quite make it, still needing the assistance of a cane.)

But his health doesn't matter to the team. And when training camp opens, there is a wonderful new spirit. Coach Dave Wohl is as pleased as a guy with a 38 percent winning percentage can dare to be. Buck is Buck. Orlando is Orlando. And Keith Lee is running. Without pain.

Weltman is, by mid-October, on the phone or in meetings all the day long. He is awaiting a medical report on four of his players who have nagging injuries. Finally, at the end of the day, knowing nothing of the outside world, he makes contact with the medico and the doctor says, "Well, the news isn't good but it's better than the stock market."

"What did the stock market do?" Weltman asks.

"Down five hundred points," from the medical maven.

And now the most wonderful feeling of relief comes over Weltman, because he knows his players are all right. Health reigns. He knows this because he knows the doctor is kidding him.

The most wonderful feeling of relief, alas, is not long in staying around the Nets' offices. All four players are hurt seriously. One of them, Woolridge, lost an argument with a scissors and would be gone for a month.

And Keith Lee would be gone indefinitely. Why indefinitely? Because they hadn't the foggiest what was wrong with him. He had gone into anguish without being touched the fourth day of training and they couldn't find the source.

But they were pretty sure it wasn't his knees.

Also Otis Birdsong would miss the opener.

Weltman is taking the phone call like Slapsie Maxie Rosenbloom now, as cruncher after cruncher lands. All he knows for sure is that his plans are out the window.

He has no small forward. (He eventually brings one in from L.A. the night before the Cleveland game.) He has no center backup. And he must start his rookie, Hopson, with all the ensuing confidence risks.

It began 2-and-19 once a few years ago in Cleveland. A start like that eats your innards to shreds. There are tears behind your eyes. You feel humiliated going to get the goddamn morning papers. You grow paranoid. Why are people turning their heads when they see me? Why are they scurrying across streets?

Whyyyyy . . . ?

The announced crowd for the Cleveland opener was just over thirteen thousand. Maybe ten thousand were actually there. And they were, as Net crowds always are, well-mannered, silent. Close your eyes, you'd think you were in L.A.

Above, in the Caesar's Palace color scheme of Byrne Arena, hangs the lone bright light of the Nets: Julius Erving's No. 32 is a constant reminder of both possibilities and failure: the Nets had him, gave him away to Philly, and destroyed the future of the franchise.

Richie Havens sang the anthem and got the words way wrong. If you didn't know the song, you wouldn't have known the song. Twenty cheerleaders with pom-poms bounded onto the floor. The teams were introduced quietly. On the bench, in street clothes, were Birdsong, Woolridge, and Lee.

Weltman, hobbling on his cane, was wearing a gray tweed jacket, a red tie. He sat quietly through the game and if you hadn't examined his face, you could have assumed he was just another Jerseyite. But the tautness of the lips, the continual whispered urgings, the way his fingers clasped and unclasped told you no fan was this involved.

The Nets played well. Adrian Branch, who flew all night from Los

Angeles, scored a career-high 20 points. Gminski had 22. Hopson, the
rookie, hit for 16. And Buck was Buck, 23 points, 16 rebounds.

With ten minutes to go it was 91–91. Weltman's silent mutterings
were continual now.

Nine minutes left: down 91–96.

Now eight: 93–100.

Seven: 93–102.

But the Nets were tough and with four minutes left, they'd cut the
lead to 5. Plenty of time.

A minute and a half left: 105–109. Still time. Weltman is sitting there
quietly, doing his incantations, skin the color of snow. An opening win
would be such a blessing. Especially an opening comeback win. Particularly an opening comeback win against the team that had fired him, a
solid professional team, which is what he planned for the Nets to be,
soon.

Buck goes for a lay-up to cut the lead to two. The lay-up is blown,
the Cavs recover, score, it's over quickly, 114–108.

Weltman and his wife go out for a drink with friends after. He is, as
always, charming. Talk circles this way, that, but it always comes back
to the game. Not just the Nets game but basketball. Because he truly
loves it. And he thinks the beauty (his word) of the college game is
being trampled by the over-dominating coaches. The beauty of the
game is just letting the players fly. But not without plan. You want to
frame a player, he says. If you do it right, each player is framed so he
can function always at what he does best, within his limitations. If you
can get a player framed properly and then a team framed properly, well
. . . what could be prettier?

That first loss, that was the high point of the first quarter of the
season, though Weltman had no way of knowing it then. The injuries
would become genuinely amazing—at one December game the Nets
only dressed nine players, had *six* on the bench in street clothes. They
lost eleven in a row. Woolridge got injured again. Hopson had trouble
with the rookie pressure and his shot was gone.

The only constant was Buck, indestructible Buck, getting his 17
points and 11-plus rebounds a game—

—then Buck, for the first time, destructed, damaging an ankle in
pursuit of Washington's Bernard King. Keith Lee might never play, the
rumors were. Other rumors had Weltman himself in trouble. He fired

the coach, brought in an interim. The rumor machine went crazy, claiming Hubie Brown was in line for the job. If he was, and Weltman hired him, surely he would get Weltman fired, if not sooner, then later.

After 21 games, the Nets had won 3. Making a projection look like this:

49
45
42
39
24
12!

Maybe twelve wins Weltman's first year of rebuilding. Worse than the Cleveland nightmare. Could a man survive?

Sure. It's a job. He was employed. He had a terrific wife, two good kids. And he was walking again, unaided—

—if only he could say as much for his team. . . .

TO THE DEATH

Certain scholars in the field of epistemology theorize that words are, truly, alive. And some words, those close in meaning, are in competition with each other. And when two words come to mean *exactly* the same thing, one of them dies.

That is as far as this book is going to get into linguistics, and the thought came to me this morning as I was going over my stats (which is my caffeine substitute now that I've given up morning coffee) and read that Mr. Bird of Boston, while leading his team to their fourth straight win this '87–'88 season, had managed to accumulate, along with 2 blocks, 3 steals, 5 assists, the quite grand total of 42 points, and 20 rebounds.

Forty-plus points and 20 rebounds in one game. That's a week for a Knick forward.

The article went on to report that it was Bird's first "40-20" game and, "it is believed," the first ever by a Celtic. Amazing. All of Boston's glorious history, all those legitimate Hall of Famers, and this is the first by a Celt. What this team tidbit does, of course, is put the special quality of Bird's feat into even stronger relief. I wonder if any other player today has ever done it? Has Barkley? Maybe. Has Akeem? Possibly. Can you come up with any other candidates? I can't.

Are we all not in agreement that this is not your ho-hum effort? I suspect we are.

Well, Wilt Chamberlain, for the first 450-plus *games* of his career, *averaged better than that.* Over the first *six seasons* of his there-are-no-words basketball life, Chamberlain put up these numbers: 40.6 points and 24.9 rebounds.

I'm going to guess now. What you're thinking is this: "Sure he was something, but the game's different now. He couldn't do that kind of thing today." I agree with you. The game is different. And he could never put up numbers like that today. Wilt is not playing anymore (although not a season goes by that someone doesn't seriously ask him to return) and no one will ever know for sure what he would do today. My feelings? I think he'd be a lot better now.

With the total dissolution of talent that exists at center today, why not? Is Alton Lister going to give him trouble? Is Mike Gminski going to beat him down the court? Kareem? Kareem didn't much damage him when Wilt was old and Kareem was young. Sure Moses would make him work and so would Olajuwon. But tell me Robert Parish is going to muscle him. And Robert Parish is going to end up in the Hall of Fame.

I guess the point is this: In their time, just as Bird and Magic are joined at the hip, once it was Wilt and Russell. Now that time has begun to take its toll I think Russell is beginning to fade. An all-time great center, no question. The greatest winner in the history of his sport? You bet. But start a franchise and you can have one or the other. Once there was argument. Now I'd guess Wilt would win breezing.

Russell is beginning to die.

Reasons? Many and, to coin a phrase, varied. Russell, since his Celtic days, has turned out to be a most mediocre coach and a putrescent broadcaster.

Also (and yes, I know Russell was voted the greatest player in league history less than a decade ago), as more and more of his teammates justly go into the Hall of Fame, it's clearer that Russell was brilliantly framed by Mr. Auerbach. He never had to do what he couldn't do. (Like Balanchine, revered among dancers for changing the steps to suit the performer: If a guy can't do a double air turn,

Balanchine would change it to something within the dancer's limitations.) And Russell's limitations? He was a shitty shooter. Put him on
today's Boston or L.A. teams, he'd be fabulous. Put him on today's
Indiana or Phoenix, he'd be exposed. As a great defensive player who
couldn't score. A world-class Tree Rollins.

And Wilt? The knocks against him were two in his playing days: few
championships and a dreadful free throw shooter. Well, yes, he was
only on two championship teams, but one of them, the lesser of them,
set I think an unassailable mark of 33 straight wins. And the other,
Philly, '66–'67, is increasingly regarded as the greatest team in history
and has been so voted from time to time. And of course he stunk at free
throws (51 percent). But so did Russell (56 percent). And put Wilt
anywhere, either the L.A. Lakers or the L.A. Clippers, and he would be
devastating.

Plus, history comes to Wilt.

While Russell is out tarnishing the old image as he seeks the spot-
light, Wilt is quiet in L.A. But the news finds him. Either when some
team wants him to come back and play for them . . .

. . . or whenever a record is talked of.

During Michael Jordan's amazing '86–'87, Wilt was always in the
papers because Jordan was always scoring the most *this*'s since Wilt
Chamberlain or taking the most *that*'s since Wilt Chamberlain.

And *that* ain't gonna change, folks. Not in *this* century.

Take big-scoring games, for example. Michael Jordan hit 60 points,
twice last year. In the eighties, only two other men have done it, each
once: Bernard King and Larry Bird. Four times this decade.

Seven other guys did it once: Fulks (the first), Mikan, Gervin,
West, Barry, Maravich, and David "oh-what-a-fall-was-there" Thompson. Elgin Baylor did it thrice.

And Wilt? Well, it's been done 46 times so you substract. Wilt: 32.
The rest of basketball: 14. At the present rate, we will be well into the
twenty-first century before the NBA catches up.

Switching briefly to baseball. During my formative years, this was
the all-time baseball team. (When two vied, they're listed alphabetically.)

    1B   Gehrig, Sisler
    2B   Lajoie
    SS   Wagner
    3B   Traynor

OF   Cobb, Ruth, Speaker
C   Cochrane

Today, I suspect, the team would look like this:

1B   Gehrig
2B   Morgan
SS   Wagner
3B   Robinson/Schmidt
OF   Aaron/Mays, Ruth
C   Bench/Berra/Campanella

What happened to George Sisler? He didn't lose a step after he died. In 1920, he hit .407 and had 257 hits. (Not to mention 49 doubles, 18 triples, 19 home runs, 137 runs scored, 122 runs batted in, 42 stolen bases; he was also the Keith Hernandez of his era, leading the league's first basemen in assists 6 times.) And 1920 wasn't a freak Norm Cash year. The year after, he slipped to .371. The year after that he atoned, going .420 for the season. (With 51 stolen bases, 134 runs scored in just 142 games. He also knocked in over a hundred.) He ended up with a lifetime .340, but before he was struck down with an illness in his prime—he'd just finished the .420 season and although he was still a force, was never the same after—his average was over .360.

He stopped being a figure of conjecture. He collided with Gehrig and just as there can't be two identical words, there can't be two identical greatest anything else's, first basemen included. Sisler was the greatest. Then Gehrig came along. The two ran step-for-step. Gehrig died more glamorously—Gary Cooper never played George Sisler.

Baseball today, probably except in St. Louis, is as if he never happened. The same is true of many others on the first list: Nap Lajoie is not much mentioned anymore.

And Bird and Magic's time is coming.

It's easy being fans of theirs now. But wait. Give it a decade. If God grants us a year 2000, when they'll be trotted out for Old Timer's Games, people will look at Magic and say, "Well, for his time, sure, he was good, but he couldn't shoot with anybody guarding him and he played with Kareem behind him covering his defensive weaknesses." And Bird? "Too slow for today's games—not a good percentage shooter under pressure—never shot even .500 when it counted, in a playoff final—got undressed by even mediocre one-on-one forwards—sure he was good, so was Magic—

"But they couldn't play today."

I have no idea which of today's giants will maintain their size, who will shrink and who will commence to tower even more. But I do know that after a player's career is ended, his real struggle begins. In 2000 will Payton be another who "couldn't have played today—too small." Kareem? "Couldn't have played today, too soft, maybe the worst rebounder for his size ever."

Each era is so arrogant, so dismissive. Everybody *knows* that George Mikan, voted the greatest player of the half century, "couldn't have played today—too slow." And soon, trust me, they'll start sniping at Mays—"only .302 lifetime, couldn't have played today." Not this decade, but next; that surely will happen.

The greatest struggle an athlete undergoes is the battle for our memories. It's gradual. It begins before you're aware it's begun, and it ends with a terrible fall from grace. Stripped of medals, sent to Siberia. West and Robertson, the two supreme guards, have fought successfully so far. Frazier made a run; Magic's making one now. Will they survive or will they end up like George Gervin is already—"Oh, he could score all right, good enough for his time, but don't think about Gervin, couldn't have played today."

It really is a battle to the death.

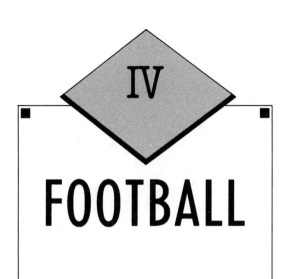

IV

FOOTBALL

THE
REPORTER'S NOTEBOOK

"SOMEONE SPIT
AT MARK'S WINDOW ..."

The strike by the National Football League Players Association—Affiliate of Federation of Professional Athletes, AFL-CIO—had arrived. September 21 had become September 22. It was past midnight in the locker room of the New York Jets at Giants Stadium. The Jets had just trounced the New England Patriots on national television, 43–24. The victory brought the Jets' record to 2–0, at a time when the Giants' record was 0–2. This was no small thing. The Jets were the Other Team in New York and New Jersey. Even when Joe Namath had guaranteed the win over the Colts in Super Bowl III, when Namath had been drinking his Johnny Walker Scotch and owning Manhattan as few New York athletes ever had, the Jets had been the Other Team to the Giants. The Jets had the Super Bowl, but the Giants had history.

The Giants had tradition, throw that in there.

And the Giants had romance. Buy an old Giants fan a couple of drinks, get him talking about Chuckin' Charlie Conerly and Gifford, and what it was like against the Bears in '56, and just cue the tears, okay?

In those days, even with the Giants down and Namath all the way up, the Giants had Yankee Stadium.

The Jets, they were Shea Stadium, Flushing Bay, Queens. Even there, the Jets were the Other Team to the Mets.

The Giants, they were the Old Blue, and the Jets were green.

Mostly with envy.

The Giants moved across the river to New Jersey. Still, they owned New York. And finally they won their own Super Bowl in January of 1987. They were as big as ever.

The Jets, who had started off the previous season 10–1 before going into this tuck position that was the envy of every living platform diver, were more the Other Team than they had ever been.

Except now it was a new season, and the defending champion Giants were 0–2 and looked like shit, and the Jets had just danced all over the Patriots to get to 2–0. Maybe the Jets could do some business. Maybe, if the *Jets* could win a Super Bowl—and, sonofabitch, they had looked good against the Patriots—they could stop being the goddamn Other Team—for a little while, anyway.

Except.

The strike was here. Staring all of them in the face. Official. Stroke of midnight. When the game was over, nobody spent much time talking about Jets 43, Patriots 24. The Jets were all worried about tomorrow. Strikes, even for athletes, are about tomorrow, wondering how it was going to look. The Jets showered in silence, dressed in silence, occasionally bitched to the writers and to each other.

Well, not all the Jets.

Mark Gastineau, he was okay.

Gastineau was letting everybody in the room know that come tomorrow, he was going to be in good shape, you bet.

"Leon Hess (Jets owner) and Jim Kensil (Jets team president) have been very good to me," Gastineau said in the middle of the Jets locker room. There was a crowd of writers around him. The television lights were all over him, just the way he liked.

Gastineau—once the most flamboyant defensive lineman in the game but now just another aging bum—was making it clear that the strike of the NFLPA wasn't going to affect *his* rich ass one bit.

"I'm not in favor of walking out on people who have been very good to me," Mark Gastineau said.

Gastineau, as he spoke, was well past his prime. He had become a joke. Jets fans remembered him the previous January, costing his team a chance at the AFC championship game with a mindless, late-game roughing penalty against the Cleveland Browns' quarterback, keeping a critical Browns drive alive.

Wasn't important.

This was important: Aging bum or no, Gastineau had a contract that said Leon Hess was going to pay him $725,000 for the 1987 NFL season.

Rocky Klever, a Jets tight end known for his heart on the field and facile wit off it, watched the Gastineau show from his corner locker.

"A typical Gastineau move," Klever said. "You tell me who's going to get the most attention if the whole team goes out and one guy doesn't."

In the middle of the room, cameras rolling, pens aflame in notebooks, Gastineau was saying that he just wanted to play football, was that a crime, a man wanting to play football?

Klever laughed.

"*Now* he wants to play football?"

Klever meant, nobody in the room could remember the last time Gastineau had looked anything like the player he had been in the early 1980s, when the Jets defensive line was known as the Sack Exchange, and Gastineau would celebrate sacking another quarterback with his own boogie.

"I mean, that's really funny, Mark wanting to play football," Rocky Klever said, toweling himself dry.

The next day the Jets—at least the Jets who were going out on strike—showed up at the team's Hofstra University training facility, picking up what would be their last paychecks for the month the strike would last.

In the parking lot outside the Jets practice fields, Gastineau still dominated the conversation of his teammates.

Player representative Kurt Sohn said, "I don't know about Mark. He hasn't been coming to meetings. He's never been a part of all this. I asked Mark to attend a meeting this morning, but he said he had made up his mind about not honoring the strike, and there was nothing anybody could do to change his mind."

Freeman McNeil, the Jets star running back throughout the 1980s, had vaguely suggested in the days leading up to the strike that he might not honor a picket line, either. But now, with the reality of the strike at hand and the Jets in the parking lot, McNeil softly said, "I'm supporting my teammates." And safety Harry Hamilton, another veteran who had wondered out loud about whether he would go out on strike with the rest of the Jets, the rest of the Players Association, said, "To take the field with the scabs they're going to bring in would be cheating the fans, the coaches, and the sport in general."

Linebacker Bob Crable said, "The scabs are going to think they're fulfilling a dream, playing in the NFL, but they won't be playing in the NFL."

And so the players' strike of 1987 began to unfold with the Jets and the rest of the NFL. It was just a little uglier with the Jets, and a little more visible because of the New York stage, and nobody really knew it at the time because nobody knew how long the strike was going to last, but the Jets began to die.

On Wednesday, Gastineau defended his decision to cross the picket line.

Again.

Again making it sound like he was on PT 109 and Leon Hess was Jack Kennedy.

"Leon Hess has never gotten up from a table after I've sat down in front of him," Gastineau said in the Jets locker room.

The writers just looked at each other as he rambled on.

"I've had players on this team do that," Gastineau continued. "Mr. Hess has never not talked to me. I've had people on this team not talk to me. Mr. Hess is always there with a pat on the back. I'm willing to suffer whatever I have to."

Gastineau, even in the role of aging bum, was a name player, a former star, and the word of his defection from the strike was already drawing responses from striking players around the league. Redskins linebacker Neal Olkewicz said, "He's a jerk and his teammates know it." Bears defensive end Dan Hampton said, "What he's doing figures. Gastineau has an IQ of about room temperature."

The Jets assistant player rep, Reggie McElroy, suggested that the only reason Dan Hampton hadn't equated Gastineau's IQ with his uniform number—99—was "because the uniform number is too high."

That night, Gastineau's estranged wife, Lisa, went on a Fox Network television program called *A Current Affair*. She said she found Gastineau's prestrike claims that alimony and child support would make honoring a strike impossible, well, sort of interesting.

Lisa Gastineau said, "His sudden concern for alimony payments *is* sudden, because we've gone months without seeing any. As for my daughter, he's gone three months without picking up the phone to call her and four months without seeing her."

She was asked about Gastineau's touching pledge of allegiance to Hess.

"Well, it's very honorable to say, 'I have to fulfill my obligations,'" she said. "Or to say, 'I have responsibilities.' But if Mark feels that way, it would definitely be a change of personality."

Gastineau's teammates were laughing at him.

Players around the league were insulting him.

His wife went on television, called him a deadbeat.

A week later, on October 1, Gastineau's teammate, Reggie McElroy, said he wasn't really sure which Jet it was who tried to spit on old No. 99.

The first days of scab football were lively.

On Thursday, September 24, the Jets management hired a bus to transport thirty-one replacement players from the Long Island Marriott to Hofstra.

When it got to Hofstra, the Jets on the picket lines pelted the bus with eggs, screamed insults at the players inside the bus. Jets team president Jim Kensil called the police. The next day, this is what the pro football season looked like at the Jets training facility at Hofstra:

A presidential motorcade.

The bus from the Long Island Marriott was escorted by police motorcycles, three squad cars, an ambulance, a tow truck, two campus security guards. Placekicker Pat Ragusa, a St. John's graduate who had come straight to replacement football from a job as a gas station attendant, looked at the way the escort cars and motorcycles and two trucks were organized around the bus.

Ragusa said, "Is there a police convention here?" And got into the bus for the short ride to the Hofstra facility where he would try to be a New York Jet. Mark Gastineau was already inside the locker room, having driven his car through a back gate so as to avoid his teammates on the other side of the picket line.

On Sunday, when the Jets would have been playing the Steelers if that week's games had not been canceled by the league owners, the picketing Jets decided to hold "Fan Appreciation Day" at Eisenhower Park in East Meadow, Long Island. It was an Open House–type picnic and autographing session, and more than five hundred Jets fans showed up to essentially spend an afternoon being part of the 1987 strike by the National Football League Players Association, Affiliate of Federation of Professional Athletes, AFL-CIO.

Most of the talk was about Gastineau.

Again: Long time since he had been a star, leading the league in sacks, doing his stupid dance for the people in the stands.

But it didn't stop him from being a star, or a veteran, but he was now officially over there and they were over here, and everybody knew what a fragile thing team unity was in sports, and it was like there was this small cut the Jets had, but they couldn't stop the bleeding. . . .

"The only negative thing I heard from the fans all day was about Mark," tight end Mickey Shuler said.

Indeed. Dave Hoff, a Jets fan who had come all the way to Fan Appreciation Day from Laurence Harbor, New Jersey, dressed up a stuffed animal he called "My pet monster" in Gastineau's No. 99 jersey, hung the stuffed animal in effigy from a tree in Eisenhower Park.

George Kaywood, a Jets fan from Uniondale, Long Island, wore a red T-shirt that had SCABINEAU written on the back.

Kaywood, a member of the Teamsters Union, said, "Gastineau should be over here with the rest of the guys. Who does he think he is?"

That was easy.

Gastineau was the guy who couldn't get up from Leon Hess's table, which is why Guy Bingham tried to spit through the window of Gastineau's gray Mercedes on October 1.

There were twenty-five Jets on the picket line in the Hofstra parking lot. Security had been beefed up each day. Gastineau's car approached the Oak Street Gate. He was on the passenger side of the front seat. A female companion was driving.

The car stopped. A security man went to open the gate, recognizing that it was Gastineau.

Reggie McElroy, striking Jet, assistant player representative, went to Gastineau's side of the car, put his hands on the roof, and yelled in at Gastineau.

"Scab," McElroy said.

For the Jets, the strike, right there at Gastineau's car, first of October, got as ugly as it was going to get.

It wasn't just McElroy. It was all of them, surrounding the Mercedes, blocking its way, yelling "Scab" at the man who had once been the best defensive end in football.

Bingham spit.

Gastineau, who had been yelling back at his teammates, suddenly flung open the car door and began to chase Bingham (some of Gastineau's teammates would express wonder later, noting that Gastineau had pursued a real National Football League player with a sort of speed he hadn't showed in years).

McElroy chased Gastineau, caught him from behind, got him in a bear hug. With the help of other picketing Jets, McElroy sat Gastineau back down in the Mercedes. Gastineau's shirt was torn.

Gastineau (safely inside the Jets locker room later): "When somebody spits at you, you have to get out and defend yourself. Your grandmother would do that. When you get spit in the face, it's not right."

Joe Klecko crossed the line the next day.

Klecko was thirty-three years old, perhaps the greatest Jets player since Namath: Klecko in *his* prime was perhaps the greatest NFL nose tackle of all time. Klecko's career had nearly ended because of a knee injury the season before. Klecko was still in the process of an agonizing rehabilitation. The team doctors had already advised him to retire. Klecko refused.

Now he limped across the line, telling his striking teammates it might be his last salary-earning year, and that he had already lost $50,000 out of his $812,000 contract for the '87 season.

Rocky Klever watched Klecko enter the locker room door, shook his head.

"All week," Klever said, "Joe's been telling us that the first guy who talks to Gastineau gets punched in the face." Klever smiled. "So I guess what I'm wondering is if Joe has punched himself in the face yet."

Marty Lyons, a thirty-year-old defensive end also living off a past reputation as the member of the old Sack Exchange, also crossed with Klecko. Lyons, earning $425,000 for the 1987 season, said he had to do it because of loyalty to his family.

That's what Lyons told the writers, anyway.

He told his teammates he was doing it to try to help the Jets stay unbeaten.

Klever (who by now had become the Jets unofficial anti-scab spokesman): "We'd respect Marty a lot more if he'd told *us* he was doing it for the money, and for his family. It's like that scene in *Fatal Attraction* where Michael Douglas is telling Glenn Close he can't see her anymore. She says, 'I'd have more respect for you if you just told me to fuck off.' "

Kurt Sohn said, "Marty didn't totally turn his back on us, but in the final analysis his reason was money, and he denied that to our faces. He told us he wanted to help the Jets win. We tried to explain to him that he was speaking to the Jets, that *we* were the Jets, but he'd made up his mind."

The Jets, scab Jets, played their first strike game against the Dallas Cowboys, lost 38–24, before 12,370 fans at Giants Stadium. Klever and quarterbacks Ken O'Brien and Pat Ryan watched the game on television at Manhattan's tony Sporting Club. Klever later said, "We were going to chug a beer every time Gastineau got a sack, but after the first quarter, we got kind of thirsty. So we said we'd chug a beer every time he made a tackle, but by halftime, we were *really* thirsty. So then we just decided to chug a beer every time he lined up."

Mark Gastineau, No. 99, playing against gas station attendants and the like, had two tackles for the game.

One assist.

No sacks.

Three days later, Joe Fields—known as "The General" to the Jets—became the fourth Jet past the age of thirty to cross the line. The General, he said he needed the money too, he was getting old. Like Klecko, Fields was thirty-three years old.

Freeman McNeil said, "There are some things worth fighting for. I happen to think my teammates are worth more than a few thousand bucks."

And the Jets died a little more. It was one thing for the Jets, Other Team at Giants Stadium, Other Team forever, to be an odd mixture of talented youth and over-the-hill names. It was quite another for young players on a professional sports team to watch older players fold under the pressures of a strike, seemingly within minutes after the strike was called. Now the world knew there was no foundation to this team, no center, that 2–0 was a fake, that the Jets were a fake.

They couldn't stop the bleeding.

Didn't matter whether Gastineau and Klecko and Lyons and Fields (The General) were bullshitting their teammates, or just telling them to fuck off.

Once the strike was called, the Jets could not stop the bleeding. . . .

SCAB FOOTBALL

There is an expression that goes something like this: When a Jew is dumb he's really dumb. Your Fan is really dumb for many reasons, but certainly none more than this: I was absolutely convinced, no matter what I read in the papers or heard on the tube, that the owners would never turn so scummy as to actually perpetrate scab football.

A few days before the event Bob Rosen of the Elias Sports Bureau told me that the teams had sent in the names of all the scab players to be inserted into Elias's computers.

Had to be a ploy.

The networks announced one by one that they would indeed cover the games.

Another management tactic. Had to be. (If you don't think the networks and the NFL owners are both NFL management, then kiss your tooth fairy for me.)

So, virginal and pure, I turned on my trusty Advent on Sunday where the Browns were supposed to be tiffing with the Patriots in Foxboro. And lo, the voice of Don Criqui was audible to all. "The National Broadcasting Company presents . . ."

Now a pause.

Now he drops his voice half an octave and reverentially says: "The National Football League." And during these words, glowing like The Tablet, the Vince Lombardi trophy rises, turning into view. Then a shot of the stadium with a few shivering souls and it came to me, late but thudding, that these asshole owners were going to piss on the product that had made them rich.

Criqui and Trumpy appear on the screen and are quite honest. "I don't know what's going to happen," Criqui says. Trumpy concurs:

"These players haven't had a scrimmage, there's been no live tack-ling. What we're going to see is like a lab experiment."

Now we go to the field and some Cleveland Brown players are taking pictures of each other on the playing field. (See, Ma?—I really did get to Pike's Peak.)

Then the game begins. And I must admit I am, against all my better notions, intrigued. I decided to watch the first exchange of possessions.

Cleveland kicks off. It looks like a kickoff, anyway. I mean, it wasn't a party joke—the ball didn't explode. The ball has a hang time of 3.21 seconds and lands on New England's 14, is run out to the 30.

New England, first and ten. Now, in all this uncertainty there is one known quantity: Tony Collins, a former pro bowler, has crossed the picket line and is in the backfield for New England. Walter Payton holds the league record of 275 yards in one game. I figure Collins for an outside shot.

First play: Collins rumbles left and immediately fumbles the ball, which bounces forward where New England recovers. Second and 6. Next play: The quarterback rolls to his right, hits Collins for a first and ten on the New England 40.

Third play: Collins darts to his left, is hit, immediately fumbles again (this is their star, remember) and Cleveland recovers.

Oooops—Cleveland is offside. Still New England ball. And now a genuinely memorable play happens. The New England quarterback fades to pass, it's a high, arching spiral, and (I've never seen this, maybe you have), there are four—*four*—football players within touch-ing distance of where the ball is thrown. And all four of them are Cleveland defensive players. Any of the four could make the intercep-tion, but so stunned are they at the limitless possibilities, they drop the ball.

The next play is a retreat from audacity: a run sort of where the middle is, not much gain. Third down now. New England goes into the shotgun. The quarterback, however, does not pass, he slips the ball to Tony Collins, who doesn't even come close to not fumbling. Six plays into the game and Collins has fumbled thrice. (Replays showed that this one wasn't entirely his fault. The quarterback instead of handing off the ball in the numbers area delivers it in the proximity of Collins's thigh bone.)

Their first drive thwarted, New England punts. Hang time is 3:23 seconds, maybe average for high school.

Now the Browns' offensive unit gets to display its wares. The first play is a run, stuffed for no gain. The second play is also a run, also stuffed, but the runner falls forward for a yard. Third and nine: trickery—a draw play. It is so slow developing it's amazing it gains another yard. Cleveland has to punt.

And if the New England pass to the four Brown defenders was great theater, it was, impossible as it may seem, about to be topped.

The Cleveland punter is standing on his 22-yard line. The two teams are, for a moment, frozen. And then this genuinely remarkable snap from center happens. You had to be there. It's not just that the snap is off line—it is probably a good yard to the punter's left. But that's nothing. What etched this moment for me was that the snap was also at least *two yards short.*

Imagine, for a moment, you're the punter. And punters are not like team players—if you can do it, there's a job for you. And this is this guy's shot. And he's mentally preparing for the snap, going through his mechanics. He signals for the ball and whoops—

—first he's taking a left step toward where the ball will come, at least in theory—and then he realizes it's not going to come anywhere near him. He takes a half step forward, the ball bounces, he tries to move forward and smother it, only no chance. A wild scramble and it's New England's ball and I turn off my set, contented.

Because now I realize what scab football is: It's a *Saturday Night Live* sketch. Chevy Chase is the quarterback with great suave leadership qualities except he can't throw, John Belushi is the old pro runner who keeps fumbling, Dan Aykroyd would be great as the center who can't center.

And I also realized this: The product was so impoverished it would never happen again. Trivia heaven was what it would become next Sunday.

Thus freed, I could turn my mind to the really crucial competition of the weekend, the kind of conflict that happens so rarely that you know your grandchildren will hear of it from you, many, many times. The competition that had not just me but any sports nut worthy of the name excited was this: Who would make more announcing mistakes in the ensuing hours, Joe Namath or Frank Gifford?

For those not plugged into the more arcane aspects of sports, Namath and Gifford are famed for screwing up the names in the games they broadcast when they *know* the players. Now, with hordes of lumberjacks and mixologists (don't you love our language—a bartender is now a mixologist; an "incursion" is something that used to be called "war") and high school teachers inhabiting the uniforms, what kind of heights could these two reach?

Alas, I never found out. Namath, if he was working, was not within reach of my TV set. So I restructured my priorities and decided to give my all to *Monday Night Football.*

I think it's safe to say that this is the most famous sports program in history. (It's not only safe to say it, it's dumb not to, not when Marlin Perkins is probably in second place.)

And it's a controversial show. At least it was during its first decade-plus when Howard Cosell was one of the booth's triumvirate. Today, when Cosell is old and pretty much out of it, it's difficult to remember the power of the original shows. Cosell, with that nasal New York voice, his outrageous vocabulary, the fact that he actually, *gulp,* criticized the athletes. Heady stuff. A lot of people think the show has been, over the years, pretty decent. A lot more have hated the three people jabbering and think it is not only no good now, it was never any good.

They are wrong. It was good. It was better than good, it was different and startling. But only for one year. That first year. When Cosell made a star out of Don Meredith (and boy, didn't his act sour fast) and when Keith Jackson, solid, accurate, pertinent, handled the play-by-play.

But in the second year Jackson was replaced by Gifford and the show has suffered irreparably ever since.

Frank Gifford wasn't just a great football player. He was something rarer still: He *looked* like a great football player. As matinee-idol handsome as a muscular man can be. I remember I happened to watch his first New York local telecast, replacing some vacationing fellow, giving the sports news of the day. Well, he was, to be kind, sheer embarrassment. He was panicked and got the names wrong and you could see him sweat and his hands tremble.

Well, he's famous now, and I assume rich, and certainly celebrated. And experienced. And the panic, if it's there, is well hidden. Personally, I hear he's a genuinely wonderful human being. I think he would have been the most successful insurance salesman in the history of the world.

But as a sports announcer, he still gets the names wrong.

When Cosell's valedictory book came out, he was vilified in the media for saying among other things, that Gifford got the names wrong. I mean, Cosell took a unanimous pasting.

Within two months, a sports writer said, when appraising *Monday Night Football,* that "Gifford, of course, made his unusual number of gaffes."

Cosell was dead right in his appraisal of his ex-partner. But Wilt remarked that "nobody loves Goliath" and the messenger from Corinth will always rank below Bill Cosby in popularity ratings.

When nine o'clock Monday came to my house, was I ever ready. The Giants going against the Niners. Yum. I had my bowl of nonmicrowave Orville Redenbacher Popcorn (that is not a plug, he makes the best popcorn) and a yellow pad with all kinds of numbers listed on the left for Gifford's goofs.

A total wrap. He doesn't do play-by-play anymore so the pressure was off. I mean, sure, he let you know he could still defend his title if a real contender came along. *Dan* Ditka was the coach of the Chicago Bears. He got a New York borough confused with a New York high school. He had a little trouble talking about "artistic integrity." But on the whole it was a disappointment.

Not the program, though. Gifford and Al Michaels and Dan Dierdorf (and don't forget ABC, recognized as sports leaders around the world) put on what was, for me, three-plus hours that were as sickening and unprofessional as I've ever heard. I'd rather be on a desert island with nothing but *Laverne and Shirley* reruns.

I can't really be precise about what produced my nausea; you'd have to watch the program under the conditions that existed—the Giants 0–2, about to fall out of it maybe. The huge national audience, the expectations.

But did you ever see a really awful, well-intended movie called *King of Comedy?* It starred Robert De Niro as a frustrated stand-up comic who eventually kidnaps Jerry Lewis. Why was the movie awful? Well, I've seen a lot of stand-up comics in my life and I've met some and they arrive in various shapes and sizes and there are really only a couple of things they have in common: the knowledge that stand-up comedy is the hardest single thing a performer can attempt; and rhythm. There's a pace to their speech, in life or on stage. They have a finger-snappy quality to their existence.

De Niro, a superb actor when violence is nearby (for me he's the urban Eastwood) was, for all his skills, totally wrong and unbelievable in every foot of film. And why? Because he ain't funny, folks. And I didn't believe for one instant that that character would have that ambition.

Well, they weren't funny on *Monday Night Football*, either. These are clumsy, heavy-witted men and when they decided (I'm sure it was decided for them by ABC) that what they should do was not announce the game so much as mock it, we were left with three really humorless guys knocking each other out topping each other. They reminded me of three giggling schoolgirls who've just seen something phallic in science class and decide to tell each other how hysterically funny it was.

For three-plus hours we had three men telling us the game was beneath them. And when they weren't assuring us that what was on the screen was contemptible, they showed us interviews. I think *two* touchdowns were scored while the camera plumbed the depths of the minds of Miami owner Joe Robbie (and I really feel sorry for the poor guy, a new stadium and nothing to put in it this week) or scabs like Gary Hogeboom, who had thrown five touchdown passes the day before and was therefore the closest they could scrounge up for a hero.

Among the more repellent aspects of it is that the three announcers are all men of wealth—they earn a ton for doing with arguable competency what literally hundreds of others could do. (I'm not saying there aren't great announcers—bless Madden and McCarver.) And these three aren't getting their high six-figure or low seven-figure incomes because of skill—it's because of the announcers' equivalent of free agency: If ABC won't give them what they want, they are free, once they have fulfilled their contracts, to go elsewhere. That right is all the players want.

I'm not pro-strike. I abominate strikes. I think they should be illegal and binding arbitration made the law of the land. But why is free agency so terrible? Shit, since free agency, baseball has boomed beyond the dreams of even an owner's avarice, and there is parity.

The football game dragged endlessly on. I was drinking by this time, anything to dull the pain. When I watch football, my mind is often full of legends, of Hutson and Luckman, Baugh and the Bronk. Now I was listening to Frank Gifford trying to be cute and clever. I needed numbing.

By the time the 49ers had erased the Giants, 41–21, I knew

two things. One: I would never watch shit-scab football again. Two: If Ronald Reagan had a public relations avalanche half as powerful as the NFL owners, Robert Bork would be destroying America today. . . .

THE
REPORTER'S NOTEBOOK

"I KEPT THINKING IT WOULD GET BETTER TOMORROW . . ."

Until Karl Nelson's chest X ray, it had been a relatively quiet spring and summer for the defending Super Bowl champions.

There had been some big news the week after the Super Bowl, when it was reported that the Atlanta Falcons were trying to hire Bill Parcells as coach and head of their football operation. The figure reported was $4 million spread across five years.

The problem was that Parcells's contract with the Giants still had two years to run.

But the offer was out there.

Robert Fraley, Parcells's Florida-based agent, was aware of it. He went to the Giants and asked them for permission to talk to the Falcons. Without the Giants' permission, the Falcons—whose position was that they had never officially tendered an offer to Fraley or Parcells—could be charged with tampering by National Football League commissioner Pete Rozelle, be subject to a heavy fine.

The Giants, through general manager George Young, said, forget about it.

Fraley then went straight to Rozelle himself, asked Rozelle for permission to talk to the Falcons, that it was in his client's best interest to at least know what was out there.

Rozelle—who had hand-picked George Young to be general manager of the Giants back in 1979 and who knew full well how important it was for his league to have a championship-caliber team playing in the New York area—said to Robert Fraley what George Young said.

Forget it.

The Falcons' interest was genuine, everybody in football knew it, knew they were tampering without actually tampering. The money was real. But Parcells had a contract, so it never went any further than that.

Would Parcells have left the Giants after a Super Bowl victory, gone down to Atlanta and started all over again? Even he admitted that he didn't know what he would have done if he'd been given permission to talk to the Falcons and all that money had been dropped on the table.

What he did know was that he didn't trust George Young, his immediate boss. And he knew he was never going to have more leverage than he did as coach of the No. 1 team in pro football. He could either take the money from the Falcons and run, or get the same kind of money from Young and stay.

Parcells's distrust of Young went back to 1983, Parcells's first year as head coach of the Giants. Ray Perkins had been the Giants coach, and had hired Parcells for his staff, first to coach the linebackers, then to be defensive coordinator. When Perkins announced (in December 1982) he was leaving the Giants to succeed Bear Bryant at the University of Alabama, Perkins's alma mater, Young hired Parcells immediately to replace him.

But the Giants went 3–12–1 in 1983, and by December of '83, Young was courting his old friend Howard Schnellenberger, then-coach of a University of Miami team that would win the national championship. Young wanted Schnellenberger for five years, starting in 1984, goodbye Parcells.

Young denied he was courting Schnellenberger.

Parcells knew differently.

Young kept denying he was talking to Schnellenberger, Parcells didn't believe him for a second, the Giants kept losing, Parcells became more and more certain he was going to lose his job. He even went so far as to set himself up with a backup job in case Young fired him. One of Parcells's best friends, Dan Henning, was coaching the Atlanta Falcons at the time. Henning told him that he had a job as defensive coordinator as soon as his feet hit the pavement.

Parcells said to Hennings, "That means a lot to me. Let's see what happens. I may even decide to quit before he fires me."

It never came to that. The negotiations between Young and Schnellenberger (they had worked together with the Baltimore Colts) broke down, Parcells got to stay, the Giants made the playoffs the next season, Parcells got a four-year contract extension, the Giants won the Super Bowl two seasons after that.

But Parcells never forgot that Young tried to pull the plug on him, even as he kept saying he wouldn't dream of such a thing. They were able to work together quite well, but they were never going to be Hope and Crosby in *Road to the Super Bowl*.

When the Falcons came around making more than bird noises, he at least wanted to listen.

Didn't happen. The Giants offered him a contract extension for bigger money, Parcells said he'd think about it, and set about plotting to defend the Super Bowl title.

Then there was Lawrence Taylor's book.

Taylor, the Giants' outside linebacker who was the best player in football, was one of several members of the Giants family to write a book about his life and his times and, most importantly, his role in the Super Bowl season. Parcells wrote his autobiography, defensive end Leonard Marshall wrote his, nose tackle Jim Burt wrote his, Phil Simms and Phil McConkey each had one written, even conditioning coach Johnny Parker became a writer. The books were fairly routine sports autobiographies, all of them looking to capitalize on the Giants' first title since they were NFL champions in 1956, thirty years before. It was a little life, some high times, and an awful lot of Super Bowl season.

Except for Lawrence Taylor's book, which was a pip, even in an age of tell-all star stories.

Taylor's book talked about addiction to the drug crack, cheating on urine tests, lying to his coaches and teammates about his drug problems, having his wife and a friend show up at a crack room in Harlem so they could get the best linebacker in NFL history out and bring him home. It told of his brief flirtation with a rehabilitation hospital in Houston, and how, in Taylor's own humble opinion, he went on to cure himself of his drug problem by touring America and playing the country's great golf courses.

The book's title was *LT: Living on the Edge*. Some of its spicier content was excerpted in *Sport* magazine, which came out about the time the Giants showed up for training camp in Pleasantville.

The book, of course, caused a brief, but memorable, shitstorm.

Because of some curious editing at *Sport*, readers of the excerpts came away with the sensational notion that the Giants—in the person of Parcells—had known about Taylor's drug problems across the previous few seasons, and had done nothing about them because Taylor was still peforming at such a high level, better than linebackers who wouldn't have known crack from a Contac cold capsule.

(Actually, Taylor exonerated Parcells in the book, since Taylor knew full well that Parcells had confronted him about drugs before the Super Bowl season, told him, "This shit can't go on much longer." Taylor checked himself into Houston's Methodist Hospital not long after, checked out after a week, said he went out and cured himself at places like Pebble Beach.)

In the first days after the *Sport* excerpts were released to the press, there were back-page tabloid headlines, and generally the kind of controversy the Giants had not experienced for one minute during their Super Bowl season. When Taylor made his appearance at the Giants' camp, he glared ominously and refused to talk to the writers.

Parcells, with the first storm clouds hovering over his camp and his team's defense of the title, reacted calmly.

"It won't be a factor," he told me. "Lawrence and I understand each other. We get along fine. I promise you, this will not be a factor."

I said, "The sonofabitch made you out to be the bad guy."

Parcells: "It will not be a factor. I will handle it. Lawrence will not be a problem."

Taylor, a volatile man in the best of times, bringing the same excesses and passions to his life away from the field as he did to his extraordinary play in NFL games, finally issued an angry statement, in which he accused the press of trying to destroy him, and said he would never do anything to hurt the Giants.

He said his dying words would be "Go Giants."

Taylor-watchers were amused. A few years before, he had signed a multimillion-dollar contract with Donald Trump, owner of the New Jersey Generals of the United States Football League, that would have taken effect after Taylor's standing contract with the Giants expired. It cost the Giants a million dollars—paid to Trump—to get him out of that USFL contract and keep him.

And Taylor-watchers were well aware that Taylor, even after his problems with cocaine, was still seen frequenting bars around the Giants' training site in Pleasantville, loving a party as much as he ever did, occasionally drinking right through the shank of the evening.

Taylor-watchers felt that Taylor's dying words were as likely to be

"Another round, please" or "More money" as they were to be "Go Giants."

But Taylor went to work as a football player after that, his book sold moderately well and the rest of the Giants' books sold not at all, and Parcells coached his team, and nobody knew that the Falcons were a trifle and books were a trifle compared to the tumor that Dr. Russ Warren found on August 18 in Karl Nelson's upper chest.

The results of Nelson's X rays showed he had cancer, Hodgkin's disease, which attacks the lymphatic system. It is the most treatable form of the disease, with a cure rate of over 90 percent.

But the Giants' right tackle had cancer.

(Two other Giants football players—Doug Kotar and John Tuggle—had died of cancer in the 1980s. Another, linebacker Dan Lloyd, had been forced to retire from football when his own lymphatic cancer was discovered a few years previous to Nelson's. The announcement of Nelson's tumor prompted a series of stories in the New York–New Jersey newspapers, suggesting a possible link, noting the fact that the Meadowlands Complex in East Rutherford, of which Giants Stadium was a part, had been built on what had been a waste dump. Press conferences were held, commissions were commissioned, and nothing further came of it. Officials of the Meadowlands denied their site caused cancer. There were some blind quotes from some of the Giants about how the water sure was a funny color sometimes. And two of Nelson's teammates, he still won't say which ones, called him up and told him they were having CAT-scans done. "Just to see if there was anything inside them," Nelson said. And when Parcells got the phone call from Dr. Warren about the tumor in Nelson's chest, his reaction was, "Not again." He said he immediately thought of Tuggle and Lloyd.)

The tumor was four centimeters by six centimeters. The first procedure had been a thoracotomy. Open up the chest, take a piece of the rib away, partially collapse a lung, get at the tumor for a biopsy. The biopsy said the tumor was malignant. One day Nelson was worried about whether or not he could get a nagging shoulder quick-fixed for the damn Bears game, and the next they were opening him up, taking some rib, playing with the lung, and telling him the tumor up there in his chest was malignant.

Nelson: "I never felt any fear. I never felt I was in a life-threatening situation. The doctors explained that I was young and strong, and how high the cure rate is for Hodgkin's when they find it as early as they did with me. I never thought I was going to die."

More surgery was performed. This was a splenectomy, to remove his spleen. And a laparotomy was performed. The doctors opened the abdomen for inspection and took sample tissue, wanting to check other lymph nodes, see if the cancer had spread anywhere else.

It hadn't. By October, Nelson had begun the first of forty radiation treatments at Memorial Sloan-Kettering in Manhattan. The radiation was for shrinking the tumor. Five days a week, Nelson would make the trip by car from his home in Montvale, New Jersey. The trip could take as little as thirty minutes, as many as ninety, depending on the traffic from New Jersey into Manhattan. Nelson joked to his wife that the commute was tougher than the radiation. When he got to Kerbs Hall at Memorial Sloan-Kettering, on East 68th Street between York and First, he would take the elevator to the second floor, and every morning he would ask the nurse how it looked for "244."

"244" was a linear accelerator. It produced photons. We know the process as radiation.

Sometimes there would be others ahead of Nelson to use 244; cancer is big business, in New York City and everywhere else, and Memorial Sloan-Kettering is perhaps the most famous place in the world where cancer is treated. If there were others ahead of him, Nelson would sit down in the waiting area, filled mostly with people wearing blue gowns. On the radiation/oncology floor of Kerbs, blue gowns meant cancer. If one of the linear accelerators was down—it happened a lot, because of the load—there would be more blue gowns than usual, and Nelson would just wait with everyone else. Sometimes he would be back in Montvale by eleven o'clock, sometimes by noon, sometimes as late as three in the afternoon, depending on the machines and the crowd.

But once he got into the room with 244, the process was brisk. Nelson took his shirt off, and the attendants checked the "tattoos" (black dots) that had been applied to Nelson's chest the first time he had the radiation, so they knew the machine was working on the exact same area every time. "Like looking for longitude and latitude," Nelson said. The pinpointing of the right spot was called "triangulation." It took the attendants about five minutes to get him lined up properly; they used laser beams to be precise. Then the radiation took about thirty-five seconds. Nelson would flip over on the table, the attendants would find the black dots on his back, line him up with the lasers, give him thirty-five more seconds of photons, and Nelson would be done until the next day.

Nelson got tired sometimes. He lost eighteen pounds during the radiation treatment. His throat would get a little sore, and orange juice, something citric, would make it burn. He said he felt like he was carrying around a permanent case of heartburn. There was a constant queasiness, though he never stopped eating. The shoulder wasn't any better; he planned to give himself a month after the radiation ended in December, then have the shoulder, finally, cleaned out. He eventually felt well enough to become part of the Giants radio announcing team on WNEW-AM in New York, working with play-by-play man Jim Gordon and analyst Dick Lynch.

When people asked him about the future, Nelson said, "I'll be playing tackle for the Giants next season."

The radiation, according to Nelson and his doctors, became "a textbook treatment." The tumor just caved in on itself. Nelson will be checked every three months. If the tumor does not reappear, then twice a year. If there is no recurrence in five years, he will be officially classified as being in remission.

In November, Karl Nelson said, "If you think about it, it was the luckiest shoulder injury in history."

It was. The tumor could have been allowed until Nelson's postseason physical. It wasn't. They found it. It was Hodgkin's, which cancer patients call a "lay-up." Karl Nelson was lucky.

His team was not so lucky. By the time Nelson began his radiation treatments in October, the defending Super Bowl champions were already dead.

A *Fan's Notes*

PRECIOUS SONS

*B*eing dead is sometimes not so terrible. . . .

280–1754.

If that is the general information number of the school, you suspect you're not dealing with a football power. And that is, in fact, the number of Columbia University in New York City.

Should you want further proof that this is not an athletic power-house, look for the number of the Athletic Department. There is no listing. Okay, try the Sports Department. There isn't one.

So it should come as no surprise at all to learn the city was not aboil about the coming 1:00 P.M. clash between the home team blue and the green of Dartmouth on a perfect November afternoon.

Dartmouth was a 12½-point favorite.

Dartmouth was traveling to New York and they were still the solid 12½-point favorite.

Understand this: Dartmouth has had some glorious football teams but the '87 edition wasn't one of them. They had been outscored 224–91. They had lost to New Hampshire by 38 points. To Holy Cross by 39. To Harvard, Yale, and Princeton by a combined 80. They had managed one victory all year, that against Davidson.

And they were *still* 12½-point favorites.

And a lot of people thought it should be more.

Welcome to Columbia football.

How bad, one might ask, is Columbia? Hard to put a fine point on it. This year they had averaged losing at home by 22 points, much better than their away record of 34 points—and this year's team is *a lot* better than last year's team. (Ivy League record '86: 0–7. Points allowed—257. Points scored—28. This year's team had already scored 21 points in the Ivy League with three games yet to go.)

But it is not for the size of their defeats that Columbia has become famous. We are dealing here with eons. Columbia's last *tie* was in 1983. Their Division I losing streak had reached an all-time record of 38. And if they lost to Dartmouth at home, what with their final two games being on the road, the streak would be at an unprecedented 41. (The fact that Columbia has not beaten Dartmouth in sixteen years, has been outscored 465–136 over the past decade and a half, only added to the tension.)

And tension there was. Believe that.

Columbia was ahead 2–0 in the second half. Not only that, they were clearly better. But could they hold on? Could they finally rip away the past? They could and did, winning 4–1. And if that strikes you as an impossible football score you are quite correct—it was the result of the soccer game that was going on at a neighboring field.

The football team itself, the big blue, made their appearance at 12:04, their cleats the only sound as they walked from one building along a walk to Wien Stadium. Do you realize how amazing that is? Here's the football team, going in for final warmups, moving through hundreds of spectators, and *no one applauds*. (And the way they walked, heads mostly down, slowly, a thin straggling line, you sensed they didn't expect anything different than what they were receiving.)

They also looked, for a football team in full gear, small. Which is true. Their linebackers, for example, averaged 207.

But heart, as we shall see, has nothing to do with size.

Purchasing my seat at noon, I entered the stadium after checking out the soccer score. My seat, among the best ten bucks I've spent lately, was printed thus:

SEC	ROW	SEAT
C	EE	28

I entered section C, walked up the stairs, and looked around. For Manhattan, there can't be many prettier places. Not that it's all bucolic—there are the inevitable high rises in view. But straight ahead, beneath the perfectly arched Henry Hudson Parkway Bridge, was the Hudson River. And beyond that, every color you'd want, the Palisades. I felt, at that moment, no reason to attack New England to catch the turning of the leaves.

Up I trudged, until I found it: row EE—

and my God, I was on the 30-yard line. A wonderful seat. High enough and close enough. Even a favored alum couldn't complain. Then I noticed the seat number. It was "1". And seat "2" was on the 31-yard line. In other words, as I walked down the empty row I was coming closer and closer to midfield.

I was stunned—you don't just walk in and get seats like this. On I walked. Now I was past the 40-yard line and the seat numbers were in the twenties. Seat 26 was on the 48-yard line. Seat 27 was on the 49—

—and seat 28, *my* seat was on the . . .

Hmmm. After seat 27 came an aisle. Ah, I realized, the numbers simply went on. I crossed the aisle, started to sit—

—I was back to a different number "1" again.

I am not blessed with much sense of direction. I get confused easily in public places when I don't know where I'm going.

And I sure didn't know where I was going now.

Back I went to my original seat "1". Maybe I'd gone the other way. I checked. I hadn't gone the other way—I was facing another goddamn seat 27. (Right now you're probably thinking what a fool I was for not asking the usher. Well, I would have, but they don't have ushers. You probably still think I'm a fool for not asking someone else to see what his or her ticket looked like and find my way after that. Well, I did ask him *and* her. I asked a bunch of people—and *nobody was in their proper seat.* "Oh, just sit anywhere, it won't fill up"—that was the message of the day. Eventually, I did sit anywhere on the 40 and was only asked to move once by someone who actually did sit in his own seat. Forget him. The point is this: A school with a phone number of 280–1754 sells football tickets for seats that are nonexistent. And you wonder why the team has trouble.)

At precisely 1:03 P.M. the set-to started. Both teams chomping. Temperature in the perfect fifties. Bright sunlight favoring neither side. Dartmouth's kicker went into motion—

—when the ball fell off the kicking tee.

This is worth noting for one reason only: There was no wind at the time.

The ball is replaced, Dartmouth kicks off, Columbia returns to its own 16. Not an auspicious beginning. "Well, at least the boy wasn't hurt," said an ancient Old Blue immediately behind me as the players all unpiled. (Understand, these fans are so battered that a noninjury brings smiles.)

First down. The Columbia quarterback rolls left, fumbles, recovers, loses two. "So much for our trick play," says another Ancient beside him. Columbia works it to fourth and nine—

—and then their first punt is blocked for a safety.

After 1:54 of play, they're down 2–0. "I suppose we had to come," says the wife of one of the Ancients. He nods. "Well, it *is* a lovely day."

It was that.

With 2:30 left in the first quarter, Columbia actually crossed into Dartmouth territory. They immediately punted, but they had done it. "A confidence builder," both elders agreed as the quarter ended.

(An aside: It's wonderful watching Ivy League football. Because not only are there no hateful TV time-outs—this game, in its entirety, took less than two hours, forty minutes. More than that, you can *see* the game. Everything's slowed down; the players are clearly bigger than high school kids so there's some sense of size. But at the pro colleges, or the pro pros, they're all so quick and deceptive you don't sense the runner trying to cut, not having quite enough quick to bring it off. Here, you see the strain, feel the effort. Worth a detour.)

In the second quarter, with 11:11 left to play, aided by the quality of the opposition, effort, and penalties, No. 11 of the home team scores.

It is only the second time all season Columbia has been ahead. Extra point made. 7–2.

De-leer-ium.

But Dartmouth comes right back. With 5:30 left, it's first and goal on the 2. First down. No gain. Second down, an eked-out yard. Third down, Columbia as good as stops them. The fans are all up and there is such pleading in their tones.

"Hold 'em . . . please . . ."

They practically do. Dartmouth needs six inches to score, gets at least ten, goes ahead 8–7, the extra point doubling their lead.

Only Columbia is not folding, not this day, and they march right back into Dartmouth territory, keep at it, keep at it until it's first and goal on the 8 with 46 seconds left. Two passes fail, so does a run, the field goal kicker is in—

—Dartmouth calls time out to freeze him.

Dumb. The kid nails it.

10–9 *Columbia* at the half.

Quarter three was neanderthal football. Clubbing and grunting, finesse put aside. But Dartmouth clearly had the better of it and Columbia was almost always deep in its own territory where a fumble could have crushed them. Because even though they were ahead, this much was clear: Columbia was not a team to make a long march with the game on the line. They wanted it, yes, but the talent simply was not there.

But they don't break and all around people are saying, "This is really something" and "This is amazing, they've never played like this."

I am now, for the first time, conscious of a young man, maybe twenty, short-haired, and he is truly into the game. I am looking at a Columbia football *fan*—

—do you realize how hard that is? He's probably a senior and he's never seen his team win and how easy it would be to absent himself or scoff.

This kid, you can see it in his bright eyes, lives and dies with this forlorn football team.

"... amazing ..." he keeps saying. "... amazing."

Columbia still leads as the quarter ends.

"... amazing ..."

And now the ultimate quarter. In what is fifteen minutes away from being Columbia's greatest triumph since Sid Luckman single-handedly upset Army half a century ago. If Columbia wins, bet it makes the front page of *The New York Times*. And every New York paper. And *USA Today*. And all the sports shows: "The greatest losing streak of all time came to an end today ..."

Can they hold? The answer was yes. They could and did, forcing punts. Could they move? Alas, the negative. They punted back.

But it was okay.

They were ahead.

They didn't have to score any more.

Ten minutes left in the game, then nine and eight and seven and still the one-point lead. Columbia has to punt. A horrible shanked punt—

—but it's okay. It takes a great roll. Now 5:16 to go in the game. Dartmouth's ball on their own 19. And then the most terrible thing happens to Columbia: Dartmouth begins resembling a football team. Not SMU or the other cheats in the Southwest Conference. Not Miami or the other I-don't-want-to-think-whats who've recently been flourishing in Florida. But a small-time—definitely *quality* small-time—football team.

First and 10 Dartmouth, the Dartmouth 19.

First and 10 Dartmouth, the Dartmouth 37.

First and 10 Dartmouth, the 39 (but Columbia's now).

First and 10, the Columbia 24.

Columbia holds.

Now, with 1:45 on the clock, Dartmouth lines up for a 32-yard goal. Columbia calls a time-out. Still dumb. It's nailed. Now 12–10 Dartmouth and everybody understands the seemingly everlasting truth: ashes again. It will now be five years between victories. Or maybe that's being optimistic. Maybe it'll be ten years, they're halfway there.

Maybe Columbia will never win another game. Pluto will be colonized. The biggest stock market in the world will be in Moscow. And the humiliation will still be there. Johnny Carson's grandchildren will be making jokes on *The Tonight Show* and the humiliation will still be there. Ronald Reagan will teach courses in nuclear physics at Harvard. And still and still and still the stigma.

Behind me, one of the Ancients says, "Well, I suppose we had our one brief shining moment."

Behind me, two musicians start talking about Ralph Vaughan Williams. "It was really majestically played," one of them says. "Exquisite."

Beside me, the fan is staring, body aching and wracked with pain. He cannot dislodge the knife in his heart.

But . . .

But unbeknownst . . .

But unbeknownst to the assembled, on the far end of the field, the precious sons of Columbia were bunching. Then spreading into position to receive. Probably they had lifted a million pounds of weights to get to where they stood now. Lord alone knows the smirks they had endured.

Now 1:37 left and Dartmouth makes its final kickoff—

—bad for Columbia—it's a deep kick—

—good for Columbia, it's going out of bounds—

—death for Columbia, because one of their runners is so caught up in the moment he fails to let the ball go where it wanted to, scoops it up inbounds very deep in Columbia territory—

—*and bolts to midfield.*

Columbia ball, 50 yards for 6, less for the winning field goal—

—"We don't have enough time," one of the Ancients says.

"Go, sweet Jesus," one of the musicians says, Vaughan Williams banished now.

And the fan is on his feet screaming and shouting because he's seen it—

—Dartmouth has committed a major penalty.

Fifteen yards.

First down. Columbia, on the Dartmouth 35.

Just 1:32 to go.

A Columbia back drops a pass on first down. A Columbia end catches a pass on the 27. Third and 2.

Third and 2.

Columbia calls time.

The players stand there on the field, the slanting sun making them shadows 15 yards long.

Third down. Another dropped pass—

—but Dartmouth face masks.

First and ten, Columbia. The Dartmouth 22.

With 1:14 remaining, the precious sons huddle. The fans are dying. Most have their faces buried in their hands.

Columbia tries a trick run. It gains only 2. The clock is running. Second down and Columbia gets called for an obvious procedure penalty. On third down, they complete a pass to the 19.

The kicker comes in.

Now :24 to go.

The teams line up.

It's a 35-yard try.

And in the stands now, the fans are turning their backs to the field. They stand there, many of them, facing dead away.

The ball is snapped.

The kicker nails it.

Dead solid perfect.

Columbia wins—the longest streak in major collegiate football can rest in the record books now—

—except for one official who slowly signals that the ball was wide, no good, Columbia loses, the game ends, the players shake hands numbly on the darkening green. The fans file silently out.

And then, behind us now, standing on his seat is the fan, waving his arms and shouting to us: "What's the matter with you people?—it was good. It was. It was good. I saw it. It was good."

And now a man in front of me spins toward the sound of the fan. "It *was* good," he says.

And then, off to the right, another voice:

"It was good."

"It was good." This from a shaken woman, nodding her head.

"It was good."

These words are coming from all over the stands now—not a chant, just individuals echoing a common thought.

"IT WAS GOOD."

"IT WAS GOOD."

"IT WAS GOOD."

"IT WAS GOOD."

"IT WAS GOOD."

"IT WAS GOOD."

"IT WAS GOOD."

"IT WAS GOOD."

"IT WAS GOOD."

"IT WAS GOOD."

And the fan, above us all now, waves his arms, flails them as he gives one final aching cry: "It was *very* good. . . ."

THE
REPORTER'S NOTEBOOK

OCTOBER: "GREED. IT'S ALWAYS ABOUT GREED ..."

Bill Parcells couldn't really decide whether it was the alarm clock that finally woke him up or the crying of his wife, Judy, since he heard the one sound right after he heard the other.

It was six o'clock in the morning, October 6, Parcells's home in Upper Saddle River, New Jersey. The night before, Parcells's team, known as the New York Giants, had been humiliated by the San Francisco 49ers in ABC's *Monday Night Football* game. These were not the Giants who had won Super Bowl XXI in Pasadena. Those Giants were out on strike with most of the membership of the National Football League Players Association, had been on strike for nearly two weeks now. A lot of those Giants had walked in a picket line with members of the New York Jets in a muddy lot across the street from Giants Stadium before the Giants–49ers game, joined by Giant fans and members of other local unions.

The football players Parcells had coached the night before, they were different. The game, it counted in the standings, same as it would have if Lawrence Taylor and Phil Simms and Joe Morris and Mark Bavaro had been wearing their regular uniforms.

But the "replacement players," the scabs, the New York Giants for this game and the one before it and the one to follow, they comprised perhaps the worst team in the history of pro football in the United States.

They were semi-pro players, and players who had been cut by the Giants and other teams, and college players who had never given pro football a chance, and football gypsies who simply went from training camp to training camp until their legs and dreams and youth were all used up. But now had a chance to be a part of pro football for a couple of weeks. The National Football League owners had vowed after a 1982 strike that if another strike ever came, they would not shut down their league. So they had not shut down their league. The result was Replacement Football.

Scab Football.

And Parcells, eight months after his team won the Vince Lombardi Trophy in Pasadena, had the sorriest scabs of all:

1987 NEW YORK GIANTS
ALPHABETICAL REPLACEMENT ROSTER

NO.	NAME	POS.	HT.	WT.	BIRTH DATE	COLLEGE
10	Almodar, Beau	WR	5–9	180	10/25/62	Norwich
12	Andrade, Henry	WR	5–11	165	04/17/62	SMU
26	Beecham, Earl	RB	5–8	180	09/08/65	Bucknell
87	Bennett, Lewis	WR	5–11	175	08/04/63	Florida A&B
3	Benyola, George	K	5–10	195	09/17/64	Louisiana Tech
98	Bini, Scott	DE	6–2	270	07/31/63	Fairleigh-Dickinson
47	Brown, Don	CB	5–11	189	11/28/63	Maryland
91	Burgess, Chas.	LB	6–0	230	12/29/62	Carson Newman
8	Busch, Mike	QB	6–4	214	02/08/63	South Dakota State
21	Byrd, Boris	CB	6–0	210	04/15/62	Austin Peay

"We got," Parcells had said after he had watched his replacement players practice a few times, "several guys I believe the Heisman Trophy voters overlooked."

Before the strike, the Giants had started off badly. In the most ballyhooed regular season opener the NFL had ever known, the Bears, winners of Super Bowl XX, had beaten the Giants soundly. That was also a Monday night game. The next Sunday, at Giants Stadium, the Giants had stumbled against an inferior opponent, the Dallas Cowboys, finally lost when Raul Allegre, one of the stars of the Super Bowl season, missed a last-second field goal attempt. The offensive line missed Nelson. Joe Morris missed Nelson. Morris had infuriated Parcells during the Dallas game by asking to be taken out for what Parcells deemed to be less than a life-threatening shoulder injury.

0–2.

Now the scabs were 0–1.

The scabs had absolutely no connection to the Super Bowl champions except temporary name tags over lockers and Giants uniforms they were leasing like tuxedos from a formal shop, but the standings didn't care about that, the standings just said that the champions of the world were 0–3 and sinking deeper and deeper into the shit of the strike every week the strike lasted, and Parcells was dying on the sidelines, dying at practice, dying inside.

His friends could see it. His assistant coaches could see it. His secretary, Kim Kolbe, known as Midnight, could see it. And the writers could see it. And the scab football players calling themselves Giants, they sure as hell could see it. Parcells was coaching a team that could not compete on the major college level. He could wander over to the sidelines during practice, and stand there with the writers, and not be able to keep himself from laughing at what he was seeing on the field.

And the games *counted*. And were going to keep on counting as long as the strike lasted.

Parcells had come into the season with high hopes for this team, even after losing Karl Nelson to the cancer. Parcells believed the Giants would be the first NFL team since the Steelers of 1979–80 to repeat. Now the Giants were 0–3. The Redskins had a replacement team; Redskins general manager Bobby Beathard had been ready when the strike came, even if Giants general manager George Young had not. The Redskins scabs would beat the Giants scabs the next Sunday, and the Giants would be 0–4, still looking for their first win since the Super Bowl. Parcells was frigging *dying*.

Judy Parcells could see it best of all.

And never more clearly than on the morning of October 5, 1987.

Her husband was still in bed when the alarm clock went off. She could never remember that happening during the football season. At

Wichita State and Army and Vanderbilt and Florida State and Texas
Tech and Air Force, with the New England Patriots and finally the
Giants, in Parcells's own gypsy years as a football coach, he was always
up and out of bed and having a cup of coffee at some diner by dawn,
getting ready for that day's practice or film-watching session or game.
Depending on the size of the city where he coached, Parcells would
usually have two or three diners he would hit on the way to work,
regulars with whom he would discuss football and sports in general and
the world. There was very little about coaching that Parcells didn't
love, even in all the years when it seemed like he had to pack up Judy
and the three girls and move every other season because there was a
slightly better job available. Parcells liked to stretch out the coaching
days, from the dawn cups of coffee to the last midnight look at films.
"I've never been one of those Robert Young–type husband or father
guys," Parcells said. "I never had breakfast with my family." Every
night he would set the alarm clock, like some kind of silly ritual, and by
the time it went off the next morning, Judy Parcells might be in bed, but
her husband was sure gone.

Until today.

The alarm went off and the first thing Parcells saw was his wife
sitting up in bed, crying.

He asked her what time it was, and she told him, and now he knew
why she was upset.

"Sonofabitch," Parcells said.

"You're not going to work today, are you?" she said.

She had seen the strike, and the scab players, and the losses, and the
drudgery of coaching these bums eating at him for a week, had heard
him fume every night after another practice, had seen how defeated he
had looked every time the ABC cameras showed him on the sidelines
the night before.

Judy Parcells thought her husband, coach of the Super Bowl champions, was going to quit.

He didn't say anything.

"You're not, are you?"

Parcells pulled himself up and out of the bed.

"Yeah," he said, "I am."

He showered, shaved, dressed, drove to his favorite diner, Hagler's,
in Oradell, New Jersey, didn't stay long, drove the few minutes to
Giants Stadium. Parcells drove through his regular gate and down a

ramp and through the dark bowels of the Stadium, on the field level, until he got to his personal parking space. He shut off the radio and the engine and sat there.

He couldn't get out of the car.

Didn't want to get out of bed. Couldn't get out of the car. The strike might end today, or it might last the season, which meant he might be coaching these bums all the way to the twenty-seventh of December. The idea paralyzed him.

"I don't even know how long I sat there," he would say later, recounting the morning to a friend. "Finally, I just felt silly and decided to go to work. I knew I had no shot of beating the Redskins on Sunday. The whole thing with the new guys was a fucking joke. But the Maras were paying me to do a job, whether I was having a pleasant fucking time or not. So I finally got my ass out of the car."

Parcells didn't even know at the time that ABC had provided the most memorable shot of the NFL strike during the Giants game, even more memorable than all the shots taken of empty stadiums.

An ABC camera had found Reggie Carr, a replacement defensive tackle, asleep on the Giants bench toward the end of the Giants–49ers game.

NO.	NAME	POS.	HT.	WT.	BIRTH DATE	COLLEGE
99	Carr, Reggie	DT	6–3	300	02/17/63	Jackson
66	Clark, Corey	LB	6–2	220	10/22/62	San Francisco State
83	Coleman, Chas.	TE	6–4	222	09/16/63	Alcorn State
29	Covington, Jamie	RB	6–1	234	12/12/62	Syracuse
19	Crocicchia, Jim	QB	6–2	209	02/19/64	Pennsylvania
19	Cummings, Mack	WR	6–0	195	03/03/60	East Tenn. St.
95	Davis, Chris	LB	6–1	225	07/26/63	San Diego St.
72	Davis, Kelvin	G	6–2	260	02/07/63	Johnson Smith
39	Derose, Dan	LB	6–0	230	01/25/62	So. Colorado
41	Direnzo, Fred	RB	5–11	234	01/28/61	New Haven
36	Dirico, Robert	RB	5–10	202	11/22/63	Kutztown St.
68	Dugan, William	G	6–3	290	06/05/59	Penn State

The first bargaining session between the National Football League Players Association, headed by ex-Raider Gene Upshaw, and the National Football League Management Council, its negotiating team headed by a man named Jack Donlan, had taken place back in April of 1987.

The nineteenth and final session before the old collective bargaining agreement expired took place on August 14.

On August 31, the old contract expired. Upshaw and his membership decided on a strike date, but did not announce the date.

On September 8, the NFLPA announced a September 22 strike deadline.

Following the Monday night game between the New York Jets and the New England Patriots, the 1,585-member Players Association went on strike for the second time in the 1980s.

The next day bargaining resumed in Philadelphia. Two quarterbacks, Marc Wilson of the Los Angeles Raiders and Gary Hogeboom of the Indianapolis Colts, were among the first players to cross the picket line.

On September 24, NFL Commissioner Pete Rozelle announced that games for Week 3 of the NFL season had been canceled. On September 25, talks broke off. By then, teams all around the league were beginning to assemble replacement teams.

September 29, the Management Committee decided to lift the home-team television blackout during the strike. It meant that no matter how empty the stadiums were for replacement football, scab football, the games would be shown in the home team's market.

SCTV, it was called.

Scab television.

As long as the NFL games were played, and the three major networks televised those games, the NFL owners got their television money every week.

It worked out to about a million dollars, per owner, per week.

On October 4 and 5, the replacement games took place. For the real National Football League, attendance had averaged 57,205 the first week of the season and 59,824 the second week of the season.

For scab football, shown on SCTV, the average attendance was 16,947.

But the games were played. Players continued to cross picket lines. Twelve members of the San Francisco 49ers crossed on Wednesday, October 7, bringing the total number of players who had crossed the line to 129.

The night before the replacement Giants played the replacement 49ers, and a few nights before so many of the real 49ers would cross the line, a seventy-two-year-old man named Marvin Miller sat in a waiting room outside the CNN studio near Madison Square Garden on the West Side of Manhattan, waiting to tape an appearance on the *Coors Sports Page,* a Sunday night sports wraparound show broadcast on Ted Turner's superstation, WTBS. (Turner also owns CNN, if you've been out of the country.) Miller was at the CNN studio to talk about the football strike. It was nothing new for Miller, except that the subject was a labor dispute in football, not baseball.

Miller was asked what the real issues of the strike were, and he barked out a laugh in a baritone ravaged by years of cigarette smoking and sitting in bargaining rooms thick with his smoke and everybody else's.

"Greed," Marvin Miller said. "It's always about greed."

He is the former executive director of the Major League Baseball Players Association. He came out of the steelworkers union in 1966 and took over the raggedy-ass baseball union and over the next fifteen years defined the sports union in America, became the most successful, really legendary, labor leader of his time. During Miller's tenure, the players won free agency and forever altered the salary structure of professional sports.

The last baseball strike for Marvin Miller had been in 1981. The owners wanted to take free agency away. They said they only wanted to weaken it. They really wanted to kill it. Miller laughed. Miller's players walked, and when they came back almost two months later, they still had free agency, and the free agency they still had was the reason why the owners had to resort to collusion over the winters of 1985 and 1986.

The owners never laid a glove on Marvin Miller, who retired after 1982 to his tennis game and his writing, but remained the soul of the Players Association, the standard against which all its present and future leaders would be measured. Marvin Miller kept his players in line. Marvin Miller kept his players informed. Marvin Miller won all the big ones of his time. Everybody else always got tired or discouraged, but Marvin Miller never did. He was always the toughest one in the room.

Now he was watching the strike go wrong for the football players. The picket line was being crossed. Scab football was being shown on television. The owners were losing some money because of the strike;

but they weren't paying the regular salaries, and they were getting that million dollars every week from television, and so none of them had yet shown up in a soup line.

Marvin Miller said it meant that CBS and NBC and ABC were financing strike-breaking in the fall of 1988.

"I used to think that the lowest form of humanity was a scab," Marvin Miller said. "But now I am thinking that it is anyone, from owners to network sports presidents, who finance and support scab football."

Miller shook his head disgustedly.

"But, my God, what wimps these football players are," he said. "What babies. It's sickening. Where's their resolve? They miss one paycheck, or two, and they're ready to cave in? Gutless wonders is all they are. What did they think this was going to be, a day at the beach? Strikes are hard. They eat at your bones. But if you can't hold out for more than two weeks, how can you ever expect to be strong enough to beat an operation as powerful as the National Football League?"

The football players wanted real free agency. Miller, like everyone else, knew there was no real free agency in the National Football League; it had been bargained away in the 1970s by a man named Ed Garvey, then—executive director of the players union. A player could ostensibly become a free agent in pro football, but if another team signed him, it had to compensate the player's former team with draft picks. For instance, a seven-year player with a salary of $210,000 or more was worth a No. 1 pick, in a league where No. 1 picks were considered lifeblood.

A ten-year player was worth *two* No. 1 picks.

When Walter Payton, perhaps the greatest all-around running back in the history of the NFL and the man who would retire with more yards gained than any back in history, had been a free agent a couple of years before, not one NFL team had called to inquire about signing him.

Bottom line? Check it out: If Walter Payton wasn't a free agent, no one was.

But from April 20 on, the Management Council had said there was no chance the players would ever get true free agency.

Marvin Miller had an idea about that, which he talked about that night in the waiting room, then on the *Coors Sports Page*.

"Upshaw should call off the strike," Marvin Miller said. "If they [the owners] don't want to deal in good-faith bargaining, Upshaw should send everybody back to work, play under the terms of the old agreement, and take their asses to court. The NFL is so guilty of so many per se antitrust violations, it isn't even funny. Their draft will not stand up to investigation in a court of law. Neither will the lack of free agency. A free agent like Walter Payton not getting one offer as a free agent, as part of an obvious conspiracy to restrict his movement and generally drive down salaries, will not stand up in court either. Everybody thinks Gene Upshaw is losing on the strike. If he folds his hand, everybody will say the players lost. But if he takes them to court, he'll eventually win."

Miller was asked if anybody from the football union had called to ask him for advice.

"No," he said.

They called nine days later. Marvin Miller told Dick Bertelsen from the NFLPA pretty much what he had said in the CNN studio. Bertelsen told Miller that an antitrust suit was just one of their options.

"It's your only option," Miller said.

A total of 139 players had crossed the line, and there were rumors of a mass defection any day.

"It's your only chance," Miller said. "You just go to your membership and sell it, because the the strike isn't working."

On October 15, Gene Upshaw announced in Washington, D.C., that the union had filed an antitrust suit against the National Football League in a federal court in Minneapolis, charging that football's reserve clause (by which a player is essentially bound to his team for the length of his career if management decides to keep him) and the college draft, which simply feeds the reserve clause, were both illegal.

"The players were the bad guys," Miller said ten days before, at CNN. "The players are always the bad guys because the leagues have better PR and so the fans don't grasp the issues without some real work. They just say, 'Greedy millionaire athletes,' and leave it at that. But the football players were up against some of the richest men in this country, men who tell you they can't afford free agency. What's Leon Hess worth?"

"Around six hundred twenty-five million."

"Right," Miller said. "So you're telling me Leon Hess can't afford free agency? Come *on.* These players are simply trying to have an illegal system declared illegal. You only do that in court."

So the players took the owners to court. If it went the way Marvin Miller thought it would, then the old man had won another one, just as he had been winning them from the fifties on in Pittsburgh for the steelworkers, and then for the baseball players, as he became the Gompers of his time. It had started, as it always did, with Marvin Miller talking, making sense, in a room where people were willing to listen to him. It was a room next to a CNN television studio, but it was a room, and Miller's words eventually found their way to Gene Upshaw.

None of this, however, did a frigging thing for Bill Parcells and his "fucking bums". . . .

NO.	NAME	POS.	HT.	WT.	BIRTH DATE	COLLEGE
34	Fontes, Royce	RB	5–11	218	08/29/61	New Haven
94	Garrtett, Curtis	NT	6–5	302	06/09/62	Ill. State
13	Haysbert, Adam	WR	6–0	185	02/16/62	Brigham Young
71	Howard, Anthony	G	6–3	267	07/16/60	Tennessee
90	Jones, Chris	C	6–3	263	06/26/64	Delaware St.
62	Jones, James	DE	6–5	250	10/24/64	No. Car. A&T
15	Kelly, Paul	QB	6–1	205	03/20/64	New Haven
88	Lovelady, Edwin	WR	5–9	180	04/23/63	Memphis State
18	McGowan, Reggie	WR	5–8	165	09/25/64	Abilene Christian
78	Meuth, Kevin	T	6–5	270	05/04/64	Southwest Texas State
74	Mitchell, Russell	C	6–5	288	12/28/60	Mississippi
6	Moore, Dana	P	5–10	180	09/07/61	Miss. State
37	Morrison, Pat	S	6–2	194	03/21/65	So. Conn.
96	Nicholson, Frank	LB	6–2	205	03/06/61	Delaware St.
49	Norris, Jimmy	CB	5–11	188	08/12/65	Upsala
79	Peterson, Marty	T	6–5	272	10/26/65	Pennsylvania

Between the first and second weeks of scab football, the Giants signed a fullback named Park, from Hawaii. Every day, after practice, he would dress in a native-Hawaiian skirt.

Jeff Rutledge, the backup to Giants quarterback Phil Simms, had crossed the picket line by then.

He watched Park get dressed after one practice and said, "A guy in a skirt. Is that a fitting statement about this team, or what?"

A Fan's Notes

THE NATURAL

*I*t's got a 78 of Jerry Lee Lewis belting "Great Balls of Fire." And The Righteous Brothers doing "Unchained Melody." The Ronettes are represented, as are The Dells and Roy Orbison. Mathis and Presley and Chuck Berry killing the world with "Maybelline."

And that's just part of the good stuff. Yes, we can argue about many things, summits and strike zones, artificial grass and artificial breasts, but we cannot argue about this: The juke box that dominates the living room of Bob Costas's East 50's apartment is a work of modern art.

A '47 Wurlitzer, restored and resplendent, with yellow and red push tabs, a green "make selection" sign. Four and a half feet high, all bright chrome and shined wood, it tells a lot about the taste of the owner. (Chubby Checker, it is rumored, sang "The Twist" at his wedding.)

There are other things of note in the living room. A baby ladder (son Keith is one and a half), shelves of sports books, books on rock and poetry and the Marx Brothers, not to mention a tome on French and English philosophy stolen, it looks like, from a Syracuse public library, the number:

808.8
H26
v34

Now the thief appears, making a final tug on his double-breasted blazer. Hair in place, clothes immaculate, he takes a final glance around the room, pausing for a moment not at the juke box but at the top of it where there is a fielder's glove—not his, no, it's his son's security blanket. Costas nods, exits, off to do another Sunday's *NFL Live*, the wraparound show he does each week for NBC during the football season, for which for four years he has served nominally as host, actually as core.

Robert Quinlan Costas grew up as much as anyplace in Commack, Long Island, where he fell in love with (1) sports, (2) baseball, and (3) Mickey Mantle. He attended, naturally, Syracuse (Marty Glickman, Marv Albert, etc., etc.) and got his first break when Harry Weltman, now general manager of the Nets, then with the old Spirits of St. Louis of the ABA, chose him to do Spirits' games on radio. Costas was then way over twenty-two. In many ways, his age is still as remarkable as anything about him. He was by far the youngest ever honored as Sportscaster of the Year, beating out such as Vin Scully in so doing.

He has been with NBC since he was in his twenties, doing college basketball, pro football, the game-of-the-week baseball broadcasts, and, on occasion, elevator race announcing on the David Letterman show. He has a unique combination of solid knowledge and consistent irreverence that sets him apart from his peers. If you had to guess who is going to be covering network sports in the year 2000, you've got to bet Costas.

NFL Live, on NBC, is not as popular as the enemy, the CBS entrant, hosted by Brent Musburger. But it is a better show. For many reasons, but primarily because Musburger, skilled and seasoned as he is, has become to sports fans, at least this one (though he was once a decent newspaperman), nothing but a shill. I've heard Musburger exaggerate and distort the greatest of the crummy contests he was covering and I don't believe him anymore. (I don't even think that Musburger believes Musburger anymore.)

Costas is no phony. One of his least gloried moments was when he, in essence, walked away in the middle of a horse race show because he was so clearly ignorant of the subject matter. (Musburger would have blabbed on and on about the greatness of the race just run.)

Costas arrives at the studio on West 50th at 10:00, says hello to lots of people, remembers lots of names. At 10:15 he gets light makeup. Ahmad Rashad walks in with a small toy dog for Keith. The dog does flips. Costas is grateful, says thanks, plays with the dog. He and Rashad have the same camaraderie off screen as on. I have no idea what the truth is, but they seem to enjoy each other.

The room where *NFL Live* takes place is the *Late Night with David Letterman* set. Letterman's desk is covered and so are the musicians' instruments, and the audience's seats are stored away. (A technical crew comes in after five each Sunday morning, sets things up, fifteen hours later takes things down. The set for Costas's show, then, is really only a more frequent *Brigadoon*.)

The room is very cold, kept that way because of some technical reasons with the lights. Everything about the exercise is whatever way it is because of technical reasons. To an outsider, it might be Mars. There are stage managers and people pushing cameras and in the main room maybe eight TV monitors with signs below them giving what games they'll show and in another room off the main room there are more than a dozen TV monitors covering every game with signs explaining which, and in yet another room, the control room, there are dozens of people and probably fifty monitors covering God knows what and a couple of floors down there are dozens more people and maybe a hundred more monitors and by these monitors the people seem to be measuring everything by the millisecond, making what they call "packages," and what I think they mean is those ten-second or fifty-second pro football highlight shots that are on all over the country as the day goes on.

Now, it's 11:30, and there is a lot of tension, but Costas seems totally ignorant of any of it, he just scuffs his way politely along singing an old Jimmy Webb song, "Wichita Lineman," and then he is into pretaping various segments. Because of time zones, various parts of the show are seen live and various other parts are on tape, so now Costas begins taping the Paul Maguire section, Maguire being the point spread specialist telling you where to bet your money.

(A prissy note: I think this is shit, this and the aging puerile mouthings of Jimmy El Greco. I'm not against gambling. I wish gambling were legal. It just seems to me that since it isn't, it's a bit on the smeevy side for the media to go around breaking the law—which is essentially what the papers and the tube are doing—during Sunday cartoon time in America. End of prissy note.)

There is a mild snafu on the Maguire start so they begin again and immediately one of Costas's idiosyncracies is apparent: He always gives a slightly different intro. It's going to be that way all day: In a way, he's continually improvising. The third time he throws yet another slightly different intro and this goes smoothly and the Maguire piece is done and now it's time to talk to Coach Ron Meyer of Indianapolis in the Hoosier Dome and there is Meyer's picture on a large TV monitor but no sound and Costas says casually, "Since I don't read lips, you'll have to fix this." And now a voice comes in from the control room into Costas's earpiece saying, "Bob, we're short on time, whatever's germane, ask it on top," and Costas nods as behind him now Meyer is audible but Meyer can't hear Costas and Costas says, "Ask him if it's okay if we work this interview in later, maybe sometime in the second quarter," and now Meyer is talking to the officials, saying, "There'll always be a captain out there," and they chat on, Meyer and the crew, and finally NBC makes connections and Costas says, "You won't have as much trouble with Fouts today as you have with this interview," and they chat on, Costas asking questions about how much Meyer hopes to use Eric Dickerson who has just joined the club and Meyer answers and all the time in Costas's earpiece is this voice going, "have to end this, Bob—Bob, we have to edit this so end it—Bob, we really have to edit this or we won't make air."

Costas easily maintains sanity, the interview is a success. (Sidebar: During much of this, just a few feet off camera and at the same table as Costas, Frank Deford, the splendid *Sports Illustrated* writer who does one piece a week for the program, sits reading the morning paper, in a print world of his own.)

At 12:30, the program itself comes on the air. It goes well. No problems. None that bled anyway.

Now comes the hard part of Costas's day. For the next half a dozen hours he will do interviews, scores, updates, you name it. And it all must be, for his peace of mind, dead accurate.

He intros a live piece with Brian Bosworth: "This is an exclusive with the Boz, in that it's the only one he's doing for the next five minutes." Bosworth has, in point of fact, been spreading himself a bit on the thin side of late. Ubiquitous, you might say. (Dumb aside: When I was younger, Jayne Mansfield starred on Broadway in a George Axelrod play entitled *Will Success Spoil Rock Hunter?* And during that time in New York, she established herself as a, I don't know, national *thing*. Nobody ever worked harder. You couldn't open a hardware store in the Five Boroughs without La Mansfield being there, cutting the ceremonial ribbon. The papers began referring to her as "The Ubiquitous Jayne Mansfield." For years I thought the word, instead of meaning "capable of being everywhere," meant "large breasted." Anyway, Brian Bosworth has certainly been ubiquitous and, who knows, perhaps he is also large breasted. Personally, I don't want to find out.)

When he's not on the air, Costas often does in-person interviews with people from out of town but he carries his earphone jack with him wherever he goes and usually keeps it plugged in. He makes an unusual sight then, carrying on conversations with guests, talking with someone while at the same time his head is half down, listening to staccato messages from the central room.

At about 2:20, the halftime updates begin. As games get to the half and throw back to the studio, Costas has to keep audiences abreast (there's Miss Mansfield again) of what's going on and the words rifle out, never a stumble, as he goes from one city to another.

Then, when the games get into their second halves, it quiets in the studio, more interviews, more introductions to visitors, he's pleasant, cheery, unruffled.

The only problem comes late, when he's heading for the home stretch and the package for the Bears game is shown. Otis Wilson, their fine linebacker, is seen being carried off the field but Costas has been given no information on the injury.

Costas is a purist about sports and during a break he speaks to the control room, explaining that if you don't have the extent of the injury, if you lack the specifics, don't show the shot. And how does he get this across? Here's what he says to the people in the control room: "My tone is only urgent because of the time constraints."

"Holy shit," someone in the control room says. "Did he really say that?"

He did. Nothing seems to ruffle him. Now he's into the lickety-split part of the broadcast, giving an entire rundown of all the games for each area when a game ends and they go back to the studio. He does one. He does another. He does another. Each of them without the hint of a stumble and each slightly different from the others. Sometimes he has to do this half a dozen times. This is an easy Sunday. Thrice. Timing his voice to passes and fumbles, interceptions and sideline anguish, each word essential to the *Reader's Digest* picture he is painting. On and on he goes, always with the instructions coming at him via his earpiece. "Wrap it up, Bob." "Pick it up, Bob." *"Bob, pick it up."* On and on he goes, more and more information coming out perfectly timed, summarizing this game, that one, now the two from the West Coast, more, more.

Done, he takes the earpiece off. He, the importer of crucial info to bettors and fans all over the country, stands, stretches, explains that after it's all over, he really knows zilch about what went on that day in pro football. Highlights, sure. But any fan, he explains, who has been watching an entire game knows infinitely more about that game than he does.

Nine hours after he's entered the building he's allowed to leave. To go back to his apartment? To collapse on the sofa and listen to Chuck Berry?

Negative. He's as bright-eyed and sassy as he was in mid-morning. And he's excited. Because he's got a two-hour live radio interview with Tom Seaver coming up in a little while and he can't wait to get going. . . .

"SIERENS, WHO IS PREGNANT . . ."

Although it may not rank with the Watergate break-in, a bit of skull-duggery surfaced the other morn that ought not to go unnoticed. Briefly, it appears that CBS pilfered a tape that was the property of NBC.

Not your ordinary tape, by the by. This, that they procured, was the final practice tape that Gayle Sierens did of the Tampa Bay–Detroit pro football game played earlier this December.

Why would mighty Columbia stoop to such an endeavor? A spokesman said the network was "curious" about Sierens's performance. Me, I suspect otherwise.

By the time this books sees print, Gayle Sierens will either be a well-known name or an asterisk. Now she is neither. What she was, until recently, was a news anchor in Tampa. NBC sports, already having scored what I suspect will be a major coup in hiring Gayle Gardner from ESPN, decided it wanted to try to let a woman have a go at play-by-playing a pro game, and come Sunday, Sierens will do her undoubtedly nervous best to call the Seattle–Kansas City contest, which will be heard over a small part of these United States.

And what CBS calls "curious," I call shitting in their pants.

Why?

Suppose Sierens isn't great. Suppose she isn't even good. Suppose, role model or not, what she turns out to be is just this: adequate. Do you know what that means?

It means she immediately jumps to the top 5 percent of all national sportscasters, and if you think I'm not serious, are you ever wrong.

Consider, if you will, these names: Al Michaels, Brent Musburger, Dick Stockton. Dick Vitale, Billy Cunningham, Terry Bradshaw, Tony Trabert, Tommy Heinsohn. Bill Russell, Bob Griese, Al Trautwig. I could go on but out of respect for your undoubtedly weakening stomachs, I shall refrain. The point is, have any of these gentlemen, *any* of them, ever *once, one time,* said a goddamn thing that pleasantly surprised you.

Très doubtful.

The fact is this: An overwhelming percentage of national sports broadcasters are not remotely ept. Throw out the incompetents—Namath, Gifford, Garagiola, etc. The marvel about these guys is not that they're so dreadful, it's that anybody ever hired them in the first place. As sports announcers, I mean.

Do this: Pick any game in any sport of any magnitude, get a pad and pencil and count the clichés. How many "greats" and "prides" will you quickly tick off? How many times will you hear that "it takes a lot of guts" for a quarterback to "stand in there" with "all that pressure coming."

Gee, I thought that's what quarterbacks got a million a year for. How many defenses will "bend but not break"?

If clichés bore you, and they should, start a clean page and start with mistakes. I saw a Redskins game this year where Jay Schroeder threw a bomb that was caught but didn't count, not because of a nullifying penalty but because the ball landed five yards out of bounds. What did the announcer say? Catch this (no pun intended): He said, *"That was a perfect pass."*

Gosh, what would have been the perfect word to describe it if the goddamn ball had landed five yards *in* bounds. (The announcer was Madden, by the way, the best I've ever heard at football. Proving nothing is perfect, either Madden's vocabulary or Schroeder's aim.)

How 'bout this?—I'm watching New Orleans and Pittsburgh. It's 20–14 New Orleans. Late in the game. New Orleans has to punt and they're *deeeep* in their own territory. Now Hank Stram and the fool he drools with go into this long harangue about is the punter a two- or three-step kicker and will the Steelers try for a block or a runback?

Now I'm not a genius but right then I feel like the jerk of all the world because what I can't figure out is why New Orleans doesn't go for a safety. That would make it 20–16. It doesn't change anything except for the bettors. Pittsburgh still needs more than a field goal. I like to think I'm a good watcher and I'm going crazy trying to figure what I've goofed up on in my scenario. A field goal is three so that only makes it 20–19. Pittsburgh has to score a touchdown and convert or they lose.

What's my mistake? I'm frothing.

New Orleans takes a safety and Stram says, and I quote exactly: "Good call."

This is the coach of a Super Bowl champion. This is the nerd who invented the "offense of the seventies." *Who hired him?* Why doesn't he mention the possibility of a safety *before* the safety?

The NBA has boomed of late, in spite of the poverty of their announcing. Tom Heinsohn was not only sickeningly jovial but really not articulate and if he said the phrase "wide bodies" one more time I didn't know if I'd make it to the latrine in time. So they fire him. *"Rayyyyy."* And bring in Cunningham, who makes Heinsohn sound like Gore Vidal.

Do the honchos at the three networks listen to the shit they put out? I doubt it. (Truly—most movie executives don't go to the movies, not the way we do. They'll have product screened for them. That ain't the same as paying your seven bucks and stepping on chewing gum in the darkness as you try and find your seat.) I'd like to kidnap the sports heads and chain them in front of their television sets and MAKE THEM SPEND THREE HOURS, THREE PRECIOUS HOURS OF THEIR LIVES LISTENING TO JOE GARAGIOLA TALK ABOUT BASEBALL.

And then keep at it, give them days of their employees rambling on.

Would it do any good? Doubtful. But it's always fun to see the big guys suffer.

Who do I like? Obviously McCarver and Madden, way over everybody. But Dick Enberg (for his intelligence), Pat Summerall (for his rare ability to listen), Bob Costas (for his humor), Bob Trumpy (for a certain honesty), Marv Albert (bright, funny), Bud Collins (all he needs is enthusiasm). Maybe a couple of others.

What these guys have in common is knowledge, a certain amount of passion, a realization that the sun will rise tomorrow, regardless of who gets the W, who has the L. It's not that much to ask for.

And none of them is a shill.

Having said some less than flattering things about Namath and Gifford, let me add this—I would love to get the chance to watch a football game with them in any living room. Because I've heard that privately they are bright and funny.

And more than that, I've watched games with pro athletes, and for a fan it is a glorious experience. They groan in agony, they see things we don't see and can explain what's really going on. They can very often predict, from what they see, when a soft spot is going to be exploited. They know who's dogging it, who's putting out. They understand about match-ups and who's got the benefit here, who's in trouble there. They are all aware of what's hard and what should be done by any pro. They realize that no one can do everything. They make the game, in such a different way, come alive.

Gayle Sierens has got a problem. Not just the pressure. It *is* strange to hear a woman doing sports. I remember when I first heard Gayle Gardner I was suspicious—the token announcer. Then I saw Gardner one night when the tape didn't roll and she ripped off what had happened in a game, going far beyond what might have been on the teleprompter, and I realized, "Hey, she *knows*." The best TV results show I've ever seen is when Gardner and Chris Berman worked together. Fun and fast and knowledgeable. I miss them already.

I wish Sierens the best. Not just from an antisexist point of view but because the more interesting announcers there are, the better off I am.

Make no mistake, though, she's entering a wildly sexist arena. Every male announcer's nuts are scudding up into their stomachs. And the print media's sweating a bit, too. I have yet to see her name written as her name—Gayle Sierens. It's always "Sierens, who is pregnant . . ." They don't say "Madden, who is fat . . ." do they?

Or "Garagiola, who is dumb . . ."

No one was quite saying the Jets were dumb, but the Eastern Division of the American Football Conference was a mess, everybody could see that (the Indianapolis Colts would end up winning). It was there for the taking after the strike, everybody seemed to have a .500 record, there was one five-way tie after another.

The Jets couldn't do anything about it.

Problem?

The Jets were a mess, too.

If the Jets found out during the strike that there was no veteran leadership on the team, with the veteran stars falling all over each other crossing the picket line for different reasons, the Jets found out *after* the strike that there was no leadership on the team at all.

A team that had been blown apart by the strike—some of them on one side of the picket line, others in the locker room, suiting up for scab football—found itself unified in only one area in November and December:

Most of the New York Jets thought Coach Joe Walton fell considerably short of genius.

Walton, finishing out his fifth year as Jets coach—during that time the Jets had made the playoffs twice, won just one playoff game—did it to himself. With another team, another coach, maybe you blame the collapse on injuries, and age, the ravages of the strike. Not with Joe Walton's Jets.

Hell, watch the man go.

Take a look at the man's act for November and December 1987:

Sunday, November 1: The Jets lose to the Indianapolis Colts, 19–14. After the game, Walton vilifies the Jets in the locker room. It is, the Jets agree, his most hysterical presentation in a season-long series of such presentations. They have heard him blow up before, often about the media, newspapers in particular. It was not uncommon for Walton to yell, "Someday, I'm going to write a book about *them!*"

Meaning the writers.

But this time, after the loss to the Colts, is different. Walton is after his own players.

And he has a big finish:

"You guys are stealing money!" he says, and stalks away from them, out of the room, like he can't stand the sight of them.

A lot of Jets had crossed the picket line. More had not. The ones who had stayed out had lost four weeks of salary. Now the coach was telling them they were stealing money.

The Jets' record, once 2–0, is now 3–4.

Wednesday, November 4: Walton benches Freeman McNeil.

Across the 1980s, McNeil has been the spiritual leader of the offense the way Joe Klecko has been the leader of the defense, in addition to being—when healthy—one of the star running backs of the NFL. McNeil has also been hurt a lot in the eighties, and his body seemed to wear down as the season wore on, but when McNeil was fit, the Jets could look like a great football team.

And his teammates respect Freeman McNeil. While other veterans crossed the line, McNeil, though he had talked about crossing, did not; the strike had cost him $181,250 out of his $725,000 salary. He has not been the McNeil of old to this point in the season (151 yards in four games, on 48 carries), but it is just assumed that he has been bothered by the strike like other veterans and is playing himself into shape.

Walton gives McNeil's starting spot to Johnny Hector. None of McNeil's teammates want to go on the record, but they feel Walton is looking for a new scapegoat that week, and McNeil is it.

McNeil, after practice, patiently answers questions about the benching, then says to the writers, "Gentlemen, until I move back into my office [starting at halfback], I bid you adieu."

Monday, November 9: The Jets surprise Walton, themselves, the Seattle Seahawks, and a national television audience with a 30–14 victory over Seattle, moving the record to 4–4. The Jets again are part of a five-way tie in the AFC East.

After the game, the Jets are pleased to discover they aren't stealing money anymore.

Walton tells them, "You're my team again."

He likes them a lot, it seems, when they win. The Jets are becoming more and more aware that the coach is awfully fickle, depending on which way the wind is blowing. It is a bad thing for any team to see in a coach. Walton has become the old coaching cliché: Sonofabitch, I coached good, but did *they* ever play bad.

He has become a weather vane.

Rocky Klever, voice full of sarcasm, says afterward, "If we didn't respond, Joe getting all pissed off would have been wasted, right?"

Wednesday, November 11: The Jets are getting ready to play the Kansas City Chiefs in Kansas City on Sunday (an ugly game the Jets will win, 16–9). The Chiefs have lost seven games in a row, but are two-and-a-half-point favorites over the Jets.

Walton, talking about network oddsmakers Jimmy (The Greek) Snyder of CBS and Paul Maguire of NBC, says, "They're all against us, anyway."

Rocky Klever informs Paul Needell of the New York *Daily News* that Walton had held private meetings with individual Jets in the days leading up to the Seattle game, telling each one what was expected of him.

Needell asks what Walton had told Klever.

Klever says, "He told me I had a big mouth. I told him I had a big mouth when we were 2–0, too."

Sunday, November 22: The Jets, playing at home, lose to the Buffalo Bills, 17–14. After the game, Walton, the weather vane, makes another turn.

This time, he attacks the leadership of the Jets.

Not his leadership, of course.

Theirs.

Walton says, "We need more leadership from guys on this team."

He is asked, "On the field or off?"

"On. We have to start pushing our own buttons."

Klever, who by now has become a hero to the writers as he constantly provides a proper sense of humor to the growing silliness of the Jets season, says, "I don't even know how to push my wife's buttons. How am I going to push [offensive lineman] Dan Alexander's?"

Monday, November 23: Walton gives the writers a speech they have never heard before.

The writers call it his "Sixty Minutes" speech.

Excerpt: "To win in this league, all you have to do is play together and play hard. Once a week. Sixty minutes. For about three hours."

Walton slows down his cadence here.

"One ... day ... a ... week. Think about it. One day a week. Sixty minutes. Interesting, isn't it? That's all it is. That's all there is to it."

Walton leaves the writers, goes into the weekly Monday meeting with the players.

"Did everybody get their paychecks?" Monday is payday.

The players nod yes.

The coach of the Jets says, "Okay, now get the fuck out of here."

Joe Klecko says, "The old man is pissed."

Linebacker Bob Crable is asked, "How pissed?"

Crable says, "We'll find out tomorrow when we see who he cuts."

Monday, December 7: On ABC's *Monday Night Football*, the Jets lose to the Dolphins, 37–28. The final score is a smokescreen. Most of America, in fact, doesn't know the final score until reading newspapers the next morning.

Most of America turned off the Dolphins–Jets game when it was Dolphins 27, Jets 0 at halftime.

Walton throws another tantrum at halftime. In the third quarter, Ken O'Brien throws a touchdown pass. When he comes off the field, Walton, weather vane, tries to shake his hand.

O'Brien snaps, "Fuck off."

(It is not the first time this had happened. There had been an incident between the two men earlier in the season. O'Brien had taken a sack. When he came off the field, Walton screamed, "Get rid of the goddamn ball!"

O'Brien screamed right back, "Fuck you! That's your fucking rule! *Your* fucking rule!"

Walton's Rule: When in doubt, O'Brien was to eat the football, not throw it up for grabs. But sometimes the Jets on the sidelines would listen to Joe Walton and think he had forgotten Walton's Rule. O'Brien would take another sack and Walton would turn to quarterback coach Zeke Bratkowski and snap, "Why doesn't he get rid of the fucking ball?")

By the Miami game, Ken O'Brien has heard enough from Joe Walton. Man wanted to call him and his teammates bums one minute, shake hands the next.

"Yeah, fuck off," O'Brien says again, and walks away.

The Jets' record is 6–6.

> *Saturday, December 12:* The Jets are playing the Patriots the next day, at Sullivan Stadium in Foxboro. The team spends the night at the Providence Marriott. (Providence is closer to Foxboro than Boston; on Sunday morning, the commute to the stadium is easier.)

All week long, Walton has been telling the writers and his players that the Jets are still "in the hunt." Obviously, he does not have to be a member of a pro football scouting combine to figure this out; *everybody* in the AFC East is in the frigging hunt.

Now, in the team meeting on Saturday, what motivational rabbit does Walton pull out of his hat?

His "real world" speech.

He tells them how difficult life is in "the real world."

Big finish: "And a lot of you are going to be finding out about what the real world is like when this season is over."

A tight team fighting injury and age and its own insecurities becomes tighter. Player rep Kurt Sohn says, "If you're constantly looking over your shoulder to see if 'The Turk' (the mythical football coach who tells you you've been cut) is tapping you on it, you play tight and make mistakes. And if you make mistakes *here,* well, you're out of here. I don't know if guys are playing that way, but I can understand it if they are."

> *Sunday, December 13:* The Jets decide the real world can't be more grisly than what they have just been a part of at Sullivan Stadium against the New England Patriots.

The Patriots beat the Jets, 42–20, after leading 35–6 at halftime. In two games against divisional opponents—December games that are the most important of the season so far—the Jets have fallen behind 62–6 in the first half.

Pat Ryan, backup quarterback, says afterward, "It doesn't say a hell of a lot for us, does it?"

The Jets are 6–7.

Monday, December 14: Two days after painting his players a picture of the real world, saying a lot of them are going to find out about the real world when the season is over, Joe Walton tells the writers, "The guys are trying too hard right now. We've got to get them relaxed and having fun again."

Friday, December 18: The Jets are growing tired, and more vocal, about Walton flitting from Good Cop to Bad Cop.

Cornerback Bobby Humphery says, "Joe can't threaten us now. He's lost us. And there isn't an awful lot he can say at this point to help us relax."

Punter David Jennings, a thirty-five-year-old veteran in his third season with the Jets after a long career with the Giants, is asked if he thinks Walton has lost the players.

Jennings smiles.

"Ask me after the season," he says. "If I'm here."

Happy ship.

Sunday, December 20: At home at Giants Stadium, the defensive secondary now ravaged by injuries, the Jets are beaten, 38–27, by the Philadelphia Eagles. There are 46,319 no-shows for the game, which means 30,372 in attendance, at least at the start. Jets fans know something about Joe Walton teams. The Jets now have a 4–11 record in December under Joe Walton. At this point, they are 17–22 under Walton in the second halves of seasons. (The records will go to 4–12 for December, 17–23 for the second halves against the Giants in the season's finale.)

Sometime in the first half, the chant goes up at Giants Stadium.

"Joe Must Go!"

"Joe Must Go!"

"Joe Must Go!"

The chant does not disappear in the second half; just grows fainter as Jets fans begin heading for the parking lot. By the end of the game, the crowd at Giants Stadium looks like something for scab football. They are still chanting that Joe Walton must go. As Walton walks into the tunnel leading to the Jets locker room, beer is thrown in his direction. At his press conference, Walton says he didn't notice.

At the press conference, he is asked if the Jets played hard.

"The vast majority of players played hard," he says.

Question from a reporter: "Is that good enough to win?"

"If you have good enough talent it is."

Players.

It is always the players.

Never Joe Walton.

In the Jets locker room, the players who aren't talented enough to win (in the estimation of the coach who helped assemble them) are still talking about a recent team meeting. In it, Walton screamed that he had too many players who were "peabrains who won't amount to anything after football."

Bob Crable suggests that perhaps the best thing for the entire organization is to have an outsider, a troubleshooter, come in and "look at the whole situation."

Crable finds out about eight days later what Joe Walton thinks of a good, constructive suggestion like that.

Walton tells Crable to decide whether he wants to play for the Jets next season, or some other team.

One thing about Walton, the players decide: The sucker's door was always open, right?

Thursday, December 24: Walton tells the Jets that team owner Leon Hess has assured him he will return to coach the Jets for the 1988 season, ending newspaper speculation that he wouldn't.

Walton also gets around to apologizing for the "peabrains" remark, not that any of the Jets care one whole hell of a lot by then.

Sunday, December 27: The Jets once again finish 0-for-December, losing the New Jersey state championship to the Giants, 20–7. Both teams finish 6–9. But the Giants are pleased that they were able to finish with two straight wins, even after their situation became hopeless. Most of the Giants linger in their locker room after the game, talking hopefully about next season. Coach Bill Parcells says there's no doubt in his mind that he's going to "get this team back to where it belongs." He points out that the Giants record was not really 6–9, but 6–6. He doesn't count scab games.

Parcells says, "Don't talk to me about *them* other guys."

At the other end of the corridor, the Jets, with about six exceptions, have disappeared within thirty minutes after the game; the locker room looks like someone called a fire drill, or pulled an air raid siren. Veteran equipment man Mickey Rendine surveys the emptiness and says, "I think they broke some kind of record getting to the bus."

Walton tells the writers about Leon Hess's vote of confidence.

Rocky Klever, one of the last Jets to leave, says, "Maybe it's bad karma around here."

He is asked what he means, exactly.

Klever grins.

"Do you suppose we could have been slow-finishing racehorses in another life?"

> *Tuesday, December 29:* Needell of the *Daily News* writes a story in which he quotes three anonymous Jets, referring to them as Player A, Player B, Player C. Needell protects them all because they are veteran players.

Player A says, "I don't think he has the respect of the players. People become paranoid, questioning all his yelling and the way he demeaned them personally, not treating them like men."

Player B says, "A lot of players didn't like him before this, but he sure didn't help himself."

Player C says, "I don't like the way he goes about motivating people, because he's *not* motivating people."

Rocky Klever is not one of the players quoted by Needell.

Klever says, "The guys who talked to him shouldn't worry about Joe figuring out who said what, because unfortunately, it could be any one of forty-four guys."

And Joe, whom the fans said must go?

Joe Walton tells the writers the week after the 1987 season ended that for the life of him, he couldn't think of anything he could have done differently. . . .

THE GENTLEMAN FROM ALABAMA

*O*ne of the pleasant surprises awaiting the fan is becoming acquainted (or reacquainted, depending on date of birth) with the most terrifying offensive force to ever step on a football field.

While you are coming up with your choice, let's make the decision on the other sports. The most terrifying offensive force to ever play basketball? Wilt, Wilt, and Wilt. I don't think a serious intellectual can dare mention another name.

And the diamond? A few names are possible without scoffing. Aaron, if power is your passion, Brock if you hunger for leadoff speed, Mays if you want to split the difference. Throw in Gehrig, Foxx, Greenberg; Cobb, if you want to stretch things.

I don't think any of them come close to Hornsby. (Lifetime .358. Hit, over five consecutive years, .397, .401, .384, .424, .403. And with power: 144 home runs those same years, with 598 RBI.)

And I don't think Hornsby matches Williams. No one knows what numbers The Kid would have plastered on the wall if two wars and assorted injuries hadn't robbed him of five prime years.

But, great as Williams was, the answer has to be Ruth. When Williams was at his peak, a lot of seers preferred Musial or DiMaggio—as batsmen.

The Babe had no challengers. Never had, and I suspect never will.

Now to football. I'm going to guess a few names that you've been balancing. Remember, the key words are "terrifying offensive force." And no, it's not Nagurski. But I think it would be valid to mention him. As well as Grange. As well as McAfee who, when he retired, was thought by most to be the greatest broken field runner. And certainly Baugh.

And most certainly Sayers. And Johnny U. Jim Brown, of course. Today? It's too soon, but give them another half dozen years and Marino and Dickerson will be worth mentioning. (Payton, by the by, whom I adore, never inspired terror. Dread, yes. "Oh, God, here he comes again.")

The answer, folks, is Don Hutson.

Many of you are either cursing me or saying "*Who*, for Chrissakes?" Well you won't be, come Super Bowl XXIII. Why? Because Steve Largent is closing in on one of the great records, most touchdowns ever, for a receiver. And as Largent plays his '88 year, you'll start to hear about how "Steve Largent is only three touchdowns away from the all-time record." And then you'll hear, in the following weeks, "Steve Largent is only two touchdowns away from Don Hutson's all-time record." And then "Steve Largent is just one touchdown short of Don Hutson's all-time record of ninety-nine."

And then finally, one of the two wraparound shows will do a profile on Hutson. (My early bet would be on Frank Deford.) And then the columnists will begin writing about Hutson. And by the time Largent breaks the record, people will be wondering about Hutson again, wondering, *"How did he do it?"*

It was then, and still is, his secret.

Hutson himself was no secret when he joined the Packers in '35. He had been a famous All-American at Alabama, the year before, one of the most extraordinary pair of college ends to ever play on one team at the same time—the other flanker, in case you don't know, was Bear Bryant.

Still, all of pro football was stunned by what he could do. He was a particular killer of the Bears, the other great team of this era. On the first play from scrimmage of the first game of his rookie year, the Bears were in Green Bay. Green Bay had slipped on the kickoff return, so it was first and 10 on the 17. Their quarterback faded, heaved it as far as he could.

Hutson was there.

Eighty-three yards. Touchdown. Packers win seven-zip.

But we crunched them when they came south. With five minutes left, the Bears led 7–3. With four minutes left, the Bears led 7–3. With three minutes left, the Bears led 14–3.

Green Bay got the ball back, fumbled, recovered, was offsides. The game was tucked away. Then the Packer quarterback, Arnie Herber, escaped a rush and threw a short pass.

Hutson was there.

He dodged through *five* defenders, outraced two more. Sixty-eight yards. Touchdown. But we still led 14–10.

Then the Bears fumbled. The Pack recovered. Not much time. Third and 3 on the Bear 3. The Packers fake a dive. The Bears stop it dead. But Herber lofts it into a corner of the end zone.

Hutson was there.

All, all alone.

How did he get there? The most-watched man on the field was by himself in the end zone. It was not possible. It simply could not happen, short of some dematerializing act out of *Twilight Zone.*

He was just different. He looked different, because he didn't wear shoulder pads. (Some of the players at this time didn't even wear helmets.) He was easy to spot. Because of the lack of pads and, most importantly, because you couldn't take your eyes off him; you didn't dare, you might miss the mystery.

When he retired, as a first-string All-Pro for the eighth consecutive year, in 1945, he held more records than any other player in history. A few examples: most passes caught, most yards gained catching passes, most touchdown passes, most total touchdowns, most points scored.

Plus these: shortest touchdown pass—4 *inches*. Most points scored one quarter: *29.* And most MVPs: *2.* Consecutive. No one else had won it more than once.

Probably you're thinking, Big deal, that was ancient history.

Point taken.

But Jim Brown is still thought of by many as the greatest runner of all, even the greatest player of all. (Note: During Brown's prime, a lot of experts not only didn't think Brown was the greatest fullback—forget player, that's an aberration—they didn't think he was the greatest fullback *of his time.* Jim Taylor was their man. Not as fast or strong as Brown, granted. But Brown, for all his skills, was incredibly limited. He simply would not or could not block. Taylor was a killer.

I believe this: If Jim Brown had been a Packer during the Hornung–Taylor era, he would never in this world have started. Lombardi would have used him—and no one knows so no one can prove me wrong—as an important spot player, the way Shula used Mercury Morris during the Kiick–Csonka days.)

Still, Brown's weaknesses have disappeared with time, and as a runner he ranks supreme for a great many. And he dominates the all-time record book. Most seasons leading league rushing: 8. Twice as much as any other runner. Most consecutive years leading rusher: 5. Almost double the nearest competitors, who are Steve Van Buren, Earl Campbell, and Brown himself, yet again. Twenty-two years after his retirement, his name is oh so much in evidence, and those records still count.

Well, forty-two years after his retirement, they're still shooting at Hutson. And they're never going to catch some of the agate lines. Most years leading league pass receiving: 8. If you throw out the old AFL records, no one else has done it more than 3 years. Most consecutive years, Hutson, 5. Most years leading league, yards gained, Hutson, 7. The runners-up, Raymond Berry and Lance Alworth, did it 3 times. Most years leading league in touchdowns, 8. The runner-up again did it 3.

Well, if Brown's records still are awesome, and they are, what do we do with Hutson? Remember, he did all this when passing was secondary, unsophisticated. He did all this, for the most part, in eleven-game seasons. The Packers never had a losing season during his tenure.

He was the focus of every enemy game plan, though that horrid word had not made its incursion into our vocabulary then. I remember seeing him when they would use him for a decoy for an entire half, and he would still end up as the leading receiver by far. Also remember he could play both ways, as did so many at this time. (A great defensive back he was, too.)

It's not possible to describe the impact he had for eleven impossible seasons. I guess to come close, I'd say he was a combination Bob Hayes/Raymond Berry. Or today, Gault/Largent. This blinding speed coupled with the most extraordinary ability to get open short. Fabulous practiced moves.

The thing you must remember about him was this: It was not possible to head him off at the pass. He would draw double coverage, go deep, and another receiver would be clear over the middle. He would go short, someone else would be clear deep. They would not throw to him and not throw to him and not throw to him and then there he was, clear, running clear and free with the ball in the air and no one ever had better hands, touchdown.

I remember, the games I saw him play, when it was close and tense and Green Bay had the ball, we would all stand in Wrigley, screaming, "Stop him. Stop him."

No need to be more specific. We all knew who the "him" was.

So will you. Next year. . . .

THE
REPORTER'S NOTEBOOK

"IT WAS GOING TO BE A SEVENTY-TWO-YARD TOUCHDOWN PASS ..."

Next year began for the Giants two weeks after the NFLPA strike was called off. The first week after the strike, the defending Super Bowl champion Giants beat the St. Louis Cardinals.

Record for defending Super Bowl champion Giants?

They were in last place in the National Football Conference's Eastern Division with a record of 1–5.

(The Redskins were first place, at 5–1.)

Phil Simms: "I was more tired after that Cardinals game than any game I'd ever played, including the Super Bowl. Shit, man, I was *exhausted*. I think everyone on the team was. Coming off the strike, we had ten games left, and we didn't know how many of them we needed to make the playoffs, but we were thinking at least nine. That meant we'd finish nine-six. I don't know, maybe in the backs of our minds we were thinking we had to win all ten. And once we got into that game with the Cardinals, we all of a sudden realized what a bitch that was gonna be. All of a sudden, every series was important, every touchdown was life or death. Fuck, every damn *down*. So we win that game, but afterward, I think it sunk in on everybody just what a hole the strike had put us in. 'Cause what we had felt against the Cardinals was what we were staring at for nine more weeks. Every series. Every touchdown. Every down."

This was in January, in San Diego, a few days before Super Bowl XXII. Simms was having breakfast at a resort called the Princess, not five minutes from the Hyatt Islandia, where the NFC champion Washington Redskins were staying. Simms was in town to do a television show for a Super Bowl preview show for Home Box Office, make some appearances for Subaru, play a lot of golf. A year after he had completed 22 of 25 passes in Super Bowl XXI and been that game's Most Valuable Player, Simms sat in a near-empty coffee shop and talked about November, first weekend in November, when the Giants made it official that they were not coming back to the Super Bowl; weren't even going to make the playoffs.

Sometimes, a team's demise is straightforward, logical, orderly in professional sports. Domino pushing against domino pushing against domino. Sometimes there are no gloomy portents or dramatic moments. *B* follows *A* and *C* follows *B*. It is not necessary for a dove to fall from the Shea Stadium sky. Or for Roger McDowell to serve up a home run ball to a fat third baseman named Pendleton.

Karl Nelson got cancer, and the Giants' running game began to get shot all to hell, and that put pressure on the passing game, just for those first two games, and the Giants started 0–2.

That was *A*.

There was a football strike. George Young, the Giant's general manager, hired himself a bunch of scabs who couldn't have made either team in the movie *M*A*S*H*. And by the time the strike ended, and you had to add 0–2 from real Giants to 0–3 for scab Giants, you had that 0–5 sinkhole, and it looked like just about everybody in the National Football Conference had a better record than the Giants.

And a better shot at the playoffs.

Which made every play for the rest of the season seem like fourth and long.

Make that *B*.

C was easy. *C* was Giants vs. Dallas, November 2, Monday night at Texas Stadium, ABC *Monday Night Football*. *C* was the reason Phil Simms ended up at the Princess resort on the last week of January and not at the Hyatt Islandia, hotel for the NFC champions.

"Dallas was all she wrote, son," Phil Simms said. "The season seemed to end in about ten minutes. And the funny thing is, the play that started it, I thought it was going to be a seventy-two-yard-touchdown pass. . . ."

That was one funny thing.

Another was that as the Monday night game between the Giants and Cowboys wore on, Phil Simms was thinking the way the Mets' Howard Johnson did back in July, when he and his teammates became convinced that they were going to catch the St. Louis Cardinals.

"I thought, Sonofabitch, we're going to get out of this," Simms said.

With ten minutes remaining in the game, the Giants led, 24–17. But they had been in control for most of the game, and Simms had been brilliant. This was the Simms of Super Bowl XXI. It was the Simms who had completed every important pass he needed to complete in the Giants' run to Super Bowl XXI. Fifty minutes into that Monday night game, he was 13 for 17, and had thrown two touchdown passes to Lionel Manuel, one for 50 yards, another for 33 yards. Now he needed one more scoring drive—score of any kind, touchdown or field goal—to put the Cowboys away. The Giants' record would become 2–5. Still a long way to go. But if they could beat New England at home the next Sunday night, then the Eagles at Philadelphia, well, 4–5 looked a hell of a lot peachier than 0–5.

They would be in the chase, anyway.

The Cowboys had just kicked a field goal. The ball was kicked off after that. Lee Rouson of the Giants, backup to Joe Morris, returned the ball to the 24-yard line. But a penalty for an illegal block made the Giants start the drive on their own 15.

Simms handed to Morris, who ran left for a yard (Morris did that a lot in 1987, ran left for a yard).

Simms completed an 11-yard pass to Manuel, first down; now he was 14 for 18.

Morris got another yard, up the middle.

It was second and 9, Giants 28-yard line. Simms dropped back to pass.

Simms: "It was a big rush, but I didn't feel like I was in trouble. When you're a quarterback, there's times you know you're in trouble, and there's times when you know they're just squeezing you, and it's time to cut it loose. I was getting squeezed on both sides, but it was all right. Because I looked down the middle, and there wasn't anybody within twenty yards of [Mark] Bavaro. He was wide open. I really did think it was going to be a touchdown, we were going to be ahead, 31–17, and that was gonna be that."

Simms threw the ball. Ed (Too Tall) Jones reached a big hand up and deflected the ball into the air.

Another Dallas lineman, Jim Jeffcoat, caught the ball and returned it 26 yards for the touchdown that tied the score at 24–24.

The 72-yard touchdown to Mark Bavaro became a touchdown the other way. Suddenly, that poststrike hole the Giants had found themselves in started to cave back in on them. The ball was kicked off. The Giants started on their 22-yard line. Morris lost five yards. There was a delay-of-game penalty, dumb mistake at any point in the game, big-time dumb in the last quarter of a tie game you have to win. They lined up again and Simms completed a short pass to Rouson.

Third down, 13 yards to go, from the Giants 19.

Now the crowd was into the game at Texas Stadium, sensing the underdog Cowboys had the Giants by the throat. The Giants were having trouble hearing Simms call the signals over the noise from the stands.

Brad Benson, left tackle, jumped before the ball was snapped.

Five yards against New York.

Third down, 18 yards to go, from the 14-yard line.

Simms started to call the signals.

Benson jumped again.

Third down, 23 yards to go, from the 9-yard line.

Benson didn't jump, but Too Tall Jones jumped all over Simms, seven yards beyond the line, and the Giants had to punt. The Cowboys drove down the field and kicked a field goal. Now they led, 27–24. There were four minutes, eleven seconds left in the game.

Still plenty of time.

The ball was kicked off to Lee Rouson. He fumbled. The Cowboys recovered. They ran three plays. Another field goal. It was 30–24. Two minutes, fifty-four seconds left.

Still plenty of time.

The ball was kicked off. The Giants started at their 21-yard line.

Phil Simms dropped back to pass. They squeezed him again. He threw. Too Tall Jones tipped. Randy White intercepted this time. Talk about dominos falling against each other. Simms sprained his knee on the play. He left the game, replaced by Jeff Rutledge. The Cowboys finally won, 33–24, having outscored the Giants 19–0 in the fourth quarter. After the game, Simms came walking out of the trainer's room, the knee in a splint. The Giants were 1–6, and the Super Bowl MVP wouldn't play again until December. It was too late by then.

The season officially ended in Dallas. The Giants had gone from cancer to the strike to ten horrific minutes at Texas Stadium. One thing pushing against another, which pushed against another. The Giants were supposed to be the darlings of the season, the big television draw from New York. Defending champs. They had opened on *Monday Night*

Football. Lost to the Bears. They had played their first scab game on *Monday Night Football.* Lost to the 49ers. Now they had lost to the Cowboys on *Monday Night Football.*

In the Princess coffee shop in January, Phil Simms said, "Well, it's not like we hid on anybody. We were always right there, messing up in prime time."

The waitress brought him an omelette. Simms smiled and thanked her. He looked out the window, saw that the sun was breaking through the clouds. At Super Bowl XXII, what would be Doug Williams's Super Bowl, the MVP of Super Bowl XXI said he might get to play golf that afternoon, after all.

Simms had been yesterday's news since Dallas.

AIR

Yesterday's news we don't much care about. But sometimes last century's news is still vital to some people. Example: the wine buff. For this person, arguably *the* vintage of the nineteenth century was 1811, the legendary "Year of the Comet."

For the True Believer, no "arguably" exists. The year of the nineteenth century was 1845. Why? Because something of Genuine Import happened. The historian might argue that a lot of important things happened that year: Texas and Florida became states. Polk became our eleventh president. The Maoris rose. Dumas père wrote the wonderful *Twenty Years After,* the sequel to *The Three Musketeers.* Mérimée wrote *Carmen.* Poe published *The Raven and Other Poems.* John Henry Newman became a Catholic. Wagner premiered *Tannhäuser.* The first submarine cable was laid across the English Channel. Kolbe synthesized acetic acid. Heilman patented his cotton and wool combing machine. Bigelow built his power loom. Annapolis opened in Maryland.

To these events and more, I say, "Piffle."

The biggie of 1845 appeared in the New York *Herald.* For in that year, that paper printed—wait for it—*the first known baseball box score.* New York beat Brooklyn, 37–19. Names were listed. Runs were listed. In other words—trumpets please—

—stats were born!

Statistics to the fan are like the actual size of the Pentagon—something that cannot be overrated. They not only provide crucial sustenance, they alert us to other people's foibles—a guy says he's a fan but he doesn't know Mays's lifetime? A phony, put him against the wall and blast away, no peep out of me.

Historically, there is, of course, only one meaningful stat: Who got the W. But I couldn't care less about "historically," I'm here *now*. And besides, only one team each year gets the final victory in any sport, and if I don't root for that team, I'm left with gruel.

Statistics are many things, among them salvation. When I was growing up there were certain numbers (just talking baseball now) that were tattooed behind my eyelids:

56

60

511

714

2130

3508

Those were the untouchables. (If you're under forty, maybe half make no sense.) But the wisdom when I was young was that never would any of these records be broken. DiMaggio's 56-consecutive-game hitting streak is still very much alive, but more about that later. Maris topped Ruth's 60 home runs in a season by one. Cy Young's 511 wins is the one record I know will never be approached. Ruth's home run totals were smashed by Aaron. Gehrig's game streak is the second hardest to break. Walter Johnson's strikeout total has been obliterated.

Of course, these were so much more than numbers. The number 60 conjured up The Bambino, sweet, uncouth, kissing babies in hospitals, promising homers to injured lads, pointing with his bat to where he was going to splat the next pitch.

I believed in numbers then.

Still try. But it's getting so much harder. Because, ironically, there are so many more people working with numbers today, telling us so much of what we didn't know.

It is now January of '88, and this last week, a lot of numbers have been nagging at me. Take Joe D's 56. That number, more than any single thing, is the proof of DiMaggio's greatness. We don't have that much film on him, so we can't see him the way we watch Ozzie Smith. And the war affected his career, so his lifetime statistics aren't remotely as impressive as his reputation.

That reputation resting, more than on any single item, on the consecutive game streak. Take 56 away from DiMaggio and he's a Mister Coffee pusher who married a hunk.

Well, alas, it was probably a phony streak. I say "probably" because we can't go to the vault and get out TV tapes of the games. And not too many people are around who saw it when it took place. (It was, by the way, a manufactured record, manufactured by the press, much as the triple-double has been invented to suit the skills of Magic Johnson. The point being that before the New York media got into it, nobody gave a shit about batting streaks. When the great Sisler hit in 41 in 1922, nobody knew or cared much—the day it ended, not one major paper so much as gave it a mention.)

But the New York media got behind DiMaggio in '41, and made the happening.

They also kept it alive.

In Game 30, DiMaggio hit a grounder to the White Sox shortstop, Luke Appling, a hall of fame hitter, (2,749 hits, lifetime .310) with minor league hands. As history goes DiMaggio's ball collided not with Luke's glove but his shoulder and there was tension in Yankee Stadium. What would the official scorer rule? Dan Daniel was the gentleman's name, a famous sportswriter of the day. And since sportswriters had invented the streak, it doesn't seem odd that Daniel did what he could to keep it going, ruling a hit. Even the *Times* the next day said it was a "lucky" hit.

DiMaggio was saved.

Until the morrow. The next game, Thornton Lee was on the mound, a 22-game winner that year, the league leader in ERA (2.37). Last time up. DiMaggio hitless. He swings. Bouncer to Appling again. Luke stops it, drops it—

—*hit.*

Guess who the scorer was this time? Dan Daniel again. Was it a single? No one will ever know with certainty. It was scored as such and as such it remains. But with a different scorer, DiMaggio might have had a 29-game hitting streak.

Not easy. But surely not the stuff of legends.

Oscar Robertson surely is. (For me, inch for inch, *the* roundball player.) And right now, the Knicks' splendid rookie guard, Mark Jackson, is challenging one of O's records, highest assist average in a rookie season.

The subtext to this is obvious: They are somehow, if not equals, players that you can mention together. "Jackson broke Robertson's record." (I think, by the by, he will shatter it.)

Why?

a. Because Jackson is a terrific player.
b. Dat ole debbil New York Media.

The last few days the papers have been full of Jackson stats. He is, after 32 games, dead on Robertson's record of 9.7 assists per game. (Magic leads the league with 11.7 as of now.) Clearly, only an outstanding talent could play at this level, which takes care of a.

But b is something of a problem, because the New York media is also dealing with this teeny discrepancy in Jackson's totals. In 18 games at home, in the friendly confines of MSG, his average is a remarkable 12.5 assists per game.

And on the road?

On the road he is averaging exactly 6 assists per game. Half of what he does on the home court. Less than. Magic, incidentally, is averaging 11.7 at home, 11.8 when visiting.

The New York press has come up with astounding reasons for the astounding difference. The Knicks don't score as much on the road. (True. They score seven-tenths of a point less.) They don't shoot as well on the road. (True. They stink both places but are a fat 2 percent better at home.) Jackson doesn't play as much. (True, true, true.) On and on go the explanations.

But it is all the purest bullshit: He has fewer assists on the road because road scorers are tougher on the enemy. He has more at home because Garden statisticians are, like Dan Daniel for DiMaggio, human and therefore homers. (This will diminish now that attention is being paid. Garden statisticians will stay as they are; roadies will smile more.)

But false as the scoring may be, it is nothing compared to the basic falseness, which is locking Jackson and Robertson in the same sentence.

When Oscar Robertson left the University of Cincinnati and joined the NBA for the '60–'61 season, he was anything but an unknown quantity. He was a triple All-American; he was a triple NCAA scoring champion; he was a triple College Player of the Year. He teamed with Jerry West on the undefeated Olympic team of 1960. (And don't you wish we had tapes of what it was like, those two, young and dazzling in the same backcourt?)

But college stars, especially scoring stars, have a way of disappointing in the NBA. The top seven single-season leaders—Maravich, Selvy, Johnny Neumann, Freeman Williams, Billy McGill, Calvin Murphy, Austin Carr—none of them found the same glory once they started getting paid for it.

Robertson made the adjustment with considerable comfort. We know he set the rookie record for assists. It should be pointed out that the 9.7 was a bit more—it was the (then) all-time league record for assists. Only one man (Cousy) had ever had as many as 9 a game before. Robertson also averaged over *10* rebounds a game—this is a guard, remember.

And he scored. Oh, not like in college, where he left with an average of over 33 points a game.

But 30.5 isn't an embarrassment.

No other guard had ever scored thirty points a game before.

Or 29.

Or 28.

Not 27.

26.

25.

23.

Only two guards (Sharman and Shue) had ever scored more than 22 points a game.

This was a rookie year that didn't foster a whole lot of criticism. (He finished fourth in shooting—this is a guard, remember. But let's not even count that.) What Robertson did was pass for a higher assist average than any player in history, grab more rebounds than any guard in history, and decimate the scoring records for his position.

Jackson will be forever linked with him when the year ends—thanks to his skill and the skill of the Knicks official scorers. Which is one of the most precious things about statistics—they can prove such wondrous things, no matter how false.

Example: Steve Garvey retired today. And in five years, when he comes knocking at the Hall of Fame, his supporters will not only rave about his offensive skills, they will prove that he was much more—a defensive whiz.

You can look it up. He did not play with infielders of Ozzie's class. Yet he managed to set some startling defensive records: fielding percentage for a first baseman (1.000 in 1984); most consecutive games in a season without committing an error (159 in 1984); most consecutive games in a career without committing an error (193 in '84–'85); most consecutive chances in a season without committing an error (1,319 in 1984).

Now, you know and I know—we *saw*—that Garvey was two steps up from a klutz at first. Nice hands, yes. But no arm and limited range. Kind of a musclebound stump.

Doesn't matter. The statistics are there to prove it and you'll read about it in 1992: The man was a gazelle.

Siwoff is not a gazelle, though definitely thin. Maybe he'd be heavy if he didn't work so hard. Thirty-five years on the job and he puts in 350 days a year. In slow years. Not because he has to. He wants to. *Needs* to.

My God, what if somebody made a mistake?

Breakdown time.

Seymour Siwoff, icon and grandfather, is the person most responsible for the statistical firestorm that has swept across the sports pages of America. Unknown to the outside world, he is the man all of the True Believers should bow to. We have, all of us, spent thousands of hours reading what he puts out. We quote him, not realizing it, every every day.

For he is the owner, and has been since '52, of the Elias Sports Bureau in Manhattan. Elias provides the official statistical record for:

Major League Baseball
The NFL
The NBA

Almost all those yummy numbers you read in *USA Today?* Elias. *Sports Illustrated* has them on retainer. Record books? Elias. Team guide books? Elias. Just about every number in your cranium came from Elias.

They are located at 42nd and 5th. Just across the street from the New York Public Library. "Two great fonts of information," said Siwoff.

The office—manned by fifteen or so lunatics—is open seven days a week, probably twenty hours a day. When a game ends, someone somewhere is on the phone with the official game records for Elias's computers.

Siwoff, no kid, is wary of the goddamn things. He took over Elias in '52, thought he'd give it a shot for a year, maybe two, see how it went. For ten years it was a struggle. Then Rozelle came to the NFL and Elias has been building ever since. In the early years, it was more hand work. But a decade or so ago, Siwoff sucked it up and brought computers. Enough for a billion bits of information.

"I'm in quicksand," he said to his wife when he did it. "All I want to do is survive."

He gives a tour of the Elias headquarters. It will never be confused with Versailles. Giant dusty ledger books with ancient stats climb up the shelves. The computer room is the center of it all.

Siwoff looks at the machines with an untrustworthy gaze, much as a city boy at camp might eye a large bug, wondering would it sting him. "The crazy thing," Siwoff says, "is that we had more time when it was manual. In the old days, it was limited. Now you can do so much." He leaves the computer room, goes to his own small office, sits at his wooden desk.

He gets calls all the time, most of which Elias hasn't the time or inclination to answer. "But a man called here over the weekend. He's involved in baseball in Switzerland. He wanted to see us. Can you turn down someone like that?" He shrugs. He didn't.

Ironically, the man who made the statistical marketplace is also the man most worried about the disappearing romance. "Never forget that's what we're talking about—it's a romance. Sports. And we live in such a contemporary society—people don't want to know about yesterday. And it's so programmed today. The teams look so much the same. The free-lancing is gone out of it and I'm afraid the audience may lose the romance."

He goes silent. On the wall are the faces of Mantle, of Mays, of Stan the Man.

"I like to think what we're doing here is creating history. Producing a heritage."

I nod.

Siwoff is silent again.

The legends watch.

Then he says it. One word. "Air."

I don't get it.

"Sports is air."

I listen.

"It's something we can talk about. It's not tangible. It's air. People talking about an event. Remembering an event. With nothing but air between them."

The talk drifts on. We shift from baseball to football, from Mays to his gridiron equivalent, Mr. Sayers.

Gale Sayers had a rookie season on a par with Oscar Robertson's. All kinds of records, six touchdowns in one game, a bunch more. There was a lot of ink. He was this new weapon. Different and strange. You never knew, when he touched the ball, if he was going to score. They say that of a lot of runners, but it was more true of Sayers than anyone.

He came to New York that rookie year and I saw him do something I'd never seen done as well before, certainly not since. Sayers was left-handed. The Bears had the ball just inside Giants' territory.

Pitch to Sayers. He starts to circle left. The defense flows with him. Sayers looks like he's going to run—

—and then suddenly his left arm raises to pass—

—and the entire Giant defense froze. Simply became riveted to the stadium turf—

—and in that frozen moment, Sayers flew 45 yards for an untouched touchdown. As I type these words I see the moment of twenty-plus years ago. Sayers flowing left. The left arm suddenly raised for the halfback option pass. The Giants' immobility. The startling blink of a run.

I start to tell Siwoff that Sayers came to town to play the Giants that rookie year—

—and suddenly, with no word of warning, *Siwoff raises his left arm exactly as Sayers had*—

—the silent room we inhabit is now so alive.

"I was at that game," Siwoff says quietly.

"I remember the moment," I reply, indicating his left arm. He brings it down now.

"Sayers was the art form," Siwoff says.

A pause.

And then we both can't stop, babbling like children, reconstructing the moment, talking of what we knew of Sayers before that moment, why we went to the game, what we expected, what we hoped for, how he went beyond anything. We talked on and on, smiling and interrupting each other, living again that blink in 1965 when we both stared in amazement; both of us caught up in what being a Fan is finally most truly about . . .

. . . air . . . .

V

WAIT TILL NEXT YEAR

THE DARK GUY

According to Phil Simms, who should know, the best thing about the Redskins' victorious "struggle" against the Broncos was this: "Let *those* SOBs answer all the questions about will they repeat or not next year." Simms, the greatest quarterback in Super Bowl history—for three hundred and sixty-some days—knows more than most about the hype that cascades on the quarterback's head. And never more than the 31st of January, when the game might as well have been billed thus:

THE DARK GUY AGAINST "THE DUKE"

Since the NFC–AFC Championship Game has given hyperbolic meaning to the word "hyperbole," it might be well to give a bit of attention to those gentlemen, Mr. Williams and Mr. Elway, in no particular order.

THE DARK GUY

TIME: Several Months Ago

PLACE: Hollywood.

FADE IN ON:

TWO DESPERATE PRODUCERS: They sit grinding out cigarettes and drinking espresso outside in the Polo Lounge of the Beverly Hills Hotel. The weather is gray. The place is pretty much empty—everyone with a job has gone back to work after lunch.

THE OLDER PRODUCER is in a sour mood—he had to wait half an hour last night at Spago's for a table and then was given one in the rear. He's fifty, wears a lot of gold chains, is tanned, trim, looks forty at the outside.

THE YOUNGER PRODUCER can almost never sit still. Thin to the
extreme, he plays good tennis which got him his start in the
picture business. He's thirty, hasn't had a snort of cocaine
in two months, looks forty at the outside.

> YOUNGER PRODUCER
> I'm tellin' ya, it's true—

> OLDER PRODUCER
> —I wouldn't mind a little proof—

> YOUNGER PRODUCER
> —Okay—I'm getting my BMW gassed
> and I'm talkin' to the attendant and
> he told me that the guy who he'd just
> gassed up was a friend of one of
> Eddie Murphy's best bodyguards and
> this friend swore it was true—
> *Eddie Murphy is big on sports.*

> OLDER PRODUCER
> *(impressed)*
> Okay, I admit it, that's proof—
> we don't know what sport he likes,
> though.

> YOUNGER PRODUCER
> *All* sports. We can pick one, come
> up with an idea—*we can be
> creative.*

> OLDER PRODUCER
> *(tripping off)*
> You know how much we'd make if we
> produced an Eddie Murphy flick?
> *(a sweet smile crosses
> his face)*

> YOUNGER PRODUCER
> *Stop daydreaming*—what about a
> tennis flick?

> OLDER PRODUCER

Stinks. In the first place, they
don't play tennis except for Ashe.
In the second place, someone made
a tennis movie—*Players*—and
it bombed.

> YOUNGER PRODUCER

Okay, basketball.

> OLDER PRODUCER
> *(lighting another*
> *Camel Unfiltered)*

C'*monnn*. Who's he gonna play?
—The only one his size is Muggsy
Bogues and Muggsy isn't a star.

> YOUNGER PRODUCER

Quit pissing on my ideas—*Hoosiers*
did okay.

> OLDER PRODUCER
> *(exploding)*

Don't tell me grosses, I know what
every picture did the last fifty
years damn near, I've copied from
all the biggest—but *Hoosiers*
took place back in history and in
the second and most important
place, it was about white players,
not schvartzes.

> YOUNGER PRODUCER
> *(chastised)*

Shit, Elliot, I'm trying, find
another throat to jump down. . . .

> OLDER PRODUCER
> *(pauses)*

. . . Sorry, kid, my prostate's been
acting up of late.
> *(raises his hand for*
> *more espresso)*

And don't mention baseball, it's
too slow, there's no climax and it's
all so obvious—a home run in
the last of the ninth of the seventh
game of a World Series—I like
to think my name means class and
that isn't a classy enough notion
to get me revved up.

              YOUNGER PRODUCER
Put shoulder pads on him, Eddie
Murphy could play football—
who was that little putz singer
they had in *Semi-Tough* playing
quarterback—Eddie's as big
as him.

              OLDER PRODUCER
It would take a genius notion to
make a football movie work . . . Mac
Davis.

              YOUNGER PRODUCER
Huh?

              OLDER PRODUCER
He was the shrimp in *Semi-Tough*—

              YOUNGER PRODUCER
—right, right—

              OLDER PRODUCER
That was a helluva picture, I
liked that picture, for me, that
was one classy venture—

              YOUNGER PRODUCER
*(suddenly on his feet—
shouting)*
—*I've got it, I've got the killer
idea*—

              OLDER PRODUCER
—tell me, for Chrissakes—

> YOUNGER PRODUCER
> —don't piss on this one, you
> sonofabitch—are you ready?—

> OLDER PRODUCER
> —go—

> YOUNGER PRODUCER
> —your heart's strong enough for
> what's coming?—

> OLDER PRODUCER
> —quit pulling your pud, tell me—

> YOUNGER PRODUCER
> *(all but shaking)*
> —*say pretty please*—

> OLDER PRODUCER
> —tell me *right now!*—

> YOUNGER PRODUCER
> *(in ecstasy)*
> —A nigger quarterback WINS THE
> SUPER BOWL!

CUT TO:

THE OLDER PRODUCER. CLOSE UP. He is silent. Then, quietly:

> OLDER PRODUCER
> I don't think the studios are
> looking for fantasy these days.

CUT TO:

THE YOUNGER PRODUCER, momentarily deflated. He sits back
down, brings his chair closer to the older man

> YOUNGER PRODUCER
> It could be very classy, Elliot.
> It could be very classy and very
> real. I'm not thinking fantasy.
> There's black quarterbacks. Good
> ones.

OLDER PRODUCER
If they're so good, how come I
can't think of any?

YOUNGER PRODUCER
There's the kid on Philly—there's
the Canadian plays for Houston—
there's the Tampa Bay one on the
'Skins.

OLDER PRODUCER
I remember him—what's his name—
William Douglas, right?

YOUNGER PRODUCER
Absolutely, so how about a picture
about William Douglas?

OLDER PRODUCER
(shakes his head slowly)
I get no zest out of that notion.
Anyway, this Douglas doesn't even
start.

YOUNGER PRODUCER
—I've got it—another killer—
it's the Super Bowl—the first-
string guy gets hurt and Douglas
goes out and wins the game.

OLDER PRODUCER
Corny.

YOUNGER PRODUCER
So we'll make him the starter—Gibbs
decides the other guy can't cut it,
he'll go with Williams—

OLDER PRODUCER
No coach would do that—he'd know
the players wouldn't work for a
schvartz. Not to mention the
stupidity factor.

                    YOUNGER PRODUCER
You're so damn negative—let's
pretend—think of the weeks of
hype—every sportswriter would be
trying to figure out a way to say
they're too stupid without saying
they're too stupid.

                    OLDER PRODUCER
I don't believe it—nobody could
perform under that kind of pressure—
he'd fold—I know it, you know it,
the whole world knows it.

CUT TO:

YOUNGER PRODUCER. On his feet again. Pacing around the
restaurant now.

                    YOUNGER PRODUCER
We'll figure out a way that the
pressure won't get to him—
          (stops)
—*he's been through worse.*

CUT TO:

THE OLDER PRODUCER, as the waiter brings new espresso, takes
the empty cups.

                    OLDER PRODUCER
What could that be?

CUT TO:

THE YOUNGER PRODUCER. Quickly back to the table.

                    YOUNGER PRODUCER
          (a pronouncement)
What if his wife died?

                    OLDER PRODUCER
Ridiculous.

                    YOUNGER PRODUCER
C'mon—we're making this up—
let's say he had a wonderful young

wife and kid and whammo, she kicks,
he's left with the kid and the
pain—the Super Bowl would be nothing
for a guy like that.

              OLDER PRODUCER
         (interested now in spite
         of himself)
We could keep flashing back—all
the writers are all over him and
nothing ruffles him and everyone
wonders how could he be that cool and
we show little slow motion scenes of
meeting his wife and the marriage and
the kid and her kicking—we do it
right, every broad in the house will
be bawling and every guy would be
dying for him not to fuck up. Let's
keep the dead wife, at least
temporarily. But there's gotta be
more—we need real drama, he can't
just go out and win the Super Bowl—
we gotta have things in his way—
obstructions are drama, I always say.

            YOUNGER PRODUCER
         (on fire)
He gets sick!

             OLDER PRODUCER
Sick might be okay—depends on
what kinda sick.

            YOUNGER PRODUCER
Flu. Maybe pneumonia.

             OLDER PRODUCER
No good—Eddie Murphy would never
play a part where he had to sweat
with fever during all the last
reels. Can't be temperature and a
cold's not enough of an obstruction.

YOUNGER PRODUCER
Toothache?

OLDER PRODUCER
Toothache's are a little wimpy—
Eddie's got this macho side to him.
I don't think he'd want to play a
guy who gives in to a toothache.

YOUNGER PRODUCER
(inspired)
Root canal!

OLDER PRODUCER
(grabbing his nuts)
The worst—nothing hurts like
root canal hurts—

YOUNGER PRODUCER
Okay, we're done, that's it—he
wins the Super Bowl coming straight
from the dentist's office for root
canal.

OLDER PRODUCER
That feels kind of manipulative to me.

YOUNGER PRODUCER
Okay, he has root canal the night
before—no one can accuse us of
being manipulative if it's the night
before.

OLDER PRODUCER
Right—but we still need something
more—an obstruction on game day.
Something before the game—

YOUNGER PRODUCER
(shouting it out)
No—no—*during* the game—
listen—he starts the game, but
he does crummy—the receivers

drop his passes—like you said,
they don't have faith in a
schvartz under center—and then
he's sacked and falls and he
crunches a knee—taken out of
the game—everyone feels relief
—he didn't have the stuff to
succeed under pressure like the
cocker on Denver, Elway—
　　(pause)
—but then the coach puts him back
in—they've stuck maybe a knee
brace on him on the sideline—

　　　　OLDER PRODUCER
—I like that—we see the agony
he's in—the knee brace isn't going
to be enough, he's going to fall on
his ass again—

　　　　YOUNGER PRODUCER
—right, right—and this'll grab
Eddie Murphy—he goes back in
limping—no chance to make it—
but a movie star is a movie star and
he does it! He's sensational.

　　　　OLDER PRODUCER
How sensational?—we wanna keep
this real, remember.

　　　　YOUNGER PRODUCER
He's gotta break some records—
shit, Eddie'll never go for it if
he doesn't do that—

　　　　OLDER PRODUCER
—what did Terry Bradshaw do?—
He threw four touchdown passes in
one game, I'm sure he did, I lost a
bundle on that fink—

YOUNGER PRODUCER
So Eddie Murphy throws five.

OLDER PRODUCER
That's not classy, that's ridiculous—

YOUNGER PRODUCER
(shouting)
I'm a genius—I'm a fucking
creative genius—

OLDER PRODUCER
—what? —what?—

YOUNGER PRODUCER
—our schvartz throws four—*but
he does it in one quarter!*

OLDER PRODUCER
Now *that's* class. I love it.
*(Now a dark look
hits his face)*

YOUNGER PRODUCER
What?

OLDER PRODUCER
Do you think people will think
we've Hollywooded it up?

YOUNGER PRODUCER
They bought Warren Beatty as a
forty-year-old quarterback in *Heaven
Can Wait*—worst impersonation of
an athlete since Tony Perkins in
Fear Strikes Out. And Beatty came
back from the dead to do it. If
they bought that, they'll buy
anything.
(smiles beatifically)
Eddie Murphy in *The William Douglas
Story.*

                    OLDER PRODUCER
          Now if only we knew someone who
          knew Eddie Murphy's bodyguard. . . .
                    (the two of them sit
                    happily, thinking of
                    grosses)

          FADE OUT.

   Doug Williams's shattering performance answered almost every question. One remains, though: Will a white quarterback ever play at that
level?
   Me, I'm not sure they're smart enough. . . .

THE DUKE

*W*ith his second consecutive depantsing in front of God and everybody, John Elway nailed down a position that is his and his alone—that of the single most overrated figure in team sports in this decade.

Not all that surprising, really. After all, he plays the most overrated position. Football, like basketball (and unlike baseball) is primarily a *team* sport. You can make an All-Star baseball team and put them together and on the first day, except for getting signals straight and a bit of work on the double play, they will play as if they've been together forever. Obviously, not true of the other two sports. And in football, where it is most ridiculous to single out any one person as the reason for the success of a forty-five-man team, the quarterback has become ridiculously singled out.

Not to say that the position isn't important. Obviously, it is. And not to say that it didn't used to be more important. Obviously, it was. But that was in the days when faking (anyone remember Eddie LeBaron?) went with the job.

Thinking, too.

Otto Graham, who only took his team to ten straight championship games, was severely criticized during his playing days for simply being an automaton—Paul Brown called the plays. Now, except for ho-hum efforts on play action stuff, faking is no longer a part of a quarterback's arsenal.

Thinking's gone, too. They're *all* automatons now.

Which was why the whole two weeks about was Doug Williams "smart" enough was so absurd. Anyone who has listened to John Elway knows he is listening to someone who would have trouble spelling "articulate." Which was why the hype was so insulting to anyone who could read without moving lips. What the media said about Elway was this: He was either (a) the greatest quarterback of his time or (b) the greatest quarterback of *all* time, pick one.

Why the fawning? Well, Elway *computes.* No one knows what makes an outstanding athlete. They can only be precise about certain things: his time in the forty, the strength of his arm, etc. Elway does wonderfully on that kind of marking—he has a very strong arm and he is fast.

He is, in fact, a very goddamn good quarterback. Maybe even one of the ten best throwing today. But he has never done much when it counted. Yes, the 98-yard march against Cleveland to put the '86 playoff game into overtime was a sterling effort for the entire Denver team. But, pray tell, was it any more difficult than what Williams accomplished in Chicago?

Bringing his team back—

—back from a two-touchdown deficit—

—against Chicago—

—against Chicago *in* Chicago—

—against Chicago in Chicago in *January?*

What the Redskins showed, and what every coach who plays Denver from now on is undoubtedly drooling over now, is this: Contain him and he's ordinary. Yes, on gadget plays and broken plays, when he's running around behind the line of scrimmage and his receivers are imitating a Chinese fire drill in front of it, Elway is excellent. Absolutely in a class with Randall Cunningham. But as a quarterback he has this one blip of a problem when he's stationary—

—he can't throw accurately.

Maybe he will learn to. God knows it's not that hard and he's certainly talented. But for now, he's a fastball pitcher who can bring it, he just can't bring it over the plate with consistency.

Only in the media a mark of "greatness."

THE
REPORTER'S NOTEBOOK

"NOBODY KNOWS ANYTHING ..."

Goldman (The Fan in this book) wrote a Hollywood book one time, *Adventures in the Screen Trade,* and in it he summed up everything he had learned about Hollywood's dream-makers:

Nobody knows anything.

Goes double in sports.

Whether you are on the inside, or on the outside, nobody knows anything. Not in New York or anyplace else.

General managers make bad trades, owners sign the wrong free agents or don't sign any at all, sportswriters make lousy predictions, gamblers lose their shirts. Oddsmakers promise you the world and they don't know anything either. Balls bounce funny. Guys get hurt. Guys take dope. People get fired. Yankees get Georged.

The Mets bitch to themselves and about themselves. The sports year 1987, the year we were writing about, ended in January. So, for all intents and purposes, did our book. But as I write this, trying to wrap the whole thing up, near the end of spring training, Darryl Strawberry is running around saying he was misquoted in *Esquire* and he *didn't* piss all over Gary Carter and Davey Johnson and Keith Hernandez and Wally Backman and just about every Met, it seemed living or dead Met, except Casey Stengel.

I have just gotten off the phone with Goldman. I am at spring training, watching another Mets circus take form. He is in New York and, as usual, he is dying.

I say, "We could follow the Mets this season the way we followed them last season, and get just as much craziness. They haven't learned anything."

Nobody knows anything.

Nobody ever learns anything.

Across 1987, New York sports fans did not merely have their hearts broken. They had their legs and arms broken too. Especially the baseball fans. The Mets teased Mets fans until the last week before finishing up their choke. The Yankees? With the craziness around the Mets, the Yankees seemed ready to take the town back. But then people started getting hurt, Piniella missed that silly phone call, Steinbrenner issued his hysterical statement, and the last two months, usually a hot time for the Yankees even when they would lose, became this agonizing, slow death.

Know what?

New York baseball fans looked ahead to 1988 with more anticipation, more hunger, than at any time I could remember in New York. Steinbrenner, the man who swallowed his wallet and had his heart shrivel up when Jack Morris was available, became a player in the free agent market, signed slugger Jack Clark of the Cardinals. And he traded for pitcher Richard Dotson of the White Sox and got Rafael Santana from the Mets, in addition to John Candelaria, a potential starting pitcher.

Steinbrenner already had Billy back.

Yankee fans wanted the season to start in January, even knowing that Steinbrenner isn't dangerous in January, it's during the summer when his balls start to ache.

Yankee fans are the same as all fans: If yesterday went wrong, forget about it. Forget the Georging of 1987. Forget that Billy had had four other cracks at managing the team.

Forget. And wait. Tomorrow will be better. Sports fans remember what they want to remember. Steinbrenner remembers what he wants to remember about Billy Martin, not the shit in the bars, or when Martin was saying "one's a born liar [Reggie], the other's convicted [Steinbrenner]" in a Chicago airport. In August of 1987, the Yankees burned Steinbrenner's statement about Piniella in Detroit. By spring training '88, Claudell Washington was saying it wasn't Steinbrenner's fault, and even Don Mattingly was saying, "It's up to us to keep George off our backs."

Sing the chorus: Nobody knows anything.

Strawberry spent the winter saying he was finished making headlines with his mouth, then sat down for an *Esquire* interview with me, and, well, you know, watered five teammates and the manager.

Carter? He quit in 1987, according to Darryl.

Hernandez? Darryl wanted to tell him to get his head out of his ass.
Dykstra? Was out for himself, not the team.
Backman? Didn't do "jackshit."
And Darryl said he wondered all the time how many games the Mets would win if Whitey Herzog, the Cardinals manager, were managing them.
I wrote the column in January. It came out in March. When first shown the copy by Bob Klapisch, by then with the *Daily News,* Darryl said, "Yeah, I said it, what's the big deal."
Two days later, after Dykstra had read the story and confronted Darryl in the Mets' Port St. Lucie clubhouse, Darryl pulled Klapisch aside, said, "See, when it's about them, they can't take it."
By that evening, Darryl decided he was misquoted.
The next day, he said his words were "twisted."
A couple of weeks later, he went on a national NBC telecast of a Mets–Dodgers game from Vero Beach, Florida, and said he would never say anything like that about his teammates, forgetting about threatening to punch Backman in the face the previous season.
Strawberry, as ever, was the one with his head buried somewhere, once again being Mr. Misunderstood and blaming everybody else for problems he had created.
The week before the *Esquire* column started to breathe real air, Strawberry had been late to Port St. Lucie and missed the team's official spring training photograph.
Said he got a flat tire.
Said he didn't have a spare for the Mercedes.
Didn't call because he didn't know the number of the Mets complex.
Had to wait for a tow truck.
I suggested that the flat tire was the excuse that he decided on, that one of the excuses that he rejected was that a UFO had landed on the highway in front of the Mercedes and he had been kidnapped by aliens.
"No one believes him anymore," One Met said.
In this case, One Met was all of them. . . .

Fans don't learn. Steinbrenner doesn't learn. Strawberry doesn't learn. Sportswriters don't learn. I thought the Knicks were simply kissing off the season when the Knicks let Bernard King leave the team and picked up a scorer to replace him, and maybe the Knicks were doing just that.
But Mark Jackson became the best rookie in pro basketball, and

Pitino, the Hot Boy, still had the magic from Providence. He got the Knicks to play with passion, every night. The team had miraculously suffered no major injuries, at least into March. The league, desperate for the Knicks to win again, had given the team every possible schedule break, including never having to play more than three consecutive games on the road. (Many teams play 5 or 6, sometimes as many as 8.)

The Knicks put together a great late-winter winning streak at home, and found themselves in an honest-to-God, no-shit run at the playoffs and even as one basketball year was ending, Knicks fans, finally, were waiting for the next one.

Goldman? All during 1987 he wanted Richard Evans, Al Bianchi, and Rick Pitino dead. But by the spring of 1988, Goldman couldn't decide whose baby he wanted to have. Everything had gone wrong in 1987. Everything would be perfect in 1988. I heard it in my job, felt it, saw it. *Knew* it. There was no logic to the flowering of this hope. Just the hope—that tomorrow would be better, Steinbrenner wouldn't screw up, Darryl would finally shut his mouth, Gooden would go back to being The Doc, Walton would learn how to win, really win, Parcells's Giants would act as if the strike never happened, would play in '88 as if they were defending the Super Bowl title.

As I write this, there is trouble around. Jack Clark has torn up his leg running around the bases for a *home run*. Gooden's Florida earned run average is 8.44. Darryl is mad at the universe. Walton is cutting Jets veterans like Joe Klecko and Joe Fields. Davey Johnson wants Frank Cashen to trade somebody so he can keep the kid, Keith Miller, on the twenty-four-man roster. The Yankees rookie center fielder, Roberto Kelly, dropped a fly ball the other day, and Steinbrenner was heard bitching.

What does it all mean?

Beats me.

In the end, we are all in it together. In this sense, 1988 is exactly like 1987, which is not so different from '67, or '77 or '89.

Pick a year.

Sports is a life sentence.

We never learn enough to graduate.

We keep coming back, hopeful, saying, Surprise us.

P.S. And boy do we need our surprises. Sports feeds our sense of wonder. That's why we need it. Sports—exasperating, repetitive, childish, trivial, all that and more, agreed, agreed—but still, sports is what helps us get through the shit . . .

. . . by which we mean, of course, daily life. . . .

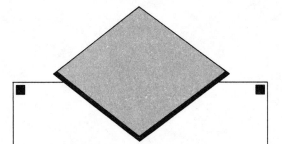

EPILOGUE

Here it is, folks
Here it is, world
NEXT YEAR

Graceful, always that, the giant stood blinking in the sun, a stick wiggling in his hands. The stick moved forward and the ball arced safely into the outfield. Dave Winfield had driven in what would prove to be the game winning RBI—

—and the crowd—

—the record-breaking opening day, April 5, 1988, Yankee Stadium crowd—

—fifty-five thousand eight hundred and two men and women, boys and girls stood and turned and glared up at the owner's box—

—and the cry "Steinbrenner sucks" was once again heard in our land. . . .

And you know what?

Doesn't matter, not now, not during these twenty-four-plus hours sent straight down to you from what can only be Up There. The Yanks win eight-zip, with Pags and Rickey parking shots.

Glory.

Almost as exciting as the Mets' behavior the day preceding—

—*Six* dingers.

The first time in world (actually baseball but they're the same thing in terms of importance) history that one team had done that on opening day. And one of Darryl's two was such a monster that even McCarver was almost at a loss for words. This baby hit so high that no one saw it—the TV cameras were pointed toward mortal destinations. No one thought to tilt up 160 feet where the ball is rumored to have collided with a bunch of lights.

And you know what?

There's more.

The football schedules were released (not Columbia's) and if the Giants can get through their first six with a W or two, they might just run the table after that. And the Jets have got to be relieved with what's on their plate, too.

The Nets lost, sure, but the glass can be half full if you let it and they weren't blown out.

And Larry Brown, who did not get the Knicks job, brought Kansas home for the NCAA championship by using a combination of Danny Manning and his own special weird ability to win wherever he goes.

And the night of the Yanks' triumph, the Knicks won *on the road,* jumping dead into the playoff picture, jokes no longer. You watch that game but it's tough, because it's clear that when you're in the room with the tube they're struggling, but when you're outside the room listening, eyes closed, they romp. So you stay outside until they're up by twenty and it's safe to go in and watch the finish.

Then you hit the streets.

Because you have to.

There's no room that can contain what these hours have given you. Anyway, you're dangerous, you might explode, taking anyone and everyone with you.

So you walk the streets of this great splintered bitch of a city, and in the warm spring darkness ahead of you kids with Polo clothes and thousands of dollars of braces on are making drug deals and marriages are ending and failure billows out of the open windows of apartments—

—and it's okay. Not good, but there are other nights to fret about the imperfections of the world.

Years ago, decades really, an elderly cab driver said to you of an inclement morning, "Sonny, this is a hackman's rain," and when you enquired he explained that it wasn't raining so hard people stayed indoors but just hard enough so that the minute they hit the pavement they were looking for a ride.

Well, this was a sports fan's night.

And you walked through it. Thinking of Darryl and Big Dave and Mark Jackson and you can't walk the streets of this city long without remembering, at least for a blink, Irwin Shaw, the master, because no one before and no one yet unborn will write as tellingly about what it's like, moving along these sidewalks. And in one story, "Welcome to the City," a young man, which you were once, alas, is robbed of his loneliness by the comfort of a sad ex-dancer who looks like Greta Garbo. But Garbo's not like that anymore, she's old now—

—except on a sports fan's night; she'll be young again—standing there ahead of you, looking just like she did in *Camille;* and beside her, that's Audrey Hepburn in *Roman Holiday,* and they're both with Elizabeth Taylor in *Ivanhoe*—

—the three of them waiting for you—

—waiting to hear you tell what it's like, having a night like this, when all the baskets drop, all the line drives clear the fences—

—their arms are out toward you now—

—their smiles are on for you now—

—they ache for you, ache for your strength, your pure male power, your unfailing wit, your special wisdom, your honest cloak of modesty, the sheer unassailable wonderfulness of you, the True Believer....

INDEX